CW00431397

The Memoirs of
Volume 3 of 6: The Eternal Quest

by

Jacques Casanova de Seingalt

1725-1798
The rare unabridged London edition of 1894 translated by
Arthur Machen to which has been added the chapters
discovered by Arthur Symons. Reproduced in 6 volumes.

The Echo Library 2007

Published by

The Echo Library

Echo Library
131 High St.
Teddington
Middlesex TW11 8HH

www.echo-library.com

Please report serious faults in the text to complaints@echo-library.com

ISBN 978-1-40682-445-2

Contents

VOLUME 3 — THE ETERNAL QUEST

EPISODE 11 — PARIS AND HOLLAND

CHAPTER I

Count Tiretta of Trevisa Abbe Coste—Lambertini, the Pope's Niece Her Nick—Name for Tiretta The Aunt and Niece—Our Talk by the Fireside—Punishment of Damien—Tiretta's Mistake Anger of Madame***—Their Reconciliation—My Happiness with Mdlle. de la Meure Silvia's Daughter—Mdlle. de la Meure Marries—My Despair and Jealousy—A Change far the Better

In the beginning of March, 1757, I received a letter from my friend Madame Manzoni, which she sent to me by a young man of good appearance, with a frank and high-born air, whom I recognized as a Venetian by his accent. He was young Count Tiretta de Trevisa, recommended to my care by Madame Manzoni, who said that he would tell me his story, which I might be sure would be a true one. The kind woman sent to me by him a small box in which she told me I should find all my manuscripts, as she did not think she would ever see me again.

I gave Tiretta the heartiest of welcomes, telling him that he could not have found a better way to my favour than through a woman to whom I was under the greatest obligations.

"And now, that you may be at your ease with me, I should like to know in what manner I can be of service to you?"

"I have need of your friendship, perhaps of your purse, but at any rate of your protection."

"You have my friendship and my protection already, and my purse is at your service."

After expressing his gratitude to me, Tiretta said,

"A year ago the Supreme Council of my country entrusted me with an employment dangerous to one of my years. I was made, with some other young gentlemen of my own age, a keeper of the Mont de Piete. The pleasures of the carnival having put us to a good deal of expense, we were short of money, and borrowed from the till hoping to be able to make up the money before balancing-day, but hoping all in vain.

"The fathers of my two companions, richer than mine, paid the sums they had taken, and I, not being able to pay, took the part of escaping by flight from the shame and the punishment I should have undergone.

"Madame Manzoni advised me to throw myself on your mercy, and she gave me a little box which you shall have to-day. I only got to Paris yesterday, and have only two louis, a little linen, and the clothes on my back. I am twenty-five, have an iron constitution, and a determination to do all in my power to make an honest living; but I can do nothing. I have not cultivated any one talent in a manner to make use of it now. I can play on the flute, but only as an amateur. I only know my own language, and I have no taste for literature. So what can you make of me? I must add that I have not a single expectation, least of all from my father, for to save the honour of the family he will be obliged to sell my portion of the estate, to which I shall have to bid an eternal farewell."

If the count's story had surprised me, the simplicity with which he told it had given me pleasure; and I was resolved to do honour to Madame Manzoni's introduction, feeling that it was my duty to serve a fellow-countryman, who was really guilty of nothing worse than gross thoughtlessness.

"Begin," said I, "by bringing your small belongings to the room next to mine, and get your meals there. I will pay for everything while I am looking out for something which may do for you.

"We will talk of business to-morrow, for as I never dine here I rarely if ever come home till late, and I do not expect to have the honour of seeing you again today. Leave me for the present, as I have got some work to do; and if you go out to walk, beware of bad company, and whatever you do keep your own counsel. You are fond of gaming, I suppose?"

"I hate it, as it has been the cause of half my troubles."

"And the other half, I'll wager, was caused by women."

"You have guessed aright—oh, those women!"

"Well, don't be angry with them, but make them pay for the ill they have done you."

"I will, with the greatest pleasure, if I can."

"If you are not too particular in your goods, you will find Paris rich in such commodities."

"What do you mean by particular? I would never be a prince's pathic."

"No, no, I was not thinking of that. I mean by 'particular' a man who cannot be affectionate unless he is in love. The man who . . . ."

"I see what you mean, and I can lay no claim to such a character. Any hag with golden eyes will always find me as affectionate as a Celadon."

"Well said! I shall soon be able to arrange matters for you."

"I hope you will."

"Are you going to the ambassador's?"

"Good God!—no! What should I do when I got there? Tell him my story? He might make things unpleasant for me."

"Not without your going to see him, but I expect he is not concerning himself with your case."

"That's all I ask him."

"Everybody, my dear count, is in mourning in Paris, so go to my tailor's and get yourself a black suit. Tell him you come from me, and say you want it by tomorrow. Good bye."

I went out soon after, and did not come back till midnight. I found the box which Madame Manzoni had sent me in my room, and in it my manuscripts and my beloved portraits, for I never pawned a snuff-box without taking the portrait out.

Next day Tiretta made his appearance all in black, and thanked me for his transformation.

"They are quick, you see, at Paris. It would have taken a week at Trevisa."

"Trevisa, my dear fellow, is not Paris."

As I said this, the Abbe de la Coste was announced. I did not know the name, but I gave orders for him to be admitted; and there presently appeared the same little priest with whom I had dined at Versailles after leaving the Abbe de la Ville.

After the customary greetings he began by complimenting me on the success of my lottery, and then remarked that I had distributed tickets for more than six thousand francs.

"Yes," I said, "and I have tickets left for several thousands more."

"Very good, then I will invest a thousand crowns in it."

"Whenever you please. If you call at my office you can choose the numbers."

"No, I don't think I'll trouble to do so; give me any numbers just as they come."

"Very good; here is the list you can choose from."

He chose numbers to the amount of three thousand francs, and then asked me for a piece of paper to write an acknowledgment.

"Why so? I can't do business that way, as I only dispose of my tickets for cash."

"But you may be certain that you will have the money to-morrow."

"I am quite sure I should, but you ought to be certain that you will have the tickets to-morrow. They are registered at my office, and I can dispose of them in no other manner."

"Give me some which are not registered."

"Impossible; I could not do it."

"Why not?"

"Because if they proved to be winning numbers I should have to pay out of my own pocket an honour I do not desire."

"Well, I think you might run the risk."

"I think not, if I wish to remain an honest man, at all events."

The abbe, who saw he could get nothing out of me, turned to Tiretta, and began to speak to him in bad Italian, and at last offered to introduce him to Madame de Lambertini, the widow of one of the Pope's nephews. Her name, her relationship to the Pope, and the abbe's spontaneous offer, made me curious to know more, so I said that my friend would accept his offer, and that I would have the honour to be of the party; whereupon we set out.

We got down at the door of the supposed niece of the Holy Father in the Rue Christine, and we proceeded to go upstairs. We saw a woman who, despite her youthful air, was, I am sure, not a day under forty. She was rather thin, had fine black eyes, a good complexion, lively but giddy manners, was a great laugher, and still capable of exciting a passing fancy. I soon made myself at home with her, and found out, when she began to talk, that she was neither a widow nor the niece of the Pope. She came from Modena, and was a mere adventuress. This discovery shewed me what sort of a man the abbe was.

I thought from his expression that the count had taken a fancy to her, and when she asked us to dinner I refused on the plea of an engagement; but Tiretta, who took my meaning, accepted. Soon after I went away with the abbe, whom I dropped at the Quai de la Ferraille, and I then went to beg a dinner at Calsabigi's.

After dinner Calsabigi took me on one side, and told me that M. du Vernai had commissioned him to warn me that I could not dispose of tickets on account.

"Does M. du Vernai take me for a fool or a knave? As I am neither, I shall complain to M. de Boulogne."

"You will be wrong; he merely wanted to warn you and not offend you."

"You offend me very much yourself, sir, in talking to me in that fashion; and you may make up your mind that no one shall talk to me thus a second time."

Calsabigi did all in his power to quiet me down, and at last persuaded me to go with him to M. du Vernai's. The worthy old gentleman seeing the rage I was in apologized to me for what he had said, and told me that a certain Abbe de la Coste had informed him that I did so. At this I was highly indignant, and I told him what had happened that morning, which let M. du Vernai know what kind of a man the abbe was. I never saw him again, either because he got wind of my discovery, or because a happy chance kept him out of my way; but I heard, three years after, that he had been condemned to the hulks for selling tickets of a Trevaux lottery which was non-existent, and in the hulks he died.

Next day Tiretta came in, and said he had only just returned.

"You have been sleeping out, have you, master profligate?"

"Yes, I was so charmed with the she-pope that I kept her company all the night."

"You were not afraid of being in the way?"

"On the contrary, I think she was thoroughly satisfied with my conversation."

"As far as I can see, you had to bring into play all your powers of eloquence."

"She is so well pleased with my fluency that she has begged me to accept a room in her house, and to allow her to introduce me as a cousin to M. le Noir, who, I suppose, is her lover."

"You will be a trio, then; and how do you think you will get on together?"

"That's her business. She says this gentleman will give me a good situation in the Inland Revenue."

"Have you accepted her offer?"

"I did not refuse it, but I told her that I could do nothing without your advice. She entreated me to get you to come to dinner with her on Sunday."

"I shall be happy to go."

I went with my friend, and as soon as the harebrain saw us she fell on Tiretta's neck, calling him dear Count "Six-times"—a name which stuck to him all the time he was at Paris.

"What has gained my friend so fine a title, madam?"

"His erotic achievements. He is lord of an honour of which little is known in France, and I am desirous of being the lady."

"I commend you for so noble an ambition."

After telling me of his feats with a freedom which chewed her exemption from vulgar prejudice, she informed me that she wished her cousin to live in the same house, and had already obtained M. le Noir's permission, which was given freely.

"M. le Noir," added the fair Lambertini, "will drop in after dinner, and I am dying to introduce Count 'Sixtimes' to him."

After dinner she kept on speaking of the mighty deeds of my countryman, and began to stir him up, while he, no doubt, pleased to have a witness to his exploits, reduced her to silence. I confess that I witnessed the scene without excitement, but as I could not help seeing the athletic person of the count, I concluded that he might fare well everywhere with the ladies.

About three o'clock two elderly women arrived, to whom the Lambertini eagerly introduced Count "Six-times." In great astonishment they enquired the origin of his title, and the heroine of the story having whispered it to them, my friend became an object of interest.

"I can't believe it," said one of these ladies, ogling the count, while his face seemed to say,

"Would you like to try?"

Shortly after, a coach stopped at the door, and a fat woman of middle-aged appearance and a very pretty girl were ushered in; after them came a pale man in a black suit and a long wig. After greeting them in a manner which implied intimacy, the Pope's niece introduced her cousin Count "Six-strokes". The elderly woman seemed to be astonished at such a name, but the Lambertini gave no explanation. Nevertheless, people seemed to think it rather curious that a man who did not know a word of French should be living in Paris, and that in spite of his ignorance he continued to jabber away in an easy manner, though nobody could understand what he was talking about.

After some foolish conversation, the Pope's niece proposed a game at Loo. She asked me to play but on my refusing did not make a point of it, but she insisted on her cousin being her partner.

"He knows nothing about cards," said she; "but that's no matter, he will learn, and I will undertake to instruct him."

As the girl, by whose beauty I was struck, did not understand the game, I offered her a seat by the fire, asking her to grant me the honour of keeping her company, whereupon the elderly woman who had brought her began to laugh, and said I should have some difficulty in getting her niece to talk about anything, adding, in a polite manner, that she hoped I would be lenient with her as she had only just left a convent. I assured her that I should have no difficulty in amusing myself with one so amiable, and the game having begun I took up my position near the pretty niece.

I had been near her for several minutes, and solely occupied in mute admiration of her beauty, when she asked me who was that handsome gentleman who talked so oddly.

"He is a nobleman, and a fellow-countryman of mine, whom an affair of honour has banished from his country."

"He speaks a curious dialect."

"Yes, but the fact is that French is very little spoken in Italy; he will soon pick it up in Paris, and then he will be laughed at no longer. I am sorry to have brought him here, for in less than twenty-four hours he was spoiled."

"How spoiled?"

"I daren't tell you as, perhaps, your aunt would not like it."

"I don't think I should tell her, but, perhaps, I should not have asked."

"Oh, yes! you should; and as you wish to know I will make no mystery of it. Madame Lambertini took a fancy to him; they passed the night together, and in token of the satisfaction he gave her she has given him the ridiculous nickname of 'Count Sixtimes.' That's all. I am vexed about it, as my friend was no profligate."

Astonishment—and very reasonable astonishment—will be expressed that I dared to talk in this way to a girl fresh from a convent; but I should have been astonished myself at the bare idea of any respectable girl coming to Lambertini's house. I fixed my gaze on my fair companion, and saw the blush of shame mounting over her pretty face; but I thought that might have more than one meaning.

Judge of my surprise when, two minutes afterwards, I heard this question:

"But what has 'Sixtimes' got to do with sleeping with Madame Lambertini?"

"My dear young lady, the explanation is perfectly simple: my friend in a single night did what a husband often takes six weeks to do."

"And you think me silly enough to tell my aunt of what we have been talking? Don't believe it."

"But there's another thing I am sorry about."

"You shall tell me what that is directly."

The reason which obliged the charming niece to retire for a few minutes may be guessed without our going into explanations. When she came back she went behind her aunt's chair, her eyes fixed on Tiretta, and then came up to me, and taking her seat again, said:

"Now, what else is it that you are sorry about?" her eyes sparkling as she asked the question.

"May I tell you, do you think?"

"You have said so much already, that I don't think you need have any scruples in telling me the rest."

"Very good: you must know, then, that this very day and in my presence he—— -her."

"If that displeased you, you must be jealous."

"Possibly, but the fact is that I was humbled by a circumstance I dare not tell you."

"I think you are laughing at me with your 'dare not tell you.'"

"God forbid, mademoiselle! I will confess, then, that I was humbled because Madame Lambertini made me see that my friend was taller than myself by two inches."

"Then she imposed on you, for you are taller than your friend."

"I am not speaking of that kind of tallness, but another; you know what I mean, and there my friend is really monstrous."

"Monstrous! then what have you to be sorry about? Isn't it better not to be monstrous?"

"Certainly; but in the article we are discussing, some women, unlike you, prefer monstrosity."

"I think that's absurd of them, or rather mad; or perhaps, I have not sufficiently clear ideas on the subject to imagine what size it would be to be called monstrous; and I think it is odd that such a thing should humble you."

"You would not have thought it of me, to see me?"

"Certainly not, for when I came into the room I thought you looked a well-proportioned man, but if you are not I am sorry for you."

"I won't leave you in doubt on the subject; look for yourself, and tell me what you think."

"Why, it's you who are the monster! I declare you make me feel quite afraid."

At this she began to perspire violently, and went behind her aunt's chair. I did not stir, as I was sure she would soon come back, putting her down in my own mind as very far removed from silliness or innocence either. I supposed she wished to affect what she did not possess. I was, moreover, delighted at having taken the opportunity so well. I had punished her for having tried to impose on me; and as I had taken a great fancy to her, I was pleased that she seemed to like her punishment. As for her possession of wit, there could be no doubt on that point, for it was she who had sustained the chief part in our dialogue, and my sayings and doings were all prompted by her questions, and the persevering way in which she kept to the subject.

She had not been behind her aunt's chair for five minutes when the latter was looed. She, not knowing whom to attack, turned on her niece and said, "Get you gone, little silly, you are bringing me bad luck! Besides, it is bad manners to leave the gentleman who so kindly offered to keep you company all by himself."

The amiable niece made not answer, and came back to me smiling. "If my aunt knew," said she, "what you had done to me, she would not have accused me of bad manners."

"I can't tell you how sorry I am. I want you to have some evidence of my repentance, but all that I can do is to go. Will you be offended if I do?"

"If you leave me, my aunt will call me a dreadful stupid, and will say that I have tired you out."

"Would you like me to stay, then?"

"You can't go."

"Had you no idea what I shewed you was like till just now?"

"My ideas on the subject were inaccurate. My aunt only took me out of the convent a month ago, and I had been there since I was seven."

"How old are you now?"

"Seventeen. They tried to make me take the veil, but not having any relish for the fooleries of the cloister I refused."

"Are you vexed with me?"

"I ought to be very angry with you, but I know it was my fault, so I will only ask you to be discreet."

"Don't be afraid, if I were indiscreet I should be the first to suffer."

"You have given me a lesson which will come in useful. Stop! stop! or I will go away."

"No, keep quiet; it's done now."

I had taken her pretty hand, with which she let me do as I liked, and at last when she drew it back she was astonished to find it wanted wiping.

"What is that?"

"The most pleasant of substances, which renovates the world."

"I see you are an excellent master. Your pupils make rapid progress, and you give your lessons with such a learned air."

"Now don't be angry with me for what has happened. I should never have dared to go so far if your beauty had not inspired me."

"Am I to take that speech as a declaration of love?"

"Yes, it is bold, sweetheart, but it is sincere. If it were not, I should be unworthy both of you and of myself."

"Can I believe you?"

"Yes, with all your heart. But tell me if I may hope for your love?"

"I don't know. All I know at present is that I ought to hate you, for in the space of a quarter of an hour you have taught me what I thought I should never know till I was married."

"Are you sorry?"

"I ought to be, although I feel that I have nothing more to learn on a matter which I never dared to think about. But how is it that you have got so quiet?"

"Because we are talking reasonably and after the rapture love requires some repose. But look at this!"

"What! again? Is that the rest of the lesson?"

"It is the natural result of it."

"How is it that you don't frighten me now?"

"The soldier gets used to fire."

"I see our fire is going out."

With these words she took up a stick to poke the fire, and as she was stooping down in a favourable position my rash hand dared to approach the porch of the temple, and found the door closed in such sort that it would be necessary to break it open if one wished to enter the sanctuary. She got up in a dignified way, and told me in a polite and feeling manner that she was a well-born girl and worthy of respect. Pretending to be confused I made a thousand excuses, and I soon saw the amiable expression return to the face which it became so well. I said that in spite of my repentance I was glad to know that she had never made another man happy.

"Believe me," she said, "that if I make anyone happy it will be my husband, to whom I have given my hand and heart."

I took her hand, which she abandoned to my rapturous kisses. I had reached this pleasant stage in the proceedings when M. le Noir was announced, he having come to enquire what the Pope's niece had to say to him.

M. le Noir, a man of a certain age and of a simple appearance, begged the company to remain seated. The Lambertini introduced me to him, and he asked if I were the artist; but on being informed that I was his elder brother, he congratulated me on my lottery and the esteem in which M. du Vernai held me. But what interested him most was the cousin whom the fair niece of the Pope introduced to him under his real name of Tiretta, thinking, doubtless, that his new title would not carry much weight with M. le Noir. Taking up the discourse, I told him that the count was commanded to me by a lady whom I greatly esteemed, and that he had been obliged to leave his country for the present on account of an affair of honour. The Lambertini added that she wished to accommodate him, but had not liked to do so till she had consulted M. le Noir. "Madam," said the worthy man, "you have sovereign power in your house, and I shall be delighted to see the count in your society."

As M. le Noir spoke Italian very well, Tiretta left the table, and we sat down all four of us by the fire, where my fresh conquest had an opportunity of shewing her wit. M. le Noir was a man of much intelligence and great experience. He made her talk of the convent where she had been, and as soon as he knew her name he began to speak of her father, with whom he had been well acquainted. He was a councillor of the Parliament of Rouen, and had enjoyed a great reputation during his lifetime.

My sweetheart was above the ordinary height, her hair was a fine golden colour, and her regular features, despite the brilliance of her eyes, expressed candour and modesty. Her dress allowed me to follow all the lines of her figure, and the eyes dwelt pleasantly on the beauty of her form, and on the two spheres which seemed to lament their too close confinement. Although M. le Noir said nothing of all this, it was easy to see that in his own way he admired her perfections no less than I. He left us at eight o'clock, and half an hour afterwards the fat aunt went away followed by her charming niece and the pale man who had come with them. I lost no time in taking leave with Tiretta, who promised the Pope's niece to join her on the morrow, which he did.

Three or four days later I received at my office a letter from Mdlle. de la Meure—the pretty niece. It ran as follows: "Madame, my aunt, my late mother's sister, is a devotee, fond of gaming, rich, stingy, and unjust. She does not like me, and not having succeeded in persuading me to take the veil, she wants to marry me to a wealthy Dunkirk merchant, whom I do not know, but (mark this) whom she does not know any more than I do. The matrimonial agent has praised him very much, and very naturally, as a man must praise his own goods. This gentleman is satisfied with an income of twelve hundred francs per annum, but he promises to leave me in his will no less than a hundred and fifty thousand francs. You must know that by my mother's will my aunt is obliged to pay me on my wedding day twenty-five thousand crowns.

"If what has taken place between us has not made me contemptible in your sight, I offer you my hand and heart with sixty-five thousand francs, and as much more on my aunt's death.

"Don't send me any answer, as I don't know how or by whom to receive your letter. You can answer me in your own person next Sunday at Madame Lambertini's. You will thus have four days whereon to consider this most important question. I do not exactly know whether I love you, but I am quite sure that I prefer you to any other man. I know that each of us has still to gain the other's esteem, but I am sure you would make my life a happy one, and that I should be a faithful wife. If you think that the happiness I seek can add to your own, I must warn you that you will need the aid of a lawyer, as my aunt is miserly, and will stick at trifles.

"If you decide in the affirmative you must find a convent for me to take refuge in before I commit myself to anything, as otherwise I should be exposed to the harsh treatment I wish to avoid. If, on the other hand, my proposal does not meet your views, I have one favour to ask by granting which you will earn my everlasting gratitude. This is that you will endeavour to see me no more, and will take care not to be present in any company in which you think I am to be found. Thus you will help me to forget you, and this is the least you can do for me. You may guess that I shall never be happy till I have become your wife or have forgotten you. Farewell! I reckon upon seeing you on Sunday."

This letter affected me. I felt that it was dictated by prudent, virtuous, and honourable feelings, and I found even more merit in the intellectual endowments of the girl than in her beauty. I blushed at having in a manner led her astray, and I should have thought myself worthy of punishment if I had been capable of refusing the hand offered to me with so much nobility of feeling. And a second but still a powerful consideration made me look complacently upon a fortune larger than I could reasonably expect to win. Nevertheless, the idea of the marriage state, for which I felt I had no vocation, made me tremble.

I knew myself too well not to be aware that as a married man I should be unhappy, and, consequently, with the best intentions I should fail in making the woman's life a happy one. My uncertainty in the four days which she had wisely left me convinced me that I was not in love with her. In spite of that, so weak was I that I could not summon up courage to reject her offer—still less to tell her so frankly, which would have made her esteem me.

During these four days I was entirely absorbed in this one subject. I bitterly repented of having outraged her modesty, for I now esteemed and respected her, but yet I could not make up my mind to repair the wrong I had done her. I could not bear to incur her dislike, but the idea of tying myself down was dreadful to me; and such is the condition of a man who has to choose between two alternatives, and cannot make up his mind.

Fearing lest my evil genius should take me to the opera or elsewhere, and in spite of myself make me miss my appointment, I resolved to dine with the Lambertini without having come to any decision. The pious niece of the Pope was at mass when I reached her house. I found Tiretta engaged in playing on the flute, but as soon as he saw me he dropped the instrument, ran up to me, embraced me, and gave me back the money his suit had cost me.

"I see you are in cash, old fellow; I congratulate you."

"It's a grievous piece of luck to me, for the money is stolen, and I am sorry I have got it though I was an accomplice in the theft."

"What! the money is stolen?"

"Yes, sharping is done here, and I have been taught to help. I share in their ill-gotten gains because I have not the strength of mind to refuse. My landlady and two or three women of the same sort pluck the pigeons. The business does not suit me, and I am thinking of leaving it. Sooner or later I shall kill or be killed, and either event will be the death of me, so I am thinking of leaving this cutthroat place as soon as possible."

"I advise you—nay, I bid you do so by all means, and I should think you had better be gone to-day than to-morrow."

"I don't want to do anything suddenly, as M. le Noir is a gentleman and my friend, and he thinks me a cousin to this wretched woman. As he knows nothing of the infamous trade she carries on, he would suspect something, and perhaps would leave her after learning the reason of my departure. I shall find some excuse or other in the course of the next five or six days, and then I will make haste and return to you."

The Lambertini thanked me for coming to dinner in a friendly manner, and told me that we should have the company of Mdlle. de la Meure and her aunt. I asked her if she was still satisfied with my friend "Sixtimes," and she told me that though the count did not always reside on his manor, she was for all that delighted with him; and said she,

"I am too good a monarch to ask too much of my vassals."

I congratulated her, and we continued to jest till the arrival of the two other guests.

As soon as Mdlle. de la Meure saw me she could scarcely conceal her pleasure. She was in half mourning, and looked so pretty in this costume, which threw up the whiteness of her skin, that I still wonder why that instant did not determine my fate.

Tiretta, who had been making his toilette, rejoined us, and as nothing prevented me from shewing the liking I had taken for the amiable girl I paid her all possible attention. I told the aunt that I found her niece so pretty that I would renounce my bachelorhood if I could find such a mate.

"My niece is a virtuous and sweet-tempered 'girl, sir, but she is utterly devoid either of intelligence or piety."

"Never mind the intelligence," said the niece, "but I was never found wanting in piety at the convent."

"I dare say the nuns are of the jesuitical party."

"What has that got to do with it, aunt?"

"Very much, child; the Jesuits and their adherents are well known to have no vital religion. But let us talk of something else. All that I want you to do is to know how to please your future husband."

"Is mademoiselle about to marry, then?"

"Her intended will probably arrive at the beginning of next month."

"Is he a lawyer?"

"No, sir; he is a well-to-do merchant."

"M. le Noir told me that your niece was the daughter of a councillor, and I did not imagine that you would sanction her marrying beneath her."

"There will be no question of such a thing in this instance, sir; and, after all, what is marrying beneath one? My niece's intended is an honest, and therefore a noble, man, and I am sure it will be her fault if she does not lead a life of perfect happiness with him."

"Quite so, supposing she loves him."

"Oh! love and all that kind of thing will come in good time, you know."

As these remarks could only give pain to the young lady, who listened in silence, I changed the conversation to the enormous crowd which would be present at the execution of Damien, and finding them extremely desirous of witnessing this horrible sight I offered them a large window with an excellent view. The ladies accepted with great pleasure, and I promised to escort them in good time.

I had no such thing as a window, but I knew that in Paris, as everywhere, money will procure anything. After dinner I went out on the plea of business, and, taking the first coach I came across, in a quarter of an hour I succeeded in renting a first floor window in excellent position for three louis. I paid in advance, taking care to have a receipt.

My business over, I hastened to rejoin the company, and found them engaged in piquet. Mdlle. de la Meure, who knew nothing about it, was tired of looking on. I came up to her, and having something to say we went to the other end of the room.

"Your letter, dearest, has made me the happiest of men. You have displayed in it such intelligence and such admirable characteristics as would win you the fervent adoration of every man of good sense."

"I only want one man's love. I will be content with the esteem of the rest."

"My angel, I will make you my wife, and I shall bless till my latest breath the lucky audacity to which I owe my being chosen before other men who would not have refused your hand, even without the fifty thousand crowns, which are nothing in comparison with your beauty and your wit."

"I am very glad you like me so much."

"Could I do otherwise? And now that you know my heart, do nothing hastily, but trust in me."

"You will not forget how I am placed."

"I will bear it in mind. Let me have time to take a house, to furnish it and to put myself in a position in which I shall be worthy of your hand. You must remember that I am only in furnished apartments; that you are well connected, and that I should not like to be regarded as a fortune-hunter."

"You know that my intended husband will soon arrive?"

"Yes, I will take care of that."

"When he does come, you know, matters will be pushed on rapidly."

"Not too rapidly for me to be able to set you free in twenty-four hours, and without letting your aunt know that the blow comes from me. You may rest assured, dearest, that the minister for foreign affairs, on being assured that you wish to marry me, and me only, will get you an inviolable asylum in the best convent in Paris. He will also retain counsel on your behalf, and if your mother's will is properly drawn out your aunt will soon be obliged to hand over your dowry, and to give security for the rest of the property. Do not trouble yourself about the matter, but let the Dunkirk merchant come when he likes. At all hazards, you may reckon upon me, and you may be sure you will not be in your aunt's house on the day fixed for the wedding."

"I confide in you entirely, but for goodness' sake say no more on a circumstance which wounds my sense of modesty. You said that I offered you marriage because you took liberties with me?"

"Was I wrong?"

"Yes, partly, at all events; and you ought to know that if I had not good reasons I should have done a very foolish thing in offering to marry you, but I may as well tell you that, liberties or no liberties, I should always have liked you better than anyone."

I was beside myself with joy, and seizing her hand I covered it with tender and respectful kisses; and I feel certain that if a notary and priest had been then and there available, I should have married her without the smallest hesitation.

Full of each other, like all lovers, we paid no attention to the horrible racket that was going on at the other end of the room. At last I thought it my duty to see what was happening, and leaving my intended I rejoined the company to quiet Tiretta.

I saw on the table a casket, its lid open, and full of all sorts of jewels; close by were two men who were disputing with Tiretta, who held a book in one hand. I saw at once that they were talking about a lottery, but why were they disputing? Tiretta told me they were a pair of knaves who had won thirty or forty louis of him by means of the book, which he handed to me.

"Sir," said one of the gamesters, "this book treats of a lottery in which all the calculations are made in the fairest manner possible. It contains twelve hundred leaves, two hundred being winning leaves, while the rest are blanks. Anyone who wants to play has only to pay a crown, and then to put a pin's point at random between two leaves of the closed book. The book is then opened at the place where the pin is, and if the leaf is blank the player loses; but if, on the other hand, the leaf bears a number, he is given the corresponding ticket, and an article of the value indicated on the ticket is then handed to him. Please to observe, sir, that the lowest prize is twelve francs, and there are some numbers worth as much as six hundred francs, and even one to the value of twelve hundred. We have been playing for an hour, and have lost several costly articles, and madam," pointing to my sweetheart's aunt, "has won a ring worth six louis, but as she preferred cash, she continued playing and lost the money she had gained."

"Yes," said the aunt, "and these gentlemen have won everybody's money with their accursed game; which proves it is all a mere cheat."

"It proves they are rogues," said Tiretta.

"But gentlemen," answered one of them, "in that case the receivers of the Government lottery are rogues too"; whereon Tiretta gave him a box on the ear. I threw myself between the two combatants, and told them not to speak a word.

"All lotteries," said I, "are advantageous to the holders, but the king is at the head of the Government lottery, and I am the principal receiver, in which character I shall proceed to confiscate this casket, and give you the choice of the following alternatives: You can, if you like, return to the persons present the money you have unlawfully won from them, whereupon I will let you go with your box. If you refuse to do so, I shall send for a policeman, who will take you to prison, and to-morrow you will be tried by M. Berier, to whom I shall take this book in the morning. We shall soon see whether we are rogues as well as they."

Seeing that they had to do with a man of determination, and that resistance would only result in their losing all, they resolved with as good a grace as they could muster to return all their winnings, and for all I know double the sum, for they were forced to return forty louis, though they swore they had only won twenty. The company was too select for me to venture to decide between them. In point of fact I was rather inclined to believe the rascals, but I was angry with them, and I wanted them to pay a good price for having made a comparison, quite right in the main, but odious to me in the extreme. The same reason, doubtless, prevented me from giving them back their book, which I had no earthly right to keep, and which they asked me in vain to return to them. My firmness and my threats, and perhaps also the fear of the police, made them think themselves lucky to get off with their jewel-box. As soon as they were gone the ladies, like the kindly creatures they were, began to pity them. "You might have given them back their book," they said to me.

"And you, ladies, might have let them keep their money."

"But they cheated us of it."

"Did they? Well, their cheating was done with the book, and I have done them a kindness by taking it from them."

They felt the force of my remarks, and the conversation took another turn.

Early next morning the two gamesters paid me a visit bringing with them as a bribe a beautiful casket containing twenty-four lovely pieces of Dresden china. I found this argument irresistible, and I felt obliged to return them the book, threatening them at the same time with imprisonment if they dared to carry on their business in Paris for the future. They promised me to abstain from doing so—no doubt with a mental reservation, but I cared nothing about that.

I resolved to offer this beautiful gift to Mdlle. de la Meure, and I took it to her the same day. I had a hearty welcome, and the aunt loaded me with thanks.

On March the 28th, the day of Damien's martyrdom, I went to fetch the ladies in good time; and as the carriage would scarcely hold us all, no objection was made to my taking my sweetheart on my knee, and in this order we reached the Place de Greve. The three ladies packing themselves together as tightly as possible took up their positions at the window, leaning forward on their elbows, so as to prevent us seeing from behind. The window had two steps to it, and they stood on the second; and in order to see we had to stand on the same step, for if we had stood on the first we should not have been able to see over their heads. I have my reasons for giving these minutiae, as otherwise the reader would have some difficulty in guessing at the details which I am obliged to pass over in silence.

We had the courage to watch the dreadful sight for four hours. The circumstances of Damien's execution are too well known to render it necessary for me to speak of them; indeed, the account would be too long a one, and in my opinion such horrors are an offence to our common humanity.

Damien was a fanatic, who, with the idea of doing a good work and obtaining a heavenly reward, had tried to assassinate Louis XV.; and though the attempt was a failure, and he only gave the king a slight wound, he was torn to pieces as if his crime had been consummated.

While this victim of the Jesuits was being executed, I was several times obliged to turn away my face and to stop my ears as I heard his piercing shrieks, half of his body having been torn from him, but the Lambertini and the fat aunt did not budge an inch. Was it because their hearts were hardened? They told me, and I pretended to believe them, that their horror at the wretch's wickedness prevented Them feeling that compassion which his unheard-of torments should have excited. The fact was that Tiretta kept the pious aunt curiously engaged during the whole time of the execution, and this, perhaps, was what prevented the virtuous lady from moving or even turning her head round.

Finding himself behind her, he had taken the precaution to lift up her dress to avoid treading on it. That, no doubt, was according to the rule; but soon after, on giving an involuntary glance in their direction, I found that Tiretta had carried his precautions rather far, and, not wishing to interrupt my friend or to make the lady feel awkward, I turned my head and stood in such a way that my sweetheart could see nothing of what was going on; this put the good lady at her ease. For two hours after I heard a continuous rustling, and relishing the joke I kept quiet the whole time. I admired Tiretta's hearty appetite still more than his courage, but what pleased me most was the touching resignation with which the pious aunt bore it all.

At the end of this long session I saw Madame turn round, and doing the same I fixed my gaze on Tiretta, and found him looking as fresh and cool as if nothing had happened, but the aunt seemed to me to have a rather pensive appearance. She had been under the fatal necessity of keeping quiet and letting Tiretta do what he liked for fear of the Lambertini's jests, and lest her niece might be scandalized by the revelation of mysteries of which she was supposed to know nothing.

We set out, and having dropped the Pope's niece at her door, I begged her to lend me Tiretta for a few hours, and I then took Madame to her house in the Rue St. Andre-des-Arts. She asked me to come and see her the following day as she had something to tell me, and I remarked that she took no notice of my friend as she left us. We went to the "Hotel de Russie," where they gave you an excellent dinner for six francs a head, and I thought my mad friend stood in need of recruiting his strength.

"What were you doing behind Madame—?" said I.

"I am sure you saw nothing, or anybody else either."

"No, because when I saw the beginning of your manoeuvres, and guessed what was coming, I stood in such a way that neither the Lambertini or the pretty niece could see you. I can guess what your goal was, and I must say I admire your hearty appetite. But your wretched victim appears to be rather angry."

"Oh! my dear fellow, that's all the affectation of an old maid. She may pretend to be put out, but as she kept quiet the whole time I am certain she would be glad to begin all over again."

"I think so, too, in her heart of hearts; but her pride might suggest that you had been lacking in respect, and the suggestion would be by no means groundless."

"Respect, you say; but must one not always be lacking in respect to women when one wants to come to the point?"

"Quite so, but there's a distinction between what lovers may do when they are together, and what is proper in the presence of a mixed company."

"Yes, but I snatched four distinct favours from her, without the least opposition; had I not therefore good reasons for taking her consent for granted?"

"You reason well, but you see she is out of humour with you. She wants to speak to me to-morrow, and I have no doubt that you will be the subject of our conversation."

"Possibly, but still I should think she would not speak to you of the comic piece of business; it would be very silly of her."

"Why so? You don't know these pious women. They are brought up by Jesuits, who often give them some good lessons on the subject, and they are delighted to confess to a third party; and these confessions with a seasoning of tears gives them in their own eyes quite a halo of saintliness."

"Well, let her tell you if she likes. We shall see what comes of it."

"Possibly she may demand satisfaction; in which case I shall be glad to do my best for her."

"You make me laugh! I can't imagine what sort of satisfaction she could claim, unless she wants to punish me by the 'Lex talionis', which would be hardly practicable without a repetition of the original offence. If she had not liked the game, all she had to do was to give me a push which would have sent me backwards."

"Yes, but that would have let us know what you had been trying to do."

"Well, if it comes to that, the slightest movement would have rendered the whole process null and void; but as it was she stood in the proper position as quiet as a lamb; nothing could be easier."

"It's an amusing business altogether. But did you notice that the Lambertini was angry with you, too? She, perhaps, saw what you were doing, and felt hurt."

"Oh! she has got another cause of complaint against me. We have fallen out, and I am leaving her this evening."

"Really?"

"Yes, I will tell you all about it. Yesterday evening, a young fellow in the Inland Revenue who had been seduced to sup with us by a hussy of Genoa, after losing forty louis, threw, the cards in the face of my landlady and called her a thief. On the impulse of the moment I took a candle and put it out on his face. I might have destroyed one of his eyes, but I fortunately hit him on the cheek. He immediately ran for his sword, mine was ready, and if the Genoese had not thrown herself between us murder might have been committed. When the poor wretch saw his cheek in the glass, he became so furious that nothing short of the return of all his money would appease him. They gave it him back, in spite of my advice, for in doing so they admitted, tacitly at all events, that it had been won by cheating. This caused a sharp dispute between the Lambertini and myself after he had gone. She said we should have kept the forty louis, and nothing would have happened except for my interference, that it was her and not me whom the young man had insulted. The Genoese added that if we had kept cool we should have had the plucking of him, but that God alone knew what he would do now with the mark of the burn on his face. Tired of the talk of these infamous women, I was about to leave them, but my landlady began to ride the high horse, and went so far as to call me a beggar.

"If M. le Noir had not come in just then, she would have had a bad time of it, as my stick was already in my hand. As soon as they saw him they told me to hold my tongue, but my blood was up; and turning towards the worthy man I told him that his mistress had called me a beggar, that she was a common prostitute, that I was not her cousin, nor in any way related to her, and that I should leave her that very day. As soon as I had come to the end of this short and swift discourse, I went out and shut myself up in my room. In the course of the next two hours I shall go and fetch my linen, and I hope to breakfast with you to-morrow."

Tiretta did well. His heart was in the right place, and he was wise not to allow the foolish impulses of youth to plunge him in the sink of corruption. As long as a man has not committed a dishonourable action, as long as his heart is sound, though his head may go astray, the path of duty is still open to him. I should say the same of women if prejudice were not so strong in their case, and if they were not much more under the influence of the heart than the head.

After a good dinner washed down by some delicious Sillery we parted, and I spent the evening in writing. Next morning I did some business, and at noon went to see the distressed devotee, whom I found at home with her charming niece. We talked a few minutes about the weather, and she then told my sweetheart to leave us as she wanted to speak to me. I was prepared for what was coming and I waited for her to break the silence which all women of her position observe. "You will be surprised, sir, at what I am going to tell you, for I have determined to bring before you a complaint of an unheard-of character. The case is really of the most delicate nature, and I am impelled to make a confidant of you by the impression you made on me when I first saw you. I consider you to be a man of discretion, of honour, and above all a moral man; in short, I believe you have experienced religion, and if I am making a mistake it will be a pity, for though I have been insulted I don't lack means of avenging myself, and as you are his friend you will be sorry for him."

"Is Tiretta the guilty party, madam?"

"The same."

"And what is his crime?"

"He is a villain; he has insulted me in the most monstrous manner."

"I should not have thought him capable of doing so."

"I daresay not, but then you are a moral man."

"But what was the nature of his offence? You may confide in my secrecy."

"I really couldn't tell you, it's quite out of the question; but I trust you will be able to guess it. Yesterday, during the execution of the wretched Damien, he strongly abused the position in which he found himself behind me."

"I see; I understand what you mean; you need say no more. You have cause for anger, and he is to blame for acting in such a manner. But allow me to say that the case is not unexampled or even uncommon, and I think you might make some allowance for the strength of love, the close quarters, and above all for the youth and passion of the sinner. Moreover, the offence is one which may be expiated in a number of ways, provided the parties come to an agreement. Tiretta is young and a perfect gentleman, he is handsome and at bottom a good fellow; could not a marriage be arranged?"

I waited for a reply, but perceiving that the injured party kept silence (a circumstance which seemed to me a good omen) I went on.

"If marriage should not meet your views, we might try a lasting friendship, in which he could shew his repentance and prove himself deserving of pardon. Remember, madam, that Tiretta is only a man, and therefore subject to all the weaknesses of our poor human nature; and even you have your share of the blame."

"I, sir?"

"Involuntarily, madam, involuntarily; not you but your charms led him astray. Nevertheless, without this incentive the circumstance would never have taken place, and I think you should consider your beauty as a mitigation of the offence."

"You plead your cause well, sir, but I will do you justice and confess that all your remarks have been characterized by much Christian feeling. However, you are reasoning on false premises; you are ignorant of his real crime, yet how should you guess it?"

With this she burst into tears, leading me completely off the scent, and not knowing what to think.

"He can't have stolen her purse," said I to myself, "as I don't think him capable of such an action; and if I did I'd blow his brains out."

The afflicted lady soon dried her tears, and went on as follows:

"You are thinking of a deed which one might possibly succeed in reconciling with reason, and in making amends for; but the crime of which that brute has been guilty I dare scarcely imagine, as it is almost enough to drive me mad."

"Good heavens! you can't mean it? This is dreadful; do I hear you aright?"

"Yes. You are moved, I see, but such are the circumstances of the case. Pardon my tears, which flow from anger and the shame with which I am covered."

"Yes, and from outraged religion, too."

"Certainly, certainly. That is the chief source of my grief, and I should have mentioned it if I had not feared you were not so strongly attached to religion as myself."

"Nobody, God be praised! could be more strongly attached to religion than I, and nothing can ever unloose the ties which bind me to it:"

"You will be grieved, then, to hear that I am destined to suffer eternal punishment, for I must and will be avenged."

"Not so, madam, perish the thought, as I could not become your accomplice in such a design, and if you will not abandon it at least say nothing to me on the subject. I will promise you to tell him nothing, although as he lives with me the sacred laws of hospitality oblige me to give him due warning."

"I thought he lived with the Lambertini"

"He left her yesterday. The connection between them was a criminal one, and I have drawn him back from the brink of the precipice."

"You don't mean to say so!"

"Yes, upon my word of honour:"

"You astonish one. This is very edifying. I don't wish the young man's death, but you must confess he owes me some reparation."

"He does indeed. A charming Frenchwoman is not to be handled in the Italian manner without signal amends, but I can think of nothing at all commensurate with the offence. There is only one plan, which I will endeavour to carry out if you will agree to it."

"What is that?"

"I will put the guilty party in your power without his knowing what is to happen, and I will leave you alone, so that you can wreak all your wrath upon him, provided you will allow me to be, unknown to him, in the next room, as I shall regard myself as responsible for his safety."

"I consent. You will stay in this room, and he must be left in the other where I shall receive you, but take care he has no suspicion of your presence."

"He shan't dream of it. He will not even know where I am taking him, for he must not think that I have been informed of his misdoings. As soon as we be there, and the conversation becomes general, I shall leave the room, pretending to be going away."

"When will you bring him? I long to cover him with confusion. I will make him tremble. I am curious to hear how he will justify himself for such an offence."

"I can't say, but I think and hope that your presence will make him eloquent, as I should like to see your differences adjusted."

At one o'clock the Abbe des Forges arrived, and she made me sit down to dinner with them. This abbe was a pupil of the famous Bishop of Auxerre, who was still living. I talked so well on the subject of grace, and made so many quotations from St. Augustine, that the abbe and the devotee took me for a zealous Jansenista character with which my dress and appearance did not at all correspond. My sweetheart did not give me a single glance while the meal was going on, and thinking she had some motives I abstained from speaking to her.

After dinner, which, by the way, was a very good one, I promised the offended lady to bring her the culprit bound hand and foot next day, after the play was over. To put her at her ease I said I should walk, as I was certain that he would not recognize the house in the dark.

As soon as I saw Tiretta, I began with a seriocomic air to reproach him for the dreadful crime he had committed on the body of a lady in every way virtuous and respectable, but the mad fellow began to laugh, and it would have been waste of time for me to try to stop him.

"What!" said he, "she has had the courage to tell you all?"

"You don't deny the fact, then?"

"If she says it is so, I don't think I can give her the lie, but I am ready to swear that I don't know how the land lay. In the position I was in it was impossible for me to say where I took up my dwelling. However, I will quiet her indignation, as I shall come to the point quickly, and not let her wait."

"You will ruin the business if you don't take care; be as long as you can; she will like that best, and it will be to your interest. Don't hurry yourself, and never mind me, as I am sure to get on all right while you are changing anger into a softer passion. Remember not to know that I am in the house, and if you only stay with her a short time (which I don't think will be the case) take a coach and be off. You know the least a pious woman like her can do will be to provide me with fire and company. Don't forget that she is well-born like yourself. These women of quality are, no doubt, as immoral as any other women, since they are constructed of the same material, but they like to have their pride flattered by certain attentions. She is rich, a devote, and, what is more, inclined to pleasure; strive to gain her friendship 'faciem ad faciem', as the King of Prussia says. You may, perhaps, make your fortune."

"If she asks you why you have left the Pope's niece, take care not to tell her the reason. She will be pleased with your discretion. In short, do your best to expiate the enormity of your offence."

"I have only to speak the truth. I went in in the dark."

"That's an odd reason, but it may seem convincing to a Frenchwoman."

I need not tell the reader that I gave Tiretta a full account of my conversation with the lady. If any complain of this breach of honour, I must tell them that I had made a mental reservation not to keep my promise, and those who are acquainted with the morality of the children of Ignatius will understand that I was completely at my ease.

Next day we went to the opera, and afterwards, our plans made out, we walked to the house of the insulted and virtuous lady. She received us with great dignity, but yet there was an agreeable undercurrent in her voice and manner which I thought very promising.

"I never take supper," she said, "but if you had forewarned me of your visit I should have got something for you."

After telling her all the news I had heard in the theatre, I pretended to be obliged to go, and begged her to let me leave the count with her for a few minutes.

"If I am more than a quarter of an hour," said I to the count, "don't wait. Take a coach home and we shall see each other to-morrow."

Instead of going downstairs I went into the next room, and two minutes after who should enter but my sweetheart, who looked charmed and yet puzzled at my appearance.

"I think I must be dreaming," said she, "but my aunt has charged me not to leave you alone, and to tell her woman not to come upstairs unless she rings the bell. Your friend is with her, and she told me to speak low as he is not to know that you are here. What does it all mean?"

"You are curious, are you?"

"I confess I am in this instance, for all this mystery seems designed to excite curiosity."

"Dearest, you shall know all; but how cold it is."

"My aunt has told me to make a good fire, she has become liberal or rather lavish all of a sudden; look at the wax candles."

"That's a new thing, is it?"

"Oh, quite new."

As soon as we were seated in front of the fire I began to tell her the story, to which she listened with all the attention a young girl can give to such a matter; but as I had thought it well to pass over some of the details, she could not properly understand what crime it was that Tiretta had committed. I was not sorry to be obliged to tell her the story in plain language, and to give more expression I employed the language of gesture, which made her blush and laugh at the same time. I then told her that, having taken up the question of the reparation that was due to her aunt, I had so arranged matters that I was certain of being alone with her all the time my friend was engaged. Thereupon I began to cover her pretty face with kisses, and as I allowed myself no other liberties she received my caresses as a proof of the greatness of my love and the purity of my feelings.

"Dearest," she said, "what you say puzzles me; there are two things which I can't understand. How could Tiretta succeed in committing this crime with my aunt, which I think would only be possible with the consent of the party attacked, but quite impossible without it; and this makes me believe that if the thing was done it was done with her hearty good will."

"Very true, for if she did not like it she had only to change her position."

"Not so much as that; she need only have kept the door shut."

"There, sweetheart, you are wrong, for a properly-made man only asks you to keep still and he will overcome all obstacles. Moreover, I don't expect that your aunt's door is so well shut as yours."

"I believe that I could defy all the Tirettas in the world.

"There's another thing I don't understand, and that is how my blessed aunt came to tell you all about it; for if she had any sense she might have known that it would only make you laugh. And what satisfaction does she expect to get from a brute like that, who possibly thinks the affair a matter of no consequence. I should think he would do the same to any woman who occupied the same position as my aunt."

"You are right, for he told me he went in like a blind man, not knowing where he was going."

"Your friend is a queer fellow, and if other men are like him I am sure I should have no feeling but contempt for them."

"She has told me nothing about the satisfaction she is thinking of, and which she possibly feels quite sure of attaining; but I think I can guess what it will be namely, a formal declaration of love; and I suppose he will expiate his crime by becoming her lover, and doubtless this will be their wedding night."

"The affair is getting amusing. I can't believe it. My dear aunt is too anxious about her salvation; and how do you imagine the young man can ever fall in love with her, or play the part with such a face as hers before his eyes. Have you ever seen a countenance as disgusting as my aunt's? Her skin is covered with pimples, her eyes distil humours, and her teeth and breath are enough to discourage any man. She's hideous."

"All that is nothing to a young spark of twenty-five; one is always ready for an assault at that age; not like me who only feel myself a man in presence of charms like yours, of which I long to be the lawful possessor."

"You will find me the most affectionate of wives, and I feel quite sure that I shall have your heart in such good keeping that I shall never be afraid of losing it."

We had talked thus pleasantly for an hour, and Tiretta was still with the aunt. I thought things pointed towards a reconciliation, and judged the matter was getting serious. I told my sweetheart my opinion, and asked her to give me something to eat.

"I can only give you," said she, "some bread and cheese, a slice of ham, and some wine which my aunt pronounces excellent."

"Bring them quick, then; I am fainting with hunger."

She soon laid the table for two, and put on it all the food she had. The cheese was Roquefort, and the ham had been covered with jelly. About ten persons with reasonable appetites should have been able to sup on what there was; but (how I know not) the whole disappeared, and also two bottles of Chambertin, which I seem to taste now. My sweetheart's eyes gleamed with pleasure: truly Chambertin and Roquefort are excellent thinks to restore an old love and to ripen a young one.

"Don't you want to know what your aunt has been doing the last two hours with M. Sixtimes?"

"They are playing, perhaps; but there is a small hole in the wall, and I will look and see. I can only see the two candles, and the wicks are an inch long."

"Didn't I say so? Give me a coverlet and I will sleep on the sofa here, and do you go to bed. But let me look at it first:"

She made me come into her little room, where I saw a pretty bed, a prayer desk, and a large crucifix.

"Your bed is too small for you, dear heart."

"Oh, not at all! I am very comfortable"; and so saying she laid down at full length.

"What a beautiful wife I shall have! Nay, don't move, let me look at you so." My hand began to press the bosom of her dress, where were imprisoned two spheres which seemed to lament their captivity. I went farther, I began to untie strings . . . for where does desire stop short?

"Sweetheart, I cannot resist, but you will not love me afterwards."

"I will always love you:"

Soon her beautiful breasts were exposed to my burning kisses. The flame of my love lit another in her heart, and forgetting her former self she opened her arms to me, making me promise not to despise her, and what would one not promise! The modesty inherent in the sex, the fear of results, perhaps a kind of instinct which reveals to them the natural faithlessness of men make women ask for such promises, but what mistress, if really amorous, would even think of asking her lover to respect her in the moment of delirious ecstacy, when all one's being is centred on the fulfilment of desire?

After we had passed an hour in these amorous toyings, which set my sweetheart on fire, her charms having never before been exposed to the burning lips or the free caresses of a man, I said to her,

"I grieve to leave you without having rendered to your beauty the greatest homage which it deserves so well."

A sigh was her only answer.

It was cold, the fire was out, and I had to spend the night on the sofa.

"Give me a coverlet, dearest, that I may go away from you, for I should die here between love and cold if you made me abstain."

"Lie where I have been, sweetheart. I will get up and rekindle the fire."

She got up in all her naked charms, and as she put a stick to the fire the flame leapt up; I rose, I found her standing so as to display all her beauties, and I could refrain no longer. I pressed her to my heart, she returned my caresses, and till day-break we gave ourselves up to an ecstacy of pleasure.

We had spent four or five delicious hours on the sofa. She then left me, and after making a good fire she went to her room, and I remained on the sofa and slept till noon. I was awakened by Madame, who wore a graceful undress.

"Still asleep, M. Casanova?"

"Ah! good morning, madam, good morning. And what has become of my friend?"

"He has become mine, I have forgiven him."

"What has he done to be worthy of so generous a pardon?"

"He proved to me that he made a mistake."

"I am delighted to hear it; where is he?"

"He has gone home, where you will find him; but don't say anything about your spending the night here, or he will think it was spent with my niece. I am very much obliged to you for what you have done, and I have only to ask you to be discreet."

"You can count on me entirely, for I am grateful to you for having forgiven my friend."

"Who would not do so? The dear young man is something more than mortal. If you knew how he loved me! I am grateful to him, and I have taken him to board for a year; he will be well lodged, well fed, and so on."

"What a delightful plan! You have arranged the terms, I suppose."

"All that will be settled in a friendly way, and we shall not need to have recourse to arbitration. We shall set out to-day for Villette, where I have a nice little house; for you know that it is necessary, at first, to act in such a way as to give no opportunity to slanderers. My lover will have all he wants, and whenever you, sir, honour us with your presence you will find a pretty room and a good bed at your disposal. All I am sorry for is that you will find it tedious; my poor niece is so dull."

"Madam, your niece is delightful; she gave me yesterday evening an excellent supper and kept me company till three o'clock this morning."

"Really? I can't make it out how she gave you anything, as there was nothing in the house."

"At any rate, madam, she gave me an excellent supper, of which there are no remains, and after keeping me company she went to bed, and I have had a good night on this comfortable sofa."

"I am glad that you, like myself, were pleased with everything, but I did not think my niece so clever."

"She is very clever, madam—in my eyes, at all events:"

"Oh, sir! you are a judge of wit, let us go and see her. She has locked her door. Come open the door, why have you shut yourself up, you little prude? what are you afraid of. My Casanova is incapable of hurting you."

The niece opened her door and apologized for the disorder of her dress, but what costume could have suited her better? Her costume was dazzling."

"There she is," said the aunt, "and she is not so bad looking after all, but it is a pity she is so stupid. You were very right to give this gentleman a supper. I am much obliged to you for doing so. I have been playing all night, and when one is playing one only thinks of the game. I have determined on taking young Tiretta to board with us. He is an excellent and clever young man, and I am sure he will learn to speak French before long. Get dressed, my dear, as we must begin to pack. We shall set out this afternoon for Villette, and shall spend there the whole of the spring. There is no need, you know, to say anything about this to my sister:"

"I, aunt? Certainly not. Did I ever tell her anything on the other occasions?"

"Other occasions! You see what a silly girl it is. Do you mean by 'other occasions,' that I have been circumstanced like this before?"

"No, aunt. I only meant to say that I had never told her anything of what you did."

"That's right, my dear, but you must learn to express yourself properly. We dine at two, and I hope to have the pleasure of M. Casanova's company at dinner; we will start immediately after the meal. Tiretta promised to bring his small portmanteau with him, and it will go with our luggage."

After promising to dine with them, I bade the ladies good-bye; and I went home as fast as I could walk, for I was as curious as a woman to know what arrangements had been made.

"Well," said I to Tiretta, "I find you have got a place. Tell me all about it."

"My dear fellow, I have sold myself for a year. My pay is to be twenty-five louis a month, a good table, good lodging, etc., etc."

"I congratulate you."

"Do you think it is worth the trouble?"

"There's no rose without a thorn. She told me you were something more than mortal."

"I worked hard all night to prove it to her; but I am quite sure your time was better employed than mine."

"I slept like a king. Dress yourself, as I am coming to dinner, and I want to see you set out for Villette. I shall come and see you there now and then, as your sweetheart has told me that a room shall be set apart for my convenience."

We arrived at two o'clock. Madame dressed in a girlish style presented a singular appearance, but Mdlle. de la Meure's beauty shone like a star. Love and pleasure had given her a new life, a new being. We had a capital dinner, as the good lady had made the repast dainty like herself; but in the dishes there was nothing absurd, while her whole appearance was comic in the highest degree. At four they all set out, and I spent my evening at the Italian comedy.

I was in love with Mdlle. de la Meure, but Silvia's daughter, whose company at supper was all I had of her, weakened a love which now left nothing more to desire.

We complain of women who, though loving us and sure of our love, refuse us their favours; but we are wrong in doing so, for if they love they have good reason to fear lest they lose us in the moment of satisfying our desires. Naturally they should do all in their power to retain our hearts, and the best way to do so is to cherish our desire of possessing them; but desire is only kept alive by being denied: enjoyment kills it, since one cannot desire what one has got. I am, therefore, of opinion that women are quite right to refuse us. But if it be granted that the passions of the two sexes are of equal strength, how comes it that a man never refuses to gratify a woman who loves him and entreats him to be kind?

We cannot receive the argument founded on the fear of results, as that is a particular and not a general consideration. Our conclusion, then, will be that the reason lies in the fact that a man thinks more of the pleasure he imparts than that which he receives, and is therefore eager to impart his bliss to another. We know, also, that, as a general rule, women, when once enjoyed, double their love and affection. On the other hand, women think more of the pleasure they receive than of that which they impart, and therefore put off enjoyment as long as possible, since they fear that in giving themselves up they lose their chief good—their own pleasure. This feeling is peculiar to the sex, and is the only cause of coquetry, pardonable in a woman, detestable in a man.

Silvia's daughter loved me, and she knew I loved her, although I had never said so, but women's wit is keen. At the same time she endeavoured not to let me know her feelings, as she was afraid of encouraging me to ask favours of her, and she did not feel sure of her strength to refuse them; and she knew my inconstant nature. Her relations intended her for Clement, who had been teaching her the clavichord for the last three years. She knew of the arrangement and had no objection, for though she did not love him she liked him very well. Most girls are wedded without love, and they are not sorry for it afterwards. They know that by marriage they become of some consequence in the world, and they marry to have a house of their own and a good position in society. They seem to know that a husband and a lover need not be synonymous terms. At Paris men are actuated by the same views, and most marriages are matters of convenience. The French are jealous of their mistresses, but never of their wives.

There could be no doubt that M. Clement was very much in love, and Mdlle. Baletti was delighted that I noticed it, as she thought this would bring me to a declaration, and she was quite right. The departure of Mdlle. de la Meure had a good deal to do with my determination to declare myself; and I was very sorry to have done so afterwards, for after I had told her I loved her Clement was dismissed, and my position was worse than before. The man who declares his love for a woman in words wants to be sent to school again.

Three days after the departure of Tiretta, I took him what small belongings he had, and Madame seemed very glad to see me. The Abbe des Forges arrived just as we were sitting down to dinner, and though he had been very friendly to me at Paris he did not so much as look at me all through the meal, and treated Tiretta in the same way. I, for my part, took no notice of him, but Tiretta, not so patient as I, at last lost his temper and got up, begging Madame to tell him when she was going to have that fellow to dine with her. We rose from table without saying a word, and the silent abbe went with madam into another room.

Tiretta took me to see his room, which was handsomely furnished, and, as was right, adjoined his sweetheart's. Whilst he was putting his things in order, Mdlle. de la Meure made me come and see my apartment. It was a very nice room on the ground floor, and facing hers. I took care to point out to her how easily I could pay her a visit after everyone was in bed, but she said we should not be comfortable in her room, and that she would consequently save me the trouble of getting out of bed. It will be guessed that I had no objections to make to this arrangement.

She then told me of her aunt's folly about Tiretta.

"She believes," said she, "that we do not know he sleeps with her."

"Believes, or pretends to believe."

"Possibly. She rang for me at eleven o'clock this morning and told me to go and ask him what kind of night he had passed. I did so, but seeing his bed had not been slept in I asked him if he had not been to sleep.

"'No,' said he, 'I have been writing all night, but please don't say anything about it to your aunt: I promised with all my heart to be as silent as the grave."

"Does he make sheep's eyes at you?"

"No, but if he did it would be all the same. Though he is not over sharp he knows, I think, what I think of him."

"Why have you such a poor opinion of him?"

"Why? My aunt pays him. I think selling one's self is a dreadful idea."

"But you pay me."

"Yes, but in the same coin as you give me."

The old aunt was always calling her niece stupid, but on the contrary I thought her very clever, and as virtuous as clever. I should never have seduced her if she had not been brought up in a convent.

I went back to Tiretta, and had some pleasant conversation with him. I asked him how he liked his place.

"I don't like it much, but as it costs me nothing I am not absolutely wretched."

"But her face!"

"I don't look at it, and there's one thing I like about her—she is so clean."

"Does she take good care of you?"

"O yes, she is full of feeling for me. This morning she refused the greeting I offered her. 'I am sure,' said she, 'that my refusal will pain you, but your health is so dear to me that I feel bound to look after it."

As soon as the gloomy Abbe des Forges was gone and Madame was alone, we rejoined her. She treated me as her gossip, and played the timid child for Tiretta's benefit, and he played up to her admirably, much to my admiration.

"I shall see no more of that foolish priest," said she; "for after telling me that I was lost both in this world and the next he threatened to abandon me, and I took him at his word."

An actress named Quinault, who had left the stage and lived close by, came to call, and soon after Madame Favart and the Abbe de Voisenon arrived, followed by Madame Amelin with a handsome lad named Calabre, whom she called her nephew. He was as like her as two peas, but she did not seem to think that a sufficient reason for confessing she was his mother. M. Patron, a Piedmontese, who also came with her, made a bank at faro and in a couple of hours won everybody's money with the exception of mine, as I knew better than to play. My time was better occupied in the company of my sweet mistress. I saw through the Piedmontese, and had put him down as a knave; but Tiretta was not so sharp, and consequently lost all the money he had in his pockets and a hundred louis besides. The banker having reaped a good harvest put down the cards, and Tiretta told him in good Italian that he was a cheat, to which the Piedmontese replied with the greatest coolness that he lied. Thinking that the quarrel might have an unpleasant ending, I told him that Tiretta was only jesting, and I made my friend say so, too. He then left the company and went to his room.

Eight years afterwards I saw this Patron at St. Petersburg, and in the year 1767 he was assassinated in Poland.

The same evening I preached Tiretta a severe yet friendly sermon. I pointed out to him that when he played he was at the mercy of the banker, who might be a rogue but a man of courage too, and so in calling him a cheat he was risking his life.

"Am I to let myself be robbed, then?"

"Yes, you have a free choice in the matter; nobody will make you play."

"I certainly will not pay him that hundred louis."

"I advise you to do so, and to do so before you are asked."

"You have a knack of persuading one to do what you will, even though one be disposed to take no notice of your advice."

"That's because I speak from heart and head at once, and have some experience in these affairs as well."

Three quarters of an hour afterwards I went to bed and my mistress came to me before long. We spent a sweeter night than before, for it is often a matter of some difficulty to pluck the first flower; and the price which most men put on this little trifle is founded more on egotism than any feeling of pleasure.

Next day, after dining with the family and admiring the roses on my sweetheart's cheeks, I returned to Paris. Three or four days later Tiretta came to tell me that the Dunkirk merchant had arrived, that he was coming to dine at Madame's, and that she requested me to make one of the party. I was prepared for the news, but the blood rushed into my face. Tiretta saw it, and to a certain extent divined my feelings. "You are in love with the niece," said he.

"Why do you think so?"

"By the mystery you make about her; but love betrays itself even by its silence."

"You are a knowing fellow, Tiretta. I will come to dinner, but don't say a word to anybody."

My heart was rent in twain. Possibly if the merchant had put off his arrival for a month I should have welcomed it; but to have only just lifted the nectar to my lips, and to see the precious vessel escape from my hands! To this day I can recall my feelings, and the very recollection is not devoid of bitterness.

I was in a fearful state of perplexity, as I always was whenever it was necessary for me to resolve, and I felt that I could not do so. If the reader has been placed in the same position he will understand my feelings. I could not make up my mind to consent to her marrying, nor could I resolve to wed her myself and gain certain happiness.

I went to Villette and was a little surprised to find Mdlle. de la Meure more elaborately dressed than usual.

"Your intended," I said, "would have pronounced you charming without all that."

"My aunt doesn't think so"

"You have not seen him yet?"

"No, but I should like to, although I trust with your help never to become his wife."

Soon after, she arrived with Corneman, the banker, who had been the agent in this business transaction. The merchant was a fine man, about forty, with a frank and open face. His dress was good though not elaborate. He introduced himself simply but in a polite manner to Madame, and he did not look at his future wife till the aunt presented her to him. His manner immediately became more pleasing; and without making use of flowers of speech he said in a very feeling way that he trusted the impression he had made on her was equal to that which she had made on him. Her only answer was a low curtsy, but she studied him carefully.

Dinner was served, and in the course of the meal we talked of almost everything—except marriage. The happy pair only caught each other's eyes by chance, and did not speak to one another. After dinner Mdlle. de la Meure went to her room, and the aunt went into her closet with the banker and the merchant, and they were in close conversation for two hours. At the end of that time the gentlemen were obliged to return to Paris, and Madame, after summoning her niece, told the merchant she would expect him to dinner on the day following, and that she was sure that her niece would be glad to see him again.

"Won't you, my dear?"

"Yes, aunt, I shall be very glad to see the gentleman again."

If she had not answered thus, the merchant would have gone away without hearing his future bride speak.

"Well," said the aunt, "what do you think of your husband?"

"Allow me to put off my answer till to-morrow; but be good enough, when we are at table, to draw me into the conversation, for it is very possible that my face has not repelled him, but so far he knows nothing of my mental powers; possibly my want of wit may destroy any slight impression my face may have made."

"Yes, I am afraid you will begin to talk nonsense, and make him lose the good opinion he seems to have formed of you."

"It is not right to deceive anybody. If he is disabused of his fictitious ideas by the appearance of the truth, so much the better for him; and so much the worse for both of us, if we decide on marrying without the slightest knowledge of each other's habits and ways of thought."

"What do you think of him?"

"I think he is rather nice-looking, and his manners are kind and polite; but let us wait till to-morrow."

"Perhaps he will have nothing more to say to me; I am so stupid."

"I know very well that you think yourself very clever, and that's where your fault lies; it's your self-conceit which makes you stupid, although M. Casanova takes you for a wit."

"Perhaps he may know what he is talking about."

"My poor dear, he is only laughing at you."

"I have good reasons for thinking otherwise, aunt."

"There you go; you will never get any sense."

"Pardon me, madam, if I cannot be of your opinion. Mademoiselle is quite right in saying that I do not laugh at her. I dare to say that to-morrow she will shine in the conversation."

"You think so? I am glad to hear it. Now let us have a game at piquet, and I will play against you and my niece, for she must learn the game."

Tiretta asked leave of his darling to go to the play, and we played on till supper-time. On his return, Tiretta made us almost die of laughing with his attempts to tell us in his broken French the plot of the play he had seen.

I had been in my bedroom for a quarter of an hour, expecting to see my sweetheart in some pretty kind of undress, when all of a sudden I saw her come in with all her clothes on. I was surprised at this circumstance, and it seemed to me of evil omen.

"You are astonished to see me thus," said she, "but I want to speak to you for a moment, and then I will take off my clothes. Tell me plainly whether I am to consent to this marriage or no?"

"How do you like him?"

"Fairly well."

"Consent, then!"

"Very good; farewell! From this moment our love ends, and our friendship begins. Get you to bed, and I will go and do the same. Farewell!"

"No, stay, and let our friendship begin to-morrow."

"Not so, were my refusal to cost the lives of both of us. You know what it must cost me to speak thus, but it is my irrevocable determination. If I am to become another's wife, I must take care to be worthy of him; perhaps I may be happy. Do not hold me, let me go. You know how well I love you."

"At least, let us have one final embrace."

"Alas! no."

"You are weeping."

"No, I am not. In God's name let me go."

"Dear heart, you go but to weep in your chamber; stay here. I will marry you."

"Nay, no more of that."

With these words she made an effort, escaped from my hands, and fled from the room. I was covered with shame and regret, and could not sleep. I hated myself, for I knew not whether I had sinned most grievously in seducing her or in abandoning her to another.

I stayed to dinner next day in spite of my heartbreak and my sadness. Mdlle. de la Meure talked so brilliantly and sensibly to her intended that one could easily see he was enchanted with her. As for me, feeling that I had nothing pleasant to say, I pretended to have the toothache as an excuse for not talking. Sick at heart, absent-minded, and feeling the effects of a sleepless night, I was well-nigh mad with love, jealousy, and despair. Mdlle. de la Meure did not speak to me once, did not so much as look at me. She was quite right, but I did not think so then. I thought the dinner would never come to an end, and I do not think I was ever present at so painful a meal.

As we rose from the table, Madame went into her closet with her niece and nephew that was to be, and the niece came out in the course of an hour and bade us congratulate her, as she was to be married in a week, and after the wedding she would accompany her husband to Dunkirk. "To-morrow," she added, "we are all to dine with M. Corneman, where the deed of settlement will be signed."

I cannot imagine how it was I did not fall dead on the spot. My anguish cannot be expressed.

Before long it was proposed that we should go to the play, but excusing myself on the plea of business I returned to Paris. As I got to my door I seemed to be in a fever, and I lay down on my bed, but instead of the rest I needed I experienced only remorse and fruitless repentance-the torments of the damned. I began to think it was my duty to stop the marriage or die. I was sure that Mdlle. de la Meure loved me, and I fancied she would not say no if I told her that her refusal to marry me would cost me my life. Full of that idea I rose and wrote her a letter, strong with all the strength of tumultuous passion. This was some relief, and getting into bed I slept till morning. As soon as I was awake I summoned a messenger and promised him twelve francs if he would deliver my letter, and report its receipt in an hour and a half. My letter was under cover of a note addressed to Tiretta, in which I told him that I should not leave the house till I had got an answer. I had my answer four hours after; it ran as follows: "Dearest, it is too late; you have decided on my destiny, and I cannot go back from my word. Come to dinner at M. Corneman's, and be sure that in a few weeks we shall be congratulating ourselves on having won a great victory. Our love, crowned all too soon, will soon live only in our memories. I beg of you to write to me no more."

Such was my fate. Her refusal, with the still more cruel charge not to write to her again, made me furious. In it I only saw inconstancy. I thought she had fallen in love with the merchant. My state of mind may be judged from the fact that I determined to kill my rival. The most savage plans, the most cruel designs, ran a race through my bewildered brain. I was jealous, in love, a different being from my ordinary self; anger, vanity, and shame had destroyed my powers of reasoning. The charming girl whom I was forced to admire, whom I should have esteemed all the more for the course she had taken, whom I had regarded as an angel, became in my eyes a hateful monster, a meet object for punishment. At last I determined on a sure method of revenge, which I knew to be both dishonourable and cowardly, but in my blind passion I did not hesitate for a moment. I resolved to go to the merchant at M. Corneman's, where he was staying, to tell him all that had passed between the lady and myself, and if that did not make him renounce the idea of marrying her I would tell him that one of us must die, and if he refused my challenge I determined to assassinate him.

With this terrible plan in my brain, which makes me shudder now when I think of it, I ate with the appetite of a wild beast, lay down and slept till day. I was in the same mind when I awoke, and dressed myself hastily yet carefully, put two good pistols in my pocket and went to M. Corneman's. My rival was still asleep; I waited for him, and for a quarter of an hour my thoughts only grew more bitter and my determination more fixed. All at once he came into the room, in his dressing-gown, and received me with open arms, telling me in the kindest of voices that he had been expecting me to call, as he could guess what feelings I, a friend of his future wife's, could have for him, and saying that his friendship for me should always be as warm as hers. His honest open face, his straightforward words, overwhelmed me, and I was silent for a few minutes—in fact I did not know what to say. Luckily he gave me enough time to recollect myself, as he talked on for a quarter of an hour without noticing that I did not open my lips.

M. Corneman then came in; coffee was served, and my speech returned to me; but I am happy to say I refrained from playing the dishonourable part I had intended; the crisis was passed.

It may be remarked that the fiercest spirits are like a cord stretched too tight, which either breaks or relaxes. I have known several persons of that temperament—the Chevalier L——, amongst others, who in a fit of passion used to feel his soul escaping by every pore. If at the moment when his anger burst forth he was able to break something and make a great noise, he calmed down in a moment; reason resumed her sway, and the raging lion became as mild as a lamb.

After I had taken a cup of coffee, I felt myself calmed but yet dizzy in the head, so I bade them good morning and went out. I was astonished but delighted that I had not carried my detestable scheme into effect. I was humbled by being forced to confess to myself that chance and chance alone had saved me from becoming a villain. As I was reflecting on what had happened I met my brother, and he completed my cure. I took him to dine at Silvia's and stayed there till midnight. I saw that Mdlle. Baletti would make me forget the fair inconstant, whom I wisely determined not to see again before the wedding. To make sure I set out the next day for Versailles, to look after my interests with the Government.

CHAPTER II

The Abby de la Ville—The Abby Galiani—The Neapolitan Dialect—I Set Out
for Dunkirk on a Secret Mission—I Succeed—I Return to Paris by Amiens—
My Adventure by the Way—M. de la Bretonniere—My Report Gives
Satisfaction—I Am Paid Five Hundred Louis—Reflections.

A new career was opening before me. Fortune was still my friend, and I had
all the necessary qualities to second the efforts of the blind goddess on my
behalf save one—perseverance. My immoderate life of pleasure annulled the
effect of all my other qualities.

M. de Bernis received me in his usual manner, that is more like a friend than
a minister. He asked me if I had any inclination for a secret mission.

"Have I the necessary talents?"

"I think so."

"I have an inclination for all honest means of earning a livelihood, and as for
my talents I will take your excellency's opinion for granted."

This last observation made him smile, as I had intended.

After a few words spoken at random on the memories of bygone years
which time had not entirely defaced, the minister told me to go to the Abbe de
la Ville and use his name.

This abbe, the chief permanent official of the foreign office, was a man of
cold temperament, a profound diplomatist, and the soul of the department, and
high in favour with his excellency the minister. He had served the state well as
an agent at The Hague, and his grateful king rewarded him by giving him a
bishopric on the day of his death. It was a little late, but kings have not always
sufficient leisure to remember things. His heir was a wealthy man named
Gamier, who had formerly been chief cook at M. d'Argenson's, and had become
rich by profiting by the friendship the Abbe de la Ville had always had for him.
These two friends, who were nearly of the same age, had deposited their wills in
the hands of the same attorney, and each had made the other his residuary
legatee.

After the abbe had delivered a brief discourse on the nature of secret
missions and the discretion necessary to those charged with them, he told me
that he would let me know when anything suitable for me presented itself.

I made the acquaintance of the Abbe Galiani, the secretary of the
Neapolitan Embassy. He was a brother to the Marquis de Galiani, of whom I
shall speak when we come to my Italian travels. The Abbe Galiani was a man of
wit. He had a knack of making the most serious subjects appear comic; and
being a good talker, speaking French with the ineradicable Neapolitan accent, he
was a favourite in every circle he cared to enter. The Abbe de la Ville told him
that Voltaire had complained that his Henriade had been translated into
Neapolitan verse in such sort that it excited laughter.

"Voltaire is wrong," said Galiani, "for the Neapolitan dialect is of such a
nature that it is impossible to write verses in it that are not laughable. And why

should he be vexed; he who makes people laugh is sure of being beloved. The Neapolitan dialect is truly a singular one; we have it in translations of the Bible and of the Iliad, and both are comic."

"I can imagine that the Bible would be, but I should not have thought that would have been the case with the Iliad."

"It is, nevertheless."

I did not return to Paris till the day before the departure of Mdlle. de la Meure, now Madame P———. I felt in duty bound to go and see her, to give her my congratulations, and to wish her a pleasant journey. I found her in good spirits and quite at her ease, and, far from being vexed at this, I was pleased, a certain sign that I was cured. We talked without the slightest constraint, and I thought her husband a perfect gentleman. He invited us to visit him at Dunkirk, and I promised to go without intending to do so, but the fates willed otherwise.

Tiretta was now left alone with his darling, who grew more infatuated with her Strephon every day, so well did he prove his love for her.

With a mind at ease, I now set myself to sentimentalize with Mdlle. Baletti, who gave me every day some new mark of the progress I was making.

The friendship and respect I bore her family made the idea of seduction out of the question, but as I grew more and more in love with her, and had no thoughts of marriage, I should have been puzzled to say at what end I was aiming, so I let myself glide along the stream without thinking where I was going.

In the beginning of May the Abbe de Bernis told me to come and call on him at Versailles, but first to see the Abbe de la Ville. The first question the abbe asked me was whether I thought myself capable of paying a visit to eight or ten men-of-war in the roads at Dunkirk, of making the acquaintance of the officers, and of completing a minute and circumstantial report on the victualling, the number of seamen, the guns, ammunition, discipline, etc., etc.

"I will make the attempt," I said, "and will hand you in my report on my return, and it will be for you to say if I have succeeded or not."

"As this is a secret mission, I cannot give you a letter of commendation; I can only give you some money and wish you a pleasant journey."

"I do not wish to be paid in advance—on my return you can give me what you think fit. I shall want three or four days before setting out, as I must procure some letters of introduction."

"Very good. Try to come back before the end of the month. I have no further instructions to give you."

On the same day I had some conversation at the Palais Bourbon with my patron, who could not admire sufficiently my delicacy in refusing payment in advance; and taking advantage of my having done so he made me accept a packet of a hundred Louis. This was the last occasion on which I made use of his purse; I did not borrow from him at Rome fourteen years afterwards.

"As you are on a secret mission, my dear Casanova, I cannot give you a passport. I am sorry for it, but if I did so your object would be suspected. However, you will easily be able to get one from the first gentleman of the chamber, on some pretext or other. Silvia will be more useful to you in that way than anybody else. You quite understand how discreet your behaviour must be. Above all, do not get into any trouble; for I suppose you know that, if anything happened to you, it would be of no use to talk of your mission. We should be obliged to know nothing about you, for ambassadors are the only avowed spies. Remember that you must be even more careful and reserved than they, and yet, if you wish to succeed, all this must be concealed, and you must have an air of freedom from constraint that you may inspire confidence. If, on your return, you like to shew me your report before handing it in, I will tell you what may require to be left out or added."

Full of this affair, the importance of which I exaggerated in proportion to my inexperience, I told Silvia that I wanted to accompany some English friends as far as Calais, and that she would oblige me by getting me a passport from the Duc de Gesvres. Always ready to oblige me, she sat down directly and wrote the duke a letter, telling me to deliver it myself since my personal description was necessary. These passports carry legal weight in the Isle de France only, but they procure one respect in all the northern parts of the kingdom.

Fortified with Silvia's letter, and accompanied by her husband, I went to the duke who was at his estate at St. Toro, and he had scarcely read the letter through before he gave me the passport. Satisfied on this point I went to Villette, and asked Madame if she had anything I could take to her niece. "You can take her the box of china statuettes," said she, "if M. Corneman has not sent them already." I called on the banker who gave me the box, and in return for a hundred Louis a letter of credit on a Dunkirk house. I begged him to name me in the letter in a special manner, as I was going for the sake of pleasure. He seemed glad to oblige me, and I started the same evening, and three days later I was at the "Hotel de la Conciergerie," in Dunkirk.

An hour after my arrival I gave the charming Madame P—— an agreeable surprise by handing her the box, and giving her her aunt's messages. Just as she was praising her husband, and telling me how happy she was, he came in, saying he was delighted to see me and asked me to stay in his house, without enquiring whether my stay in Dunkirk would be a long or short one. I of course thanked him, and after promising to dine now and again at his house I begged him to take me to the banker on whom I had a letter.

The banker read my letter, and gave me the hundred louis, and asked me to wait for him at my inn where he would come for me with the governor, a M. de Barail. This gentleman who, like most Frenchmen, was very polite, after making some ordinary enquiries, asked me to sup with him and his wife who was still at the play. The lady gave me as kind a reception as I had received from her husband. After we had partaken of an excellent supper several persons arrived, and play commenced in which I did not join, as I wished to study the society of the place, and above all certain officers of both services who were present. By means of speaking with an air of authority about naval matters, and by saying that I had served in the navy of the Venetian Republic, in three days I not only knew but was intimate with all the captains of the Dunkirk fleet. I talked at random about naval architecture, on the Venetian system of manoeuvres, and I noticed that the jolly sailors were better pleased at my blunders than at my sensible remarks.

Four days after I had been at Dunkirk, one of the captains asked me to dinner on his ship, and after that all the others did the same; and on every occasion I stayed in the ship for the rest of the day. I was curious about everything—and Jack is so trustful! I went into the hold, I asked questions innumerable, and I found plenty of young officers delighted to shew their own importance, who gossipped without needing any encouragement from me. I took care, however, to learn everything which would be of service to me, and in the evenings I put down on paper all the mental notes I had made during the day. Four or five hours was all I allowed myself for sleep, and in fifteen days I had learnt enough.

Pleasure, gaming, and idleness—my usual companions—had no part in this expedition, and I devoted all my energies to the object of my mission. I dined once with the banker, once with Madame P——, in the town, and once in a pretty country house which her husband had, at about a league's distance from Dunkirk. She took me there herself, and on finding myself alone with the woman I had loved so well I delighted her by the delicacy of my behaviour, which was marked only by respect and friendship. As I still thought her charming, and as our connection had only ended six weeks ago, I was astonished to see myself so quiet, knowing my disposition too well to attribute my restraint to virtue. What, then, was the reason? An Italian proverb, speaking for nature, gives the true solution of the riddle.

'La Mona non vuol pensieri', and my head was full of thought.

My task was done, and bidding good-bye to all my friends, I set out in my post-chaise for Paris, going by another way for the sake of the change. About midnight, on my asking for horses at some stage, the name of which I forget, they told me that the next stage was the fortified town of Aire, which we should not be allowed to pass through at midnight.

"Get me the horses," said I, "I will make them open the gates."

I was obeyed, and in due time we reached the gates.

The postillion cracked his whip and the sentry called out, "Who goes there?"

"Express messenger."

After making me wait for an hour the gate was opened, and I was told that I must go and speak to the governor. I did so, fretting and fuming on my way as if I were some great person, and I was taken to a room where a man in an elegant nightcap was lying beside a very pretty woman.

"Whose messenger are you?"

"Nobody's, but as I am in a hurry."

"That will do. We will talk the matter over tomorrow. In the meanwhile you will accept the hospitality of the guard-room."

"But, sir . . ."

"But me no buts, if you please; leave the room."

I was taken to the guard-room where I spent the night seated on the ground. The daylight appeared. I shouted, swore, made all the racket I could, said I wanted to go on, but nobody took any notice of me.

Ten o'clock struck. More impatient than I can say, I raised my voice and spoke to the officer, telling him that the governor might assassinate me if he liked, but had no right to deny me pen and paper, or to deprive me of the power of sending a messenger to Paris.

"Your name, sir?"

"Here is my passport."

He told me that he would take it to the governor, but I snatched it away from him.

"Would you like to see the governor?"

"Yes, I should."

We started for the governor's apartments. The officer was the first to enter, and in two minutes came out again and brought me in. I gave up my passport in proud silence. The governor read it through, examining me all the while to see if I was the person described; he then gave it me back, telling me that I was free to go where I liked.

"Not so fast, sir, I am not in such a hurry now. I shall send a messenger to Paris and wait his return; for by stopping me on my journey you have violated all the rights of the subject."

"You violated them yourself in calling yourself a messenger."

"Not at all; I told you that I was not one."

"Yes, but you told your postillion that you were, and that comes to the same thing."

"The postillion is a liar, I told him nothing of the kind."

"Why didn't you shew your passport?"

"Why didn't you give me time to do so? In the course of the next few days we shall see who is right."

"Just as you please."

I went out with the officer who took me to the posting-place, and a minute afterwards my carriage drew up. The posting-place was also an inn, and I told the landlord to have a special messenger ready to carry out my orders, to give me a good room and a good bed, and to serve me some rich soup immediately; and I warned him that I was accustomed to good fare. I had my portmanteau and all my belongings taken into my room, and having washed and put on my dressing-gown I sat down to write, to whom I did not know, for I was quite wrong in my contention. However, I had begun by playing the great man, and I thought myself bound in honour to sustain the part, without thinking whether I stood to have to back out of it or no. All the same I was vexed at having to wait in Aire till the return of the messenger, whom I was about to send to the-moon! In the meanwhile, not having closed an eye all night, I determined to take a rest. I was sitting in my shirt-sleeves and eating the soup which had been served to me, when the governor came in unaccompanied. I was both surprised and delighted to see him.

"I am sorry for what has happened, sir, and above all that you think you have good reason for complaint, inasmuch as I only did my duty, for how was I to imagine that your postillion had called you a messenger on his own responsibility."

"That's all very well, sir, but your sense of duty need not have made you drive me from your room."

"I was in need of sleep."

"I am in the same position at the present moment, but a feeling of politeness prevents me from imitating your example."

"May I ask if you have ever been in the service?"

"I have served by land and sea, and have left off when most people are only beginning."

"In that case you will be aware that the gates of a fortified town are only opened by night to the king's messengers or to military superiors."

"Yes, I know; but since they were opened the thing was done, and you might as well have been polite."

"Will you not put on your clothes, and walk a short distance with me!"

His invitation pleased me as well as his pride had displeased me. I had been thinking of a duel as a possible solution of the difficulty, but the present course took all trouble out of my hands. I answered quietly and politely that the honour of walking with him would be enough to make me put off all other calls, and I asked him to be seated while I made haste to dress myself.

I drew on my breeches, throwing the splendid pistols in my pockets on to the bed, called up the barber, and in ten minutes was ready. I put on my sword, and we went out.

We walked silently enough along two or three streets, passed through a gate, up a court, till we got to a door where my guide stopped short. He asked me to come in, and I found myself in a fine room full of people. I did not think of going back, but behaved as if I had been in my own house.

"Sir-my wife," said the governor; and turning to her without pausing, "here is M. de Casanova, who has come to dinner with us."

"I am delighted to hear it, sir, as otherwise I should have had no chance of forgiving you for waking me up the other night."

"I paid dearly for my fault, madam, but after the purgatory I had endured I am sure you will allow me to be happy in this paradise."

She answered with a charming smile, and after asking me to sit beside her she continued whatever conversation was possible in the midst of a game at cards.

I found myself completely outwitted, but the thing was done so pleasantly that all I could do was to put a good face on it—a feat which I found sufficiently easy from the relief I felt at no longer being bound to send a messenger to I did not know whom.

The governor well satisfied with his victory, got all at once into high spirits, and began to talk about military matters, the Court, and on general topics, often addressing me with that friendly ease which good French society knows so well how to reconcile with the rules of politeness; no one could have guessed that there had ever been the slightest difference between us. He had made himself the hero of the piece by the dexterous manner in which he had led up to the situation, but I had a fair claim to the second place, for I had made an experienced officer high in command give me the most flattering kind of satisfaction, which bore witness to the esteem with which I had inspired him.

The dinner was served. The success of my part depended on the manner in which it was played, and my wit has seldom been keener than during this meal. The whole conversation was in a pleasant vein, and I took great care to give the governor's wife opportunities for shining in it. She was a charming and pretty woman, still quite youthful, for she was at least thirty years younger than the governor. Nothing was said about my six hours' stay in the guard-room, but at dessert the governor escaped speaking plainly by a joke that was not worth the trouble of making.

"You're a nice man," said he, "to think I was going to fight you. Ah! ha! I have caught you, haven't I?"

"Who told you that I was meditating a duel?"

"Confess that such was the case?"

"I protest; there is a great difference between believing and supposing; the one is positive, the other merely hypothetical. I must confess, however, that your invitation to take a walk roused my curiosity as to what was to come next, and I admire your wit. But you must believe me that I do not regard myself as caught in a trap—far from that, I am so well pleased that I feel grateful to you."

In the afternoon we all took a walk, and I gave my arm to the charming mistress of the house. In the evening I took my leave, and set out early the next day having made a fair copy of my report.

At five o'clock in the morning I was fast asleep in my carriage, when I was suddenly awakened. We were at the gate of Amiens. The fellow at the door was an exciseman—a race everywhere detested and with good cause, for besides the insolence of their manners nothing makes a man feel more like a slave than the inquisitorial search they are accustomed to make through one's clothes and most secret possessions. He asked me if I had anything contraband; and being in a bad temper at being deprived of my sleep to answer such a question I replied with an oath that I had nothing of the sort, and that he would have done better to let me sleep.

"As you talk in that style," said the creature, "we will see what we can see."

He ordered the postillion to pass on with the carriage. He had my luggage hauled down, and not being able to hinder him I fumed in silence.

I saw my mistake, but there was nothing to be done; and having no contraband goods I had nothing to fear, but my bad temper cost me two weary hours of delay. The joys of vengeance were depicted on the features of the exciseman. At the time of which I am writing these gaugers were the dregs of the people, but would become tractable on being treated with a little politeness. The sum of twenty-four sous given with good grace would make them as supple as a pair of gloves; they would bow to the travellers, wish them a pleasant journey, and give no trouble. I knew all this, but there are times when a man acts mechanically as I had done, unfortunately.

The scoundrels emptied my boxes and unfolded everything even to my shirts, between which they said I might have concealed English lace.

After searching everything they gave me back my keys, but they had not yet done with us; they began to search my carriage. The rascal who was at the head of them began to shout "victory," he had discovered the remainder of a pound of snuff which I had bought at St. Omer on my way to Dunkirk.

With a voice of triumph the chief exciseman gave orders that my carriage should be seized, and warned me that I would have to pay a fine of twelve hundred francs.

For the nonce my patience was exhausted, and I leave the names I called them to the imagination of the reader; but they were proof against words. I told them to take me to the superintendent's.

"You can go if you like," said they, "we are not your servants."

Surrounded by a curious crowd, whom the noise had drawn together, I began to walk hurriedly towards the town, and entering the first open shop I came to, I begged the shopkeeper to take me to the superintendent's. As I was telling the circumstances of the case, a man of good appearance, who happened to be in the shop, said that he would be glad to show me the way himself, though he did not think I should find the superintendent in, as he would doubtless be warned of my coming.

"Without your paying either the fine or caution money," said he, "you will find it a hard matter to get yourself out of the difficulty."

I entreated him to shew me the way to the superintendent's, and not to trouble about anything else. He advised me to give the rabble a louis to buy drink, and thus to rid myself of them, on which I gave him the louis, begging him to see to it himself, and the bargain was soon struck. He was a worthy attorney, and knew his men.

We got to the superintendent's; but, as my guide had warned me, my gentleman was not to be seen. The porter told us that he had gone out alone, that he would not be back before night, and that he did not know where he had gone.

"There's a whole day lost, then," said the attorney.

"Let us go and hunt him up; he must have well-known resorts and friends, and we will find them out. I will give you a louis for the day's work; will that be enough?"

"Ample."

We spent in vain four hours in looking for the superintendent in ten or twelve houses. I spoke to the masters of all of them, exaggerating considerably the injury that had been done to me. I was listened to, condoled with, and comforted with the remark that he would certainly be obliged to return to his house at night, and then he could not help hearing what I had to say. That would not suit me, so I continued the chase.

At one o'clock the attorney took me to an old lady, who was thought a great deal of in the town. She was dining all by herself. After giving great attention to my story, she said that she did not think she could be doing wrong in telling a stranger the whereabouts of an individual who, in virtue of his office, ought never to be inaccessible.

"And so, sir, I may reveal to you what after all is no secret. My daughter told me yesterday evening that she was going to dine at Madame N———'s, and that the superintendent was to be there. Do you go after him now, and you will find him at table in the best society in Amiens, but," said she, with a smile, "I advise you not to give your name at the door. The numerous servants will shew you the way without asking for your name. You can then speak to him whether he likes it or not, and though you don't know him he will hear all you say. I am sorry that I cannot be present at so fine a situation."

I gratefully took leave of the worthy lady, and I set off in all haste to the house I had been told of, the attorney, who was almost tired out, accompanying me. Without the least difficulty he and I slipped in between the crowds of servants till we got to a hall where there were more than twenty people sitting down to a rich and delicate repast.

"Ladies and gentlemen, you will excuse my troubling your quiet on this festive occasion with a tale of terror."

At these words, uttered in the voice of Jupiter Tonans, everybody rose. The surprise of the high-born company of knights and ladies at my apparition can easily be imagined.

"Since seven o'clock this morning I have been searching from door to door and from street to street for his honour the superintendent, whom I have at last been fortunate enough to find here, for I know perfectly well that he is present, and that if he have ears he hears me now. I am come to request him to order his scoundrelly myrmidons who have seized my carriage to give it up, so that I may continue my journey. If the laws bid me pay twelve hundred francs for seven ounces of snuff for my own private use, I renounce those laws and declare that I will not pay a farthing. I shall stay here and send a messenger to my ambassador, who will complain that the 'jus gentium' has been violated in the Ile-de-France in my person, and I will have reparation. Louis XV. is great enough to refuse to become an accomplice in this strange onslaught. And if that satisfaction which is my lawful right is not granted me, I will make the thing an affair of state, and my Republic will not revenge itself by assaulting Frenchmen for a few pinches of snuff, but will expel them all root and branch. If you want to know whom I am, read this."

Foaming with rage, I threw my passport on the table.

A man picked it up and read it, and I knew him to be the superintendent. While my papers were being handed round I saw expressed on every face surprise and indignation, but the superintendent replied haughtily that he was at Amiens to administer justice, and that I could not leave the town unless I paid the fine or gave surety.

"If you are here to do justice, you will look upon my passport as a positive command to speed me on my way, and I bid you yourself be my surety if you are a gentleman."

"Does high birth go bail for breaches of the law in your country?"

"In my country men of high birth do not condescend to take dishonourable employments."

"No service under the king can be dishonourable."

"The hangman would say the same thing."

"Take care what you say."

"Take care what you do. Know, sir, that I am a free man who has been grievously outraged, and know, too, that I fear no one. Throw me out of the window, if you dare."

"Sir," said a lady to me in the voice of the mistress of the house, "in my house there is no throwing out of windows."

"Madam, an angry man makes use of terms which his better reason disowns. I am wronged by a most cruel act of injustice, and I humbly crave your pardon for having offended you. Please to reflect that for the first time in my life I have been oppressed and insulted, and that in a kingdom where I thought myself safe from all but highway robbers. For them I have my pistols, and for the worthy superintendents I have a passport, but I find the latter useless. For the sake of seven ounces of snuff which I bought at St. Omer three weeks ago, this gentleman robs me and interrupts my journey, though the king's majesty is my surety that no one shall interfere with me; he calls on me to pay fifty louis, he delivers me to the rage of his impudent menials and to the derision of the mob, from whom I had to rid myself by my money and the aid of this worthy man beside me. I am treated like a scoundrel, and the man who should have been my defender and deliverer slinks away and hides himself, and adds to the insults I have received. His myrmidons have turned my clothes upside down, and pitchforked my linen at the foot of the town gates, to revenge themselves on me for not giving them twenty, four sous. To-morrow the manner in which I have been treated will be known to the diplomatic bodies at Versailles and Paris, and in a few days it will be in all the newspapers. I will pay not a farthing because I owe not a farthing. Now, sir, am I to send a courier to the Duc de Gesvres?"

"What you have got to do is to pay, and if you do not care to pay, you may do whatever you like."

"Then, ladies and gentlemen, good-bye. As for you, sir, we shall meet again."

As I was rushing out of the room like a madman, I heard somebody calling out to me in good Italian to wait a minute. I turned round, and saw the voice had proceeded from a man past middle age, who addressed the superintendent thus:—

"Let this gentleman proceed on his journey; I will go bail for him. Do you understand me, superintendent? I will be his surety. You don't know these Italians. I went through the whole of the last war in Italy, and I understand the national character. Besides, I think the gentleman is in the right."

"Very good," said the official, turning to me. "All you have to do is to pay a matter of thirty or forty francs at the customs' office as the affair is already booked."

"I thought I told you that I would not pay a single farthing, and I tell it you again. But who are you, sir," said I, turning to the worthy old man, "who are good enough to become surety for me without knowing me?"

"I am a commissary of musters, sir, and my name is de la Bretonniere. I live in Paris at the 'Hotel de Saxe,' Rue Colombien, where I shall be glad to see you after to-morrow. We will go together to M. Britard, who, after hearing your case, will discharge my bail."

After I had expressed my gratitude, and told him that I would wait upon him without fail, I made my excuses to the mistress of the house and the guests, and left them.

I took my worthy attorney to dinner at the best inn in the place, and I gave him two louis for his trouble. Without his help and that of the commissary I should have been in great difficulty; it would have been a case of the earthen pot and the iron pot over again; for with jacks-in-office reason is of no use, and though I had plenty of money I would never have let the wretches rob me of fifty louis.

My carriage was drawn up at the door of the tavern; and just as I was getting in, one of the excisemen who had searched my luggage came and told me that I should find everything just as I left it:—

"I wonder at that since it has been left in the hands of men of your stamp; shall I find the snuff?"

"The snuff has been confiscated, my lord."

"I am sorry for you, then; for if it had been there I would have given you a louis."

"I will go and look for it directly."

"I have no time to wait for it. Drive on, postillion."

I got to Paris the next day, and four days after I waited on M. de la Bretonniere, who gave me a hearty welcome, and took me to M. Britard, the fermier-general, who discharged his bail. This M. Britard was a pleasant young man. He blushed when he heard all I had gone through.

I took my report to M. de Bernis, at the "Hotel Bourbon," and his excellence spent two hours over it, making me take out all unnecessary matter. I spent the time in making a fair copy, and the next day I took it to M. de la Ville, who read it through in silence, and told me that he would let me know the result. A month after I received five hundred louis, and I had the pleasure of hearing that M. de Cremille, the first lord of the admiralty, had pronounced my report to be not only perfectly accurate but very suggestive. Certain reasonable apprehensions prevented me from making myself known to him—an honour which M. de Bernis wished to procure for me.

When I told him my adventures on the way back, he laughed, but said that the highest merit of a secret agent was to keep out of difficulties; for though he might have the tact to extricate himself from them, yet he got talked of, which it should be his chief care to avoid.

This mission cost the admiralty twelve thousand francs, and the minister might easily have procured all the information I gave him without spending a penny. Any intelligent young naval officer would have done it just as well, and would have acquitted himself with zeal and discretion, to gain the good opinion of the ministers. But all the French ministers are the same. They lavished money which came out of other people's pockets to enrich their creatures, and they were absolute; the downtrodden people counted for nothing, and of this course the indebtedness of the state and the confusion of the finances were the inevitable results. It is quite true that the Revolution was a necessity, but it should have been marked with patriotism and right feeling, not with blood. However, the nobility and clergy were not men of sufficient generosity to make the necessary sacrifices to the king, the state, and to themselves.

Silvia was much amused at my adventures at Aire and Amiens, and her charming daughter shewed much pity for the bad night I had passed in the guard-room. I told her that the hardship would have been much less if I had had a wife beside me. She replied that a wife, if a good one, would have been only too happy to alleviate my troubles by sharing in them, but her mother observed that a woman of parts, after seeing to the safety of my baggage and my coach, would have busied herself in taking the necessary steps for setting me at liberty, and I supported this opinion as best indicating the real duty of a good wife.

CHAPTER III

The Count de la Tour D'Auvergne and Madame D'Urfe—Camille—My Passion for the Count's Mistress—The Ridiculous Incident Which Cured Me—The Count de St. Germain

In spite of my love for Mdlle. Baletti, I did not omit to pay my court to the most noted ladies of the pavement; but I was chiefly interested in kept women, and those who consider themselves as belonging to the public only in playing before them night by night, queens or chamber-maids.

In spite of this affection, they enjoy what they call their independence, either by devoting themselves to Cupid or to Plutus, and more frequently to both together. As it is not very difficult to make the acquaintance of these priestesses of pleasure and dissipation, I soon got to know several of them.

The halls of the theatres are capital places for amateurs to exercise their talents in intriguing, and I had profited tolerably well by the lessons I had learnt in this fine school.

I began by becoming the friend of their lovers, and I often succeeded by pretending to be a man of whom nobody need be afraid.

Camille, an actress and dancer at the Italian play, with whom I had fallen in love at Fontainebleu seven years ago, was one of those of whom I was most fond, liking the society at her pretty little house, where she lived with the Count d'Eigreville, who was a friend of mine, and fond of my company. He was a brother of the Marquis de Gamache and of the Countess du Rumain, and was a fine young fellow of an excellent disposition. He was never so well pleased as when he saw his mistress surrounded by people—a taste which is rarely found, but which is very convenient, and the sign of a temperament not afflicted by jealousy. Camille had no other lovers—an astonishing thing in an actress of the kind, but being full of tact and wit she drove none of her admirers to despair. She was neither over sparing nor over generous in the distribution of her favours, and knew how to make the whole town rave about her without fearing the results of indiscretion or sorrows of being abandoned.

The gentleman of whom, after her lover, she took most notice, was the Count de la Tour d'Auvergne, a nobleman of an old family, who idolized her, and, not being rich enough to possess her entirely, had to be content with what she gave him. Camille had given him a young girl, for whose keep she paid, who lived with Tour d'Auvergne in furnished apartments in the Rue de Taranne, and whom he said he loved as one loves a portrait, because she came from Camille. The count often took her with him to Camille's to supper. She was fifteen, simple in her manners, and quite devoid of ambition. She told her lover that she would never forgive him an act of infidelity except with Camille, to whom she felt bound to yield all since to her she owed all.

I became so much in love with her that I often went to Camille's solely to see her and to enjoy those artless speeches with which she delighted the company. I strove as best I could to conceal my flame, but often I found myself looking quite sad at the thought of the impossibility of my love being crowned with success. If I had let my passion be suspected I should have been laughed at, and should have made myself a mark for the pitiless sarcasms of Camille. However, I got my cure in the following ridiculous manner:—

Camille lived at the Barriere Blanche, and on leaving her house, one rainy evening, I sought in vain for a coach to take me home.

"My dear Casanova," said Tour d'Auvergne, "I can drop you at your own door without giving myself the slightest inconvenience, though my carriage is only seated for two; however, my sweetheart can sit on our knees."

I accepted his offer with pleasure, and we seated ourselves in the carriage, the count on my left hand and Babet on both our knees.

Burning with amorous passion I thought I would take the opportunity, and, to lose no time, as the coachman was driving fast, I took her hand and pressed it softly. The pressure was returned. Joy! I carried the hand to my lips, and covered it with affectionate though noiseless kisses. Longing to convince her of the ardour of my passion, and thinking that her hand would not refuse to do me a sweet service, I . . . but just at critical moment,

"I am really very much obliged to you, my dear fellow," said the Count de la Tour d'Auvergne, "for a piece of politeness thoroughly Italian, of which, however, I do not feel worthy; at least, I hope it's meant as politeness and not as a sign of contempt."

At these dreadful words I stretched out my hand and felt the sleeve of his coat. Presence of mind was no good in a situation like this, when his words were followed by a peal of loud laughter which would have confounded the hardiest spirit. As for me, I could neither join in his laughter nor deny his accusation; the situation was a fearful one, or would have been if the friendly shades of night had not covered my confusion. Babet did her best to find out from the count why he laughed so much, but he could not tell her for laughing, for which I gave thanks with all my heart. At last the carriage stopped at my house, and as soon as my servant had opened the door of my carriage I got down as fast as I could, and wished them good night—a compliment which Tour d'Auvergne returned with fresh peals of laughter. I entered my house in a state of stupefaction, and half an hour elapsed before I, too, began to laugh at the adventure. What vexed me most was the expectation of having malicious jests passed upon me, for I had not the least right to reckon on the count's discretion. However, I had enough sense to determine to join in the laughter if I could, and if not, to take it well, for this is, and always will be, the best way to get the laughers on one's own side at Paris.

For three days I saw nothing of the delightful count, and on the fourth I resolved to ask him to take breakfast with me, as Camille had sent to my house to enquire how I was. My adventure would not prevent me visiting her house, but I was anxious to know how it had been taken.

As soon as Tour d'Auvergne saw me he began to roar with laughter, and I joined in, and we greeted each other in the friendliest manner possible. "My dear count," said I, "let us forget this foolish story. You have no business to attack me, as I do not know how to defend myself."

"Why should you defend yourself, my dear fellow. We like you all the better for it, and this humorous adventure makes us merry every evening."

"Everybody knows it, then?"

"Of course, why not? It makes Camille choke with laughter. Come this evening; I will bring Babet, and she will amuse you as she maintains that you were not mistaken."

"She is right."

"Eh? what? You do me too much honour, and I don't believe you; but have it as you like."

"I can't do better, but I must confess when all's said that you were not the person to whom my fevered imagination offered such ardent homage."

At supper I jested, pretended to be astonished at the count's indiscretion, and boasted of being cured of my passion. Babet called me a villain, and maintained that I was far from cured; but she was wrong, as the incident had disgusted me with her, and had attached me to the count, who, indeed, was a man of the most amiable character. Nevertheless, our friendship might have been a fatal one, as the reader will see presently.

One evening, when I was at the Italian theatre, Tour d'Auvergne came up to me and asked me to lend him a hundred louis, promising to repay me next Saturday.

"I haven't got the money," I said, "but my purse and all it contains is at your service."

"I want a hundred louis, my dear fellow, and immediately, as I lost them at play yesterday evening at the Princess of Anhalt's."

"But I haven't got them."

"The receiver of the lottery ought always to be able to put his hand on a hundred louis."

"Yes, but I can't touch my cash-box; I have to give it up this day week."

"So you can; as I will repay you on Saturday. Take a hundred louis from the box, and put in my word of honour instead; don't you think that is worth a hundred Louis?"

"I have nothing to say to that, wait for me a minute."

I ran to my office, took out the money and gave it to him. Saturday came but no count, and as I had no money I pawned my diamond ring and replaced the hundred louis I owed the till. Three or four days afterwards, as I was at the Comedie Francaise, the Count de la Tour d'Auvergne came up to me and began to apologize. I replied by shewing my hand, and telling him that I had pawned my ring to save my honour. He said, with a melancholy air, that a man had failed to keep his word with him, but he would be sure to give me the hundred louis on the Saturday following, adding, "I give you my word of honour."

"Your word of honour is in my box, so let's say nothing about that. You can repay me when you like."

The count grew as pale as death.

"My word of honour, my dear Casanova, is more precious to me than my life; and I will give you the hundred louis at nine o'clock to-morrow morning at a hundred paces from the cafe at the end of the Champs-Elysees. I will give you them in person, and nobody will see us. I hope you will not fail to be there, and that you will bring your sword. I shall have mine."

"Faith, count! that's making me pay rather dear for my jest. You certainly do me a great honour, but I would rather beg your pardon, if that would prevent this troublesome affair from going any further."

"No, I am more to blame than you, and the blame can only be removed by the sword's point. Will you meet me?

"I do not see how I can refuse you, although I am very much averse to the affair."

I left him and went to Silvia's, and took my supper sadly, for I really liked this amiable nobleman, and in my opinion the game we were going to play was not worth the candle. I would not have fought if I could have convinced myself that I was in the wrong, but after turning the matter well-over, and looking at it from every point of view, I could not help seeing that the fault lay in the count's excessive touchiness, and I resolved to give him satisfaction. At all hazards I would not fail to keep the appointment.

I reached the cafe a moment after him. We took breakfast together and he payed. We then went out and walked towards the Etoile. When we got to a sheltered place he drew a bundle of a hundred louis from his pocket, gave it to me with the greatest courtesy, and said that one stroke of the sword would be sufficient. I could not reply.

He went off four paces and drew his sword. I did the same without saying a word, and stepping forward almost as soon as our blades crossed I thrust and hit him. I drew back my sword and summoned him to keep his word, feeling sure that I had wounded him in his chest.

He gently kissed his sword, and putting his hand into his breast he drew it out covered with blood, and said pleasantly to me, "I am satisfied."

I said to him all that I could, and all that it was my duty to say in the way of compliment, while he was stanching the blood with his handkerchief, and on looking at the point of my sword I was delighted to find that the wound was of the slightest. I told him so offering to see him home. He thanked me and begged me to keep my own counsel, and to reckon him henceforth amongst my truest friends. After I had embraced him, mingling my tears with my embraces, I returned home, sad at heart but having learnt a most useful lesson. No one ever knew of our meeting, and a week afterwards we supped together at Camille's.

A few days after, I received from M. de la Ville the five hundred louis for my Dunkirk mission. On my going to see Camille she told me that Tour d'Auvergne was kept in bed by an attack of sciatica, and that if I liked we could pay him a visit the next day. I agreed, and we went. After breakfast was over I told him in a serious voice that if he would give me a free hand I could cure him, as he was not suffering from sciatica but from a moist and windy humour which I could disperse my means of the Talisman of Solomon and five mystic words. He began to laugh, but told me to do what I liked.

"Very good, then I will go out and buy a brush."

"I will send a servant."

"No, I must get it myself, as I want some drugs as well." I bought some nitre, mercury, flower of sulphur, and a small brush, and on my return said, "I must have a little of your——, this liquid is indispensable, and it must be quite fresh."

Camille and he began to laugh, but I succeeded in keeping the serious face suitable to my office. I handed him a mug and modestly lowered the curtains, and he then did what I wanted.

I made a mixture of the various ingredients, and I told Camille that she must rub his thigh whilst I spoke the charm, but I warned her that if she laughed while she was about it it would spoil all. This threat only increased their good humour, and they laughed without cessation; for as soon as they thought they had got over it, they would look at one another, and after repressing themselves as long as they could would burst out afresh, till I began to think that I had bound them to an impossible condition. At last, after holding their sides for half an hour, they set themselves to be serious in real earnest, taking my imperturbable gravity for their example. De la Tour d'Auvergne was the first to regain a serious face, and he then offered Camille his thigh, and she, fancying herself on the boards, began to rub the sick man, whilst I mumbled in an undertone words which they would not have understood however clearly I had spoken, seeing that I did not understand them myself.

I was nearly spoiling the efficacy of the operation when I saw the grimaces they made in trying to keep serious. Nothing could be more amusing than the expression on Camille's face. At last I told her that she had rubbed enough, and dipping the brush into the mixture I drew on his thigh the five-pointed star called Solomon's seal. I then wrapped up the thigh in three napkins, and I told him that if he would keep quiet for twenty-four hours without taking off—his napkins, I would guarantee a cure.

The most amusing part of it all was, that by the time I had done the count and Camille laughed no more, their faces wore a bewildered look, and as for me . . . I could have sworn I had performed the most wonderful work in the world. If one tells a lie a sufficient number of times, one ends by believing it.

A few minutes after this operation, which I had performed as if by instinct and on the spur of the moment, Camille and I went away in a coach, and I told her so many wonderful tales that when she got out at her door she looked quite mazed.

Four or five days after, when I had almost forgotten the farce, I heard a carriage stopping at my door, and looking out of my window saw M. de la Tour d'Auvergne skipping nimbly out of the carriage.

"You were sure of success, then," said he, "as you did not come to see me the day after your astounding operation."

"Of course I was sure, but if I had not been too busy you would have seen me, for all that."

"May I take a bath?"

"No, don't bathe till you feel quite well."

"Very good. Everybody is in a state of astonishment at your feat, as I could not help telling the miracle to all my acquaintances. There are certainly some sceptics who laugh at me, but I let them talk."

"You should have kept your own counsel; you know what Paris is like. Everybody will be considering me as a master-quack."

"Not at all, not at all. I have come to ask a favour of you."

"What's that?"

"I have an aunt who enjoys a great reputation for her skill in the occult sciences, especially in alchemy. She is a woman of wit, very, rich, and sole mistress of her fortune; in short, knowing her will do you no harm. She longs to see you, for she pretends to know you, and says that you are not what you seem. She has entreated me to take you to dine with her, and I hope you will accept the invitation. Her name is the Marchioness d'Urfe."

I did not know this lady, but the name of d'Urfe caught my attention directly, as I knew all about the famous Anne d'Urfe who flourished towards the end of the seventeenth century. The lady was the widow of his great-grandson, and on marrying into the family became a believer in the mystical doctrines of a science in which I was much interested, though I gave it little credit. I therefore replied that I should be glad to go, but on the condition that the party should not exceed the count, his aunt, and myself.

"She has twelve people every day to dinner, and you will find yourself in the company of the best society in Paris."

"My dear fellow, that's exactly what I don't want; for I hate to be thought a magician, which must have been the effect of the tales you have told."

"Oh, no! not at all; your character is well known, and you will find yourself in the society of people who have the greatest regard for you."

"Are you sure of that?"

"The Duchess de l'Oragnais told me, that, four or five years ago, you were often to be seen at the Palais Royal, and that you used to spend whole days with the Duchess d'Orleans; Madame de Bouffers, Madame de Blots, and Madame de Melfort have also talked to me about you. You are wrong not to keep up your old acquaintances. I know at least a hundred people of the first rank who are suffering from the same malady as that of which you cured me, and would give the half of their goods to be cured."

De la Tour d'Auvergne had reason on his side, but as I knew his wonderful cure had been due to a singular coincidence, I had no desire to expose myself to public ridicule. I therefore told him that I did not wish to become a public character, and that he must tell Madame d'Urfe that I would have the honour of calling on her in strict privacy only, and that she might tell me the day and hour on which I should kneel before her.

The same evening I had a letter from the count making an appointment at the Tuileries for the morrow; he was to meet me there, and take me to his aunt's to dinner. No one else was to be present.

The next day we met each other as had been arranged, and went to see Madame d'Urfe, who lived on the Quai des Theatins, on the same side as the "Hotel Bouillon."

Madame d'Urfe, a woman advanced in years, but still handsome, received me with all the courtly grace of the Court of the Regency. We spent an hour and a half in indifferent conversation, occupied in studying each other's character. Each was trying to get at the bottom of the other.

I had not much trouble in playing the part of the unenlightened, for such, in point of fact, was my state of mind, and Madame d'Urfe unconsciously betrayed the desire of shewing her learning; this put me at my ease, for I felt sure I could make her pleased with me if I succeeded in making her pleased with herself.

At two o'clock the same dinner that was prepared every day for twelve was served for us three. Nothing worthy of note (so far as conversation went) was done at dinner, as we talked commonplace after the manner of people of fashion.

After the dessert Tour d'Auvergne left us to go and see the Prince de Turenne, who was in a high fever, and after he was gone Madame d'Urfe began to discuss alchemy and magic, and all the other branches of her beloved science, or rather infatuation. When we got on to the magnum opus, and I asked her if she knew the nature of the first matter, it was only her politeness which prevented her from laughing; but controlling herself, she replied graciously that she already possessed the philosopher's stone, and that she was acquainted with all the operations of the work. She then shewed me a collection of books which had belonged to the great d'Urfe, and Renee of Savoy, his wife; but she had added to it manuscripts which had cost her more than a hundred thousand francs. Paracelsus was her favourite author, and according to her he was neither man, woman, nor hermaphrodite, and had the misfortune to poison himself with an overdose of his panacea, or universal medicine. She shewed me a short manuscript in French, where the great work was clearly explained. She told me that she did not keep it under lock and key, because it was written in a cypher, the secret of which was known only to herself.

"You do not believe, then, in steganography."

"No, sir, and if you would like it, I will give you this which has been copied from the original."

"I accept it, madam, with all the more gratitude in that I know its worth."

From the library we went into the laboratory, at which I was truly astonished. She shewed me matter that had been in the furnace for fifteen years, and was to be there for four or five years more. It was a powder of projection which was to transform instantaneously all metals into the finest gold. She shewed me a pipe by which the coal descended to the furnace, keeping it always at the same heat. The lumps of coal were impelled by their own weight at proper intervals and in equal quantities, so that she was often three months without looking at the furnace, the temperature remaining the same the whole time. The cinders were removed by another pipe, most ingeniously contrived, which also answered the purpose of a ventilator.

The calcination of mercury was mere child's play to this wonderful woman. She shewed me the calcined matter, and said that whenever I liked she would instruct me as to the process. I next saw the Tree of Diana of the famous Taliamed, whose pupil she was. His real name was Maillot, and according to Madame d'Urfe he had not, as was supposed, died at Marseilles, but was still alive; "and," added she, with a slight smile, "I often get letters from him. If the Regent of France," said she, "had listened to me he would be alive now. He was my first friend; he gave me the name of Egeria, and he married me to M. d'Urfe."

She possessed a commentary on Raymond Lully, which cleared up all difficult points in the comments of Arnold de Villanova on the works of Roger Bacon and Heber, who, according to her, were still alive. This precious manuscript was in an ivory casket, the key of which she kept religiously; indeed her laboratory was a closed room to all but myself. I saw a small cask full of 'platina del Pinto', which she told me she could transmute into gold when she pleased. It had been given her by M. Vood himself in 1743. She shewed me the same metal in four phials. In the first three the platinum remained intact in sulphuric, nitric, and muriatic acid, but in the fourth, which contained 'aqua regia', the metal had not been able to resist the action of the acid. She melted it with the burning-glass, and said it could be melted in no other way, which proved, in her opinion, its superiority to gold. She shewed me some precipitated by sal ammoniac, which would not precipitate gold.

Her athanor had been alight for fifteen years. The top was full of black coal, which made me conclude that she had been in the laboratory two or three days before. Stopping before the Tree of Diana, I asked her, in a respectful voice, if she agreed with those who said it was only fit to amuse children. She replied, in a dignified manner, that she had made it to divert herself with the crystallization of the silver, spirit of nitre, and mercury, and that she looked upon it as a piece of metallic vegetation, representing in little what nature performed on a larger scale; but she added, very seriously, that she could make a Tree of Diana which should be a very Tree of the Sun, which would produce golden fruit, which might be gathered, and which would continue to be produced till no more remained of a certain ingredient. I said modestly that I could not believe the thing possible without the powder of projection, but her only answer was a pleased smile.

She then pointed out a china basin containing nitre, mercury, and sulphur, and a fixed salt on a plate.

"You know the ingredients, I suppose?" said she.

"Yes; this fixed salt is a salt of urine."

"You are right."

"I admire your sagacity, madam. You have made an analysis of the mixture with which I traced the pentacle on your nephew's thigh, but in what way can you discover the words which give the pentacle its efficacy?"

"In the manuscript of an adept, which I will shew you, and where you will find the very words you used."

I bowed my head in reply, and we left this curious laboratory.

We had scarcely arrived in her room before Madame d'Urfe drew from a handsome casket a little book, bound in black, which she put on the table while she searched for a match. While she was looking about, I opened the book behind her back, and found it to be full of pentacles, and by good luck found the pentacle I had traced on the count's thigh. It was surrounded by the names of the spirits of the planets, with the exception of those of Saturn and Mars. I shut up the book quickly. The spirits named were the same as those in the works of Agrippa, with which I was acquainted. With an unmoved countenance I drew near her, and she soon found the match, and her appearance surprised me a good deal; but I will speak of that another time.

The marchioness sat down on her sofa, and making me to do the like she asked me if I was acquainted with the talismans of the Count de Treves?

"I have never heard of them, madam, but I know those of Poliphilus:"

"It is said they are the same."

"I don't believe it."

"We shall see. If you will write the words you uttered, as you drew the pentacle on my nephew's thigh, and if I find the same talisman with the same words around it, the identity will be proved."

"It will, I confess. I will write the words immediately."

I wrote out the names of the spirits. Madame d'Urfe found the pentacle and read out the names, while I pretending astonishment, gave her the paper, and much to her delight she found the names to be the same.

"You see," said she, "that Poliphilus and the Count de Treves possessed the same art."

"I shall be convinced that it is so, if your book contains the manner of pronouncing the ineffable names. Do you know the theory of the planetary hours?"

"I think so, but they are not needed in this operation."

"They are indispensable, madam, for without them one cannot work with any certainty. I drew Solomon's pentacle on the thigh of Count de la Tour d'Auvergne in the hour of Venus, and if I had not begun with Arael, the spirit of Venus, the operation would have had no effect."

"I did not know that. And after Arael?"

"Next comes Mercury, then the Moon, then Jupiter, and then the Sun. It is, you see, the magic cycle of Zoroaster, in which Saturn and Mars are omitted."

"And how would you have proceeded if you had gone to work in the hour of the Moon?"

"I should have begun with Jupiter, passed to the Sun, then to Arael or Venus, and I should have finished at Mercury."

"I see sir, that you are most apt in the calculation of the planetary hours."

"Without it one can do nothing in magic, as one would have no proper data; however, it is an easy matter to learn. Anyone could pick it up in a month's time. The practical use, however, is much more difficult than the theory; this, indeed, is a complicated affair. I never leave my house without ascertaining the exact number of minutes in the day, and take care that my watch is exact to the time, for a minute more or less would make all the difference in the world."

"Would you have the goodness to explain the theory to me."

"You will find it in Artephius and more clearly in Sandivogius."

"I have both works, but they are in Latin."

"I will make you a translation of them."

"You are very kind; I shall be extremely obliged to you."

"I have seen such things here, madam, that I could not refuse, for reasons which I may, perhaps, tell you to-morrow."

"Why not to-day?"

"Because I ought to know the name of your familiar spirit before I tell you."

"You know, then, that I have a familiar? You should have one, if it is true that you possess the powder of projection."

"I have one."

"Give me the oath of the order."

"I dare not, and you know why."

"Perhaps I shall be able to remove your fears by tomorrow."

This absurd oath was none other than that of the princes of the Rosy Cross, who never pronounce it without being certain that each party is a Rosicrucian, so Madame d'Urfe was quite right in her caution, and as for me I had to pretend to be afraid myself. The fact is I wanted to gain time, for I knew perfectly well the nature of the oath. It may be given between men without any indecency, but a woman like Madame d'Urfe would probably not relish giving it to a man whom she saw for the first time.

"When we find this oath alluded to in the Holy Scriptures," she said, "it is indicated by the words 'he swore to him by laying his hand on his thigh.'"

"But the thigh is not really what is meant; and consequently we never find any notice of a man taking this oath to a woman, as a woman has no 'verbum'."

The Count de la Tour d'Auvergne came back at nine o'clock in the evening, and he skewed no little astonishment at seeing me still with his aunt. He told us that his cousin's fever had increased, and that small-pox had declared itself; "and I am going to take leave of you, my dear aunt, at least for a month, as I intend to shut myself up with the sick man."

Madame d'Urfe praised his zeal, and gave him a little bag on his promising to return it to her after the cure of the prince.

"Hang it round his neck and the eruption will come out well, and he will be perfectly cured."

He promised to do so, and having wished us good evening he went out.

"I do not know, madam, what your bag contains, but if it have aught to do with magic, I have no confidence in its efficacy, as you have neglected to observe the planetary hour."

"It is an electrum, and magic and the observance of the hour have nothing to do with it."

"I beg your pardon."

She then said that she thought my desire for privacy praiseworthy, but she was sure I should not be ill pleased with her small circle, if I would but enter it.

"I will introduce you to all my friends," said she, "by asking them one at a time, and you will then be able to enjoy the company of them all."

I accepted her proposition.

In consequence of this arrangement I dined the next day with M. Grin and his niece, but neither of them took my fancy. The day after, I dined with an Irishman named Macartney, a physician of the old school, who bored me terribly. The next day the guest was a monk who talked literature, and spoke a thousand follies against Voltaire, whom I then much admired, and against the "Esprit des Lois," a favourite work of mine, which the cowled idiot refused to attribute to Montesquieu, maintaining it had been written by a monk. He might as well have said that a Capuchin created the heavens and the earth.

On the day following Madame d'Urfe asked me to dine with the Chevalier d'Arzigny, a man upwards of eighty, vain, foppish, and consequently ridiculous, known as "The Last of the Beaus." However, as he had moved in the court of Louis XIV., he was interesting enough, speaking with all the courtesy of the school, and having a fund of anecdote relating to the Court of that despotic and luxurious monarch.

His follies amused me greatly. He used rouge, his clothes were cut in the style which obtained in the days of Madame de Sevigne, he professed himself still the devoted lover of his mistress, with whom he supped every night in the company of his lady friends, who were all young and all delightful, and preferred his society to all others; however, in spite of these seductions, he remained faithful to his mistress.

The Chevalier d'Arzigny had an amiability of character which gave whatever he said an appearance of truth, although in his capacity of courtier truth was probably quite unknown to him. He always wore a bouquet of the most strongly-smelling flowers, such as tuberoses, jonquils, and Spanish jasmine; his wig was plastered down with amber-scented pomade, his teeth were made of ivory, and his eyebrows dyed and perfumed, and his whole person exhaled an odour to which Madame d'Urfe did not object, but which I could scarcely bear. If it had not been for this drawback I should probably have cultivated his society. He was a professed Epicurean, and carried out the system with an amazing tranquillity. He said that he would undertake to receive twenty-four blows with the stick every morning on the condition that he should not die within the twenty-four hours, and that the older he grew the more blows he would gladly submit to. This was being in love with life with a vengeance.

Another day I dined with M. Charon, who was a counsellor, and in charge of a suit between Madame d'Urfe and her daughter Madame du Chatelet, whom she disliked heartily. The old counsellor had been the favoured lover of the marchioness forty years before, and he thought himself bound by the remembrance of their love-passages to support the cause of his old sweetheart. In those days French magistrates thought they had a right to take the side of their friends, or of persons in whom they had an interest, sometimes for friendship's sake, and sometimes for a monetary consideration; they thought, in fact, that they were justified in selling justice.

M. Charon bored me like the others, as was natural, considering we had no two tastes in common.

The scene was changed the next day when I was amused with the company of M. de Viarme, a young counsellor, a nephew of Madame d'Urfe's, and his pretty and charming wife. He was the author of the "Remonstrances to the King," a work which got him a great reputation, and had been read eagerly by the whole town. He told me that the business of a counsellor was to oppose everything done by the crown, good and bad. His reasons for this theory were those given by all minorities, and I do not think I need trouble my readers with them.

The most enjoyable dinner I had was with Madame de Gergi, who came with the famous adventurer, known by the name of the Count de St. Germain. This individual, instead of eating, talked from the beginning of the meal to the end, and I followed his example in one respect as I did not eat, but listened to him with the greatest attention. It may safely be said that as a conversationalist he was unequalled.

St. Germain gave himself out for a marvel and always aimed at exciting amazement, which he often succeeded in doing. He was scholar, linguist, musician, and chemist, good-looking, and a perfect ladies' man. For awhile he gave them paints and cosmetics; he flattered them, not that he would make them young again (which he modestly confessed was beyond him) but that their beauty would be preserved by means of a wash which, he said, cost him a lot of money, but which he gave away freely.

He had contrived to gain the favour of Madame de Pompadour, who had spoken about him to the king, for whom he had made a laboratory, in which the monarch—a martyr to boredom—tried to find a little pleasure or distraction, at all events, by making dyes. The king had given him a suite of rooms at Chambord, and a hundred thousand francs for the construction of a laboratory, and according to St. Germain the dyes discovered by the king would have a materially beneficial influence on the quality of French fabrics.

This extraordinary man, intended by nature to be the king of impostors and quacks, would say in an easy, assured manner that he was three hundred years old, that he knew the secret of the Universal Medicine, that he possessed a mastery over nature, that he could melt diamonds, professing himself capable of forming, out of ten or twelve small diamonds, one large one of the finest water without any loss of weight. All this, he said, was a mere trifle to him.

Notwithstanding his boastings, his bare-faced lies, and his manifold eccentricities, I cannot say I thought him offensive. In spite of my knowledge of what he was and in spite of my own feelings, I thought him an astonishing man as he was always astonishing me. I shall have something more to say of this character further on.

When Madame d'Urfe had introduced me to all her friends, I told her that I would dine with her whenever she wished, but that with the exception of her relations and St. Germain, whose wild talk amused me, I should prefer her to invite no company. St. Germain often dined with the best society in the capital, but he never ate anything, saying that he was kept alive by mysterious food known only to himself. One soon got used to his eccentricities, but not to his wonderful flow of words which made him the soul of whatever company he was in.

By this time I had fathomed all the depths of Madame d'Urfe's character. She firmly believed me to be an adept of the first order, making use of another name for purposes of my own; and five or six weeks later she was confirmed in this wild idea on her asking me if I had diciphered the manuscript which pretended to explain the Magnum Opus.

"Yes," said I, "I have deciphered it, and consequently read it, and I now beg to return it you with my word of honour that I have not made a copy; in fact, I found nothing in it that I did not know before."

"Without the key you mean, but of course you could never find out that."

"Shall I tell you the key?"

"Pray do so."

I gave her the word, which belonged to no language that I know of, and the marchioness was quite thunderstruck.

"This is too amazing," said she; "I thought myself the sole possessor of that mysterious word—for I had never written it down, laying it up in my memory—and I am sure I have never told anyone of it."

I might have informed her that the calculation which enabled me to decipher the manuscript furnished me also with the key, but the whim took me to tell her that a spirit had revealed it to me. This foolish tale completed my mastery over this truly learned and sensible woman on everything but her hobby. This false confidence gave me an immense ascendancy over Madame d'Urfe, and I often abused my power over her. Now that I am no longer the victim of those illusions which pursued me throughout my life, I blush at the remembrance of my conduct, and the penance I impose on myself is to tell the whole truth, and to extenuate nothing in these Memoirs.

The wildest notion in the good marchioness's brain was a firm belief in the possibility of communication between mortals and elementary spirits. She would have given all her goods to attain to such communication, and she had several times been deceived by impostors who made her believe that she attained her aim.

"I did not think," said she, sadly, "that your spirit would have been able to force mine to reveal my secrets."

"There was no need to force your spirit, madam, as mine knows all things of his own power."

"Does he know the inmost secrets of my soul?"

"Certainly, and if I ask him he is forced to disclose all to me."

"Can you ask him when you like?"

"Oh, yes! provided I have paper and ink. I can even ask him questions through you by telling you his name."

"And will you tell it me?"

"I can do what I say; and, to convince you, his name is Paralis. Ask him a simple question in writing, as you would ask a common mortal. Ask him, for instance, how I deciphered your manuscript, and you shall see I will compel him to answer you."

Trembling with joy, Madame d'Urfe put her question, expressed it in numbers, then following my method in pyramid shape; and I made her extract the answer, which she wrote down in letters. At first she only obtained consonants, but by a second process which supplied the vowels she received a clear and sufficient answer. Her every feature expressed astonishment, for she had drawn from the pyramid the word which was the key to her manuscript. I left her, carrying with me her heart, her soul, her mind, and all the common sense which she had left.

CHAPTER IV

Absurd Ideas of Madame D'Urfe on My Supernatural Powers—Marriage of My Brother—I Conceive a Plan on His Wedding Day—I Go to Holland on a Financial Mission—The Jew Boaz Gives Me a Lesson—M. d'Afri—Esther—Another Casanova—I Find Therese Imer Again

By the time that the Prince du Turenne had recovered from the small-pox and the Count de la Tour d'Auvergne had left him, the latter, knowing his aunt's taste for the occult sciences, was not surprised to find me become her confident and most intimate friend.

I was glad so see him and all the relations of the marchioness at dinner, as I was delighted with the courtesy with which they treated me. I am referring more especially to her brothers MM. de Pont-Carre and de Viarme who had lately been chosen head of the trade companies, and his son. I have already spoken of Madame du Chatelet, the marchioness's daughter, but an unlucky lawsuit separated them, and she no longer formed one of the family circle.

De la Tour d'Auvergne having been obliged to rejoin his regiment which was in garrison in Brittany, the marchioness and I dined together almost every day and people looked upon me as her husband, and despite the improbability of the supposition this was the only way in which they could account for the long hours we spent together. Madame d'Urfe thought that I was rich and looked upon my position at the lottery as a mere device for preserving my incognito.

I was the possessor in her estimation, not only of the philosopher's stone, but also of the power of speaking with the whole host of elementary spirits; from which premises she drew the very logical deduction that I could turn the world upside down if I liked, and be the blessing or the plague of France; and she thought my object in remaining incognito was to guard myself from arrest and imprisonment; which according to her would be the inevitable result of the minister's discovering my real character. These wild notions were the fruit of the nocturnal revelations of her genius, that is, of the dreams of her disordered spirit, which seemed to her realities. She did not seem to think that if I was endowed as she supposed no one would have been able to arrest me, in the first place, because I should have had foreknowledge of the attempt, and in the second place because my power would have been too strong for all bolts and bars. All this was clear enough, but strong passion and prejudice cannot reason.

One day, in the course of conversation, she said, with the utmost seriousness, that her genius had advised her that not even I had power to give her speech with the spirits, since she was a woman, and the genii only communicated with men, whose nature is more perfect. Nevertheless, by a process which was well known to me, I might make her soul pass into the body of a male child born of the mystic connection between a mortal and an immortal, or, in other words, between an ordinary man and a woman of a divine nature.

If I had thought it possible to lead back Madame d'Urfe to the right use of her senses I would have made the attempt, but I felt sure that her disease was without remedy, and the only course before me seemed to abet her in her ravings and to profit by them.

If I had spoken out like an honest man and told her that her theories were nonsensical, she would not have believed me; she would have thought me jealous of her knowledge, and I should have lost her favour without any gain to her or to myself. I thus let things take their course, and to speak the truth I was flattered to see myself treated as one of the most profound brothers of the Rosy Cross, as the most powerful of men by so distinguished a lady, who was in high repute for her learning, who entertained and was related to the first families of France, and had an income of eighty thousand francs, a splendid estate, and several magnificent houses in Paris. I was quite sure that she would refuse me nothing, and though I had no definite plan of profiting by her wealth I experienced a certain pleasure at the thought that I could do so if I would.

In spite of her immense fortune and her belief in her ability to make gold, Madame d'Urfe was miserly in her habits, for she never spent more than thirty thousand francs in a year, and she invested her savings in the exchange, and in this way had nearly doubled them. A brother used to buy her in Government securities at their lowest rate and sell at their rise, and in this manner, being able to wait for their rise, and fall, she had amassed a considerable sum.

She had told me more than once that she would give all she possessed to become a man, and that she knew I could do this for her if I would. One day, as she was speaking to me on this subject in a tone of persuasion almost irresistible, I told her that I must confess I had the power to do what she wanted, but that I could not make up my mind to perform the operation upon her as I should have to kill her first. I thought this would effectually check her wish to go any further, but what was my surprise to hear her say,

"I know that, and what is more I know the death I shall have to die; but for all that I am ready."

"What, then, is that death, madam?"

"It is by the same poison which killed Paracelsus."

"Do you think that Paracelsus obtained the hypostasis?"

"No, but I know the reason of his not doing so."

"What is the reason?"

"It is that he was neither man or woman, and a composite nature is incapable of the hypostasis, to obtain which one must be either the one or the other."

"Very true, but do you know how to make the poison, and that the thing is impossible without the aid of a salamander?"

"That may or may not be! I beseech you to enquire of the oracle whether there be anyone in Paris in possession of this potion."

It was easy to see that she thought herself in possession of it, so I had no hesitation in extracting her name from the oracular pyramid. I pretended to be astonished at the answer, but she said boastfully,

"You see that all we want is a male child born of an immortal. This, I am advised, will be provided by you; and I do not think you will be found wanting out of a foolish pity for this poor old body of mine."

At these words I rose and went to the window, where I stayed for more than a quarter of an hour reflecting on her infatuation. When I returned to the table where she was seated she scanned my features attentively, and said, with much emotion, "Can it be done, my dear friend? I see that you have been weeping."

I did not try to undeceive her, and, taking my sword and hat, I took leave of her sadly. Her carriage, which was always at my disposal, was at the door, and I drove to the Boulevards, where I walked till the evening, wondering all the while at the extraordinary fantasies of the marchioness.

My brother had been made a member of the Academy, on the exhibition of a battle piece which had taken all the critics by storm. The picture was purchased by the Academy for five hundred louis.

He had fallen in love with Caroline, and would have married her but for a piece of infidelity on her part, which so enraged him that in a week after he married an Italian dancer. M. de Sanci, the ecclesiastical commissioner, gave the wedding party. He was fond of the girl, and out of gratitude to my brother for marrying her he got him numerous orders among his friends, which paved the way to the large fortune and high repute which my brother afterwards attained.

M. Corneman, the banker, who was at my brother's wedding, spoke to me at considerable length on the great dearth of money, and asked me to discuss the matter with the comptroller-general.

He told me that one might dispose of Government securities to an association of brokers at Amsterdam, and take in exchange the securities of any other country whose credit was higher than that of France, and that these securities could easily be realized. I begged him to say no more about it, and promised to see what I could do.

The plan pleased me, and I turned it over all night; and the next day I went to the Palais Bourbon to discuss the question with M. de Bernis. He thought the whole idea an excellent one, and advised me to go to Holland with a letter from M. de Choiseul for M. d'Afri, the ambassador at the Hague. He thought that the first person I should consult with M. de Boulogne, with whom he warned me to appear as if I was sure of my ground.

"As you do not require money in advance," said he, "you will be able to get as many letters of recommendation as you like."

The same day I went to the comptroller-general, who approved of my plan, and told me that M. le Duc de Choiseul would be at the Invalides the next day, and that I should speak to him at once, and take a letter he would write for me.

"For my part," said he, "I will credit our ambassador with twenty millions, and if, contrary to my hopes, you do not succeed, the paper can be sent back to France."

I answered that there would be no question of the paper being returned, if they would be content with a fair price.

"The margin will be a small one; however, you will hear about that from the ambassador, who will have full instructions."

I felt so flattered by this mission that I passed the night in thinking it over. The next day I went to the Invalides, and M. de Choiseul, so famous for taking decisive action, had no sooner read M. de Boulogne's letter and spoken a few words to me on the subject, than he got me to write a letter for M. d'Afri, which he signed, sealed, returned to me, and wished me a prosperous journey.

I immediately got a passport from M. de Berkenrode, and the same day took leave of Madame Baletti and all my friends except Madame d'Urfe, with whom I was to spend the whole of the next day. I gave my clerk at the lottery office full authority to sign all tickets.

About a month before, a girl from Brussels, as excellent as she was pretty, had been married under my auspices to an Italian named Gaetan, by trade a broker. This fellow, in his fit of jealousy, used to ill-treat her shamefully; I had reconciled them several times already, and they regarded me as a kind of go-between. They came to see me on the day on which I was making my preparations for going to Holland. My brother and Tiretta were with me, and as I was still living in furnished apartments I took them all to Laudel's, where they gave one an excellent dinner. Tiretta, drove his coach-and-four; he was ruining his ex-methodist, who was still desperately in love with him.

In the course of dinner Tiretta, who was always in high spirits and loved a jest, began to flirt with the girl, whom he saw for the first time. She, who neither meant nor suspected any ill, was quite at her ease, and we should have enjoyed the joke, and everything would have gone on pleasantly, if her husband had possessed some modicum of manners and common sense, but he began to get into a perfect fury of jealousy. He ate nothing, changed colour ten times in a minute, and looked daggers at his wife, as much as to say he did not see the joke. To crown all, Tiretta began to crack jests at the poor wretch's expense, and I, foreseeing unpleasantness, endeavoured, though all in vain, to moderate his high spirits and his sallies. An oyster chanced to fall on Madame Gaetan's beautiful breast; and Tiretta, who was sitting near her, took it up with his lips as quick as lightning. Gaetan was mad with rage and gave his wife such a furious box on the ear that his hand passed on from her cheek to that of her neighbour. Tiretta now as enraged as Gaetan took him by his middle and threw him down, where, having no arms, he defended himself with kicks and fisticuffs, till the waiter came, and we put him out of the room.

The poor wife in tears, and, like Tiretta, bleeding at the nose, besought me to take her away somewhere, as she feared her husband would kill her if she returned to him. So, leaving Tiretta with my brother, I got into a carriage with her and I took her, according to her request, to her kinsman, an old attorney who lived in the fourth story of a house in the Quai de Gevres. He received us politely, and after having heard the tale, he said,

"I am a poor man, and I can do nothing for this unfortunate girl; while if I had a hundred crowns I could do everything."

"Don't let that stand in your way," said I, and drawing three hundred francs from my pockets I gave him the money.

"Now, sir," said he, "I will be the ruin of her husband, who shall never know where his wife is."

She thanked me and I left her there; the reader shall hear what became of her when I return from my journey.

On my informing Madame d'Urfe that I was going to Holland for the good of France, and that I should be coming back at the beginning of February, she begged me to take charge of some shares of hers and to sell them for her. They amounted in value to sixty thousand francs, but she could not dispose of them on the Paris Exchange owing to the tightness in the money market. In addition, she could not obtain the interest due to her, which had mounted up considerably, as she had not had a dividend for three years.

I agreed to sell the shares for her, but it was necessary for me to be constituted depositary and owner of the property by a deed, which was executed the same day before a notary, to whose office we both went.

On returning to her house I wished to give her an I O U for the moneys, but she would not hear of such a thing, and I let her remain satisfied of my honesty.

I called on M. Corneman who gave me a bill of exchange for three hundred florins on M. Boaz, a Jewish banker at the Hague, and I then set out on my journey. I reached Anvers in two days, and finding a yacht ready to start I got on board and arrived at Rotterdam the next day. I got to the Hague on the day following, and after depositing my effects at the "Hotel d'Angleterre" I proceeded to M. d'Afri's, and found him reading M. de Choiseul's letter, which informed him of my business. He asked me to dine in his company and in that of the ambassador of the King of Poland, who encouraged me to proceed in my undertaking though he had not much opinion of my chances of success.

Leaving the ambassador I went to see Boaz, whom I found at table in the midst of a numerous and ugly family. He read my letter and told me he had just received a letter from M. Corneman in which I was highly commended to him. By way of a joke he said that as it was Christmas Eve he supposed I should be going to rock the infant Jesus asleep, but I answered that I was come to keep the Feast of the Maccabees with him—a reply which gained me the applause of the whole family and an invitation to stay with them. I accepted the offer without hesitation, and I told my servant to fetch my baggage from the hotel. Before leaving the banker I asked him to shew me some way of making twenty thousand florins in the short time I was going to stay in Holland.

Taking me quite seriously he replied that the thing might easily be done and that he would think it over.

The next morning after breakfast, Boaz said,

"I have solved your problem, sir; come in here and I will tell you about it."

He took me into his private office, and, after counting out three thousand florins in notes and gold, he told me that if I liked I could undoubtedly make the twenty thousand florins I had spoken of.

Much surprised at the ease with which money may be got in Holland, as I had been merely jesting in the remarks I had made, I thanked him for his kindness, and listened to his explanation.

"Look at this note," said he, "which I received this morning from the Mint. It informs me that an issue of four hundred thousand ducats is about to be made which will be disposed of at the current rate of gold, which is fortunately not high just now. Each ducat will fetch five florins, two stivers and three-fifths. This is the rate of exchange with Frankfort. Buy in four hundred thousand ducats; take them or send them to Frankfort, with bills of exchange on Amsterdam, and your business is done. On every ducat you will make a stiver and one-ninth, which comes to twenty-two thousand, two hundred and twenty-two of our florins. Get hold of the gold to-day, and in a week you will have your clear profit. That's my idea."

"But," said I, "will the clerks of the Mint trust me with such a sum?"

"Certainly not, unless you pay them in current money or in good paper."

"My dear sir, I have neither money nor credit to that amount."

"Then you will certainly never make twenty thousand florins in a week. By the way you talked yesterday I took you for a millionaire."

"I am very sorry you were so mistaken."

"I shall get one of my sons to transact the business to-day."

After giving me this rather sharp lesson, M. Boaz went into his office, and I went to dress.

M. d'Afri had paid his call on me at the "Hotel d'Angleterre," and not finding me there he had written me a letter asking me to come and see him. I did so, and he kept me to dinner, shewing me a letter he had received from M. de Boulogne, in which he was instructed not to let me dispose of the twenty millions at a greater loss than eight per cent., as peace was imminent. We both of us laughed at this calm confidence of the Parisian minister, while we who were in a country where people saw deeper into affairs knew that the truth was quite otherwise.

On M. d'Afri's hearing that I was staying with a Jew, he advised me to keep my own counsel when with Jews, "because," said he, "in business, most honest and least knavish mean pretty much the same thing. If you like," he added, "I will give you a letter of introduction to M. Pels, of Amsterdam." I accepted his offer with gratitude, and in the hope of being useful to me in the matter of my foreign shares he introduced me to the Swedish ambassador, who sent me to M. d'O——.

Wanting to be present at a great festival of Freemasons on St. John's Day, I remained at the Hague till the day after the celebration. The Comte de Tot, brother of the baron, who lost all his money at the seraglio, and whom I had met again at the Hague, introduced me. I was not sorry to be in company with all the best society in Holland.

M. d'Afri introduced me to the mother of the stadtholder, who was only twelve, and whom I thought too grave for his years. His mother was a worthy, patient kind of woman, who fell asleep every minute, even while she was speaking. She died shortly after, and it was discovered at the postmortem examination that she had a disease of the brain which caused her extreme propensity to sleep. Beside her I saw Count Philip de Zinzendorf, who was looking for twelve millions for the empress—a task which was not very difficult, as he offered five per cent. interest.

At the play I found myself sitting next to the Turkish minister, and I thought he would die with laughter before my eyes. It happened thus:

They were playing Iphigenia, that masterpiece of Racine's. The statue of Diana stood in the midst of the stage, and at the end of one act Iphigenia and her train of priestesses, while passing before it, all made a profound bow to the goddess. The candlesnuffer, who perhaps may have been a bad wit, crossed the stage just after wards, and likewise bowed to the goddess. This put pit and boxes in a good humour, and peals of laughter sounded from all parts of the house. All this had to be explained to the Turk, and he fell into such a fit of laughter that I thought he would burst. At last he was carried to his inn still laughing but almost senseless.

To have taken no notice of the Dutchman's heavy wit would have been, I confess, a mark of stupidity, but no one but a Turk could have laughed like that. It may be said that a great Greek philosopher died of laughter at seeing a toothless old woman trying to eat figs. But there is a great difference between a Turk and a Greek, especially an ancient Greek.

Those who laugh a good deal are more fortunate than those who do not laugh at all, as laughter is good for the digestion; but there is a just mean in everything.

When I had gone two leagues from Amsterdam in my posting-chaise on two wheels, my servant sitting beside me, I met a carriage on four wheels, drawn like mine by two horses, and containing a fine-looking young man and his servant. His coachman called out to mine to make way for him. My coachman answered that if he did he might turn me into the ditch, but the other insisted on it. I spoke to the master, begging him to tell his coachman to make way for me.

"I am posting, sir," said I; "and, moreover, I am a foreigner."

"Sir," answered he, "in Holland we take no notice of posting or not posting; and if you are foreigner, as you say, you must confess that you have fewer rights than I who am in my own country."

The blood rushed to my face. I flung open the door with one hand and took my sword with the other; and leaping into the snow, which was up to my knees, I drew my sword, and summoned the Dutchman to give way or defend himself. He was cooler than I, and replied, smiling, that he was not going to fight for so foolish a cause, and that I might get into my carriage again, as he would make way for me. I was somewhat interested in his cool but pleasant manner. I got back into my chaise, and the next night reached Amsterdam.

I put up at the excellent inn "L'Etoile d'Orient," and in the morning I went on 'Change and found M. Pels. He told me he would think my business over, and finding M, d'O—— directly afterwards he offered to do me my sixty bills and give me twelve per cent. M. Pels told me to wait, as he said he could get me fifteen per cent. He asked me to dinner, and, on my admiring his Cape wine, he told me with a laugh that he had made it himself by mixing Bordeaux and Malaga.

M. d'O—— asked me to dinner on the day following; and on calling I found him with his daughter Esther, a young lady of fourteen, well developed for her age, and exquisite in all respects except her teeth, which were somewhat irregular. M. d'O was a widower, and had this only child; consequently, Esther was heiress to a large fortune. Her excellent father loved her blindly, and she deserved his love. Her skin was snow white, delicately tinted with red; her hair was black as ebony, and she had the most beautiful eyes I have ever seen. She made an impression on me. Her father had given her an excellent education; she spoke French perfectly, played the piano admirably, and was passionately fond of reading.

After dinner M. d'O—— shewed me the uninhabited part of the house, for since the death of his wife, whose memory was dear to him, he lived on the ground floor only. He shewed me a set of rooms where he kept a treasure in the way of old pottery. The walls and windows were covered with plates of marble, each room a different colour, and the floors were of mosaic, with Persian carpets. The dining-hall was cased in alabaster, and the table and the cupboards were of cedar wood. The whole house looked like a block of solid marble, for it was covered with marble without as well as within, and must have cost immense sums. Every Saturday half-a-dozen servant girls, perched on ladders, washed down these splendid walls. These girls wore wide hoops, being obliged to put on breeches, as otherwise they would have interested the passers by in an unseemly manner. After looking at the house we went down again, and M. d'O—— left me alone with Esther in the antechamber, where he worked with his clerks. As it was New Year's Day there was not business going on.

After playing a sonata, Mdlle. d'O—— asked me if I would go to a concert. I replied that, being in her company, nothing could make me stir. "But would you, mademoiselle, like to go?"

"Yes, I should like to go very well, but I cannot go by myself."

"If I might presume to offer to escort you . . . but I dare not think you would accept."

"I should be delighted, and if you were to ask my father I am sure he would not refuse his permission."

"Are you sure of that?"

"Quite sure, for otherwise he would be guilty of impoliteness, and my father would not do such a thing. But I see you don't know the manners of the country."

"I confess I do not:"

"Young ladies enjoy great liberty here—liberty which they lose only by marrying. Go and ask, and you will see:"

I went to M. d'O—— and made my request, trembling lest I should meet with a refusal.

"Have you a carriage?"

"Yes, sir."

"Then I need not give orders to get mine ready. Esther!"

"Yes, father."

"Go and dress, my dear; M. Casanova has been kind enough to offer to take you to the concert."

"How good of him! Thank you, papa, for letting me go."

She threw her arms around his neck, ran to dress, and reappeared an hour after, as fair as the joy which was expressed on her every feature. I could have wished she had used a little powder, but Esther was jealous of her ebon tresses, which displayed the whiteness of her skin to admiration. The chief aim of women in making their toilette is to please men, but how poor is the judgment of most men in such matters compared to the unerring instinct of the generality of women!

A beautiful lace kerchief veiled her bosom, whose glories made my heart beat faster.

We went down the stair, I helped her into the carriage, and stopped, thinking she would be accompanied by one of her women; but seeing nobody I got in myself. The door was shut, and we were off. I was overwhelmed with astonishment. A treasure like this in my keeping I could hardly think. I asked myself whether I was to remember that I was a free-lance of love, or whether honour bade me forget it. Esther, in the highest spirits, told me that we were going to hear an Italian singer whose voice was exquisite, and noticing my confusion she asked what was the matter. I did not know what to say, and began to stammer out something, but at last succeeded in saying that she was a treasure of whom I was not worthy to be the keeper.

"I know that in other countries a young girl would not be trusted alone with a gentleman, but here they teach us discretion and how to look after ourselves."

"Happy the man who is charged with your welfare, and happier still he on whom your choice has fallen!"

"That choice is not for me to make; 'tis my father's business."

"But supposing your father's choice is not pleasing to you, or supposing you love another?"

"We are not allowed to love a man until we know he is to be our husband."

"Then you are not in love with anyone?"

"No, and I have never felt the desire to love."

"Then I may kiss your hand?"

"Why should you kiss my hand?"

She drew away her hand and offered me her lovely lips. I took a kiss, which she gave modestly enough, but which went to my heart. My delight was a little alloyed when she said that she would give me another kiss before her father whenever I liked.

We reached the concert-room, where Esther found many of her young friends—all daughters of rich merchants, some pretty, some plain, and all curious to know who I was. The fair Esther, who knew no more than my name, could not satisfy them. All at once seeing a fair young girl a little way off she pointed her out to me and asked me my opinion of her. Naturally enough I replied that I did not care for fair girls.

"All the same, I must introduce you to her, for she may be a relation of yours. Her name is the same; that is her father over there:"

"M. Casanova," said she, speaking to a gentleman, "I beg to introduce to you M. Casanova, a friend of my father's."

"Really? The same name; I wish, sir, you were my friend, as we are, perhaps, related. I belong to the Naples branch."

"Then we are related, though distantly, as my father came from Parma. Have you your pedigree?"

"I ought to have such a thing, but to tell you the truth, I don't think much of such matters. Besants d'or and such heraldic moneys are not currency in a mercantile republic."

"Pedigree-hunting is certainly a somewhat foolish pursuit; but it may nevertheless afford us a few minutes' amusement without our making any parade of our ancestry."

"With all my heart."

"I shall have the honour of calling on you to-morrow, and I will bring my family-tree with me. Will you be vexed if you find the root of your family also?"

"Not at all; I shall be delighted. I will call on you myself to-morrow. May I ask if you are a business man?"

"No, I am a financial agent in the employ of the French ministry. I am staying with M. Pels."

M. Casanova made a sign to his daughter and introduced me to her. She was Esther's dearest friend, and I sat down between them, and the concert began.

After a fine symphony, a concerto for the violin, another for the hautbois, the Italian singer whose repute was so great and who was styled Madame Trend made her appearance. What was my surprise when I recognized in her Therese Imer, wife of the dancer Pompeati, whose name the reader may remember. I had made her acquaintance eighteen years ago, when the old senator Malipiero had struck me because we were playing together. I had seen her again at Venice in 1753, and then our pastime had been of a more serious nature. She had gone to Bayreuth, where she had been the margrave's mistress. I had promised to go and see her, but C—— C—— and my fair nun M—— M—— had left me neither the time nor the wish to do so. Soon after I was put under the Leads, and then I had other things to think about. I was sufficiently self-controlled not to shew my astonishment, and listened to an aria which she was singing, with her exquisite voice, beginning "Eccoti giunta al fin, donna infelice," words which seemed made for the case.

The applause seemed as if it would never come to an end. Esther told me that it was not known who she was, but that she was said to be a woman with a history, and to be very badly off. "She goes from one town to another, singing at all the public concerts, and all she receives is what those present choose to give her on a plate which she takes round."

"Does she find that pay?"

"I should suspect not, as everyone has paid already at coming in. She cannot get more than thirty or forty florins. The day after to-morrow she will go to the Hague, then to Rotterdam, then back here again. She had been performing for six months, and she is always well received."

"Has she a lover?"

"She is said to have lovers in every town, but instead of enriching her they make her poorer. She always wears black, not only because she is a widow, but also on account of a great grief she is reported to have gone through. She will soon be coming round." I took out my purse; and counted out twelve ducats, which I wrapped in paper; my heart beating all the while in a ridiculous manner, for I had really nothing to be excited about.

When Therese was going along the seats in front of me, I glanced at her for an instant, and I saw that she looked surprised. I turned my head to speak to Esther, and when she was directly in front of me I put my little packet on the plate without looking at her, and she passed on. A little girl, four or five years old, followed her, and when she got to the end of the bench she came back to kiss my hand. I could not help recognizing in her a facsimile of myself, but I concealed my emotion. The child stood still, and gazed at me fixedly, to my no small confusion. "Would you like some sweets, my dear?" said I, giving her my box, which I should have been glad to turn into gold. The little girl took it smilingly, made me a curtsy, and went on.

"Does it strike you, M. Casanova," said Esther, with a laugh, "that you and that little girl are as like each other as two peas?"

"Yes, indeed," added Mdlle. Casanova, "there is a striking likeness."

"These resemblances are often the work of chance."

"Just so," said Esther, with a wicked smile, "but you admit a likeness, don't you?"

"I confess I was struck with it, though of course I cannot judge so well as you."

After the concert M. d'O—— arrived, and giving back his daughter to his care I betook myself to my lodging. I was just sitting down to a dish of oysters, before going to bed, when Therese made her appearance, holding her child by the hand. Although I had not expected her to visit me that evening, I was nevertheless not much surprised to see her. I, of course, rose to greet her, when all at once she fell fainting on the sofa, though whether the fainting fit was real or assumed I cannot say. Thinking that she might be really ill I played my part properly, and brought her to herself by sprinkling her with cold water and putting my vinaigrette to her nose. As soon as she came to herself she began to gaze at me without saying a word. At last, tired of her silence, I asked her if she would take any supper; and on her replying in the affirmative, I rang the bell and ordered a good supper for three, which kept us at the table till seven o'clock in the morning, talking over our various fortunes and misfortunes. She was already acquainted with most of my recent adventures, but I knew nothing at all about hers, and she entertained me with a recital of them for five or six hours.

Sophie, the little girl, slept in my bed till day, and her mother, keeping the best of her tale to the last, told me that she was my daughter, and shewed me her baptismal certificate. The birth of the child fell in with the period at which I had been intimate with Therese, and her perfect likeness to myself left no room for doubt. I therefore raised no objections, but told the mother that I was persuaded of my paternity, and that, being in a position to give the child a good education, I was ready to be a father to her.

"She is too precious a treasure in my sight; if we were separated I should die."

"You are wrong; for if I took charge of the little girl I should see that she was well provided for."

"I have a son of twelve to whom I cannot give a proper education; take charge of him instead of Sophie."

"Where is he?"

"He is boarding, or rather in pawn, at Rotterdam."

"What do you mean by in pawn?"

"I mean that he will not be returned to me until I pay the person who has got him all my debts."

"How much do you owe?"

"Eighty florins. You have already given me sixty-two, give me four ducats more; you can then take my son, and I shall be the happiest of mothers. I will send my son to you at the Hague next week, as I think you will be there."

"Yes, my dear Therese; and instead of four ducats, here are twenty."

"We shall see each other again at the Hague."

She was grateful to excess, but I only felt pity for her and a sort of friendly interest, and kept quite cool, despite the ardour of her embraces. Seeing that her trouble was of no avail, she sighed, shed some tears, and, taking her daughter, she bid me adieu, promising once more to send me her son.

Therese was two years older than I. She was still pretty, and even handsome, but her charms no longer retained their first beauty, and my passion for her, having been a merely physical one, it was no wonder that she had no longer any attraction for me. Her adventures during the six years in which I had lost her would certainly interest my readers, and form a pleasing episode in my book, and I would tell the tale if it were a true one; but not being a romance writer, I am anxious that this work shall contain the truth and nothing but the truth. Convicted by her amorous and jealous margrave of infidelity, she had been sent about her business. She was separated from her husband Pompeati, had followed a new lover to Brussels, and there had caught the fancy of Prince Charles de Lorraine, who had obtained her the direction of all the theatres in the Austrian Low Countries. She had then undertaken this vast responsibility, entailing heavy expenditure, till at last, after selling all her diamonds and lace, she had fled to Holland to avoid arrest. Her husband killed himself at Vienna in a paroxysm caused by internal pain—he had cut open his stomach with a razor, and died tearing at his entrails.

My business left me no time for sleep. M. Casanova came and asked me to dinner, telling me to meet him on the Exchange—a place well worth seeing. Millionaires are as plentiful as blackberries, and anyone who is not worth more than a hundred thousand florins is considered a poor man. I found M. d'O—— there, and was asked by him to dinner the following day at a small house he had on the Amstel. M. Casanova treated me with the greatest courtesy. After reading my pedigree he went for his own, and found it exactly the same; but he merely laughed, and seemed to care little about it, differing in that respect from Don Antonio of Naples, who set such store by my pedigree, and treated me with such politeness on that account. Nevertheless, he bade me make use of him in anything relating to business if I did anything in that way. I thought his daughter pretty, but neither her charms nor her wit made any impression on me. My thoughts were taken up with Esther, and I talked so much about her at dinner that at last my cousin declared that she did not consider her pretty. Oh, you women! beauty is the only unpardonable offence in your eyes. Mdlle. Casanova was Esther's friend, and yet she could not bear to hear her praised.

On my seeing M. d'O—— again after dinner, he told me that if I cared to take fifteen per cent. on my shares, he would take them from me and save broker's expenses. I thought the offer a good one, and I accepted it, taking a bill of exchange on Tourton & Baur. At the rate of exchange at Hamburg I found I should have seventy-two thousand francs, although at five per cent. I had only expected sixty-nine thousand. This transaction won me high favour with Madame d'Urfe, who, perhaps, had not expected me to be so honest.

In the evening I went with M. Pels to Zaandam, in a boat placed on a sleigh and impelled by a sail. It was an extraordinary, but at the same time an amusing and agreeable, mode of travelling. The wind was strong, and we did fifteen miles an hour; we seemed to pass through the air as swiftly as an arrow. A safer and more convenient method of travelling cannot be imagined; it would be an ideal way of journeying round the world if there were such a thing as a frozen sea all round. The wind, however, must be behind, as one cannot sail on a side wind, there being no rudder. I was pleased and astonished at the skill of our two sailors in lowering sail exactly at the proper time; for the sleigh ran a good way, from the impetus it had already received, and we stopped just at the bank of the river, whereas if the sail had been lowered a moment later the sleigh might have been broken to pieces. We had some excellent perch for dinner, but the strength of the wind prevented us from walking about. I went there again, but as Zaandam is well known as the haunt of the millionaire merchants who retire and enjoy life there in their own way, I will say no more about it. We returned in a fine sleigh drawn by two horses, belonging to M. Pels, and he kept me to supper. This worthy man, whose face bore witness to his entire honesty, told me that as I was now the friend of M. d'O—— and himself, I should have nothing whatever to do with the Jews, but should address myself to them alone. I was pleased with this proposal, which made a good many of my difficulties disappear, and the reader will see the results of this course.

Next day snow fell in large flakes, and I went early to M. d'O——'s, where I found Esther in the highest of spirits. She gave me a warm welcome, and began to rally me on having spent the whole night with Madame Trenti.

I might possibly have shewn some slight confusion, but her father said an honest man had nothing to be ashamed of in admiring talent. Then, turning to me, he said,

"Tell me, M. Casanova, who this woman is?"

"She is a Venetian whose husband died recently; I knew her when I was a lad, and it was six years since I had seen her last."

"You were agreeably surprised, then, to see your daughter?" said Esther.

"Why do you think the child is my daughter? Madame Trenti was married then."

"The likeness is really too strong. And how about your falling asleep yesterday when you were supping with M. Pels?"

"It was no wonder that I went asleep, as I had not closed an eye the night before."

"I am envious of anyone who possesses the secret of getting a good sleep, for I have always to wait long hours before sleep comes to me, and when I awake, instead of being refreshed, I feel heavy and languid from fatigue."

"Try passing the night in listening to one in whom you take an interest, telling the story of her life, and I promise you that you will sleep well the night after."

"There is no such person for me."

"No, because you have as yet only seen fourteen summers; but afterwards there will be someone."

"Maybe, but what I want just now is books, and the help of someone who will guide my reading."

"That would be an easy matter for anyone who knew your tastes."

"I like history and travels, but for a book to please me it must be all true, as I lay it down at the slightest suspicion of its veracity."

"Now I think I may venture to offer my services, and if you will accept them I believe I shall be able to give satisfaction."

"I accept your offer, and shall keep you to your word."

"You need not be afraid of my breaking it, and before I leave for the Hague I will prove that I am reliable."

She then began to rally me on the pleasure I should have at the Hague, where I should see Madame Trenti again. Her freedom, mirth, and extreme beauty set my blood on fire, and M. d'O—— laughed heartily at the war his charming daughter waged on me. At eleven o'clock we got into a well-appointed sleigh and we set out for his small house, where she told me I should find Mdlle. Casanova and her betrothed.

"Nevertheless," said I, "you will continue to be my only attraction."

She made no answer, but it was easy to perceive that my avowal had not displeased her.

When we had gone some distance we saw the lovers, who had come out, in spite of the snow, to meet us. We got down, and after taking off our furs we entered the house. I gazed at the young gentleman, who looked at me a moment in return and then whispered in Mdlle. Casanova's ear. She smiled and whispered something to Esther. Esther stepped up to her father and said a few words to him in a low voice, and everybody began to laugh at once. They all looked at me and I felt certain that I was somehow the point of the joke, but I put on an indifferent air.

"There may be a mistake," said M. d'O——; "at any rate we should ascertain the truth of the matter."

"M. Casanova, had you any adventures on your journey from the Hague to Amsterdam?"

At this I looked again at the young gentleman, and I guessed what they were talking about.

"No adventure to speak of," I answered, "except a meeting with a fine fellow who desired to see my carriage turn upside down into the ditch, and who I think is present now."

At these words the laughter broke out afresh, and the gentleman and I embraced each other; but after he had given the true account of the adventure his mistress pretended to be angry, and told him that he ought to have fought. Esther observed that he had shewn more true courage in listening to reason, and M. d'O—— said he was strongly of his daughter's opinion; however, Mdlle. Casanova, after airing her high-flown ideas, began to sulk with her lover.

To restore the general mirth, Esther said, gaily, "Come, come, let us put on our skates, and try the Amstel, for I am afraid that unless we go forthwith the ice will have melted." I was ashamed to ask her to let me off, though I would gladly have done so! but what will not love do! M. d'O—— left us to our own devices. Mdlle. Casanova's intended put on my skates, and the ladies put on their short petticoats with black velvet drawers to guard against certain accidents. We reached the river, and as I was a perfect neophyte in this sport the figure I cut may be imagined. However, I resolutely determined to conquer my awkwardness, and twenty times, to the peril of my spine, did I fall down upon the ice. I should have been wiser to have left off, but I was ashamed to do so, and I did not stop till, to my huge delight, we were summoned in to dinner. But I paid dear for my obstinacy, for when I tried to rise from the table I felt as if I had lost the use of my limbs. Esther pitied me, and said she would cure me. There was a good deal of laughter at my expense, and I let them laugh, as I felt certain that the whole thing had been contrived to turn me into derision, and wishing to make Esther love me I thought it best to stimulate a good temper. I passed the afternoon with M. d'O——, letting the young people go by themselves on the Amstel, where they stopped till dusk.

Next morning when I awoke I thought I was a lost man. I suffered a martyrdom of pain. The last of my vertebral bones, called by doctors the os sacrum, felt as if it had been crushed to atoms, although I had used almost the whole of a pot of ointment which Esther had given me for that purpose. In spite of my torments I did not forget my promise, and I had myself taken to a bookseller's where I bought all the books I thought likely to interest her. She was very grateful, and told me to come and embrace her before I started if I wanted a pretty present.

It was not likely that I was going to refuse such an invitation as that, so I went early in the morning, leaving my post-chaise at the door Her governess took me to her bed, where she was lying as fair and gay as Venus herself.

"I am quite sure," said she, "that you would not have come at all unless I had asked you to come and embrace me."

At this my lips were fastened on her mouth, her eyes, and on every spot of her lovely face. But seeing my eyes straying towards her bosom, and guessing that I should make myself master of it, she stopped laughing and put herself on the defensive.

"Go away," said she, slyly, "go away and enjoy yourself at the Hague with the fair Trenti, who possesses so pretty a token of your love."

"My dear Esther, I am going to the Hague to talk business with the ambassador, and for no other reason, and in six days at latest you will see me back again, as much your lover as before, and desiring nothing better than to please you."

"I rely upon your word of honour, but mind you do not deceive me."

With these words she put up her mouth and gave me so tender and passionate a kiss that I went away feeling certain of my bliss being crowned on my return. That evening, at supper-time, I reached Boaz's house.

EPISODE 12 — RETURN TO PARIS

CHAPTER V

My Fortune in Holland—My Return to Paris with Young Pompeati

Amongst the letters which were waiting for me was one from the comptroller-general, which advised me that twenty millions in Government securities had been placed in the hands of M. d'Afri, who was not to go beyond a loss of eight per cent.; and another letter from my good patron, M. de Bernis, telling me to do the best I could, and to be assured that the ambassador would be instructed to consent to whatever bargain might be made, provided the rate was not more disadvantageous than that of the exchange at Paris. Boaz, who was astonished at the bargain I had made with my shares, wanted to discount the Government securities for me, and I should very likely have agreed to his terms if he had not required me to give him three months, and the promise that the agreement should hold even in the case of peace being concluded in the meanwhile. It was not long before I saw that I should do well to get back to Amsterdam, but I did not care to break my word to Therese, whom I had promised to meet at the Hague. I received a letter from her while I was at the play, and the servant who brought it told me he was waiting to conduct me to her. I sent my own servant home, and set out on my quest.

My guide made me climb to the fourth floor of a somewhat wretched house, and there I found this strange woman in a small room, attended by her son and daughter. The table stood in the midst of the room, and was covered with a black cloth, and the two candles standing upon it made it look like some sort of sepulchral altar. The Hague was a Court town. I was richly dressed; my elaborate attire made the saddest possible contrast with the gloom of my surroundings. Therese, dressed in black and seated between her children at that black table, reminded me of Medea. To see these two fair young creatures vowed to a lot of misery and disgrace was a sad and touching sight. I took the boy between my arms, and pressing him to my breast called him my son. His mother told him to look upon me as his father from henceforth. The lad recognized me; he remembered, much to my delight, seeing me in the May of 1753, in Venice, at Madame Manzoni's. He was slight but strong; his limbs were well proportioned, and his features intellectual. He was thirteen years old.

His sister sat perfectly still, apparently waiting for her turn to come. I took her on my knee, and as I embraced her, nature herself seemed to tell me that she was my daughter. She took my kisses in silence, but it was easy to see that she thought herself preferred to her brother, and was charmed with the idea. All her clothing was a slight frock, and I was able to feel every limb and to kiss her pretty little body all over, delighted that so sweet a being owed her existence to me.

"Mamma, dear," said she, "is not this fine gentleman the same we saw at Amsterdam, and who was taken for my papa because I am like him? But that cannot be, for my papa is dead."

"So he is, sweetheart; but I may be your dear friend, mayn't I? Would you like to have me for a friend?"

"Yes, yes!" she cried, and throwing her arms about my neck gave me a thousand kisses, which I returned with delight.

After we had talked and laughed together we sat down at table, and the heroine Therese gave me a delicate supper accompanied by exquisite wines. "I have never given the margrave better fare," said she, "at those nice little suppers we used to take together."

Wishing to probe the disposition of her son, whom I had engaged to take away with me, I addressed several remarks to him, and soon discovered that he was of a false and deceitful nature, always on his guard, taking care of what he said, and consequently speaking only from his head and not from his heart. Every word was delivered with a quiet politeness which, no doubt, was intended to please me.

I told him that this sort of thing was all very well on occasion; but that there were times when a man's happiness depended on his freedom from constraint; then and only then was his amiability, if he had any, displayed. His mother, thinking to praise him, told me that reserve was his chief characteristic, that she had trained him to keep his counsel at all times and places, and that she was thus used to his being reserved with her as with everyone else.

"All I can say is," said I, "your system is an abominable one. You may have strangled in their infancy all the finer qualities with which nature has endowed your son, and have fairly set him on the way to become a monster instead of an angel. I don't see how the most devoted father can possibly have any affection for a son who keeps all his emotions under lock and key."

This outburst, which proceeded from the tenderness I would fain have felt for the boy, seemed to strike his mother dumb.

"Tell me, my dear, if you feel yourself capable of shewing me that confidence which a father has a right to expect of a good son, and if you can promise to be perfectly open and unreserved towards me?"

"I promise that I will die rather than tell you a falsehood."

"That's just like him," said the mother. "I have succeeded in inspiring him with the utmost horror of untruthfulness."

"That's all very well, my dear madam, but you might have pursued a still better course, and one which would have been still more conducive to his happiness."

"What is that?"

"I will tell you. It was necessary to make him detest a lie; you should have rather endeavoured to make him a lover of the truth by displaying it to him in all its native beauty. This is the only way to make him lovable, and love is the sole bestower of happiness in this world."

"But isn't it the same thing not to lie and to tell the truth," said the boy, with a smile which charmed his mother and displeased me.

"Certainly not; there is a great difference—for to avoid lying you have only to hold your tongue; and do you think that comes to the same thing as speaking the truth? You must open your mind to me, my son, and tell me all your thoughts, even if you blush in the recital. I will teach you how to blush, and soon you will have nothing to fear in laying open all your thoughts and deeds. When we know each other a little longer we shall see how we agree together. You must understand that I cannot look upon you as my son until I see cause to love you, and I cannot have you call me father till you treat me as the best friend you have. You may be quite sure that I shall find a way to discover your thoughts, however cleverly you try to hide them. If I find you deceitful and suspicious I shall certainly entertain no regard for you. As soon as I have finished my business at Amsterdam we will set out for Paris. I am leaving the Hague to-morrow, and on my return I hope to find you instructed by your mother in a system of morality more consonant with my views, and more likely to lead to your happiness."

On glancing at my little daughter, who had been listening to me with the greatest attention, I saw that her eyes were swimming with tears, which she could hardly retain.

"Why are you crying?" said the mother; "it is silly to cry." And with that the child ran to her mother and threw her arms round her neck.

"Would you like to come to Paris, too?" said I to her.

"Oh, yes! But mamma must come too, as she would die without me."

"What would you do if I told you to go?" said the mother.

"I would obey you, mamma, but how could I exist away from you?"

Thereupon my little daughter pretended to cry. I say pretended, as it was quite evident that the child did not mean what she said, and I am sure that her mother knew it as well as I.

It was really a melancholy thing to see the effects of a bad education on this young child, to whom nature had given intelligence and feeling. I took the mother on one side, and said that if she had intended to make actors of her children she had succeeded to admiration; but if she wished them to become useful members of society her system had failed lamentably, as they were in a fair way to become monsters of deceit. I continued making her the most pointed remonstrances until, in spite of her efforts to control herself, she burst into tears. However, she soon recovered her composure, and begged me to stay at the Hague a day longer, but I told her it was out of the question, and left the room. I came in again a few minutes after, and Sophie came up to me and said, in a loving little voice,

"If you are really my friend, you will give me some proof of your friendship."

"And what proof do you want, my dear?"

"I want you to come and sup with me to-morrow."

"I can't, Sophie dear, for I have just said no to your mother, and she would be offended if I granted you what I had refused her."

"Oh, no! she wouldn't; it was she who told me to ask you just now."

I naturally began to laugh, but on her mother calling the girl a little fool, and the brother adding that he had never committed such an indiscretion, the poor child began to tremble all over, and looked abashed. I reassured her as best I could, not caring whether what I said displeased her mother or not, and I endeavoured to instill into her principles of a very different nature to those in which she had been reared, while she listened with an eagerness which proved that her heart was still ready to learn the right way. Little by little her face cleared, and I saw that I had made an impression, and though I could not flatter myself that any good I might do her would be lasting in its effects as long as she remained under the bad influence of her mother, I promised to come and sup with her next evening, "but on the condition," I said, "that you give me a plain meal, and one bottle of chambertin only, for you are not too well off."

"I know that, but mamma says that you pay for everything."

This reply made me go off into a roar of laughter; and in spite of her vexation the mother was obliged to follow my example. The poor woman, hardened by the life she led, took the child's simplicity for stupidity, but I saw in her a rough diamond which only wanted polishing.

Therese told me that the wine did not cost her anything, as the son of the Rotterdam burgomaster furnished her with it, and that he would sup with us the next day if I would allow him to be present. I answered smilingly that I should be delighted to see him, and I went away after giving my daughter, of whom I felt fond, a tender embrace. I would have done anything to be entrusted with her, but I saw it would be no good trying to get possession of her, as the mother was evidently keeping her as a resource for her old age. This is a common way for adventuresses to look upon their daughters, and Therese was an adventuress in the widest acceptation of the term. I gave her twenty ducats to get clothes for my adopted son and Sophie, who, with spontaneous gratitude, and her eyes filled with tears, came and gave me a kiss. Joseph was going to kiss my hand, but I told him that it was degrading for one man to kiss another's hand, and that for the future he was to shew his gratitude by embracing me as a son embraces his father.

Just as I was leaving, Therese took me to the closet where the two children were sleeping. I knew what she was thinking of; but all that was over long ago; I could think of no one but Esther.

The next day I found the burgomaster's son at my actress's house. He was a fine young fellow of twenty or twenty-one, but totally devoid of manner. He was Therese's lover, but he should have regulated his behaviour in my presence. Therese, seeing that he was posing as master of the field, and that his manners disgusted me, began to snub him, much to his displeasure, and after sneering at the poorness of the dishes, and praising the wine which he had supplied, he went out leaving us to finish our dessert by ourselves. I left myself at eleven, telling Therese that I should see her again before I went away. The Princesse de

Galitzin, a Cantimir by birth, had asked me to dinner, and this made me lose another day.

Next day I heard from Madame d'Urfe, who enclosed a bill of exchange on Boaz for twelve thousand francs. She said that she had bought her shares for sixty thousand, that she did not wish to make anything of them, and that she hoped I would accept the overplus as my broker's fee. She worded her offer with too much courtesy for me to refuse it. The remainder of the letter was devoted to the wildest fancies. She said that her genius had revealed to her that I should bring back to Paris a boy born of the Mystical Marriage, and she hoped I would take pity on her. It was a strange coincidence, and seemed likely to attach the woman still more closely to her visionary theories. I laughed when I though how she would be impressed by Therese's son, who was certainly not born of the Mystical Marriage.

Boaz paid me my twelve thousand francs in ducats, and I made him my friend, as he thanked me for receiving the moneys in ducats, and he doubtless made a profit on the transaction, gold being a commodity in Holland, and all payments being made in silver or paper money.

At that time gold was at a low rate, and nobody would take ducats.

After having an excellent dinner with the Princesse de Galitzin, I put on my cloak and went to the cafe. I found there the burgomaster's son, who was just beginning a game of billiards. He whispered to me that I might back him with advantage, and thinking he was sure of his stroke I thanked him and followed his advice. However, after losing three games one after the other, I took his measure and began to lay against him without his knowledge. After playing for three hours and losing all the time, he stopped play and came to condole with me on my heavy loss. It is impossible to describe his amazed expression when I shewed him a handful of ducats, and assured him that I had spent a very profitable evening in laying against him. Everybody in the room began to laugh at him, but he was the sort of young man who doesn't understand a joke, and he went out in a rage. Soon after I left the billiard-room myself, and, according to my promise went to see Therese, as I was leaving for Amsterdam the next day.

Therese was waiting for her young wine merchant, but on my recounting his adventures she expected him no longer. I took my little daughter on my knee and lavished my caresses on her, and so left them, telling them that we should see each other again in the course of three weeks or a month at latest.

As I was going home in the moonlight by myself, my sword under my arm, I was encountered all of a sudden by the poor dupe of a burgomaster's son.

"I want to know," said he, "if your sword has as sharp a point as your tongue."

I tried to quiet him by speaking common sense, and I kept my sword wrapped in my cloak, though his was bared and directed against me.

"You are wrong to take my jests in such bad part," said I; "however, I apologize to you."

"No apologies; look to yourself."

"Wait till to-morrow, you will be cooler then, but if you still wish it I will give you satisfaction in the midst of the billiard-room."

"The only satisfaction you can give me is to fight; I want to kill you."

As evidence of his determination, and to provoke me beyond recall, he struck me with the flat of his sword, the first and last time in my life in which I have received such and insult. I drew my sword, but still hoping to bring him to his senses I kept strictly on the defensive and endeavoured to make him leave off. This conduct the Dutchman mistook for fear, and pushed hard on me, lunging in a manner that made me look to myself. His sword passed through my necktie; a quarter of an inch farther in would have done my business.

I leapt to one side, and, my danger no longer admitting of my fighting on the defensive, I lunged out and wounded him in the chest. I thought this would have been enough for him, so I proposed we should terminate our engagement.

"I'm not dead yet," said he; "I want to kill you."

This was his watchword; and, as he leapt on me in a paroxysm of rage, more like a madman than a sensible being, I hit him four times. At the fourth wound he stepped back, and, saying he had had enough, begged me to leave him.

I went off as fast as I could, and was very glad to see from the look of my sword that his wounds were slight. I found Boaz still up, and on hearing what had taken place he advised me to go to Amsterdam at once, though I assured him that the wounds were not mortal. I gave in to his advice, and as my carriage was at the saddler's he lent me his, and I set out, bidding my servant to come on the next day with my luggage, and to rejoin me at the "Old Bible," in Amsterdam. I reached Amsterdam at noon and my man arrived in the evening.

I was curious to hear if my duel had made any noise, but as my servant had left at an early hour he had heard nothing about it. Fortunately for me nothing whatever was known about it at Amsterdam for a week after; otherwise, things might not have gone well with me, as the reputation of being a duellist is not a recommendation to financiers with whom one is about to transact business of importance.

The reader will not be surprised when I tell him that my first call was on M. d'O, or rather on his charming daughter Esther, for she it was on whom I waited. It will be remembered that the way in which we parted did a good deal towards augmenting the warmth of my affection for her. On entering the room I found Esther writing at a table.

"What are you doing Esther, dear?"

"An arithmetical problem."

"Do you like problems?"

"I am passionately fond of anything which contains difficulties and offers curious results."

"I will give you something which will please you."

I made her, by way of jest, two magic squares, which delighted her. In return, she spewed me some trifles with which I was well acquainted, but which I pretended to think very astonishing. My good genius then inspired me with the idea of trying divination by the cabala. I told her to ask a question in writing, and assured her that by a certain kind of calculation a satisfactory answer would be obtained. She smiled, and asked why I had returned to Amsterdam so soon. I shewed her how to make the pyramid with the proper numbers and the other ceremonies, then I made her extract the answer in numbers, translating it into French, and greatly was she surprised to find that the cause which had made me return to Amsterdam so soon was—love.

Quite confounded, she said it was very wonderful, even though the answer might not be true, and she wished to know what masters could teach this mode of calculation.

"Those who know it cannot teach it to anyone."

"How did you learn it, then?"

"From a precious manuscript I inherited from my father."

"Sell it me."

"I have burnt it; and I am not empowered to communicate the secret to anyone before I reach the age of fifty."

"Why fifty?"

"I don't know; but I do know that if I communicated it to anyone before that age I should run the risk of losing it myself. The elementary spirit who is attached to the oracle would leave it."

"How do you know that?"

"I saw it so stated in the manuscript I have spoken of."

"Then you are able to discover all secrets?"

"Yes, or I should be if the replies were not sometimes too obscure to be understood."

"As it does not take much time, will you be kind enough to get me an answer to another question?"

"With pleasure; you can command me in anything not forbidden by my familiar spirit."

She asked what her destiny would be, and the oracle replied that she had not yet taken the first step towards it. Esther was astonished and called her governess to see the two answers, but the good woman saw nothing wonderful in them whatever. Esther impatiently called her a blockhead, and entreated me to let her ask another question. I begged her to do so, and she asked,

"Who loves me most in Amsterdam?" The oracle replied that no one loved her as well as he who had given her being: Poor Esther then told me that I had made her miserable, and that she would die of grief if she could not succeed in learning the method of calculation. I gave no answer, and pretended to feel sad at heart. She began to write down another question, putting her hand in front so as to screen the paper. I rose as if to get out of her way, but while she was arranging the pyramid I cast my eyes on the paper whilst walking up and down the room, and read her question. After she had gone as far as I had taught her, she asked me to extract the answer, saying that I could do so without reading the question. I agreed to do so on the condition that she would not ask a second time.

As I had seen her question, it was easy for me to answer it. She had asked the oracle if she might shew the questions she had propounded to her father, and the answer was that she would be happy as long as she had no secrets from her father.

When she read these words she gave a cry of surprise, and could find no words wherewith to express her gratitude to me. I left her for the Exchange, where I had a long business conversation with M. Pels.

Next morning a handsome and gentlemanly man came with a letter of introduction from Therese, who told me that he would be useful in case I wanted any assistance in business. His name was Rigerboos. She informed me that the burgomaster's son was only slightly wounded, and that I had nothing to fear as the matter was not generally known, and that if I had business at the Hague I might return there in perfect safety. She said that my little Sophie talked of me all day, and that I should find my son much improved on my return. I asked M. Rigerboos to give me his address, assuring him that at the proper time I should rely on his services.

A moment after Rigerboos had gone, I got a short note from Esther, who begged me, in her father's name, to spend the day with her—at least, if I had no important engagement. I answered that, excepting a certain matter of which her father knew, I had no chiefer aim than to convince her that I desired a place in her heart, and that she might be quite sure that I would not refuse her invitation.

I went to M. d'O—— at dinner time. I found Esther and her father puzzling over the method which drew reasonable answers out of a pyramid of numbers. As soon as her father saw me, he embraced me, saying how happy he was to possess a daughter capable of attracting me.

"She will attract any man who has sufficient sense to appreciate her."

"You appreciate her, then?"

"I worship her."

"Then embrace her."

Esther opened her arms, and with a cry of delight threw them round my neck, and gave the back all my caresses, kiss for kiss.

"I have got through all my business," said M. d'O——, "and the rest of my day is at your disposal. I have known from my childhood that there is such a science as the one you profess, and I was acquainted with a Jew who by its aid made an immense fortune. He, like you, said that, under pain of losing the secret, it could only be communicated to one person, but he put off doing so so long that at last it was too late, for a high fever carried him off in a few days. I hope you will not do as the Jew did; but in the meanwhile allow me to say that if You do not draw a profit from this treasure, you do not know what it really is."

"You call this knowledge of mine a treasure, and yet you possess one far more excellent," looking at Esther as I spoke.

"We will discuss that again. Yes, sir, I call your science a treasure."

"But the answers of the oracle are often very obscure."

"Obscure! The answers my daughter received are as clear as day."

"Apparently, she is fortunate in the way she frames her questions; for on this the reply depends."

"After dinner we will try if I am so fortunate—at least, if you will be so kind as to help me."

"I can refuse you nothing, as I consider father and daughter as one being."

At table we discussed other subjects, as the chief clerks were present— notably the manager, a vulgar-looking fellow, who had very evident aspirations in the direction of my fair Esther. After dinner we went into M. d'O 's private closet, and thereupon he drew two long questions out of his pocket. In the first he desired to know how to obtain a favourable decision from the States-General in an important matter, the details of which he explained. I replied in terms, the obscurity of which would have done credit to a professed Pythoness, and I left Esther to translate the answer into common sense, and find a meaning in it.

With regard to the second answer I acted in a different manner; I was impelled to answer clearly, and did so. M. d'O asked what had become of a vessel belonging to the India Company of which nothing had been heard. It was known to have started on the return voyage, and should have arrived two months ago, and this delay gave rise to the supposition that it had gone down. M. d'O—— wished to know if it were still above water, or whether it were lost, etc. As no tidings of it had come to hand, the company were on the look-out for someone to insure it, and offered ten per cent., but nobody cared to run so great a risk, especially as a letter had been received from an English sea captain who said he had seen her sink.

I may confess to my readers, though I did not do so to M. d'O——. that with inexplicable folly I composed an answer that left no doubt as to the safety of the vessel, pronouncing it safe and sound, and that we should hear of it in a few days. No doubt I felt the need of exalting my oracle, but this method was likely to destroy its credit for ever. In truth, if I had guessed M. d'O——'s design, I would have curbed my vanity, for I had no wish to make him lose a large sum without profiting myself.

The answer made him turn pale, and tremble with joy. He told us that secrecy in the matter was of the last importance, as he had determined to insure the vessel and drive a good bargain. At this, dreading the consequences, I hastened to tell him that for all I knew there might not be a word of truth in the oracle's reply, and that I should die of grief if I were the involuntary cause of his losing an enormous sum of money through relying on an oracle, the hidden sense of which might be completely opposed to the literal translation.

"Have you ever been deceived by it?"

"Often."

Seeing my distress, Esther begged her father to take no further steps in the matter. For some moments nobody spoke.

M. d'O—— looked thoughtful and full of the project which his fancy had painted in such gay colours. He said a good deal about it, dwelling on the mystic virtues of numbers, and told his daughter to read out all the questions she had addressed to the oracle with the answers she had received. There were six or seven of them, all briefly worded, some direct and some equivocal. Esther, who had constructed the pyramids, had shone, with my potent assistance, in extracting the answers, which I had really invented, and her father, in the joy of his heart, seeing her so clever, imagined that she would become an adept in the science by the force of intelligence. The lovely Esther, who was much taken with the trifle; was quite ready to be of the same opinion.

After passing several hours in the discussion of the answers, which my host thought divine, we had supper, and at parting M. d'O—— said that as Sunday was a day for pleasure and not business he hoped I would honour them by passing the day at their pretty house on the Amstel, and they were delighted at my accepting their invitation.

I could not help pondering over the mysteries of the commercial mind, which narrows itself down to considerations of profit and loss. M. d'O—— was decidedly an honest man; but although he was rich, he was by no means devoid of the greed incident to his profession. I asked myself the question, how a man, who would consider it dishonourable to steal a ducat, or to pick one up in the street and keep it, knowing to whom it belonged, could reconcile it with his conscience to make an enormous profit by insuring a vessel of the safety of which he was perfectly certain, as he believed the oracle infallible. Such a transaction was certainly fraudulent, as it is dishonest to play when one is certain of winning.

As I was going home I passed a tea-garden, and seeing a good many people going in and coming out I went in curious to know how these places were managed in Holland. Great heavens! I found myself the witness of an orgy, the scene a sort of cellar, a perfect cesspool of vice and debauchery. The discordant noise of the two or three instruments which formed the orchestra struck gloom to the soul and added to the horrors of the cavern. The air was dense with the fumes of bad tobacco, and vapours reeking of beer and garlic issued from every mouth. The company consisted of sailors, men of the lowest-class, and a number of vile women. The sailors and the dregs of the people thought this den a garden of delight, and considered its pleasures compensation for the toils of the sea and the miseries of daily labour. There was not a single woman there whose aspect had anything redeeming about it. I was looking at the repulsive sight in silence, when a great hulking fellow, whose appearance suggested the blacksmith, and his voice the blackguard, came up to me and asked me in bad Italian if I would like to dance. I answered in the negative, but before leaving me he pointed out a Venetian woman who, he said, would oblige me if I gave her some drink.

Wishing to discover if she was anyone I knew I looked at her attentively, and seemed to recollect her features, although I could not decide who she could be. Feeling rather curious on the subject I sat down next to her, and asked if she came from Venice, and if she had left that country some time ago.

"Nearly eighteen years," she replied.

I ordered a bottle of wine, and asked if she would take any; she said yes, and added, if I liked, she would oblige me.

"I haven't time," I said; and I gave the poor wretch the change I received from the waiter. She was full of gratitude, and would have embraced me if I had allowed her.

"Do you like being at Amsterdam better than Venice?" I asked.

"Alas, no! for if I were in my own country I should not be following this dreadful trade."

"How old were you when you left Venice."

"I was only fourteen and lived happily with my father and mother, who now may have died of grief."

"Who seduced you?"

"A rascally footman."

"In what part of Venice did you live?"

"I did not live in Venice, but at Friuli, not far off."

Friuli . . . eighteen years ago . . . a footman . . . I felt moved, and looking at the wretched woman more closely I soon recognized in her Lucie of Pasean. I cannot describe my sorrow, which I concealed as best I could, and tried hard to keep up my indifferent air. A life of debauchery rather than the flight of time had tarnished her beauty, and ruined the once exquisite outlines of her form. Lucie, that innocent and pretty maiden, grown ugly, vile, a common prostitute! It was a dreadful thought. She drank like a sailor, without looking at me, and without caring who I was. I took a few ducats from my purse, and slipped them into her hand, and without waiting for her to find out how much I had given her I left that horrible den.

I went to bed full of saddening thoughts. Not even under the Leads did I pass so wretched a day. I thought I must have risen under some unhappy star! I loathed myself. With regard to Lucie I felt the sting of remorse, but at the thought of M. d'O—— I hated myself. I considered that I should cause him a loss of three or four hundred thousand florins; and the thought was a bitter drop in the cup of my affection for Esther. I fancied, she, as well as her father, would become my implacable foe; and love that is not returned is no love at all.

I spent a dreadful night. Lucie, Esther, her father, their hatred of me, and my hatred of myself, were the groundwork of my dreams. I saw Esther and her father, if not ruined, at all events impoverished by my fault, and Lucie only thirty-two years old, and already deep in the abyss of vice, with an infinite prospect of misery and shame before her. The dawn was welcome indeed, for with its appearance a calm came to my spirit; it is, the darkness which is terrible to a heart full of remorse.

I got up and dressed myself in my best, and went in a coach to do my suit to the Princesse de Galitzin, who, was staying at the "Etoile d'Orient." I found her out; she had gone to the Admiralty. I went there, and found her accompanied by M. de Reissak and the Count de Tot, who had just received news of my friend Pesselier, at whose house I made his acquaintance, and who was dangerously ill when I left Paris.

I sent away my coach and began to walk towards M. d'O——'s house on the Amsel. The extreme elegance of my costume was displeasing in the eyes of the

Dutch populace, and they hissed and hooted me, after the manner of the mob all the world over, Esther saw me coming from the window, drew the rope, and opened the door. I ran in, shut the door behind me, and as I was going up the wooden staircase, on the fourth or fifth step my foot struck against some yielding substance. I looked down and saw a green pocket-book. I stooped down to pick it up, but was awkward enough to send it through an opening in the stairs, which had been doubtless made for the purpose of giving light to a stair below. I did not stop, but went up the steps and was received with the usual hospitality, and on their expressing some wonder as to the unusual brilliance of my attire I explained the circumstances of the case. Esther smiled and said I looked quite another person, but I saw that both father and daughter were sad at heart. Esther's governess came in and said something to her in Dutch, at which, in evident distress, she ran and embraced her father.

"I see, my friends, that something has happened to you. If my presence is a restraint, treat me without ceremony, and bid me go."

"It's not so great an ill-hap after all; I have enough money left to bear the loss patiently."

"If I may ask the question, what is the nature of your loss?"

"I have lost a green pocket-book containing a good deal of money, which if I had been wise I would have left behind, as I did not require it till to-morrow."

"And you don't know where you lost it?"

"It must have been in the street, but I can't imagine how it can have happened. It contained bills of exchange for large amounts, and of course they don't matter, as I can stop payment of them, but there were also notes of the Bank of England for heavy sums, and they are gone, as they are payable to the bearer. Let us give thanks to God, my dear child, that it is no worse, and pray to Him to preserve to us what remains, and above all to keep us in good health. I have had much heavier losses than this, and I have been enabled not only to bear the misfortune but to make up the loss. Let us say no more about the matter."

While he was speaking my heart was full of joy, but I kept up the sadness befitting the scene. I had not the slightest doubt that the pocket-book in question was the one I had unluckily sent through the staircase, but which could not be lost irretrievably. My first point was how to make capital of my grand discovery in the interests of my cabalistic science. It was too fine an opportunity to be lost, especially as I still felt the sting of having been the cause of an enormous loss to the worthy man. I would give them a grand proof of the infallibility of my oracle: how many miracles are done in the same way! The thought put me into a good humour. I began to crack jokes, and my jests drew peals of laughter from Esther.

We had an excellent dinner and choice wine. After we had taken coffee I said that if they liked we would have a game of cards, but Esther said that this would be a waste of time, as she would much prefer making the oracular pyramids. This was exactly what I wanted.

"With all my heart," I said.

"We will do as you suggest."

"Shall I ask where my father lost his pocket-book?"

"Why not? It's a plain question: write it down."

She made the pyramid, and the reply was that the pocket-book had not been found by anyone. She leapt up from her seat, danced for joy, and threw her arms round her father's neck, saying,

"We shall find it, we shall find it, papa!"

"I hope so, too, my dear, that answer is really very consoling."

Wherewith Esther gave her father one kiss after another.

"Yes," said I, "there is certainly ground for hope, but the oracle will be dumb to all questions."

"Dumb! Why?"

"I was going to say it will be dumb if you do not give me as many kisses as you have given your father."

"Oh, then I will soon make it speak!" said she, laughing; and throwing her arms about my neck she began to kiss me, and I to give her kisses in return.

Ah! what happy days they seem when I recall them; and still I like dwelling on these days despite my sad old age, the foe of love. When I recall these events I grow young again and feel once more the delights of youth, despite the long years which separate me from that happy time.

At last Esther sat down again, and asked, "Where is the pocket-book?" And the pyramid told her that the pocket-book had fallen through the opening in the fifth step of the staircase.

M. d'O——— said to his daughter,

"Come, my dear Esther, let us go and test the truth of the oracle." And full of joy and hope they went to the staircase, I following them, and M. d'O shewed her the hole through which the pocket-book must have fallen. He lighted a candle and we went down to the cellar, and before long he picked up the book, which had fallen into some water. We went up again in high spirits, and there we talked for over an hour as seriously as you please on the divine powers of the oracle, which, according to them, should render its possessor the happiest of mortals.

He opened the pocket-book and shewed us the four thousand pound notes. He gave two to his daughter, and made me take the two remaining; but I took them with one hand and with the other gave them to Esther begging her to keep them for me; but before she would agree to do so I had to threaten her with the stoppage of the famous cabalistic oracle. I told M. d'O that all I asked was his friendship, and thereon he embraced me, and swore to be my friend to the death.

By making the fair Esther the depositary of my two thousand pounds, I was sure of winning her affection by an appeal, not to her interest, but to her truthfulness. This charming girl had about her so powerful an attraction that I felt as if my life was wound up with hers.

I told M. d'O that my chief object was to negotiate the twenty millions at a small loss.

"I hope to be of service to you in the matter," he said, "but as I. shall often want to speak to you, you must come and live in our house, which you must look upon as your own."

"My presence will be a restraint on you. I shall be a trouble."

"Ask Esther."

Esther joined her entreaties to her father's and I gave in, taking good care not to let them see how pleased I was. I contented myself with expressing my gratitude, to which they answered that it was I who conferred a favour.

M. d'O went into his closet, and as soon as I found myself alone with Esther I kissed her tenderly, saying that I should not be happy till I had won her heart.

"Do you love me?"

"Dearly, and I will do all in my power to shew how well I love you, if you will love me in return."

She gave me her hand, which I covered with kisses, and she went on to say, "As soon as you come and live with us, you must look out for a good opportunity for asking my hand of my father. You need not be afraid he will refuse you, but the first thing for you to do is to move into our house."

"My dear little wife! I will come to-morrow."

We said many sweet things to one another, talked about the future, and told each other our inmost thoughts; and I was undoubtedly truly in love, for not a single improper fancy rose in my mind in the presence of my dear who loved me so well.

The first thing that M. d'O said on his return was, that there would be a piece of news on the Exchange the next day.

"What is that, papa dear?"

"I have decided to take the whole risk—amounting to three hundred thousand florins-of the ship which is thought to have gone down. They will call me mad, but they themselves will be the madmen; which is what I should be if, after the proof we have had, I doubted the oracle any more."

"My dear sir, you make me frightened. I have told you that I have been often deceived by the oracle."

"That must have been, my dear fellow, when the reply was obscure, and you did not get at the real sense of it; but in the present case there is no room, for doubt. I shall make three million florins, or, if the worst comes to the worse, my loss won't ruin me."

Esther, whom the finding of the pocket-book had made enthusiastic, told her father to lose no time. As for me, I could not recall what I had done, but I was again overwhelmed with sadness. M. d'O—— saw it, and taking my hand said, "If the oracle does lie this time, I shall be none the less your friend."

"I am glad to hear it," I answered; "but as this is a matter of the utmost importance, let me consult the oracle a second time before you risk your three hundred thousand florins." This proposition pleased the father and daughter highly; they could not express their gratitude to me for being so careful of their interests.

What followed was truly surprising—enough to make one believe in fatality. My readers probably will not believe it; but as these Memoirs will not be published till I have left this world, it would be of no use for me to disguise the truth in any way, especially as the writing of them is only the amusement of my leisure hours. Well, let him who will believe it; this is absolutely what happened. I wrote down the question myself, erected the pyramid, and carried out all the magical ceremonies without letting Esther have a hand in it. I was delighted to be able to check an act of extreme imprudence, and I was determined to do so. A double meaning, which I knew how to get, would abate M. d'O——'s courage and annihilate his plans. I had thought over what I wanted to say, and I thought I had expressed it properly in the numbers. With that idea, as Esther knew the alphabet perfectly well, I let her extract the answer, and transfer it into letters. What was my surprise when I heard her read these words:

"In a matter of this kind neither fear nor hesitate. Your repentance would be too hard for you to bear."

That was enough. Father and daughter ran to embrace me, and M. d'O-said that when the vessel was sighted a tithe of the profits should be mine. My surprise prevented me giving any answer; I had intended to write trust and hazard, and I had written fear and hesitate. But thanks to his prejudice, M. d'O—— only saw in my silence confirmation of the infallibility of the oracle. In short, I could do nothing more, and I took my leave leaving everything to the care of chance, who sometimes is kind to us in spite of ourselves.

The next morning I took up my abode in a splendid suite of rooms in Esther's house, and the day after I took her to a concert, where she joked with me on the grief I should endure on account of the absence of Madame Trend and my daughter. Esther was the only mistress of my soul. I lived but to adore her, and I should have satisfied my love had not Esther been a girl of good principles. I could not gain possession of her, and was full of longing and desire.

Four or five days after my installation in my new quarters, M. d'O—— communicated to me the result of a conference which he had had with M. Pels and six other bankers on the twenty millions. They offered ten millions in hard cash and seven millions in paper money, bearing interest at five or six per cent. with a deduction of one per cent. brokerage. Furthermore, they would forgive a sum of twelve hundred thousand florins owed by the French India Company to the Dutch Company.

With such conditions I could not venture to decide on my own responsibility, although, personally, I thought them reasonable enough, the impoverished state of the French treasury being taken into consideration. I sent copies of the proposal to M. de Boulogne and M. d'Afri, begging from them an immediate reply. At the end of a week I received an answer in the writing of M. de Courteil, acting for M. de Boulogne, instructing me to refuse absolutely any such proposal, and to report myself at Paris if I saw no chance of making a better bargain. I was again informed that peace was imminent, though the Dutch were quite of another opinion.

In all probability I should have immediately left for Paris, but for a circumstance which astonished nobody but myself in the family of which I had become a member. The confidence of M. d'O—— increased every day, and as if chance was determined to make me a prophet in spite of myself, news was received of the ship which was believed to be lost, and which, on the faith of my oracle, M. d'O had bought for three hundred thousand florins. The vessel was at Madeira. The joy of Esther, and still more my own, may be imagined when we saw the worthy man enter the house triumphantly with confirmation of the good news.

"I have insured the vessel from Madeira to the mouth of the Texel for a trifle," said he, "and so," turning to me, "you may count from this moment on the tenth part of the profit, which I owe entirely to you."

The reader may imagine my delight; but there is one thing he will not imagine, unless he knows my character better than I do myself, the confusion into which I was thrown by the following remarks:

"You are now rich enough," said M. d'O——, "to set up for yourself amongst us, and you are positively certain to make an enormous fortune in a short time merely by making use of your cabala. I will be your agent; let us live together, and if you like my daughter as she likes you, you can call yourself my son as soon as you please."

In Esther's face shone forth joy and happiness, and in mine, though I adored her, there was to be seen, alas! nothing but surprise. I was stupid with happiness and the constraint in which I held myself. I did not analyze my feelings, but, though I knew it not, there can be no doubt that my insuperable objection to the marriage tie was working within my soul. A long silence followed; and last, recovering my powers of speech, I succeeded, with an effort, in speaking to them of my gratitude, my happiness, my love, and I ended by saying that, in spite of my affection for Esther, I must, before settling in Holland, return to Paris, and discharge the confidential and responsible duty which the Government had placed in my hands. I would then return to Amsterdam perfectly independent.

This long peroration won their approval. Esther was quite pleased, and we spent the rest of the day in good spirits. Next day M. d'O—gave a splendid dinner to several of his friends, who congratulated him on his good fortune, being persuaded that his courageous action was to be explained by his having had secret information of the safety of the vessel, though none of them could see from what source he, and he only, had obtained it.

A week after this lucky event he gave me an ultimatum on the matter of the twenty millions, in which he guaranteed that France should not lose more than nine per cent. in the transaction.

I immediately sent a copy of his proposal to M. d'Afri, begging him to be as prompt as possible, and another copy to the comptroller-general, with a letter in which I warned him that the thing would certainly fall through if he delayed a single day in sending full powers to M. d'Afri to give me the necessary authority to act.

I wrote to the same effect to M. de Courteil and the Duc de Choiseul, telling them that I was to receive no brokerage; but that I should all the same accept a proposal which I thought a profitable one, and saying that I had no doubt of obtaining my expenses from the French Government.

As it was a time of rejoicing with us, M. d'O——— thought it would be a good plan to give a ball. All the most distinguished people in Amsterdam were invited to it. The ball and supper were of the most splendid description, and Esther, who was a blaze of diamonds, danced all the quadrilles with me, and charmed every beholder by her grace and beauty.

I spent all my time with Esther, and every day we grew more and more in love, and more unhappy, for we were tormented by abstinence, which irritated while it increased our desires.

Esther was an affectionate mistress, but discreet rather by training than disposition the favours she accorded me were of the most insignificant description. She was lavish of nothing but her kisses, but kisses are rather irritating than soothing. I used to be nearly wild with love. She told me, like other virtuous women, that if she agreed to make me happy she was sure I would not marry her, and that as soon as I made her my wife she would be mine and mine only. She did not think I was married, for I had given her too many assurances to the contrary, but she thought I had a strong attachment to someone in Paris. I confessed that she was right, and said that I was going there to put an end to it that I might be bound to her alone. Alas! I lied when I said so, for Esther was inseparable from her father, a man of forty, and I could not make up my mind to pass the remainder of my days in Holland.

Ten or twelve days after sending the ultimatum, I received a letter from M. de Boulogne informing me that M. d'Afri had all necessary instructions for effecting the exchange of the twenty millions, and another letter from the ambassador was to the same effect. He warned me to take care that everything was right, as he should not part with the securities before receiving 18,200,000 francs in current money.

The sad time of parting at last drew near, amid many regrets and tears from all of us. Esther gave me the two thousand pounds I had won so easily, and her father at my request gave me bills of exchange to the amount of a hundred thousand florins, with a note of two hundred thousand florins authorizing me to draw upon him till the whole sum was exhausted. Just as I was going, Esther gave me fifty shirts and fifty handkerchiefs of the finest quality.

It was not my love for Manon Baletti, but a foolish vanity and a desire to cut a figure in the luxurious city of Paris, which made me leave Holland. But such was the disposition that Mother Nature had given me that fifteen months under The Leads had not been enough to cure this mental malady of mine. But when I reflect upon after events of my life I am not astonished that The Leads proved ineffectual, for the numberless vicissitudes which I have gone through since have not cured me—my disorder, indeed, being of the incurable kind. There is no such thing as destiny. We ourselves shape our lives, notwithstanding that saying of the Stoics, 'Volentem ducit, nolentem trahit'.

After promising Esther to return before the end of the year, I set out with a clerk of the company who had brought the French securities, and I reached the Hague, where Boaz received me with a mingled air of wonder and admiration. He told me that I had worked a miracle; "but," he added, "to succeed thus you must have persuaded them that peace was on the point of being concluded."

"By no means," I answered; "so far from my persuading them, they are of the opposite opinion; but all the same I may tell you that peace is really imminent."

"If you like to give me that assurance in writing," said he, "I will make you a present of fifty thousand florins' worth of diamonds."

"Well," I answered, "the French ambassador is of the same opinion as myself; but I don't think the certainty is sufficiently great as yet for you to risk your diamonds upon it."

Next day I finished my business with the ambassador, and the clerk returned to Amsterdam.

I went to supper at Therese's, and found her children very well dressed. I told her to go on to Rotterdam the next day and wait for me there with her son, as I had no wish to give scandal at the Hague.

At Rotterdam, Therese told me that she knew I had won half a million at Amsterdam, and that her fortune would be made if she could leave Holland for London. She had instructed Sophie to tell me that my good luck was the effect of the prayers she had addressed to Heaven on my behalf. I saw where the land lay, and I enjoyed a good laugh at the mother's craft and the child's piety, and gave her a hundred ducats, telling her that she should have another hundred when she wrote to me from London. It was very evident that she thought the sum a very moderate one, but I would not give her any more. She waited for the moment when I was getting into my carriage to beg me to give her another hundred ducats, and I said, in a low tone, that she should have a thousand if she would give me her daughter. She thought it over for a minute, and then said that she could not part with her.

"I know very well why," I answered; and drawing a watch from my fob I gave it to Sophie, embraced her, and went on my way. I arrived at Paris on February 10th, and took sumptuous apartments near the Rue Montorgueil.

CHAPTER VI

I Meet With a Flattering Reception From My Patron—Madame D'Urfe's Infatuation—Madame X. C. V. And Her Family—Madame du Rumain

During my journey from the Hague to Paris, short as it was, I had plenty of opportunities for seeing that the mental qualities of my adopted son were by no means equal to his physical ones.

As I had said, the chief point which his mother had impressed on him was reserve, which she had instilled into him out of regard for her own interests. My readers will understand what I mean, but the child, in following his mother's instructions, had gone beyond the bounds of moderation; he possessed reserve, it is true, but he was also full of dissimulation, suspicion, and hypocrisy—a fine trio of deceit in one who was still a boy. He not only concealed what he knew, but he pretended to know that which he did not. His idea of the one quality necessary to success in life was an impenetrable reserve, and to obtain this he had accustomed himself to silence the dictates of his heart, and to say no word that had not been carefully weighed. Giving other people wrong impressions passed with him for discretion, and his soul being incapable of a generous thought, he seemed likely to pass through life without knowing what friendship meant.

Knowing that Madame d'Urfe counted on the boy for the accomplishment of her absurd hypostasis, and that the more mystery I made of his birth the more extravagant would be her fancies about it, I told the lad that if I introduced him to a lady who questioned him by himself about his birth, he was to be perfectly open with her.

On my arrival at Paris my first visit was to my patron, whom I found in grand company amongst whom I recognized the Venetian ambassador, who pretended not to know me.

"How long have you been in Paris?" said the minister, taking me by the hand.

"I have only just stepped out of my chaise."

"Then go to Versailles. You will find the Duc de Choiseul and the comptroller-general there. You have been wonderfully successful, go and get your meed of praise and come and see me afterwards. Tell the duke that Voltaire's appointment to be a gentleman-in-ordinary to the king is ready."

I was not going to start for Versailles at midday, but ministers in Paris are always talking in this style, as if Versailles were at the end of the street. Instead of going there, I went to see Madame d'Urfe.

She received me with the words that her genius had informed her that I should come to-day, and that she was delighted with the fulfilment of the prophecy.

"Corneman tells me that you have been doing wonders in Holland; but I see more in the matter than he does, as I am quite certain that you have taken over the twenty millions yourself. The funds have risen, and a hundred millions at least will be in circulation in the course of the next week. You must not be offended at my shabby present, for, of course, twelve thousand francs are nothing to you. You must look upon them as a little token of friendship."

"I am going to tell my servants to close all the doors, for I am too glad to see you not to want to have you all to myself."

A profound bow was the only reply I made to this flattering speech, and I saw her tremble with joy when I told her that I had brought a lad of twelve with me, whom I intended to place in the best school I could find that he might have a good education.

"I will send him myself to Viar, where my nephews are. What is his name? Where is he? I know well what this boy is, I long to see him. Why did you not alight from your journey at my house?"

Her questions and replies followed one another in rapid succession. I should have found it impossible to get in a word edgeways, even if I had wanted to, but I was very glad to let her expend her enthusiasm, and took good care not to interrupt her. On the first opportunity, I told her that I should have the pleasure of presenting the young gentleman to her the day after tomorrow, as on the morrow I had an engagement at Versailles.

"Does the dear lad speak French? While I am arranging for his going to school you must really let him come and live with me."

"We will discuss that question on the day after tomorrow, madam."

"Oh, how I wish the day after to-morrow was here!"

On leaving Madame d'Urfe I went to my lottery office and found everything in perfect order. I then went to the Italian play, and found Silvia and her daughter in their dressing-room.

"My dear friend," said she when she saw me, "I know that you have achieved a wonderful success in Holland, and I congratulate you."

I gave her an agreeable surprise by saying that I had been working for her daughter, and Marion herself blushed, and lowered her eyes in a very suggestive manner. "I will be with you at supper," I added, "and then we can talk at our ease." On leaving them I went to the amphitheatre, and what was my surprise to see in one of the first boxes Madame X—— C—— V——, with all her family. My readers will be glad to hear their history.

Madame X—— C—— V——, by birth a Greek, was the widow of an Englishman, by whom she had six children, four of whom were girls. On his death-bed he became a Catholic out of deference to the tears of his wife; but as his children could not inherit his forty thousand pounds invested in England, without conforming to the Church of England, the family returned to London, where the widow complied with all the obligations of the law of England. What will people not do when their interests are at stake! though in a case like this there is no need to blame a person for yielding, to prejudices which had the sanction of the law.

It was now the beginning of the year 1758, and five years before, when I was at Padua, I fell in love with the eldest daughter, but a few months after, when we were at Venice, Madame X. C. V. thought good to exclude me from her family circle. The insult which the mother put upon me was softened by the daughter, who wrote me a charming letter, which I love to read even now. I may as well confess that my grief was the easier to bear as my time was taken up by my fair nun, M—— M——, and my dear C—— C——. Nevertheless, Mdlle. X. C. V., though only fifteen, was of a perfect beauty, and was all the more charming in that to her physical advantages she joined those of a cultured mind.

Count Algarotti, the King of Prussia's chamberlain, gave her lessons, and several young nobles were among her suitors, her preference apparently being given to the heir of the family of Memmo de St. Marcuola. He died a year afterwards, while he was procurator.

My surprise at seeing this family at such a time and place may be imagined. Mdlle. X. C. V. saw me directly, and pointed me out to her mother, who made a sign to me with her fan to come to their box.

She received me in the friendliest manner possible, telling me that we were not at Venice now, and that she hoped I would often come and see them at the "Hotel de Bretagne," in the Rue St. Andre des Arts. I told them that I did not wish to recall any events which might have happened at Venice, and her daughter having joined her entreaties to those of her mother, I promised to accept their invitation.

Mdlle. X. C. V. struck me as prettier than ever; and my love, after sleeping for five years, awoke to fresh strength and vigour. They told me that they were going to pass six months at Paris before returning to Venice. In return I informed them that I intended making Paris my home, that I had just left Holland, that I was going to Versailles the next day, so that I could not pay my respects to them till the day after. I also begged them to accept my services, in a manner which let them know I was a person of some importance.

Mdlle. X. C. V. said that she was aware that the results of my Dutch mission should render me dear to France, that she had always lived in hopes of seeing me once more, that my famous flight from The Leads had delighted them; "for," she added, "we have always been fond of you."

"I fancy your mother has kept her fondness for me very much to herself," I whispered to her.

"We won't say anything about that," said she in the same tone. "We learnt all the circumstances of your wonderful flight from a letter of sixteen pages you wrote to M. Memmo. We trembled with joy and shuddered with fear as we read it."

"How did you know I have been in Holland?"

"M. de la Popeliniere told us about it yesterday."

M. de la Popeliniere, the fermier-general, whom I had known seven years ago at Passi, came into the box just as his name was spoken. After complimenting me he said that if I could carry through the same operation for the India Company my fortune would be made.

"My advice to you is," he said, "to get yourself naturalized before it becomes generally known that you have made half a million of money."

"Half a million! I only wish I had!"

"You must have made that at the lowest calculation."

"On the contrary, I give you my assurance, that if my claim for brokerage is not allowed, the transaction will prove absolutely ruinous to me."

"Ah! no doubt you are right to take that tone. Meanwhile, everyone wants to make your acquaintance, for France is deeply indebted to you. You have caused the funds to recover in a very marked degree."

After the play was over I went to Silvia's, where I was received as if I had been the favourite child of the family; but on the other hand I gave them certain proofs that I wished to be regarded in that light. I was impressed with the idea that to their unshaken friendship I owed all my good luck, and I made the father, mother, the daughter, and the two sons, receive the presents I had got for them. The best was for the mother, who handed it on to her daughter. It was a pair of diamond ear-rings of great beauty, for which I had given fifteen thousand francs. Three days after I sent her a box containing fine linen from Holland, and choice Mechlin and Alencon lace. Mario, who liked smoking, got a gold pipe; the father a choice gold and enamelled snuff-box, and I gave a repeater to the younger son, of whom I was very fond. I shall have occasion later on to speak of this lad, whose natural qualities were far superior to his position in life. But, you will ask, was I rich enough to make such presents? No, I was not, and I knew it perfectly well; but I gave these presents because I was afraid of not being able to do so if I waited.

I set out for Versailles at day-break, and M. de Choiseul received me as before, his hair was being dressed, but for a moment he laid down his pen, which shewed that I had become a person of greater importance in his eyes. After a slight but grateful compliment, he told me that if I thought myself capable of negotiating a loan of a hundred millions to bear interest at four per cent., he would do all in his power to help me. My answer was that I would think it over when I heard how much I was to have for what I had done already.

"But everybody says that you have made two hundred thousand florins by it."

"That would not be so bad; half a million of francs would be a fair foundation on which to build a fortune; but I can assure your excellence that there is not a word of truth in the report. I defy anyone to prove it; and till some substantial proof is offered, I think I can lay claim to brokerage."

"True, true. Go to the comptroller-general and state your views to him."

M. de Boulogne stopped the occupation on which he was engaged to give me a most friendly greeting, but when I said that he owed me a hundred thousand florins he smiled sardonically.

"I happen to know," he said, "that you have bills of exchange to the amount of a hundred thousand crowns payable to yourself."

"Certainly, but that money has no connection with my mission, as I can prove to you by referring you to M. d'Afri. I have in my head an infallible project for increasing the revenue by twenty millions, in a manner which will cause no irritation."

"You don't say so! Communicate your plan, and I promise to get you a pension of a hundred thousand francs, and letters of nobility as well, if you like to become a Frenchman."

"I will think it over."

On leaving M. de Boulogne I went to the Palace, where a ballet was going on before the Marquise de Pompadour.

She bowed to me as soon as she saw me, and on my approaching her she told me that I was an able financier, and that the "gentlemen below" could not appreciate my merits. She had not forgotten what I had said to her eight years before in the theatre at Fontainebleau. I replied that all good gifts were from above, whither, with her help, I hoped to attain.

On my return to Paris I went to the "Hotel Bourbon" to inform my patron of the result of my journey. His advice to me was to continue to serve the Government well, as its good fortune would come to be mine. On my telling him of my meeting with the X. C. V.'s, he said that M. de la Popeliniere was going to marry the elder daughter.

When I got to my house my son was nowhere to be found. My landlady told me that a great lady had come to call on my lord, and that she had taken him away with her. Guessing that this was Madame d'Urfe, I went to bed without troubling myself any further. Early next morning my clerk brought me a letter. It came from the old attorney, uncle to Gaetan's wife, whom I had helped to escape from the jealous fury of her brutal husband. The attorney begged me to come and speak to him at the courts, or to make an appointment at some place where he could see me. I went to the courts and found him there.

"My niece," he began, "found herself obliged to go into a convent; and from this vantage ground she is pleading against her husband, with the aid of a barrister, who will be responsible for the costs. However, to win our case, we require the evidence of yourself, Count Tiretta, and other servants who witnessed the scene at the inn."

I did all I could, and four months afterwards Gaetan simplified matters by a fraudulent bankruptcy, which obliged him to leave France: in due time and place, I shall have something more to say about him. As for his wife, who was young and pretty, she paid her counsel in love's money, and was very happy with him, and may be happy still for all I know, but I have entirely lost sight of her.

After my interview with the old attorney I went to Madame—— to see Tiretta, who was out. Madame was still in love with him, and he continued to make a virtue of necessity. I left my address, and went to the "Hotel de Bretagne" to pay my first call on Madame X. C. V. The lady, though she was not over fond of me, received me with great politeness. I possibly cut a better figure in her eyes when rich, and at Paris, then when we were in Venice. We all know that diamonds have the strange power of fascination, and that they form an excellent substitute for virtue!

Madame X. C. V. had with her an old Greek named Zandiri, brother to M. de Bragadin's major-domo, who was just dead. I uttered some expressions of sympathy, and the boor did not take the trouble to answer me, but I was avenged for his foolish stiffness by the enthusiasm with which I was welcomed by everyone else. The eldest girl, her sisters, and the two sons, almost overwhelmed me with friendliness. The eldest son was only fourteen, and was a young fellow of charming manners, but evidently extremely independent, and sighed for the time when he would be able to devote himself to a career of profligacy for which he was well fitted. Mdlle. X. C. V. was both beautiful and charming in her manner, and had received an excellent education of which, however, she made no parade. One could not stay in her presence without loving her, but she was no flirt, and I soon saw that she held out no vain hopes to those who had the misfortune not to please her. Without being rude she knew how to be cold, and it was all the worse for those whom her coldness did not shew that their quest was useless.

The first hour I passed in her company chained me a captive to her triumphant car. I told her as much, and she replied that she was glad to have such a captive. She took the place in my heart where Esther had reigned a week before, but I freely confess that Esther yielded only because she was away. As to my attachment to Sylvia's daughter, it was of such a nature as not to hinder me falling in love with any other woman who chanced to take my fancy. In the libertine's heart love cannot exist without substantial food, and women who have had some experience of the world are well aware of this fact. The youthful Baletti was a beginner, and so knew nothing of these things.

M. Farsetti, a Venetian of noble birth, a knight of Malta, a great student of the occult sciences, and a good Latin versifier, came in at one o'clock. Dinner was just ready and Madame X. C. V. begged him to stay. She asked me also to dine with them, but wishing to dine with Madame d'Urfe I refused the invitation for the nonce.

M. Farsetti, who had known me very well at Venice, only noticed me by a side-glance, and without shewing any vexation I paid him back in the same coin. He smiled at Mdlle. X. C. V.'s praise of my courage. She noticed his expression, and as if to punish him for it went on to say that I had now the admiration of every Venetian, and that the French were anxious to have the honour of calling me a fellow-citizen. M. Farsetti asked me if my post at the lottery paid well. I replied, coolly,

"Oh, yes, well enough for me to pay my clerks' salaries."

He understood the drift of my reply, and Mdlle. X. C. V. smiled.

I found my supposed son with Madame d'Urfe, or rather in that amiable visionary's arms. She hastened to apologize for carrying him off, and I turned it off with a jest, having no other course to take.

"I made him sleep with me," she said, "but I shall be obliged to deprive myself of this privilege for the future, unless he promises to be more discreet."

I thought the idea a grand one, and the little fellow, in spite of his blushes, begged her to say how he had offended.

"We shall have the Comte de St. Germain," said Madame d'Urfe, "to dinner. I know he amuses you, and I like you to enjoy yourself in my house."

"For that, madam, your presence is all I need; nevertheless, I thank you for considering me."

In due course St. Germain arrived, and in his usual manner sat himself down, not to eat but to talk. With a face of imperturbable gravity he told the most incredible stories, which one had to pretend to believe, as he was always either the hero of the tale or an eye witness of the event. All the same, I could not help bursting into laughter when he told us of something that happened as he was dining with the Fathers of the Council of Trent.

Madame d'Urfe wore on her neck a large magnet. She said that it would one day happen that this magnet would attract the lightning, and that she would consequently soar into the sun. I longed to tell her that when, she got there she could be no higher up than on the earth, but I restrained myself; and the great charlatan hastened to say that there could be no doubt about it, and that he, and he only, could increase the force of the magnet a thousand times. I said, dryly, that I would wager twenty thousand crowns he would not so much as double its force, but Madame d'Urfe would not let us bet, and after dinner she told me in private that I should have lost, as St. Germain was a magician. Of course I agreed with her.

A few days later, the magician set out for Chambord, where the king had given him a suite of rooms and a hundred thousand francs, that he might be at liberty to work on the dyes which were to assure the superiority of French materials over those of any other country. St. Germain had got over the king by arranging a laboratory where he occasionally tried to amuse himself, though he knew little about chemistry, but the king was the victim of an almost universal weariness. To enjoy a harem recruited from amongst the most ravishing beauties, and often from the ranks of neophytes, with whom pleasure had its difficulties, one would have needed to be a god, and Louis XV. was only a man after all.

It was the famous marquise who had introduced the adept to the king in the hope of his distracting the monarch's weariness, by giving him a taste for chemistry. Indeed Madame de Pompadour was under the impression that St. Germain had given her the water of perpetual youth, and therefore felt obliged to make the chemist a good return. This wondrous water, taken according to the charlatan's directions, could not indeed make old age retire and give way to youth, but according to the marquise it would preserve one in statu quo for several centuries.

As a matter of fact, the water, or the giver of it, had worked wonders, if not on her body, at least on her mind; she assured the king that she was not getting older. The king was as much deluded by this grand impostor as she was, for one day he shewed the Duc des Deux-Ponts a diamond of the first water, weighing twelve carats, which he fancied he had made himself. "I melted down," said Louis XV., "small diamonds weighing twenty-four carats, and obtained this one large one weighing twelve." Thus it came to pass that the infatuated monarch gave the impostor the suite formerly occupied by Marshal Saxe. The Duc des

Deux-Ponts told me this story with his own lips, one evening, when I was supping with him and a Swede, the Comte de Levenhoop, at Metz.

Before I left Madame d'Urfe, I told her that the lad might be he who should make her to be born again, but that she would spoil all if she did not wait for him to attain the age of puberty. After what she had said about his misbehavior, the reader will guess what made me say this. She sent him to board with Viar, gave him masters on everything, and disguised him under the name of the Comte d'Aranda, although he was born at Bayreuth, and though his mother never had anything to do with a Spaniard of that name. It was three or four months before I went to see him, as I was afraid of being insulted on account of the name which the visionary Madame d'Urfe had given him.

One day Tiretta came to see me in a fine coach. He told me that his elderly mistress wanted to become his wife, but that he would not hear of it, though she offered to endow him with all her worldly goods. I told him that if he gave in he might pay his debts, return to Trevisa, and live pleasantly there; but his destiny would not allow him to take my advice.

I had resolved on taking a country house, and fixed on one called "Little Poland," which pleased me better than all the others I had seen. It was well furnished, and was a hundred paces distant from the Madeleine Gate. It was situated on slightly elevated ground near the royal park, behind the Duc de Grammont's garden, and its owner had given it the name of "Pleasant Warsaw." It had two gardens, one of which was on a level with the first floor, three reception rooms, large stables, coach houses, baths, a good cellar, and a splendid kitchen. The master was called "The Butter King," and always wrote himself down so; the name had been given to him by Louis XV. on the monarch's stopping at the house and liking the butter. The "Butter King" let me his house for a hundred Louis per annum, and he gave me an excellent cook called "The Pearl," a true blue-ribbon of the order of cooks, and to her he gave charge of all his furniture and the plate I should want for a dinner of six persons, engaging to get me as much plate as I wanted at the hire of a sous an ounce. He also promised to let me have what wine I wanted, and said all he had was of the best, and, moreover, cheaper than I could get it at Paris, as he had no gate-money to pay on it.

Matters having been arranged on these terms, in the course of a week I got a good coachman, two fine carriages, five horses, a groom, and two footmen. Madame d'Urfe, who was my first guest, was delighted with my new abode, and as she imagined that I had done it all for her, I left her in that flattering opinion. I never could believe in the morality of snatching from poor mortal man the delusions which make them happy. I also let her retain the notion that young d'Aranda, the count of her own making, was a scion of the nobility, that he was born for a mysterious operation unknown to the rest of mankind, that I was only his caretaker (here I spoke the truth), and that he must die and yet not cease to live. All these whimsical ideas were the products of her brain, which was only occupied with the impossible, and I thought the best thing I could do was to agree with everything. If I had tried to undeceive her, she would have accused me of want of trust in her, for she was convinced that all her knowledge was revealed to her by her genius, who spoke to her only by night. After she had dined with me I took her back to her house, full of happiness.

Camille sent me a lottery ticket, which she had invested in at my office, and which proved to be a winning one, I think, for a thousand crowns or thereabouts. She asked me to come and sup with her, and bring the money with me. I accepted her invitation, and found her surrounded by all the girls she knew and their lovers. After supper I was asked to go to the opera with them, but we had scarcely got there when I lost my party in the crowd. I had no mask on, and I soon found myself attacked by a black domino, whom I knew to be a woman, and as she told me a hundred truths about myself in a falsetto voice, I was interested, and determined on finding out who she was. At last I succeeded in persuading her to come with me into a box, and as soon as we were in and I had taken off her mask I was astonished to find she was Mdlle. X. C. V.

"I have come to the ball," said she, "with one of my sisters, my elder brother, and M. Farsetti. I left them to go into a box and change my domino:

"They must feel very uneasy."

"I dare say they do, but I am not going to take pity on them till the end of the ball."

Finding myself alone with her, and certain of having her in my company for the rest of the night, I began to talk of our old love-making; and I took care to say that I was more in love with her than ever. She listened to me kindly, did not oppose my embraces, and by the few obstacles she placed in my way I judged that the happy moment was not far off. Nevertheless I felt that I must practice restraint that evening, and she let me see that she was obliged to me.

"I heard at Versailles, my dear mademoiselle, that you are going to marry M. de la Popeliniere."

"So they say. My mother wishes me to do so, and the old financier fancies he has got me in his talons already; but he makes a mistake, as I will never consent to such a thing."

"He is old, but he is very rich."

"He is very rich and very generous, for he promises me a dowry of a million if I become a widow without children; and if I had a son he would leave me all his property."

"You wouldn't have much difficulty in complying with the second alternative."

"I shall never have anything to do with his money, for I should never make my life miserable by a marriage with a man whom I do not love, while I do love another."

"Another! Who is the fortunate mortal to whom you have given your heart's treasure?"

"I do not know if my loved one is fortunate. My lover is a Venetian, and my mother knows of it; but she says that I should not be happy, that he is not worthy of me."

"Your mother is a strange woman, always crossing your affections."

"I cannot be angry with her. She may possibly be wrong, but she certainly loves me. She would rather that I should marry M. Farsetti, who would be very glad to have me, but I detest him."

"Has he made a declaration in terms?"

"He has, and all the marks of contempt I have given him seem to have no effect."

"He clings hard to hope; but the truth is you have fascinated him."

"Possibly, but I do not think him susceptible of any tender or generous feeling. He is a visionary; surly, jealous, and envious in his disposition. When he heard me expressing myself about you in the manner you deserve, he had the impudence to say to my mother before my face that she ought not to receive you."

"He deserves that I should give him a lesson in manners, but there are other ways in which he may be punished. I shall be delighted to serve you in any way I can."

"Alas! if I could only count on your friendship I should be happy."

The sigh with which she uttered these words sent fire through my veins, and I told her that I was her devoted slave; that I had fifty thousand crowns which were at her service, and that I would risk my life to win her favours. She replied that she was truly grateful to me, and as she threw her arms about my neck our lips met, but I saw that she was weeping, so I took care that the fire which her kisses raised should be kept within bounds. She begged me to come and see her often, promising that as often as she could manage it we should be alone. I could ask no more, and after I had promised to come and dine with them on the morrow, we parted.

I passed an hour in walking behind her, enjoying my new position of intimate friend, and I then returned to my Little Poland. It was a short distance, for though I lived in the country I could get to any part of Paris in a quarter of an hour. I had a clever coachman, and capital horses not used to being spared. I got them from the royal stables, and as soon as I lost one I got another from the same place, having to pay two hundred francs. This happened to me several times, for, to my mind, going fast is one of the greatest pleasures which Paris offers.

Having accepted an invitation to dinner at the X. C. V.'s, I did not give myself much time for sleep, and I went out on foot with a cloak on. The snow was falling in large flakes, and when I got to madame's I was as white as a sheet from head to foot. She gave me a hearty welcome, laughing, and saying that her daughter had been telling her how she had puzzled me, and that she was delighted to see me come to dinner without ceremony. "But," added she, "it's Friday today, and you will have to fast, though, after all, the fish is very good. Dinner is not ready yet. You had better go and see my daughter, who is still a-bed."

As may be imagined, this invitation had not to be repeated, for a pretty woman looks better in bed than anywhere else. I found Mdlle. X. C. V. sitting up in bed writing, but she stopped as soon as she saw me.

"How is this, sweet lie-a-bed, not up yet?"

"Yes, I am staying in bed partly because I feel lazy, and partly because I am freer here."

"I was afraid you were not quite well."

"Nor am I. However, we will say no more about that now. I am just going to take some soup, as those who foolishly establish the institution of fasting were not polite enough to ask my opinion on the subject. It does not agree with my health, and I don't like it, so I am not going to get up even to sit at table, though I shall thus deprive myself of your society."

I naturally told her that in her absence dinner would have no savour; and I spoke the truth.

As the presence of her sister did not disturb us, she took out of her pocket-book an epistle in verse which I had addressed to her when her mother had forbidden me the house. "This fatal letter," said she, "which you called 'The Phoenix,' has shaped my life and may prove the cause of my death."

I had called it the Phoenix because, after bewailing my unhappy lot, I proceeded to predict how she would afterwards give her heart to a mortal whose qualities would make him deserve the name of Phoenix. A hundred lines were taken up in the description of these imaginary mental and moral characteristics, and certainly the being who should have them all would be right worthy of worship, for he would be rather a god than a man.

"Alas!" said Mdlle. X. C. V., "I fell in love with this imaginary being, and feeling certain that such an one must exist I set myself to look for him. After six months I thought I had found him. I gave him my heart, I received his, we loved each other fondly. But for the last four months we have been separated, and during the whole time I have only had one letter from him. Yet I must not blame him, for I know he cannot help it. Such, is my sorry fate: I can neither hear from him nor write to him:"

This story was a confirmation of a theory of mine namely, that the most important events in our lives proceed often from the most trifling causes. My epistle was nothing better than a number of lines of poetry more or less well written, and the being I had delineated was certainly not to be found, as he surpassed by far all human perfections, but a woman's heart travels so quickly and so far! Mdlle. X. C. V. took the thing literally, and fell in love with a chimera of goodness, and then was fain to turn this into a real lover, not thinking of the vast difference between the ideal and the real. For all that, when she thought that she had found the original of my fancy portrait, she had no difficulty in endowing him with all the good qualities I had pictured. Of course Mdlle. X. C. V. would have fallen in love if I had never written her a letter in verse, but she would have done so in a different manner, and probably with different results.

As soon as dinner was served we were summoned to do justice to the choice fish which M. de la Popeliniere had provided. Madame X. C. V. a narrowminded Greek, was naturally bigoted and superstitious. In the mind of a silly woman the idea of an alliance between the most opposite of beings, God and the Devil, seems quite natural. A priest had told her that, since she had converted her husband, her salvation was secure, for the Scriptures solemnly promised a soul for a soul to every one who would lead a heretic or a heathen within the fold of the church. And as Madame X. C. V. had converted her husband, she felt no anxiety about the life of the world to come, as she had done all that was necessary. However, she ate fish on the days appointed; the reason being that she preferred it to flesh.

Dinner over, I returned to the lady's bedside, and there stayed till nearly nine o'clock, keeping my passions well under control all the time. I was foppish enough to think that her feelings were as lively as mine, and I did not care to shew myself less self-restrained than she, though I knew then, as I know now, that this was a false line of argument. It is the same with opportunity as with fortune; one must seize them when they come to us, or else they go by, often to return no more.

Not seeing Farsetti at the table, I suspected there had been a quarrel, and I asked my sweetheart about it; but she told me I was mistaken in supposing they had quarreled with him, and that the reason of his absence was that he would never leave his house on a Friday. The deluded man had had his horoscope drawn, and learning by it that he would be assassinated on a Friday he resolved always to shut himself up on that day. He was laughed at, but persisted in the same course till he died four years ago at the age of seventy. He thought to prove by the success of his precautions that a man's destiny depends on his discretion, and on the precautions he takes to avoid the misfortunes of which he has had warning. The line of argument holds good in all cases except when the misfortunes are predicted in a horoscope; for either the ills predicted are avoidable, in which case the horoscope is a useless piece of folly, or else the horoscope is the interpreter of destiny, in which case all the precautions in the world are of no avail. The Chevalier Farsetti was therefore a fool to imagine he had proved anything at all. He would have proved a good deal for many people if he had gone out on a Friday, and had chanced to have been assassinated. Picas de la Mirandola, who believed in astrology, says, "I have no doubt truly, 'Astra influunt, non cogunt.'" But would it have been a real proof of the truth of astrology, if Farsetti had been assassinated on a Friday? In my opinion, certainly not.

The Comte d'Eigreville had introduced me to his sister, the Comtesse du Remain, who had been wanting to make my acquaintance ever since she had heard of my oracle. It was not long before I made friends with her husband and her two daughters, the elder of whom, nicknamed "Cotenfau," married M. de Polignac later on. Madame du Remain was handsome rather than pretty, but she won the love of all by her kindness, her frank courtesy, and her eagerness to be of service to her friends. She had a magnificent figure, and would have awed the whole bench of judges if she had pleaded before them.

At her house I got to know Mesdames de Valbelle and de Rancerolles, the Princess de Chimai, and many others who were then in the best society of Paris. Although Madame du Remain was not a proficient in the occult sciences, she had nevertheless consulted my oracle more frequently than Madame d'Urfe. She was of the utmost service to me in connection with an unhappy circumstance of which I shall speak presently.

The day after my long conversation with Mdlle. X. C. V., my servant told me that there was a young man waiting who wanted to give me a letter with his own hands. I had him in, and on my asking him from whom the letter came, he replied that I should find all particulars in the letter, and that he had orders to wait for an answer. The epistle ran as follows:

"I am writing this at two o'clock in the morning. I am weary and in need of rest, but a burden on my soul deprives me of sleep. The secret I am about to tell you will no longer be so grievous when I have confided in you; I shall feel eased by placing it in your breast. I am with child, and my situation drives me to despair. I was obliged to write to you because I felt I could not say it. Give me a word in reply."

My feelings on reading the above may be guessed. I was petrified with astonishment and could only write, "I will be with you at eleven o'clock."

No one should say that he has passed through great misfortunes unless they have proved too great for his mind to bear. The confidence of Mdlle. X. C. V. shewed me that she was in need of support. I congratulated myself on having the preference, and I vowed to do my best for her did it cost me my life. These were the thoughts of a lover, but for all that I could not conceal from myself the imprudence of the step she had taken. In such cases as these there is always the choice between speaking or writing, and the only feeling which can give the preference to writing is false shame, at bottom mere cowardice. If I had not been in love with her, I should have found it easier to have refused my aid in writing than if she had spoken to me, but I loved her to distraction.

"Yes," said I to myself, "she can count on me. Her mishap makes her all the dearer to me."

And below this there was another voice, a voice which whispered to me that if I succeeded in saving her my reward was sure. I am well aware that more than one grave moralist will fling stones at me for this avowal, but my answer is that such men cannot be in love as I was.

I was punctual to my appointment, and found the fair unfortunate at the door of the hotel.

"You are going out, are you? Where are you going?"

"I am going to mass at the Church of the Augustinians."

"Is this a saint's day?"

"No; but my mother makes me go every day."

"I will come with you."

"Yes do, give me your arm; we will go into the cloisters and talk there."

Mdlle. X. C. V. was accompanied by her maid, but she knew better than to be in the way, so we left her in the cloisters. As soon as we were alone she said to me,

"Have you read my letter?"

"Yes, of course; here it is, burn it yourself."

"No, keep it, and do so with your own hands."

"I see you trust in me, and I assure you I will not abuse your trust."

"I am sure you will not. I am four months with child; I can doubt it no longer, and the thought maddens me!"

"Comfort yourself, we will find some way to get over it."

"Yes; I leave all to you. You must procure an abortion."

"Never, dearest! that is a crime!"

"Alas! I know that well; but it is not a greater crime than suicide, and there lies my choice: either to destroy the wretched witness of my shame, or to poison myself. For the latter alternative I have everything ready. You are my only friend, and it is for you to decide which it shall be. Speak to me! Are you angry that I have not gone to the Chevalier Farsetti before you?"

She saw my astonishment, and stopped short, and tried to wipe away the tears which escaped from her eyes. My heart bled for her.

"Laying the question of crime on one side," said I, "abortion is out of our power. If the means employed are not violent they are uncertain, and if they are violent they are dangerous to the mother. I will never risk becoming your executioner; but reckon on me, I will not forsake you. Your honour is as dear to me as your life. Becalm, and henceforth think that the peril is mine, not yours. Make up your mind that I shall find some way of escape, and that there will be no need to cut short that life, to preserve which I would gladly die. And allow me to say that when I read your note I felt glad, I could not help it, that at such an emergency you chose me before all others to be your helper. You will find that your trust was not given in vain, for no one loves you as well as I, and no one is so fain to help you. Later you shall begin to take the remedies I will get for you, but I warn you to be on your guard, for this is a serious matter—one of life and death. Possibly you have already told somebody about it—your maid or one of your sisters?"

"I have not told anybody but you, not even the author of my shame. I tremble when I think what my mother would do and say if she found out my situation. I am afraid she will draw her conclusions from my shape."

"So far there is nothing to be observed in that direction, the beauty of the outline still remains intact."

"But every day increases its size, and for that reason we must be quick in what we do. You must find a surgeon who does not know my name and take me to him to be bled."

"I will not run the risk, it might lead to the discovery of the whole affair. I will bleed you myself; it is a simple operation."

"How grateful I am to you! I feel as if you had already brought me from death to life. What I should like you to do would be to take me to a midwife's. We can easily go without attracting any notice at the first ball at the opera."

"Yes, sweetheart, but that step is not necessary, and it might lead to our betrayal."

"No, no, in this great town there are midwives in every quarter, and we should never be known; we might keep our masks on all the time. Do me this kindness. A midwife's opinion is certainly worth having."

I could not refuse her request, but I made her agree to wait till the last ball, as the crowd was always greater, and we had a better chance of going out free from observation. I promised to be there in a black domino with a white mask in the Venetian fashion, and a rose painted beside the left eye. As soon as she saw me go out she was to follow me into a carriage. All this was carried out, but more of it anon.

I returned with her, and dined with them without taking any notice of Farsetti, who was also at the table, and had seen me come back from mass with her. We did not speak a word to one another; he did not like me and I despised him.

I must here relate a grievous mistake of which I was guilty, and which I have not yet forgiven myself.

I had promised to take Mdlle. X. C. V. to a midwife, but I certainly ought to have taken her to a respectable woman's, for all we wanted to know was how a pregnant woman should regulate her diet and manner of living. But my evil genius took me by the Rue St. Louis, and there I saw the Montigni entering her house with a pretty girl whom I did not know, and so out of curiosity I went in after them. After amusing myself there, with Mdlle. X. C. V. running in my head all the time, I asked the woman to give me the address of a midwife, as I wanted to consult one. She told me of a house in the Marais, where according to her dwelt the pearl of midwives, and began telling me some stories of her exploits, which all went to prove that the woman was an infamous character. I took her address, however, and as I should have to go there by night, I went the next day to see where the house was.

Mdlle. X. C. V. began to take the remedies which I brought her, which ought to have weakened and destroyed the result of love, but as she did not experience any benefit, she was impatient to consult a midwife. On the night of the last ball she recognized me as we had agreed, and followed me out into the coach she saw me enter, and in less than a quarter of an hour we reached the house of shame.

A woman of about fifty received us with great politeness, and asked what she could do.

Mdlle. X. C. V. told her that she believed herself pregnant, and that she desired some means of concealing her misfortune. The wretch answered with a smile that she might as well tell her plainly that it would be easy to procure abortion. "I will do your business," said she, "for fifty Louis, half to be paid in advance on account of drugs, and the rest when it's all over. I will trust in your honesty, and you will have to trust in mine. Give me the twenty-five Louis down, and come or send to-morrow for the drugs, and instructions for using them."

So saying she turned up her clothes without any ceremony, and as I, at Mdlle. X. C. V.'s request, looked away, she felt her and pronounced, as she let down her dress, that she was not beyond the fourth month.

"If my drugs," said she, "contrary to my expectation, do not do any good, we will try some other ways, and, in any case, if I do not succeed in obliging you I will return you your money."

"I don't doubt it for a moment," said I, "but would you tell me what are those other ways!"

"I should tell the lady how to destroy the foetus."

I might have told her that to kill the child meant giving a mortal wound to the mother, but I did not feel inclined to enter into a argument with this vile creature.

"If madame decides on taking your advice," said I, "I will bring you the money for drugs to-morrow."

I gave her two Louis and left. Mdlle. X. C. V. told me that she had no doubt of the infamy of this woman, as she was sure it was impossible to destroy the offspring without the risk of killing the mother also. "My only trust," said she, "is in you." I encouraged her in this idea, dissuading her from any criminal attempts, and assured her over and over again that she should not find her trust in me misplaced. All at once she complained of feeling cold, and asked if we had not time to warm ourselves in Little Poland, saying that she longed to see my pretty house. I was surprised and delighted with the idea. The night was too dark for her to see the exterior charms of my abode, she would have to satisfy herself with the inside, and leave the rest to her imagination. I thought my hour had come. I made the coach stop and we got down and walked some way, and then took another at the corner of the Rue de la Ferannerie. I promised the coachman six francs beyond his fare, and in a quarter of an hour he put us down at my door.

I rang with the touch of the master, the Pearl opened the door, and told me that there was nobody within, as I very well knew, but it was her habit to do so.

"Quick!" said I, "light us a fire, and bring some glasses and a bottle of champagne."

"Would you like an omelette?"

"Very well."

"Oh, I should like an omelette so much!" said Mdlle. X. C. V. She was ravishing, and her laughing air seemed to promise me a moment of bliss. I sat down before the blazing fire and made her sit on my knee, covering her with kisses which she gave me back as lovingly. I had almost won what I wanted when she asked me in a sweet voice to stop. I obeyed, thinking it would please her, feeling sure that she only delayed my victory to make it more complete, and that she would surrender after the champagne. I saw love, kindness, trust, and gratitude shining in her face, and I should have been sorry for her to think that I claimed her as a mere reward. No, I wanted her love, and nothing but her love.

At last we got to our last glass of champagne, we rose from the table, and sentimentally but with gentle force I laid her on a couch and held her amorously in my arms. But instead of giving herself up to my embraces she resisted them, at first by those prayers which usually make lovers more enterprising, then by serious remonstrances, and at last by force. This was too much, the mere idea of using violence has always shocked me, and I am still of opinion that the only pleasure in the amorous embrace springs from perfect union and agreement. I pleaded my cause in every way, I painted myself as the lover flattered, deceived, despised! At last I told her that I had had a cruel awakening, and I saw that the shaft went home. I fell on my knees and begged her to forgive me. "Alas!" said she, in a voice full of sadness, "I am no longer mistress of my heart, and have far greater cause for grief than you." The tears flowed fast down her cheeks, her head rested on my shoulder, and our lips met; but for all that the piece was over. The idea of renewing the attack never came into my head, and if it had I should have scornfully rejected it. After a long silence, of which we both stood in need, she to conquer her shame, and I to repress my anger, we put on our masks and returned to the opera. On our way she dared to tell me that she should be obliged to decline my friendship if she had to pay for it so dearly.

"The emotions of love," I replied, "should yield to those of honour, and your honour as well as mine require us to continue friends. What I would have done for love I will now do for devoted friendship, and for the future i wiil die rather than make another attempt to gain those favours of which I thought you deemed me worthy."

We separated at the opera, and the vast crowd made me lose sight of her in an instant. Next day she told me that she had danced all night. She possibly hoped to find in that exercise the cure which no medicine seemed likely to give her.

I returned to my house in a bad humour, trying in vain to justify a refusal which seemed humiliating and almost incredible. My good sense shewed me, in spite of all sophisms, that I had been grievously insulted. I recollected the witty saying of Populia, who was never unfaithful to her husband except when she was with child; "Non tollo vectorem," said she, "nisi navi plena."

I felt certain that I was not loved, and the thought grieved me; and I considered that it would be unworthy of me to love one whom I could no longer hope to possess. I resolved to avenge myself by leaving her to her fate, feeling that I could not allow myself to be duped as I had been.

The night brought wisdom with it, and when I awoke in the morning my mind was calm and I was still in love. I determined to act generously by the unfortunate girl. Without my aid she would be ruined; my course, then, would be to continue my services and to shew myself indifferent to her favours. The part was no easy one, but I played it right well, and at last my reward came of itself.

CHAPTER VII

I Continue My Relations With Mdlle. X. C. V.—Vain Attempts to Procure Abortion—The Aroph—She Flies From Home and Takes Refuge in a Convent

The difficulties I encountered only served to increase my love for my charming Englishwoman. I went to see her every morning, and as my interest in her condition was genuine, she could have no suspicion that I was acting a part, or attribute my care of her to anything but the most delicate feelings. For her part she seemed well pleased in the alteration of my behaviour, though her satisfaction may very probably have been assumed. I understood women well enough to know that though she did not love me she was probably annoyed at seeing my new character sit upon me so easily.

One morning in the midst of an unimportant and disconnected conversation, she complimented me upon my strength of mind in subduing my passion, adding, with a smile, that my desire could not have pricked me very sharply, seeing that I had cured myself so well in the course of a week. I quietly replied that I owed my cure not to the weakness of my passion but to my self-respect.

"I know my own character," I said, "and without undue presumption, I think I may say that I am worthy of a woman's love. Naturally, after your convincing me that you think differently, I feel humiliated and indignant. Do you know what effect such feelings have on the heart?"

"Alas!" said she, "I know too well. Their effect is to inspire one with contempt for her who gave rise to them."

"That is going too far, at least in my case. My indignation was merely succeeded by a renewed confidence in myself, and a determination to be revenged."

"To be revenged! In what way?"

"I wish to compel you to esteem me, by proving to you that I am lord of myself, and can pass by with indifference what I once so ardently desired. I do not know whether I have succeeded yet, but I may say that I can now contemplate your charms without desiring to possess them."

"You are making a mistake, for I never ceased to esteem you, and I esteemed you as much a week ago as I do to-day. Nor for a moment I did think you capable of leaving me to my fate as a punishment for having refused to give way to your transports, and I am glad that I read your character rightly."

We went on to speak of the opiate I made her take, and as she saw no change in her condition she wanted me to increase the dose—a request I took care not to grant, as I knew that more than half a drachm might kill her. I also forbade her to bleed herself again, as she might do herself a serious injury without gaining anything by it. Her maid, of whom she had been obliged to make a confidante, had had her bled by a student, her lover. I told Mdlle. X. C. V. that if she wanted these people to keep her counsel she must be liberal with them, and she replied that she had no money. I offered her money and she accepted fifty louis, assuring me that she would repay me that sum which she needed for her brother Richard. I had not as much money about me, but I sent her the same day a packet of twelve hundred francs with a note in which I begged her to have recourse to me in all her necessities. Her brother got the money, and thought himself authorized to apply to me for aid in a much more important matter.

He was a young man and a profligate, and had got into a house of ill-fame, from which he came out in sorry plight. He complained bitterly that M. Farsetti had refused to lend him four louis, and he asked me to speak to his mother that she might pay for his cure. I consented, but when his mother heard what was the matter with him, she said it would be much better to leave him as he was, as this was the third time he had been in this condition, and that to have him cured was a waste of money, as no sooner was he well than he began his dissipated life afresh. She was quite right, for I had him cured at my expense by an able surgeon, and he was in the same way a month after. This young man seemed intended by nature for shameful excesses, for at the age of fourteen he was an accomplished profligate.

His sister was now six months with child, and as her figure grew great so did her despair. She resolved not to leave her bed, and it grieved me to see her thus cast down. Thinking me perfectly cured of my passion for her, she treated me purely as a friend, making me touch her all over to convince me that she dare not shew herself any longer. I played in short the part of a midwife, but with what a struggle! I had to pretend to be calm and unconcerned when I was consumed with passion. She spoke of killing herself in a manner that made me shudder, as I saw that she had reflected on what she was saying. I was in a difficult position when fortune came to my assistance in a strange and amusing manner.

One day, as I was dining with Madame d'Urfe, I asked her if she knew of any way by which a girl, who had allowed her lover to go too far, might be protected from shame. "I know of an infallible method," she replied, "the aroph of Paracelsus to wit, and it is easy of application. Do you wish to know more about it?" she added; and without waiting for me to answer she brought a manuscript, and put it in my hands. This powerful emmenagogue was a kind of unguent composed of several drugs, such as saffron, myrrh, etc., compounded with virgin honey. To obtain the necessary result one had to employ a cylindrical machine covered with extremely soft skin, thick enough to fill the opening of the vagina, and long enough to reach the opening of the reservoir or case containing the foetus. The end of this apparatus was to be well anointed with aroph, and as it only acted at a moment of uterine excitement it was necessary to apply it with the same movement as that of coition. The dose had to be repeated five or six times a day for a whole week.

This nostrum, and the manner of administering it, struck me in so laughable a light that I could not keep my countenance. I laughed with all my heart, but for all that I spent the next two hours in reading the dreams of Paracelsus, in which

Madame d'Urfe put more trust than in the truths of the Gospel; I afterwards referred to Boerhaave, who speaks of the aroph in more reasonable terms.

Seeing, as I have remarked, the charming X. C. V. several hours a day without any kind of constraint, feeling in love with her all the time, and always restraining my feelings, it is no wonder if the hidden fire threatened at every moment to leap up from the ashes of its concealment. Her image pursued me unceasingly, of her I always thought, and every day made it more evident that I should know rest no more till I succeeded in extinguishing my passion by obtaining possession of all her charms.

As I was thinking of her by myself I resolved to tell her of my discovery, hoping she would need my help in the introduction of the cylinder. I went to see her at ten o'clock, and found her, as usual, in bed; she was weeping because the opiate I gave her did not take effect. I thought the time a good one for introducing the aroph of Paracelsus, which I assured her was an infallible means of attaining the end she desired; but whilst I was singing the praises of this application the idea came into my head to say that, to be absolutely certain, it was necessary for the aroph to be mingled with semen which had not lost its natural heat.

"This mixture," said I, "moistening several times a day the opening of the womb, weakens it to such a degree that the foetus is expelled by its own weight."

To these details I added lengthy arguments to persuade her of the efficacy of this cure, and then, seeing that she was absorbed in thought, I said that as her lover was away she would want a sure friend to live in the same house with her, and give her the dose according to the directions of Paracelsus.

All at once she burst into a peal of laughter, and asked me if I had been jesting all the time.

I thought the game was up. The remedy was an absurd one, on the face of it; and if her common sense told her as much it would also make her guess my motive. But what limits are there to the credulity of a woman in her condition?

"If you wish," said I, persuasively, "I will give you the manuscript where all that I have said is set down plainly. I will also shew you what Boerhaeve thinks about it."

I saw that these words convinced her; they had acted on her as if by magic, and I went on while the iron was hot.

"The aroph," said I, "is the most powerful agent for bringing on menstruation."

"And that is incompatible with the state I am now in; so the aroph should procure me a secret deliverance. Do you know its composition?"

"Certainly; it is quite a simple preparation composed of certain ingredients which are well known to me, and which have to be made into a paste with butter or virgin honey. But this composition must touch the orifice of the uterus at a moment of extreme excitement."

"But in that case it seems to me that the person who gives the dose must be in love."

"Certainly, unless he is a mere animal requiring only physical incentives."

She was silent for some time, for though she was quick-witted enough, a woman's natural modesty and her own frankness, prevented her from guessing at my artifice. I, too, astonished at my success in making her believe this fable, remained silent.

At last, breaking the silence, she said, sadly,

"The method seems to me an excellent one, but I do not think I ought to make use of it."

Then she asked me if the aroph took much time to make.

"Two hours at most," I answered, "if I succeed in procuring English saffron, which Paracelsus prefers to the Oriental saffron."

At that moment her mother and the Chevalier Farsetti came in, and after some talk of no consequence she asked me to stay to dinner. I was going to decline, when Mdlle. X. C. V. said she would sit at table, on which I accepted; and we all left the room to give her time to dress. She was not long in dressing, and when she appeared her figure seemed to me quite nymph-like. I was astonished, and could scarcely believe my eyes, and I was on the point of thinking that I had been imposed on, for I could not imagine how she could manage to conceal the fulness I had felt with my own hands.

M. Farsetti sat by her, and I by the mother. Mdlle. X. C. V., whose head was full of the aroph, asked her neighbour, who gave himself out for a great chemist, if he knew it.

"I fancy I know it better than anyone," answered Farsetti, in a self-satisfied manner.

"What is it good for?"

"That is too vague a question."

"What does the word mean?"

"It is an Arabic word, of which I do not know the meaning; but no doubt Paracelsus would tell us."

"The word," said I, "is neither Arabic nor Hebrew, nor, indeed, of any language at all. It is a contraction which conceals two other words."

"Can you tell us what they are?" said the chevalier.

"Certainly; aro comes from aroma, and ph is the initial of philosophorum:"

"Did you get that out of Paracelsus?" said Farsetti, evidently annoyed.

"No, sir; I saw it in Boerhaave."

"That's good," said he, sarcastically; "Boerhaave says nothing of the sort, but I like a man who quotes readily."

"Laugh, sir, if you like," said I, proudly, "but here is the test of what I say; accept the wager if you dare. I don't quote falsely, like persons who talk of words being Arabic."

So saying I flung a purse of gold on the table, but Farsetti, who was by no means sure of what he was saying, answered disdainfully that he never betted.

However, Mdlle. X. C. V., enjoying his confusion, told him that was the best way never to lose, and began to joke him on his Arabic derivation. But, for my part, I replaced my purse in my pocket, and on some trifling pretext went out and sent my servant to Madame d'Urfe's to get me Boerhaave.

On my return to the room I sat down again at table, and joined gaily in the conversation till the return of my messenger with the book. I opened it, and as I had been reading it the evening before I soon found the place I wanted, and giving it to him begged him to satisfy himself that I had quoted not readily but exactly. Instead of taking the book, he got up and went out without saying a word.

"He has gone away in a rage," said the mother; "and I would wager anything that he will not come back again."

"I wager he will," said the daughter, "he will honour us with his agreeable company before to-morrow's sun has set."

She was right. From that day Farsetti became my determined enemy, and let no opportunity slip of convincing me of his hatred.

After dinner we all went to Passy to be present at a concert given by M. de la Popeliniere, who made us stay to supper. I found there Silvia and her charming daughter, who pouted at me and not without cause, as I had neglected her. The famous adept, St. Germain, enlivened the table with his wild tirades so finely delivered. I have never seen a more intellectual or amusing charlatan than he.

Next day I shut myself up to answer a host of questions that Esther had sent me. I took care to answer all those bearing on business matters as obscurely as possible, not only for the credit of the oracle, but also for fear of misleading the father and making him lose money. The worthy man was the most honest of Dutch millionaires, but he might easily make a large hole in his fortune, if he did not absolutely ruin himself, by putting an implicit trust in my infallibility. As for Esther, I confess that she was now no more to me than a pleasant memory.

In spite of my pretence of indifference, my whole heart was given to Mdlle. X. C. V., and I dreaded the moment when she would be no longer able to hide her condition from her family. I was sorry for having spoken about the aroph, as three days had gone by without her mentioning it, and I could not very well reopen the question myself. I was afraid that she suspected my motives, and that the esteem she professed for me had been replaced by a much less friendly sentiment. I felt that her scorn would be too much for me to bear. So humiliated was I that I could not visit her, and I doubt if I should have seen her again if she had not intervened. She wrote me a note, in which she said I was her only friend, and that the only mark of friendship she wanted was that I should come and see her every day, if it were but for a moment. I hasted to take her my reply in my own person, and promised not to neglect her, assuring her that at all hazards she might rely on me. I flattered myself that she would mention the aroph, but she did not do so. I concluded that, after thinking it over, she had resolved to think no more about it.

"Would you like me," I said, "to invite your mother and the rest of you to dine with me?"

"I shall be delighted," she replied. "It will be a forbidden pleasure to me before long."

I gave them a dinner both sumptuous and delicate. I had spared no expense to have everything of the best. I had asked Silvia, her charming daughter, an

Italian musician named Magali, with whom a sister of Mdlle. X. C. V.'s was taken, and the famous bass La Garde. Mdlle. X. C. V. was in the highest spirits all the time. Sallies of wit, jests, good stories and enjoyment, were the soul of the banquet. We did not separate till midnight, and before leaving Mdlle. X. C. V. found a moment to whisper to me to come and see her early next morning, as she wanted to speak to me on matters of importance.

It will be guessed that I accepted the invitation. I waited on her before eight o'clock. She was very melancholy, and told me that she was in despair, that la Popeliniere pressed on the marriage, and that her mother persecuted her.

"She tells me that I must sign the contract, and that the dressmaker will soon be coming to take my measure for my wedding dress. To that I cannot consent, for a dressmaker would certainly see my situation. I will die rather than confide in my mother, or marry before I am delivered."

"There is always time enough to talk about dying," said I, "when all other means have failed. I think you could easily get rid of la Popeliniere, who is a man of honour. Tell him how you are situated, and he will act without compromising you, as his own interest is sufficiently involved to make him keep the secret."

"But should I be much better off then? And how about my mother?"

"Your mother? Oh! I will make her listen to reason."

"You know not what she is like. The honour of the family would oblige her to get me out of the way, but before that she would make me suffer torments to which death is preferable by far. But why have you said no more about the aroph? Is it not all a jest? It would be a very cruel one."

"On the contrary, I believe it to be infallible, though I have never been a witness of its effects; but what good is it for me to speak to you? You can guess that a delicacy of feeling has made me keep silence. Confide in your lover, who is at Venice; write him a letter, and I will take care that it is given into his hands, in five or six days, by a sure messenger. If he is not well off I will give you whatever money may be needed for him to come without delay, and save your honour and life by giving you the aroph."

"This idea is a good one and the offer generous on your part, but it is not feasible, as you would see if you knew more about my circumstances. Do not think any more of my lover; but supposing I made up my mind to receive the aroph from another, tell me how it could be done. Even if my lover were in Paris, how could he spend an entire week with me, as he would have to? And how could he give me the dose five or six times a day for a week? You see yourself that this remedy is out of the question."

"So you would give yourself to another, if you thought that would save your honour?"

"Certainly, if I were sure that the thing would be kept secret. But where shall I find such a person? Do you think he would be easy to find, or that I can go and look for him?"

I did not know what to make of this speech; for she knew I loved her, and I did not see why she should put herself to the trouble of going far when what she wanted was to her hand. I was inclined to think that she wanted me to ask her to make choice of myself as the administrator of the remedy, either to spare her modesty, or to have the merit of yielding to my love and thus obliging me to be grateful; but I might be wrong, and I did not care to expose myself to the humiliation of a refusal. On the other hand I could hardly think she wanted to insult me. Not knowing what to say or which way to turn, and wanting to draw an explanation from her, I sighed profoundly, took up my hat, and made as if I were going, exclaiming, "Cruel girl, my lot is more wretched than yours."

She raised herself in the bed and begged me with tears in her eyes to remain, and asked me how I could call myself more wretched than her. Pretending to be annoyed and yet full of love for her, I told her that the contempt in which she held me had affected me deeply, since in her necessity she preferred the offices of one who was unknown to her rather than make use of me.

"You are cruel and unjust," she said, weeping. "I see, for my part, that you love me no longer since you wish to take advantage of my cruel necessity to gain a triumph over me. This is an act of revenge not worthy of a man of feeling."

Her tears softened me, and I fell on my knees before her.

"Since you know, dearest, that I worship you, how can you think me capable of revenging myself on you? Do you think that I can bear to hear you say that since your lover cannot help you you do not know where to look for help?"

"But after refusing you my favours, could I ask this office of you with any decency? Have I not good reason to be afraid that as I refused to take pity on your love so you would refuse to take pity on my necessity?"

"Do you think that a passionate lover ceases to love on account of a refusal which may be dictated by virtue? Let me tell you all I think. I confess I once thought you did not love me, but now I am sure of the contrary; and that your heart would have led you to satisfy my love, even if you had not been thus situated. I may add that you no doubt feel vexed at my having any doubts of your love."

"You have interpreted my feelings admirably. But how we are to be together with the necessary freedom from observation remains to be seen."

"Do not be afraid. Now I am sure of your consent, it will not be long before I contrive some plan. In the meanwhile I will go and make the aroph."

I had resolved that if ever I succeeded in persuading Mdlle. X. C. V. to make use of my specific I would use nothing but honey, so the composition of the aroph would not be a very complicated process. But if one point was then plain and simple, another remained to be solved, and its solution gave me some difficulty. I should have to pass several nights in continual toils. I feared I had promised more than I could perform, and I should not be able to make any abatement without hazarding, not the success of the aroph, but the bliss I had taken such pains to win. Again, as her younger sister slept in the same room with her and close to her, the operation could not be performed there. At last chance—a divinity which often helps lovers—came to my aid.

I was obliged to climb up to the fourth floor and met the scullion on my way, who guessed where I was going, and begged me not to go any farther as the place was taken.

"But," said I, "you have just come out of it."

"Yes, but I only went in and came out again."

"Then I will wait till the coast is clear."

"For goodness' sake, sir, do not wait!"

"Ah, you rascal! I see what is going on. Well I will say nothing about it, but I must see her."

"She won't come out, for she heard your steps and shut herself in."

"She knows me, does she?"

"Yes, and you know her."

"All right, get along with you! I won't say anything about it."

He went down, and the idea immediately struck me that the adventure might be useful to me. I went up to the top, and through a chink I saw Madelaine, Mdlle. X. C. V.'s maid. I reassured her, and promised to keep the secret, whereon she opened the door, and after I had given her a louis, fled in some confusion. Soon after, I came down, and the scullion who was waiting for me on the landing begged me to make Madelaine give him half the louis.

"I will give you one all to yourself," said I, "if you will tell me the story"—an offer which pleased the rogue well enough. He told me the tale of his loves, and said he always spent the night with her in the garret, but that for three days they had been deprived of their pleasures, as madam had locked the door and taken away the key. I made him shew me the place, and looking through the keyhole I saw that there was plenty of room for a mattress. I gave the scullion a Louis, and went away to ripen my plans.

It seemed to me that there was no reason why the mistress should not sleep in the garret as well as the maid. I got a picklock and several skeleton keys, I put in a tin box several doses of the aroph-that is, some honey mixed with pounded stag's horn to make it thick enough, and the next morning I went to the "Hotel de Bretagne," and immediately tried my picklock. I could have done without it, as the first skeleton key I tried opened the wornout lock.

Proud of my idea, I went down to see Mdlle. X. C. V., and in a few words told her the plan.

"But," said she, "I should have to go through Madelaine's room to get to the garret."

"In that case, dearest, we must win the girl over."

"Tell her my secret?"

"Just so."

"Oh, I couldn't!"

"I will see to it; the golden key opens all doors."

The girl consented to all I asked her, but the scullion troubled me, for if he found us out he might be dangerous. I thought, however, that I might trust to Madelaine, who was a girl of wit, to look after him.

Before going I told the girl that I wanted to discuss some important matters with her, and I told her to meet me in the cloisters of the Augustinian Church. She came at the appointed time and I explained to her the whole plan in all its details. She soon understood me, and after telling me that she would take care to put her own bed in the new kind of boudoir, she added that, to be quite safe, we must make sure of the scullion.

"He is a sharp lad," said Madelaine, "and I think I can answer for him. However, you may leave that to me."

I gave her the key and six louis, bidding her inform her mistress of what we had agreed upon, and get the garret ready to receive us. She went away quite merry. A maid who is in love is never so happy as when she can make her mistress protect her intrigues.

Next morning the scullion called on me at my house. The first thing I told him was to take care not to betray himself to my servants, and never to come and see me except in a case of necessity. He promised discretion, and assured me of his devotion to my service. He gave me the key of the garret and told me that he had got another. I admired his forethought, and gave him a present of six louis, which had more effect on him than the finest words.

Next morning I only saw Mdlle. X. C. V. for a moment to warn her that I should be at the appointed place at ten that evening. I went there early without being seen by anybody. I was in a cloak, and carried in my pocket the aroph, flint and steel, and a candle. I found a good bed, pillows, and a thick coverlet—a very useful provision, as the nights were cold, and we should require some sleep in the intervals of the operation.

At eleven a slight noise made my heart begin to beat—always a good sign. I went out, and found my mistress by feeling for her, and reassured her by a tender kiss. I brought her in, barricaded the door, and took care to cover up the keyhole to baffle the curious, and, if the worse happened, to avoid a surprise.

On my lighting the candle she seemed uneasy, and said that the light might discover us if anybody came up to the fourth floor.

"That's not likely," I said; "and besides, we can't do without it, for how am I to give you the aroph in the dark?"

"Very good," she replied, "we can put it out afterwards."

Without staying for those preliminary dallyings which are so sweet when one is at ease, we undressed ourselves, and began with all seriousness to play our part, which we did to perfection. We looked like a medical student about to perform an operation, and she like a patient, with this difference that it was the patient who arranged the dressing. When she was ready—that is, when she had placed the aroph as neatly as a skull-cap fits a parson—she put herself in the proper position for the preparation to mix with the semen.

The most laughable part of it all was that we were both as serious as two doctors of divinity.

When the introduction of the aroph was perfect the timid lady put out the candle, but a few minutes after it had to be lighted again. I told her politely that I was delighted to begin again, and the voice in which I paid her this compliment made us both burst into laughter.

I didn't take so short a time over my second operation as my first, and my sweetheart, who had been a little put out, was now quite at her ease.

Her modesty had now been replaced by confidence, and as she was looking at the aroph fitted in its place, she shewed me with her pretty finger very evident signs of her co-operation in the work. Then with an affectionate air, she asked me if I would not like to rest, as we had still a good deal to do before our work was at an end.

"You see," said I, "that I do not need rest, and I think we had better set to again."

No doubt she found my reason a good one, for, without saying anything, she put herself ready to begin again, and afterwards we took a good long sleep. When I woke up, feeling as fresh as ever, I asked her to try another operation; and after carrying this through successfully, I determined to be guided by her and take care of myself, for we had to reserve our energies for the following nights. So, about four o'clock in the morning she left me, and softly made her way to her room, and at daybreak I left the hotel under the protection of the scullion, who took me by a private door I did not know of.

About noon, after taking an aromatic bath, I went to call on Mdlle. X. C. V., whom I found sitting up in bed as usual, elegantly attired, and with a happy smile on her lips. She spoke at such length on her gratitude, and thanked me so often, that, believing myself, and with good cause, to be her debtor, I began to get impatient.

"Is it possible," I said, "that you do not see how degrading your thanks are to me? They prove that you do not love me, or that if you love me, you think my love less strong than yours."

Our conversation then took a tender turn, and we were about to seal our mutual ardours without troubling about the aroph, when prudence bade us beware. It would not have been safe, and we had plenty of time before us. We contented ourselves with a tender embrace till the night should come.

My situation was a peculiar one, for though I was in love with this charming girl I did not feel in the least ashamed of having deceived her, especially as what I did could have no effect, the place being taken. It was my self-esteem which made me congratulate myself on the sharp practice which had procured me such pleasures. She told me that she was sorry she had denied me when I had asked her before, and said that she felt now that I had good reason to suspect the reality of her love. I did my best to reassure her, and indeed all suspicions on my part would have been but idle thoughts, as I had succeeded beyond all expectation. However, there is one point upon which I congratulate myself to this day—namely, that during those nightly toils of mine, which did so little towards the object of her desires, I succeeded in inspiring her with such a feeling of resignation that she promised, of her own accord, not to despair any more, but to trust in and be guided by me. She often told me during our nocturnal conversations that she was happy and would continue to be so, even though the aroph had no effect. Not that she had ceased to believe in it, for she continued the application of the harmless preparation till our last assaults, in which we wanted in those sweet combats to exhaust all the gifts of pleasure.

"Sweetheart," said she, just before we parted finally, "it seems to me that what we have been about is much more likely to create than to destroy, and if the aperture had not been hermetically closed we should doubtless have given the little prisoner a companion."

A doctor of the Sorbonne could not have reasoned better.

Three or four days afterwards I found her thoughtful but quiet. She told me that she had lost all hope of getting rid of her burden before the proper time. All the while, however, her mother persecuted her, and she would have to choose in a few days between making a declaration as to her state and signing the marriage contract. She would accept neither of these alternatives, and had decided on escaping from her home, and asked me to help her in doing so.

I had determined to help her, but I desired to save my reputation, for it might have been troublesome if it had been absolutely known that I had carried her off or furnished her with the means to escape. And as for any other alternative, neither of us had any idea of matrimony.

I left her and went to the Tuileries, where a sacred concert was being given. The piece was a motet composed by Moudonville, the words by the Abbe de Voisenon, whom I had furnished with the idea, "The Israelites on Mount Horeb."

As I was getting out of my carriage, I saw Madame du Remain descending alone from hers. I ran up to her, and received a hearty welcome. "I am delighted," said she, "to find you here, it is quite a piece of luck. I am going to hear this novel composition, and have two reserved seats. Will you do me the honour of accepting one?"

Although I had my ticket in my pocket I could not refuse so honourable an offer, so, giving her my arm, we walked up to two of the best places in the house.

At Paris no talking is allowed during the performance of sacred music, especially when the piece is heard for the first time; so Madame du Remain could draw no conclusions from my silence throughout the performance, but she guessed that something was the matter from the troubled and absent expression of my face, which was by no means natural to me.

"M. Casanova," said she, "be good enough to give me your company for an hour. I want to ask you-two or three questions which can only be solved by your cabala. I hope you will oblige me, as I am, very anxious to know the answers, but we must be quick as I have an engagement to sup in Paris."

It may be imagined that I did not wait to be asked twice, and as soon as we got to her house I went to work on the questions, and solved them all in less than half an hour.

When I had finished, "M. Casanova," said she, in the kindest manner possible, "what is the matter with you? You are not in your usual state of equanimity, and if I am not mistaken you are dreading some dire event. Or perhaps you are on the eve of taking some important resolution? I am not inquisitive, but if I can be of any service to you at Court, make use of me, and be sure that I will do my best. If necessary, I will go to Versailles to-morrow morning. I know all the ministers. Confide in me your troubles, if I cannot lighten them I can at least share them, and be sure I will keep your counsel."

Her words seemed to me a voice from heaven, a warning from my good genius to open my heart to this lady, who had almost read my thoughts, and had so plainly expressed her interest in my welfare.

After gazing at her for some seconds without speaking, but with a manner that shewed her how grateful I was, "Yes madam," I said, "I am indeed critically situated, may be on the serge of ruin, but your kindness has calmed my soul and made me once more acquainted with hope. You shall hear how I am placed. I am going to trust you with a secret of the most delicate description, but I can rely on your being as discreet as you are good. And if after hearing my story you deign to give me your advice, I promise to follow it and never to divulge its author."

After this beginning, which gained her close attention, I told her all the circumstances of the case, neither concealing the young lady's name nor any of the circumstances which made it my duty to watch over her welfare. All the same I said nothing about the aroph or the share I had taken in its exhibition. The incident appeared to me too farcical for a serious drama, but I confessed that I had procured the girl drugs in the hope of relieving her of her burden.

After this weighty communication I stopped, and Madame du Rumain remained silent, as if lost in thought, for nearly a quarter of an hour. At last she rose, saying,

"I am expected at Madame de la Marque's, and I must go, as I am to meet the Bishop of Montrouge, to whom I want to speak, but I hope I shall eventually be able to help you. Come here the day after tomorrow, you will find me alone; above all, do nothing before you see me. Farewell."

I left her full of hope, and resolved to follow her advice and hers only in the troublesome affair in which I was involved.

The Bishop of Montrouge whom she was going to address on an important matter, the nature of which was well known to me, was the Abbe de Voisenon, who was thus named because he often went there. Montrouge is an estate near Paris, belonging to the Duc de la Valiere.

I saw Mdlle. X. C. V. the following day, and contented myself with telling her that in a couple of days I hope to give her some good news. I was pleased with her manner, which was full of resignation and trust in my endeavours.

The day after, I went to Madame du Rumain's punctually at eight. The porter told me that I should find the doctor with my lady, but I went upstairs all the same, and as soon as the doctor saw me he took his leave. His name was Herrenschwand, and all the ladies in Paris ran after him. Poor Poinsinet put him in a little one-act play called Le Cercle, which, though of very ordinary merit, was a great success.

"My dear sir," said Madame du Rumain, as soon as we were alone, "I have succeeded in my endeavours on your behalf, and it is now for you to keep secret my share in the matter. After I had pondered over the case of conscience you submitted to me, I went to the convent of C—where the abbess is a friend of mine, and I entrusted her with the secret, relying on her discretion. We agreed that she should receive the young lady in her convent, and give her a good lay-sister to nurse her through her confinement. Now you will not deny," said she, with a smile, "that the cloisters are of some use. Your young friend must go by herself to the convent with a letter for the abbess, which I will give her, and which she must deliver to the porter. She will then be admitted and lodged in a suitable chamber. She will receive no visitors nor any letters that have not passed through my hands. The abbess will bring her answers to me, and I will pass them on to you. You must see that her only correspondent must be yourself, and you must receive news of her welfare only through me. On your hand in writing to her you must leave the address to be filled in by me. I had to tell the abbess the lady's name, but not yours as she did not require it.

"Tell your young friend all about our plans, and when she is ready come and tell me, and I will give you the letter to the abbess. Tell her to bring nothing but what is strictly necessary, above all no diamonds or trinkets of any value. You may assure her that the abbess will be friendly, will come and see her every now and then, will give her proper books—in a word, that she will be well looked after. Warn her not to confide in the laysister who will attend on her. I have no doubt she is an excellent woman, but she is a nun, and the secret might leak out. After she is safely delivered, she must go to confession and perform her Easter duties, and the abbess will give her a certificate of good behaviour; and she can then return to her mother, who will be too happy to see her to say anything more about the marriage, which, of course, she ought to give as her reason of her leaving home."

After many expressions of my gratitude to her, and of my admiration of her plan, I begged her to give me the letter on the spot, as there was no time to be lost. She was good enough to go at once to her desk, where she wrote as follows:

"My dear abbess—The young lady who will give you this letter is the same of whom we have spoken. She wishes to spend three of four months under your protection, to recover her peace of mind, to perform her devotions, and to make sure that when she returns to her mother nothing more will be said about the marriage, which is partly the cause of her temporary separation from her family."

After reading it to me, she put it into my hands unsealed that Mdlle. X. C. V. might be able to read it. The abbess in question was a princess, and her convent was consequently a place above all suspicion. As Madame du Rumain gave me the letter, I felt such an impulse of gratitude that I fell on my knees before her. This generous woman was useful to me on another occasion, of which I shall speak later on.

After leaving Madame du Rumain I went straight to the "Hotel de Bretagne," where I saw Mdlle. X. C. V., who had only time to tell me that she was engaged for the rest of the day, but that she would come to the garret at eleven o'clock that night, and that then we could talk matters over. I was overjoyed at this arrangement, as I foresaw that after this would come the awakening from a happy dream, and that I should be alone with her no more.

Before leaving the hotel I gave the word to Madelaine, who in turn got the scullion to have everything in readiness.

I kept the appointment, and had not long to wait for my mistress. After making her read the letter written by Madame du Rumain (whose name I withheld from her without her taking offence thereat) I put out the candle, and without troubling about the aroph, we set ourselves to the pleasant task of proving that we truly loved each other.

In the morning, before we separated, I gave her all the instructions I had received from Madame du Rumain; and we agreed that she should leave the house at eight o'clock with such things as she absolutely required, that she should take a coach to the Place Maubert, then send it away, and take another to the Place Antoine, and again, farther on, a third coach, in which she was to go to the convent named. I begged her not to forget to burn all the letters she had received from me, and to write to me from the convent as often as she could, to seal her letters but to leave the address blank. She promised to carry out my instructions, and I then made her accept a packet of two hundred louis, of which she might chance to be in need. She wept, more for my situation than her own, but I consoled her by saying that I had plenty of money and powerful patrons.

"I will set out," said she, "the day after to-morrow, at the hour agreed on." And thereupon, I having promised to come to the house the day after her departure, as if I knew nothing about it, and to let her know what passed, we embraced each other tenderly, and I left her.

I was troubled in thinking about her fate. She had wit and courage, but when experience is wanting wit often leads men to commit acts of great folly.

The day after the morrow I took a coach, and posted myself in a corner of the street by which she had to pass. I saw her come, get out of the coach, pay the coachman, go down a narrow street, and a few minutes after reappear again, veiled and hooded, carrying a small parcel in her hand. She then took another conveyance which went off in the direction we had agreed upon.

The day following being Low Sunday, I felt that I must present myself at the "Hotel de Bretagne," for as I went there every day before the daughter's flight I could not stop going there without strengthening any suspicions which might be entertained about me. But it was a painful task. I had to appear at my ease and cheerful in a place where I was quite sure all would be sadness and confusion. I must say that it was an affair requiring higher powers of impudence than fall to the lot of most men.

I chose a time when all the family would be together at table, and I walked straight into the dining-room. I entered with my usual cheerful manner, and sat down by madame, a little behind her, pretending not to see her surprise, which, however, was plainly to be seen, her whole face being flushed with rage and astonishment. I had not been long in the room before I asked where her daughter was. She turned round, looked me through and through, and said not a word.

"Is she ill?" said I.

"I know nothing about her."

This remark, which was pronounced in a dry manner, put me at my ease, as I now felt at liberty to look concerned. I sat there for a quarter of an hour, playing the part of grave and astonished silence, and then, rising, I asked if I could do anything, for which all my reward was a cold expression of thanks. I then left the room and went to Mdlle. X. C. V.'s chamber as if I had thought she was there, but found only Madelaine. I asked her with a meaning look where her mistress was. She replied by begging me to tell her, if I knew.

"Has she gone by herself?"

"I know nothing at all about it, sir, but they say you know all. I beg of you to leave me."

Pretending to be in the greatest astonishment, I slowly walked away and took a coach, glad to have accomplished this painful duty. After the reception I had met with I could without affectation pose as offended, and visit the family no more, for whether I were guilty or innocent, Madame X. C. V. must see that her manner had been plain enough for me to know what it meant.

I was looking out of my window at an early hour two or three days afterwards, when a coach stopped before my door, and Madame X C V-, escorted by M. Farsetti got out. I made haste to meet them on the stair, and welcomed them, saying I was glad they had done me the honour to come and take breakfast with me, pretending not to know of any other reason. I asked them to sit down before the fire, and enquired after the lady's health; but without noticing my question she said that she had not come to take breakfast, but to have some serious conversation.

"Madam," said I, "I am your humble servant; but first of all pray be seated."

She sat down, while Farsetti continued standing. I did not press him, but turning towards the lady begged her to command me.

"I am come here," she said, "to ask you to give me my daughter if she be in your power, or to tell me where she is."

"Your daughter, madam? I know nothing about her! Do you think me capable of a crime?"

"I do not accuse you of abducting her; I have not come here to reproach you nor to utter threats, I have only come to ask you to shew yourself my friend. Help me to get my daughter again this very day; you will give me my life. I am certain that you know all. You were her only confidant and her only friend; you passed hours with her every day; she must have told you of her secret. Pity a bereaved mother! So far no one knows of the facts; give her back to me and all shall be forgotten, and her honour saved."

"Madam, I feel for you acutely, but I repeat that I know nothing of your daughter."

The poor woman, whose grief touched me, fell at my feet and burst into tears. I was going to lift her from the ground, when Farsetti told her, in a voice full of indignation, that she should blush to humble herself in such a manner before a man of my description. I drew myself up, and looking at him scornfully said,

"You insolent scoundrel! What do you mean by talking of me like that?"

"Everybody is certain that you know all about it."

"Then they are impudent fools, like you. Get out of my house this instant and wait for me, I will be with you in a quarter of an hour."

So saying, I took the poor chevalier by the shoulders, and giving him sundry shakes I turned him out of the room. He came back and called to the lady to come, too, but she rose and tried to quiet me.

"You ought to be more considerate towards a lover," said she, "for he would marry my daughter now, even after what she has done."

"I am aware of the fact, madam, and I have no doubt that his courtship was one of the chief reasons which made your daughter resolve to leave her home, for she hated him even more than she hated the fermier-general."

"She has behaved very badly, but I promise not to say anything more about marrying her. But I am sure you know all about it, as you gave her fifty louis, without which she could not have done anything."

"Nay, not so."

"Do not deny it, sir; here is the evidence—a small piece of your letter to her."

She gave me a scrap of the letter I had sent the daughter, with the fifty louis for her brother. It contained the following lines,

"I hope that these wretched louis will convince you that I am ready to sacrifice everything, my life if need be, to assure you of my affection."

"I am far from disavowing this evidence of my esteem for your daughter, but to justify myself I am obliged to tell you a fact which I should have otherwise kept secret—namely, that I furnished your daughter with this sum to enable her to pay your son's debts, for which he thanked me in a letter which I can shew you."

"My son?"

"Your son, madam."

"I will make you an ample atonement for my suspicions."

Before I had time to make any objection, she ran down to fetch Farsetti, who was waiting in the courtyard, and made him come up and hear what I had just told her.

"That's not a likely tale," said the insolent fellow.

I looked at him contemptuously, and told him he was not worth convincing, but that I would beg the lady to ask her son and see whether I told the truth.

"I assure you," I added, "that I always urged your daughter to marry M. de la Popeliniere."

"How can you have the face to say that," said Farsetti, "when you talk in the letter of your affection?"

"I do not deny it," said I. "I loved her, and I was proud of my affection for her. This affection, of whatever sort it may have been (and that is not this gentleman's business), was the ordinary topic of conversation between us. If she had told me that she was going to leave her home, I should either have dissuaded her or gone with her, for I loved her as I do at this moment; but I would never have given her money to go alone."

"My dear Casanova," said the mother, "if you will help me to find her I shall believe in your innocence."

"I shall be delighted to aid you, and I promise to commence the quest to-day."

"As soon as you have any news, come and tell me."

"You may trust me to do so," said I, and we parted.

I had to play my part carefully; especially it was essential that I should behave in public in a manner consistent with my professions. Accordingly, the next day I went to M. Chaban, first commissary of police, requesting him to institute enquiries respecting the flight of Mdlle. X. C. V. I was sure that in this way the real part I had taken in the matter would be the better concealed; but the commissary, who had the true spirit of his profession, and had liked me when he first saw me six years before, began to laugh when he heard what I wanted him to do.

"Do you really want the police to discover," said he, "where the pretty Englishwoman is to be found?"

"Certainly."

It then struck me that he was trying to make me talk and to catch me tripping, and I had no doubt of it when I met Farsetti going in as I was coming out.

Next day I went to acquaint Madame X. C. V. with the steps I had taken, though as yet my efforts had not been crowned with success.

"I have been more fortunate than you," said she, "and if you will come with me to the place where my daughter has gone, and will join me in persuading her to return, all will be well."

"Certainly," said I, "I shall be most happy to accompany you."

Taking me at my word, she put on her cloak, and leaning on my arm walked along till we came to a coach. She then gave me a slip of paper, begging me to tell the coachman to drive us to the address thereon.

I was on thorns, and my heart beat fast, for I thought I should have to read out the address of the convent. I do not know what I should have done if my fears had been well grounded, but I should certainly not have gone to the convent. At last I read what was written; it was "Place Maubert," and I grew calm once more.

I told the coachman to drive us to the Place Maubert. We set off, and in a short time stopped at the opening of an obscure back street before a dirty-looking house, which did not give one a high idea of the character of its occupants. I gave Madame X. C. V. my arm, and she had the satisfaction of looking into every room in the five floors of the house, but what she sought for was not there, and I expected to see her overwhelmed with grief. I was mistaken, however. She looked distressed but satisfied, and her eyes seemed to ask pardon of me. She had found out from the coachman, who had taken her daughter on the first stage of her journey, that she had alighted in front of the house in question, and had gone down the back street. She told me that the scullion had confessed that he had taken me letters twice from his young mistress, and that

Madelaine said all the time that she was sure her mistress and I were in love with each other. They played their parts well.

As soon as I had seen Madame X. C. V. safely home, I went to Madame du Rumain to tell her what had happened; and I then wrote to my fair recluse, telling her what had gone on in the world since her disappearance.

Three or four days after this date, Madame du Rumain gave me the first letter I received from Mdlle. X. C. V. She spoke in it of the quiet life she was leading, and her gratitude to me, praised the abbess and the lay-sister, and gave me the titles of the books they lent her, which she liked reading. She also informed me what money she had spent, and said she was happy in everything, almost in being forbidden to leave her room.

I was delighted with her letter, but much more with the abbess's epistle to Madame du Rumain. She was evidently fond of the girl, and could not say too much in her praise, saying how sweet-tempered, clever, and lady-like she was; winding up by assuring her friend that she went to see her every day.

I was charmed to see the pleasure this letter afforded Madame du Rumain—pleasure which was increased by the perusal of the letter I had received. The only persons who were displeased were the poor mother, the frightful Farsetti, and the old fermier, whose misfortune was talked about in the clubs, the Palais-Royal, and the coffee-houses. Everybody put me down for some share in the business, but I laughed at their gossip, believing that I was quite safe.

All the same, la Popeliniere took the adventure philosophically and made a one-act play out of it, which he had acted at his little theatre in Paris. Three months afterwards he got married to a very pretty girl, the daughter of a Bordeaux alderman. He died in the course of two years, leaving his widow pregnant with a son, who came into the world six months after the father's death. The unworthy heir to the rich man had the face to accuse the widow of adultery, and got the child declared illegitimate to the eternal shame of the court which gave this iniquitous judgment and to the grief of every honest Frenchman. The iniquitous nature of the judgment was afterwards more clearly demonstrated—putting aside the fact that nothing could be said against the mother's character—by the same court having the face to declare a child born eleven months after the father's death legitimate.

I continued for ten days to call upon Madame X. C. V., but finding myself coldly welcomed, decided to go there no more.

CHAPTER VIII

Fresh Adventures—J. J. Rousseau—I set Up A Business— Castel—Bajac—A Lawsuit is Commenced Against Me—M. de Sartin

Mdlle. X. C. V. had now been in the convent for a month, and her affair had ceased to be a common topic of conversation. I thought I should hear no more of it, but I was mistaken. I continued, however, to amuse myself, and my pleasure in spending freely quite prevented me from thinking about the future. The Abbe de Bernis, whom I went to see regularly once a week, told me one day that the comptroller-general often enquired how I was getting on. "You are wrong," said the abbe, "to neglect him." He advised me to say no more about my claims, but to communicate to him the means I had spoken of for increasing the revenues of the state. I laid too great store by the advice of the man who had made my fortune not to follow it. I went to the comptroller, and trusting in his probity I explained my scheme to him. This was to pass a law by which every estate, except that left by father to son, should furnish the treasury with one year's income; every deed of gift formally drawn up being subject to the same provision. It seemed to me that the law could not give offence to anyone; the heir had only to imagine that he had inherited a year later than was actually the case. The minister was of the same opinion as myself, told me that there would not be the slightest difficulty involved, and assured me that my fortune was made. In a week afterwards his place was taken by M. de Silhouette, and when I called on the new minister he told me coldly that when my scheme became law he would tell me. It became law two years afterwards, and when, as the originator of the scheme, I attempted to get my just reward, they laughed in my face.

Shortly after, the Pope died, and he was succeeded by the Venetian Rezzonico, who created my patron, the Abby de Bernis, a cardinal. However, he had to go into exile by order of the king two days after his gracious majesty had presented him with the red cap: so good a thing it is to be the friend of kings!

The disgrace of my delightful abbe left me without a patron, but I had plenty of money, and so was enabled to bear this misfortune with resignation.

For having undone all the work of Cardinal Richelieu, for having changed the old enmity between France and Austria into friendship, for delivering Italy from the horrors of war which befell her whenever these countries had a bone to pick, although he was the first cardinal made by a pope who had had plenty of opportunities for discovering his character, merely because, on being asked, he had given it as his opinion that the Prince de Soubise was not a fit person to command the French armies, this great ecclesiastic was driven into exile. The moment the Pompadour heard of this opinion of his, she decreed his banishment—a sentence which was unpopular with all classes of society; but they consoled themselves with epigrams, and the new cardinal was soon forgotten. Such is the character of the French people; it cares neither for its own misfortunes nor for those of others, if only it can extract laughter from them.

In my time epigrammatists and poetasters who assailed ministers or even the king's mistresses were sent to the Bastille, but the wits still persisted in being amusing, and there were some who considered a jest incomplete that was not followed by a prosecution. A man whose name I have forgotten—a great lover of notoriety—appropriated the following verses by the younger Crebellon and went to the Bastille rather than disown them.

> "All the world's upside down!
> Jupiter has donned the gown—the King.
> Venus mounts the council stair—the Pompadour.
> Plutus trifles with the fair—M. de Boulogne.
> Mercury in mail is drest—Marechal de Richelieu.
> Mighty Mars has turned a priest—the Duc de Clermont, abbe of
> St. Germain-des-pres."

Crebillon, who was not the sort of man to conceal his writings, told the Duc de Choiseul that he had written some verses exactly like these, but that it was possible the prisoner had been inspired with precisely the same ideas. This jest was applauded, and the author of "The Sofa" was let alone.

Cardinal de Bernis passed ten years in exile, 'procul negotiis', but he was not happy, as he told me himself when I knew him in Rome fifteen years afterwards. It is said that it is better to be a minister than a king—an opinion which seems ridiculous when it is analyzed. The question is, which is the better, independence or its contrary. The axiom may possibly be verified in a despotic government under an absurd, weak, or careless king who serves as a mere mask for his master the minister; but in all other cases it is an absurdity.

Cardinal de Bernis was never recalled; there is no instance of Louis XV. having ever recalled a minister whom he had disgraced; but on the death of Rezzonico he had to go to Rome to be present at the conclave, and there he remained as French ambassador.

About this time Madame d'Urfe conceived a wish to make the acquaintance of J. J. Rousseau, and we went to call upon him at Montmorenci, on the pretext of giving him music to copy—an occupation in which he was very skilled. He was paid twice the sum given to any other copyist, but he guaranteed that the work should be faultlessly done. At that period of his life copying music was the great writer's sole means of subsistence.

We found him to be a man of a simple and modest demeanour, who talked well, but who was not otherwise distinguished either intellectually or physically. We did not think him what would be called a good-natured man, and as he was far from having the manners of good society Madame d'Urfe did not hesitate to pronounce him vulgar. We saw the woman with whom he lived, and of whom we had heard, but she scarcely looked at us. On our way home we amused ourselves by talking about Rousseau's eccentric habits.

I will here note down the visit of the Prince of Conti (father of the gentleman who is now known as the Comte de la March) to Rousseau.

The prince—a good-natured man-went by himself to Montmorenci, on purpose to spend a day in conversation with the philosopher, who was even then famous. He found him in the park, accosted him, and said that he had come to dine with him and to talk without restraint.

"Your highness will fare but badly," said Rousseau: "however, I will tell them to lay another knife and fork."

The philosopher gave his instructions, and came out and rejoined the prince, with whom he walked up and down for two or three hours. When it was dinner-time he took the prince into his dining-room, where the table was laid for three.

"Who is going to dine with us?" said the prince. "I thought we were to be alone."

"The third party," said Rousseau, "is my other self—a being who is neither my wife, nor my mistress, nor my servant-maid, nor my mother, nor my daughter, but yet personates all these characters at once."

"I daresay, my dear fellow, I daresay; but as I came to dine with you alone, I will not dine with your—other self, but will leave you with all the rest of you to keep your company."

So saying the prince bade him farewell and went out. Rousseau did not try to keep him.

About this time I witnessed the failure of a play called 'Aristides' Daughter', written by the ingenious Madame de Graffini, who died of vexation five days after her play was damned. The Abbe de Voisenon was horrified, as he had advised the lady to produce it, and was thought to have had some hand in its composition, as well as in that of the 'Lettres Peruviennes' and 'Cenie'. By a curious coincidence, just about the same date, Rezzonico's mother died of joy because her son had become pope. Grief and joy kill many more women than men, which proves that if women have mere feeling than men they have also less strength.

When Madame d'Urfe thought that my adopted son was comfortably settled in Viar's house, she made me go with her and pay him a visit. I found him lodged like a prince, well dressed, made much of, and almost looked up to. I was astonished, for this was more than I had bargained for. Madame d'Urfe had given him masters of all sorts, and a pretty little pony for him to learn riding on. He was styled M. le Comte d'Aranda. A girl of sixteen, Viar's daughter, a fine-looking young woman, was appointed to look after him, and she was quite proud to call herself my lord's governess. She assured Madame d'Urfe that she took special care of him; that as soon as he woke she brought him his breakfast in bed; that she then dressed him, and did not leave his side the whole day. Madame d'Urfe approved of everything, told the girl to take even greater care of the count, and promised that she should not go unrewarded. As for the young gentleman, he was evidently quite happy, as he told me himself again and again, but I suspected a mystery somewhere, and determined that I would go and see him by myself another time and solve it.

On our journey home I told Madame d'Urfe how grateful I was for all her goodness to the boy, and that I approved of all the arrangements that had been made with the exception of the name Aranda, "which," said I, "may some day prove a thorn in his side." She answered that the lad had said enough to convince her that he had a right to bear that name. "I had," she said, "in my desk a seal with the arms of the house of Aranda, and happening to take it up I shewed it him as we shew trinkets to children to amuse them, but as soon as he saw it he burst out,

"'How came you to have my arms?'

"Your arms!" I answered. "I got this seal from the Comte d'Aranda; how can you prove that you are a scion of that race?"

"'Do not ask me, madam; my birth is a secret I can reveal to no one.'"

The imposition and above all the impudence of the young knave astounded me. I should not have thought him capable of it, and a week after I went to see him by myself to get at the bottom of all this mystery.

I found my young count with Viar, who, judging by the awe the child shewed of me, must have thought he belonged to me. He was unsparing in his praises of his pupil, saying that he played the flute capitally, danced and fenced admirably, rode well, and wrote a good hand. He shewed me the pens he had cut himself with three, five, and even nine points, and begged to be examined on heraldry, which, as the master observed, was so necessary a science for a young nobleman.

The young gentleman then commenced in the jargon of heraldry to blazon his own pretended arms, and I felt much inclined to burst into laughter, partly because I did not understand a word he said, and partly because he seemed to think the matter as important as would a country squire with his thirty-two quarters. However, I was delighted to see his dexterity in penmanship, which was undoubtedly very great, and I expressed my satisfaction to Viar, who soon left us to ourselves. We proceeded into the garden.

"Will you kindly inform me," I said, "how you can be so foolish as to call yourself the Comte d'Aranda?"

He replied, with the utmost calmness, "I know it is foolish, but leave me my title; it is of service to me here and gains me respect."

"It is an imposition I cannot wink at, as it may be fraught with serious results, and may do harm to both of us. I should not have thought that at your age you would be capable of such a knavish trick. I know you did it out of stupidity, but after a certain limit stupidity becomes criminal; and I cannot see how I am to remedy your fault without disgracing you in the eyes of Madame d'Urfe."

I kept on scolding him till he burst into tears, saying,

"I had rather the shame of being sent back to my mother than the shame of confessing to Madame d'Urfe that I had imposed on her; and I could not bear to stay here if I had to give up my name."

Seeing that I could do nothing with him, unless, indeed, I sent him to some place far removed from Paris under his proper name, I told him to take comfort as I would try and do the best I could for both of us.

"And now tell me—and take care to tell the truth—what sort of feelings does Viar's daughter entertain for you?"

"I think, papa, that this is a case in which the reserve commended by yourself, as well as by mother, would be appropriate."

"Yes, that sort of answer tells me a good deal, but I think you are rather too knowing for your age. And you may as well observe that when you are called upon for a confession, reserve is out of place, and it's a confession I require from you."

"Well, papa, Viar's daughter is very fond of me, and she shews her love in all sorts of ways."

"And do you love her?"

"Oh, yes!"

"Is she much with you in the morning?"

"She is with me the whole day."

"She is present when you go to bed?"

"Yes, she helps me to undress."

"Nothing else?"

"I do not care to tell you."

I was astonished at the measured way in which he answered me, and as I had heard enough to guess that the boy and girl were very good friends indeed, I contented myself with warning him to take care of his health, and with this I left him.

Some time after, my thoughts were occupied with a business speculation which all my calculations assured me would be extremely profitable. The plan was to produce on silks, by means of printing, the exquisite designs which are produced at Lyons by the tedious process of weaving, and thus to give customers excellent value at much lower prices. I had the requisite knowledge of chemistry, and enough capital to make the thing a success. I obtained the assistance of a man with the necessary technical skill and knowledge, intending to make him my manager.

I told my plan to the Prince de Conti, who encouraged me to persevere, promising me his patronage, and all the privileges I could wish for. That decided me to begin.

I rented a very large house near the Temple for a thousand crowns per annum. The house contained a spacious hall, in which I meant to put my workmen; another hall which was to be the shop; numerous rooms for my workpeople to live in; and a nice room for myself in case I cared to live on the premises.

I made the scheme into a company with thirty shares, of which I gave five to my designer, keeping the remaining twenty-five to distribute to those who were inclined to join the company. I gave one to a doctor who, on giving surety, became the storekeeper, and came to live in the house with his whole family; and I engaged four servants, a waiting-maid, and a porter. I had to give another share to an accountant, who furnished me with two clerks, who also took up their abode in the house. The carpenters, blacksmiths, and painters worked hard from morning to night, and in less than three weeks the place was ready. I told the manager to engage twenty girls to paint, who were to be paid every Saturday. I stocked the warehouse with three hundred pieces of sarcenet and camlet of different shades and colours to receive the designs, and I paid for everything in ready money.

I had made an approximate calculation with my manager that I should have to spend three hundred thousand francs, and that would not break me. If the worst happened I could fall back on my shares, which produced a good income, but I hoped I should not be compelled to do so, as I wanted to have an income of two hundred thousand francs a year.

All the while I did not conceal from myself that the speculation might be my ruin, if custom did not come in, but on looking at my beautiful materials these fears were dispelled, especially as I heard everybody saying that I sold them much too cheap.

To set up the business I spent in the course of a month about sixty thousand francs, and my weekly expenses amounted to twelve hundred francs.

As for Madame d'Urfe she laughed every time she saw me, for she was quite certain that this business was only meant to put the curious off the scent and to preserve my incognito: so persuaded was she of my omnipotence.

The sight of twenty girls, all more or less pretty, the eldest of whom was not twenty-five, far from making me tremble as it ought, delighted me. I fancied myself in the midst of a seraglio, and I amused myself by watching their meek and modest looks as they did their work under the direction of the foreman. The best paid did not get more than twenty-four sous a day, and all of them had excellent reputations, for they had been selected at her own request by the manager's wife, a devout woman of ripe age, whom I hoped to find obliging if the fancy seized me to test her choice. Manon Baletti did not share my satisfaction in them. She trembled to see me the owner of a harem, well knowing that sooner or later the barque of my virtue would run on the rocks. She scolded me well about these girls, though I assured her that none of them slept in the house.

This business increased my own ideas of my importance; partly from the thought that I was on the high road to fortune, and partly because I furnished so many people with the means of subsistence. Alas! I was too fortunate; and my evil genius soon crossed my career.

It was now three months since Mdlle. X. C. V. had gone into the convent, and the time of her delivery drew near. We wrote to each other twice a week, and I considered the matter happily settled; M. de la Popeliniere had married, and when Mdlle. X. C. V. returned to her mother there would be nothing more to be said But just at this period, when my happiness seemed assured, the hidden fire leapt forth and threatened to consume me; how, the reader will see.

One day after leaving Madame d'Urfe's I went to walk in the Tuileries. I had taken a couple of turns in the chief walk when I saw that an old woman, accompanied by a man dressed in black, was looking at me closely and communicating her observations to her companion. There was nothing very astonishing in this in a public place, and I continued my walk, and on turning again saw the same couple still watching me. In my turn I looked at them, and remembered seeing the man in a gaming-house, where he was known by the name of Castel-Bajac. On scrutinizing the features of the hag, I at last succeeded in recollecting who she was; she was the woman to whom I had taken Mdlle. X. C. V. I felt certain that she had recognized me, but not troubling myself about the matter I left the gardens to walk elsewhere. The day after next, just as I was going to get into my carriage, a man of evil aspect gave me a paper and asked me to read it. I opened it, but finding it covered with an illegible scrawl I gave it him back, telling him to read it himself. He did so, and I found myself summoned to appear before the commissary of police to answer to the plea which the midwife (whose name I forget) brought against me.

Although I could guess what the charge would be, and was certain that the midwife could furnish no proofs of her accusation, I went to an attorney I knew and told him to appear for me. I instructed him that I did not know any midwife in Paris whatsoever. The attorney waited on the commissary, and on the day after brought me a copy of the pleas.

The midwife said that I came to her one night, accompanied by a young lady about five months with child, and that, holding a pistol in one hand and a packet of fifty Louis in the other, I made her promise to procure abortion. We both of us (so she said) had masks on, thus shewing that we had been at the opera ball. Fear, said she, had prevented her from flatly refusing to grant my request; but she had enough presence of mind to say that the necessary drugs were not ready, that she would have all in order by the next night; whereupon we left, promising to return. In the belief that we would not fail to keep the appointment, she went in to M. Castel-Bajac to ask him to hide in the next room that she might be protected from my fury, and that he might be a witness of what I said, but she had not seen me again. She added that she would have given information the day after the event if she had known who I was, but since M. Castel-Bajac had told her my name on her recognizing me in the Tuileries, she had thought it her bounden duty to deliver me to the law that she might be compensated for the violence I had used to her. And this document was signed by the said Castel-Bajac as a witness.

"This is an evident case of libel," said my attorney, "at least, if she can't prove the truth of her allegations. My advice to you is to take the matter before the criminal lieutenant, who will be able to give you the satisfaction you require."

I authorized him to do what he thought advisable, and three or four days after he told me that the lieutenant wished to speak to me in private, and would expect me the same day at three o'clock in the afternoon.

As will be expected, I was punctual to the appointment. I found the magistrate to be a polite and good-hearted gentleman. He was, in fact, the well-known M. de Sartine, who was the chief of police two years later. His office of criminal lieutenant was saleable, and M. de Sartine sold it when he was appointed head of the police.

As soon as I had made my bow, he asked me to sit down by him, and addressed me as follows:

"I have asked you to call upon me in the interests of both of us, as in your position our interests are inseparable. If you are innocent of the charge which has been brought against you, you are quite right to appeal to me; but before proceedings begin, you should tell me the whole truth. I am ready to forget my position as judge, and to give you my help, but you must see yourself that to prove the other side guilty of slander, you must prove yourself innocent. What I want from you is an informal and strictly confidential declaration, for the case against you is a serious one, and of such a kind as to require all your efforts to wipe off this blot upon your honour. Your enemies will not respect your delicacy of feeling. They will press you so hard that you will either be obliged to submit to a shameful sentence, or to wound your feelings of honour in proving your innocence. You see I am confiding in you, for in certain cases honour seems so precious a thing to me that I am ready to defend it with all the power of the law. Pay me back, then, in the same coin, trust in me entirely, tell me the whole story without any reserves, and you may rely upon my good offices. All will be well if you are innocent, for I shall not be the less a judge because I am your friend; but if you are guilty I am sorry for you, for I warn you that I shall be just."

After doing my best to express my gratitude to him, I said that my position did not oblige me to make any reservations on account of honour, and that I had, consequently, no informal statement to make him.

"The midwife," I added, "is absolutely unknown to me. She is most likely an abandoned woman, who with her worthy companion wants to cheat me of my money."

"I should be delighted to think so," he answered, "but admitting the fact, see how chance favours her, and makes it a most difficult thing for you to prove your innocence.

"The young lady disappeared three months ago. She was known to be your intimate friend, you called upon her at all hours; you spent a considerable time with her the day before she disappeared, and no one knows what has become of her; but everyone's suspicions point at you, and paid spies are continually dogging your steps. The midwife sent me a requisition yesterday by her counsel, Vauversin. She says that the pregnant lady you brought to her house is the same whom Madame X. C. V. is searching for. She also says that you both wore black dominoes, and the police have ascertained that you were both at the ball in black dominoes on the same night as that on which the midwife says you came to her house; you are also known to have left the ball-room together. All this, it is true, does not constitute full proof of your guilt, but it makes one tremble for your innocence."

"What cause have I to tremble?"

"What cause! Why a false witness, easily enough hired for a little money, might swear with impunity that he saw you come from the opera together; and a coachman in the same way might swear he had taken you to the midwife's. In that case I should be compelled to order your arrest and examination, with a view to ascertain the name of the person whom you took with you. Do you realize that you are accused of procuring abortion; that three months have gone by without the lady's retreat having been discovered; that she is said to be dead. Do you realize, in short, what a very serious charge murder is?"

"Certainly; but if I die innocent, you will have condemned me wrongly, and will be more to be pitied than I."

"Yes, yes, but that wouldn't make your case any better. You may be sure, however, that I will not condemn an innocent man; but I am afraid that you will be a long time in prison before you succeed in proving your innocence. To be brief, you see that in twenty-four hours the case looks very bad, and in the course of a week it might look very much worse. My interest was aroused in your favour by the evident absurdity of the accusations, but it is the other circumstances about the case which make it a serious one for you. I can partly understand the circumstances, and the feelings of love and honour which bid you be silent. I have spoken to you, and I hope you will have no reserves with me. I will spare you all the unpleasant circumstances which threaten you, believing, as I do, that you are innocent. Tell me all, and be sure that the lady's honour will not suffer; but if, on the other hand, you are unfortunately guilty of the crimes laid to your charge, I advise you to be prudent, and to take steps which it is not my business to suggest. I warn you that in three or four days I shall cite you to the bar of the court, and that you will then find in me only the judge—just, certainly, but severe and impartial."

I was petrified; for these words shewed me my danger in all its nakedness. I saw how I should esteem this worthy man's good offices, and said to him in quite another tone, that innocent as I was, I saw that my best course was to throw myself on his kindness respecting Mdlle. X. C. V., who had committed no crime, but would lose her reputation by this unhappy business.

"I know where she is," I added, "and I may tell you that she would never have left her mother if she had not endeavoured to force her into a marriage she abhorred."

"Well, but the man is now married; let her return to her mother's house, and you will be safe, unless the midwife persists in maintaining that you incited her to procure abortion."

"There is no abortion in the matter; but other reasons prevent her returning to her family. I can tell you no more without obtaining the consent of another party. If I succeed in doing so I shall be able to throw the desired light on the question. Be kind enough to give me a second hearing on the day after to-morrow."

"I understand. I shall be delighted to hear what you have to say. I thank and congratulate you. Farewell!"

I was on the brink of the precipice, but I was determined to leave the kingdom rather than betray the honour of my poor dear sweetheart. If it had been possible, I would gladly have put an end to the case with money; but it was too late. I was sure that Farsetti had the chief hand in all this trouble, that he was continually on my track, and that he paid the spies mentioned by M. de Sartine. He it was who had set Vauversin, the barrister, after me, and I had no doubt that he would do all in his power to ruin me.

I felt that my only course was to tell the whole story to M. de Sartine, but to do that I required Madame du Rumain's permission.

CHAPTER IX

My Examination I Give the Clerk Three Hundred Louis—The Midwife and Cartel-Bajac Imprisoned—Mdlle. X. C. V. Is Brought to Bed of a Son and Obliges Her Mother to Make Me Amends—The Suit Against Me Is Quashed— Mdlle. X. C. V. Goes With Her Mother to Brussels and From Thence to Venice, Where She Becomes a Great Lady—My Work-girls—Madame Baret—I Am Robbed, Put in Prison, and Set at Liberty Again—I Go to Holland—Helvetius' "Esprit"—Piccolomini

The day after my interview with M. de Sartine I waited on Madame du Rumain at an early hour. Considering the urgency of the case I took the liberty of rousing her from her slumbers, and as soon as she was ready to receive me I told her all.

"There can be no hesitation in the matter," said this delightful woman. "We must make a confidant of M. de Sartine, and I will speak to him myself to-day without fail."

Forthwith she went to her desk and wrote to the criminal lieutenant asking him to see her at three o'clock in the afternoon. In less than an hour the servant returned with a note in which he said he would expect her. We agreed that I should come again in the evening, when she would tell me the result of her interview.

I went to the house at five o'clock, and had only a few minutes to wait.

"I have concealed nothing," said she; "he knows that she is on the eve of her confinement, and that you are not the father, which speaks highly for your generosity. I told him that as soon as the confinement was over, and the young lady had recovered her health, she would return to her mother, though she would make no confession, and that the child should be well looked after. You have now nothing to fear, and can calm yourself; but as the case must go on you will be cited before the court the day after to-morrow. I advise you to see the clerk of the court on some pretext or other, and to make him accept a sum of money."

I was summoned to appear, and I appeared. I saw M. de Sartine, 'sedentem pro tribunali'. At the end of the sitting he told me that he was obliged to remand me, and that during my remand I must not leave Paris or get married, as all my civil rights were in suspense pending the decision. I promised to follow his commands.

I acknowledged in my examination that I was at the ball in a black domino on the night named in my accusation, but I denied everything else. As for Mdlle. X. C. V., I said that neither I nor anyone of her family had any suspicion that she was with child.

Recollecting that I was an alien, and that this circumstance might make Vauversin call for my arrest, on the plea that I might fly the kingdom, I thought the moment opportune for making interest with the clerk of the court, and I accordingly paid him a visit. After telling him of my fears, I slipped into his hand a packet of three hundred louis, for which I did not ask for a receipt, saying that they were to defray expenses if I were mulcted in costs. He advised me to require the midwife to give bail for her appearance, and I told my attorney to do so; but, four days after, the following incident took place:

I was walking in the Temple Gardens, when I was accosted by a Savoyard, who gave me a note in which I was informed that somebody in an alley, fifty paces off, wanted to speak to me. "Either a love affair or a challenge," I said to myself, "let's see." I stopped my carriage, which was following me, and went to the place.

I cannot say how surprised I was to see the wretched Cartel-Bajac standing before me. "I have only a word to say," said he, when he saw me. "We will not be overheard here. The midwife is quite sure that you are the man who brought a pregnant lady to her, but she is vexed that you are accused of making away with her. Give her a hundred louis; she will then declare to the court that she has been mistaken, and your trouble will be ended. You need not pay the money till she has made her declaration; we will take your word for it. Come with me and talk it over with Vauversin. I am sure he will persuade you to do as I suggest. I know where to find him, follow me at some distance."

I had listened to him in silence, and I was delighted to see that the rascals were betraying themselves. "Very good," said I to the fellow, "you go on, and I will follow." I went after him to the third floor of a house in the Rue aux Ours, where I found Vauversin the barrister. No sooner had I arrived than he went to business without any prefatory remarks.

"The midwife," he said, "will call on you with a witness apparently with the intention of maintaining to your face that you are her man; but she won't be able to recognize you. She will then proceed with the witness to the court, and will declare that she has made a mistake, and the criminal lieutenant will forthwith put an end to the proceedings. You will thus be certain of gaining your case against the lady's mother."

I thought the plan well conceived, and said that they would find me at the Temple any day up to noon.

"But the midwife wants a hundred louis badly."

"You mean that the worthy woman rates her perjury at that price. Well, never mind, I will pay the money, and you may trust to my word; but I can't do so before she has taken oath to her mistake before the court."

"Very good, but you must first give me twenty-five louis to reimburse me for my costs and fees."

"Certainly, if you will give me a formal receipt for the money."

He hesitated at first, but after talking it over the money proved too strong a bait, and he wrote out the receipt and I gave him the twenty-five louis. He thanked me, and said that though Madame X. C. V. was his client, he would let me know confidentially how best to put a stop to the proceedings. I thanked him with as much gratitude as if I had really intended to make use of his services, and I left to write and tell M. de Sartine what had taken place.

Three days afterwards I was told that a man and woman wanted to see me. I went down and asked the woman what she wanted.

"I want to speak to M. Casanova."

"I am he."

"Then I have made a mistake, for which I hope you will forgive me."

Her companion smiled, and they went off.

The same day Madame du Rumain had a letter from the abbess telling her that her young friend had given birth to a fine boy, who had been sent away to a place where he would be well looked after. She stated that the young lady could not leave the convent for the next six weeks, at the end of which time she could return to her mother with a certificate which would protect her from all annoyance.

Soon after the midwife was put in solitary confinement, Castel-Bajac was sent to The Bicetre, and Vauversin's name was struck off the rolls. The suit instituted against me by Madame X. C. V. went on till her daughter reappeared, but I knew that I had nothing to fear. The girl returned to her mother about the end of August armed with a certificate from the abbess, who said she had been under her protection for four months, during which time she had never left the convent or seen any persons from outside. This was perfectly true, but the abbess added that her only reason for her going back to her family was that she had nothing more to dread from the attentions of M. de la Popeliniere, and in this the abbess lied.

Mdlle. X. C. V. profited by the delight of her mother in seeing her again safe and sound, and made her wait on M. de Sartine with the abbess's certificate, stop all proceedings against me, and withdraw all the charges she had made. Her daughter told her that if I liked I might claim damages for libel, and that if she did not wish to injure her reputation she would say nothing more about what had happened.

The mother wrote me a letter of the most satisfactory character, which I had registered in court, thus putting an end to the prosecution. In my turn I wrote to congratulate her on the recovery of her daughter, but I never set foot in her house again, to avoid any disagreeable scenes with Farsetti.

Mdlle. X. C. V. could not stay any longer in Paris, where her tale was known to everyone, and Farsetti took her to Brussels with her sister Madelaine. Some time after, her mother followed her, and they then went on to Venice, and there in three years' time she became a great lady. Fifteen years afterwards I saw her again, and she was a widow, happy enough apparently, and enjoying a great reputation on account of her rank, wit, and social qualities, but our connection was never renewed.

In four years the reader will hear more of Castel-Bajac. Towards the end of the same year (1759), before I went to Holland, I spent several hundred francs to obtain the release of the midwife.

I lived like a prince, and men might have thought me happy, but I was not. The enormous expenses I incurred, my love of spending money, and magnificent pleasures, warned me, in spite of myself, that there were rocks ahead. My business would have kept me going for a long time, if custom had not been paralyzed by the war; but as it was, I, like everybody else, experienced the effect of bad times. My warehouse contained four hundred pieces of stuffs with designs on them, but as I could not hope to dispose of them before the peace, and as peace seemed a long way off, I was threatened with ruin.

With this fear I wrote to Esther to get her father to give me the remainder of my money, to send me a sharp clerk, and to join in my speculation. M. d'O—— said that if I would set up in Holland he would become responsible for everything and give me half profits, but I liked Paris too well to agree to so good an offer. I was sorry for it afterwards.

I spent a good deal of money at my private house, but the chief expense of my life, which was unknown to others but which was ruining me, was incurred in connection with the girls who worked in my establishment. With my complexion and my pronounced liking for variety, a score of girls, nearly all of them pretty and seductive, as most Paris girls are, was a reef on which my virtue made shipwreck every day. Curiosity had a good deal to do with it, and they profited by my impatience to take possession by selling their favours dearly. They all followed the example of the first favourite, and everyone claimed in turn an establishment, furniture, money, and jewels; and I knew too little of the value of money to care how much they asked. My fancy never lasted longer than a week, and often waned in three or four days, and the last comer always appeared the most worthy of my attentions.

As soon as I had made a new choice I saw no more of my old loves, but I continued to provide for them, and that with a good deal of money. Madame d'Urfe, who thought I was rich, gave me no trouble. I made her happy by using my oracle to second the magical ceremonies of which she grew fonder every day, although she never attained her aim. Manon Baletti, however, grieved me sorely by her jealousy and her well-founded reproaches. She would not understand— and I did not wonder at it—how I could put off marrying her if I really loved her. She accused me of deceiving her. Her mother died of consumption in our arms. Silvia had won my true friendship. I looked upon her as a most worthy woman, whose kindness of heart and purity of life deserved the esteem of all. I stayed in the family for three days after her death, sincerely sympathizing with them in their affliction.

A few days afterwards, my friend Tiretta lost his mistress through a grievous illness. Four days before her death, perceiving that she was near her end, she willed to consecrate to God that which man could have no longer, and dismissed her lover with the gift of a valuable jewel and a purse of two hundred louis. Tiretta marched off and came and told me the sad news. I got him a lodging near the Temple, and a month after, approving his idea to try his fortune in India, I gave him a letter of introduction to M. d'O——, of Amsterdam; and in the course of a week this gentleman got him a post as clerk, and shipped him aboard one of the company's ships which was bound for Batavia. If he had behaved well he might have become a rich man, but he got involved in some conspiracy and had to fly, and afterwards experienced many vicissitudes of fortune. I heard from one of his relations that he was in Bengal in 1788, in good circumstances, but unable to realize his property and so return to his native country. I do not know what became of him eventually.

In the beginning of November an official belonging to the Duc d'Elbeuf's household came to my establishment to buy a wedding dress for his daughter. I was dazzled with her beauty. She chose a fine satin, and her pretty face lighted up when she heard her father say he did not think it was too much; but she looked quite piteous when she heard the clerk tell her father that he would have to buy the whole piece, as they could not cut it. I felt that I must give in, and to avoid making an exception in her favour I beat a hasty retreat into my private room. I wish I had gone out of the house, as I should have saved a good deal of money; but what pleasure should I have also lost! In her despair the charming girl begged the manager to take her to me, and he dared not refuse to do so. She came in; two big tears falling down her cheeks and dimming the ardour of her gaze.

"Oh, sir!" she began, "you are rich, do you buy the piece and let me have enough for a dress, which will make me happy."

I looked at her father and saw he wore an apologetic air, as if deprecating the boldness of his child.

"I like your simplicity," I said to her, "and since it will make you happy, you shall have the dress."

She ran up to me, threw her arms round my neck and kissed me, while her worthy father was dying with laughter. Her kisses put the last stroke to my bewitchment. After he had paid for the dress, her father said,

"I am going to get this little madcap married next Sunday; there will be a supper and a ball, and we shall be delighted if you will honour us with your presence. My name is Gilbert. I am comptroller of the Duc d'Elbeuf's household."

I promised to be at the wedding, and the young lady gave a skip of joy which made me think her prettier than ever.

On Sunday I repaired to the house, but I could neither eat nor drink. The fair Mdlle. Gilbert kept me in a kind of enchantment which lasted while I was in company with her friends, for whom I did not care. They were all officials in noblemen's houses, with their wives and daughters, who all aped the manners of their betters in the most ridiculous way; nobody knew me and I was known to nobody, and I cut a sorry figure amongst them all, for in a company of this sort the wittiest man is the greatest fool. Everybody cracked his joke to the bride, she answered everybody, and people laughed at nothing.

Her husband, a thin and melancholy man, with a rather foolish expression, was delighted at his wife's keeping everybody amused. Although I was in love with her, I pitied rather than envied him. I guessed that he had married for monetary considerations, and I knew pretty well what kind of a head-dress his handsome, fiery wife would give her husband, who was plain-featured, and seemed not to be aware of his wife's beauty. I was seized with the desire of asking her some questions, and she gave me the opportunity by coming to sit next to me after a quadrille. She thanked me again for my kindness, and said that the beautiful dress I had supplied had won her many compliments.

"All the same," I said, "I know you are longing to take it off. I know what love is and how impatient it makes one."

"It's very funny that everyone persists in thinking that I am in love, though I saw M. Baret for the first time only a week ago. Before then I was absolutely unconscious of his existence."

"But why are you getting married in such a hurry without waiting till you know him better?"

"Because my father does everything in a hurry."

"I suppose your husband is a very rich man?"

"No, but he may become rich. We are going to open a shop for silk stockings at the corner of the Rue St. Honore and the Rue des Prouveres, and I hope that you will deal with us, as we would serve you with the best."

"I shall certainly do so—nay, I will be your first customer, if I have to wait at the door."

"You are kind! M. Baret," said she to her husband, who was standing close by, "this gentleman promises to be our first customer."

"The gentleman is very good," said the husband, "and I am sure he will be satisfied, as my stockings are genuine silk."

Next Tuesday at day-break I began to dance attendance at the corner of the Rue des Prouveres, and waited there till the servant came out to take down the shutters. I went in and the girl asked me my business.

"I want to buy some stockings," was my answer.

"Master and mistress are still in bed, so you had better come later on."

"No, I will wait here. Stop a minute," said I, giving her six francs, "go and get me some coffee; I will drink it in the shop."

"I might go and get you some coffee, but I am not so silly as to leave you in the shop by yourself."

"You are afraid I might steal something!"

"Well, one does hear of such things being done, and I don't know you from Adam."

"Very good; but I shall stay here all the same."

Before long Baret came down and scolded the poor girl for not having told him of my presence. "Go and tell my wife to come," said he, as he began opening packets of stockings for me to choose from. He kept stockings, vests, and silk drawers, and I turned one packet over after another, looking at them all and not fixing on anything till I saw his wife coming down as fresh as a rose and as bright as a lily. She smiled at me in the most seductive manner, apologized for the disorder of her dress, and thanked me for keeping my word.

"I never break my word," I said, "especially when such a charming lady is concerned!"

Madame Baret was seventeen, of a moderate height, and an exquisite figure; without being classically beautiful, a Raphael could not wish to depict a more enticing face. Her eyes were large and brilliant. Her drooping eyelids, which gave her so modest and yet so voluptuous an appearance, the ever-smiling mouth, her splendid teeth, the dazzling whiteness of her complexion, the pleasing air with which she listened to what was being said, her silvery voice, the sweetness and sparkling vivacity of her manner, her lack of conceit, or rather her unconsciousness of the power of her charms-in fine, everything about this masterpiece of nature made me wonder and admire; while she, by chance or vile monetary considerations, was in the power of Baret, who, pale and sickly, thought a good deal more of his stockings than of the treasure marriage had given him—a treasure of which he was all unworthy, since he could not see its beauty nor taste its sweetness.

I chose stockings and vests to the amount of twenty-five louis, and I paid the price without trying to cheapen them. I saw the face of the fair shopwoman light up, and I augured well for my success, though I could not expect to do much while the honeymoon lasted. I told the servant that I would give her six francs if she would bring the packet to my house, and so I left them.

Next Sunday Baret came himself with my purchases. I gave him six francs to hand over to his servant, but he hinted that he was not too proud to keep them himself. I was disgusted at this petty greed, and at his meanness in depriving his maid of the six francs after having made a good profit in what he had sold me; but I wanted to stand well with him, and I was not sorry to find so simple a way of throwing dust into his eyes. So while I resolved that the servant should not be a loser I gave the husband a good reception that I might the better mould him to my purpose. I had breakfast brought to him, asking why he had not brought his wife.

"She wanted me to take her," said he, "but I was afraid you might be offended."

"Not at all, I should have been delighted. I think your wife a charming woman."

"You are very kind to say so; but she's young, she's young."

"I don't think that's any objection; and if she cares for the walk, bring her with you another time." He said he should be very pleased to do so.

When I passed by the shop in my carriage I blew kisses to her with my hand, but I did not stop as I did not want any more stockings. Indeed, I should have been bored with the crowd of fops with which the shop was always full. She began to be a topic of conversation in the town; the Palais Royal was full of her; and I was glad to hear that she kept to herself as if she had richer prey in view. That told me that no one possessed her so far, and I hoped that I might be the prey myself; I was quite willing to be captured.

Some days after, she saw my carriage coming, and beckoned to me as I passed. I got out, and her husband with many apologies told me that he wanted me to be the first to see a new fashion in breeches he had just got in. The breeches were parti-coloured, and no man of fashion would be seen without them. They were odd-looking things, but became a well-made young man. As they had to fit exactly, I told him to measure me for six pairs, offering to pay in advance. "We have them in all sizes," said he, "go up to my wife's room and try some on."

It was a good opportunity and I accepted, especially when I heard him tell his wife to go and help me. I went upstairs, she following, and I began to undress, apologizing for doing so before her.

"I will fancy I am your valet," said she, "and I will help you."

I did not make any difficulties, and after taking off my shoes I gave her my breeches, taking care, however, to keep on my drawers, lest her modesty should receive too severe a shock. This done she took a pair of breeches, drew them on me, took them off, and tried on others, and all this without any impropriety on either side; for I had determined to behave with discretion till the opportunity came to be indiscreet. She decided that four pairs fitted me admirably, and, not wishing to contradict her, I gave her the sixteen louis she asked, and told her I should be delighted if she would bring them herself at any time when she was at leisure. She came downstairs quite proud of her knowledge of business, and Baret said that next Sunday he and his wife would have the honour of bringing me my purchase.

"I shall be charmed, M. Baret," said I, "especially if you will stay to dinner."

He answered that having an important engagement for two o'clock he could only accept on the condition that I would let him go at that time, and he would return at about five to fetch his wife. I found the plan vastly to my taste, but I knew how to conceal my joy; and I quietly said that though I should lose the pleasure of his society, he was free to go when he liked, especially as I had not to go out myself before six.

I looked forward to the Sunday, and the tradesman and his wife did not fail me. As soon as they arrived, I told my servant to say "Not at home" for the rest of the day, and as I was impatient to know what would happen in the afternoon I had dinner served at an early hour. The dishes were exquisite, and the wines delicious. The good man ate much and drank deeply, indeed to such an extent that in common politeness I was obliged to remind him that he had an important appointment at two. His wits being sharpened with champagne, the happy thought occurred to him to tell his wife to go home by herself, if he were kept later than five; and I hastened to add that I would take her home myself in my carriage. He thanked me, and I soothed his uneasiness about being punctual to his appointment by telling him that a coach was waiting, and that the fare had been paid. He went off, and I found myself alone with my jewel, whom I was certain of possessing till six o'clock.

As soon as I heard the hall door shut on the kind husband, I said to his wife,

"You are to be congratulated on having such a kind husband; with a man like that your happiness is assured."

"It is easy to say happiness, but enjoying it is a different thing. My husband's health is so delicate that I can only consider myself as his nurse; and then he contracted heavy debts to set up in business which oblige us to observe the strictest economy. We came here on foot to save the twenty-four sons. We could live on the profits of the business, if there were no debts, but as it is everything goes to pay the interest, and our sales are not large enough to cover everything."

"But you have plenty of customers, for whenever I pass I see the shop full of people."

"These customers you see are idlers, crackers of bad jokes, and profligates, who come and make my head ache with their jests. They have not a penny to bless themselves with, and we dare not let them out of our sight for fear of their hands wandering. If we had cared to give them credit, our shop would have been emptied long ago. I am rude to them, in the hopes that they may leave me alone, but it's of no use. Their impudence is astonishing. When my husband is in I retreat to my room, but he is often away, and then I am obliged to put up with them. And the scarcity of money prevents us from doing much business, but we are obliged to pay our workmen all the same. As far as I can see, we shall be obliged to dismiss them, as we shall soon have to meet several bills. Next Saturday we have got to pay six hundred francs, and we have only got two hundred."

"I am surprised at your having all this worry in these early days of your marriage. I suppose your father knew about your husband's circumstances; how about your dowry?"

"My dowry of six thousand francs has served, most of it, to stock the shop and to pay our debts. We have goods which would pay our debts three times over; but in bad times capital sunk is capital dead."

"I am sorry to hear all this, as if peace is not made your situation will become worse, for as you go on your needs will become greater."

"Yes, for when my husband is better we may have children."

"What! Do you mean to say his health prevents him from making you a mother? I can't believe it."

"I don't see how I can be a mother who am still a maid; not that I care much about the matter."

"I shouldn't have believed it! How can a man not in the agony of death feel ill beside you? He must be dead."

"Well, he is not exactly dead, but he doesn't shew many signs of life."

This piece of wit made me laugh, and under cover of my applause I embraced her without experiencing much resistance. The first kiss was like an electric spark; it fired my imagination and I increased my attentions till she became as submissive as a lamb.

"I will help you, dearest, to meet the bill on Saturday;" and so saying I drew her gently into a closet where a soft divan formed a suitable altar for the completion of an amorous sacrifice.

I was enchanted to find her submissive to my caresses and my inquisitiveness, but she surprised me greatly when, as I placed myself in readiness for the consummation of the act, and was already in the proper posture between the two columns, she moved in such a way as to hinder my advance. I thought at first that it was only one of those devices intended to make the final victory more sweet by putting difficulties in the way; but, finding that her resistance was genuine, I exclaimed,

"How was I to expect a refusal like this at a moment when I thought I saw my ardours reflected in your eyes?"

"Your eyes did not deceive you; but what would my husband say if he found me otherwise than as God has made me?"

"He can't have left you untouched!"

"He really has done so. You can see for yourself if you like. Can I, then, give to you what appertains to the genius of the marriage-bed."

"You are right, my angel; this fruit must be kept for a mouth unworthy to taste it. I pity and adore you. Come to my arms, abandon yourself to my love, and fear nothing. The fruit shall not be damaged; I will but taste the outer surface and leave no trace behind."

We passed three hours in trifling together in a manner calculated to inflame our passions despite the libations which we now and again poured forth. I was consoled by her swearing to be mine as soon as Baret had good grounds for thinking that she was his, and, after taking her on the Boulevards, I left her at her door, with a present of twenty-five Louis.

I was in love with her as I had never been before, and I passed the shop three or four times a day, going round and round, to the wrath of my coachman, who got sick of telling me that I was ruining my horses. I was happy to see her watch for the moment that I passed, and waft me a kiss by putting her pretty fingers to her mouth.

We had agreed that she should not make me a sign to leave my coach till her husband had forced a passage. At last this day, so ardently desired and so long waited for, arrived. The sign was given, and I stopped the coach and she came out and, standing on the step, told me to go and wait for her at the church door of St. Germain l'Auxerrois.

I was curious to know what the results would be, and had not been at the place appointed more than a quarter of an hour when she came towards me, her head muffled in a hood. She got into the carriage and, saying that she wanted to make some purchases, begged me to take her to the shops.

I had business of my own, and pressing business too, but who can refuse the Beloved Object anything? I told the coachman to drive to the Place Dauphine, and I prepared to loosen my purse-strings, as I had a feeling she was going to treat me as a friend. In point of fact she left few shops unvisited, going from jewels to pretty trifles and toys of different kinds, and from these to dresses of the latest fashion, which they displayed before her, addressing her as princess, and saying that this would become her admirably. She looked at me, and said it must be confessed that it was very pretty and that she would like it if it were not so dear. I was a willing dupe, and assured her that if she liked it it could not be too dear, and that I would pay.

While my sweetheart was thus choosing one trifle after another my ill-luck brought about an incident which placed me in a fearful situation four years afterwards. The chain of events is endless.

I perceived at my left hand a pretty girl of twelve or thirteen, with an old and ugly woman who was disparaging a pair of ear-rings which the girl had in her hands, and on which she had evidently set her heart: she looked sad at not being able to buy them. I heard her say to the old woman that they would make her happy, but she snatched them from the girl's hands and told her to, come away.

"I can let you have a cheaper pair and almost as fine," said the shopwoman, but the young lady said she did not; care about it, and was getting ready to go, making a profound reverence to my princess Baret.

She, no doubt flattered by this sign of respect went up to her, called her little queen, told her she was as fair as a May morning, and asked the old woman her name,

"She is Mdlle. de Boulainvilier, my niece."

"How can you be so hard-hearted," said I to the aunt, "as to refuse your charming niece a toy which would make her happy? Allow me to make her a present of them."

So saying I put the ear-rings in the girl's hands, while she blushed and looked at her aunt as if to ask her permission.

"You may have the ear-rings," said she, "as this gentleman has been kind enough to give you such a present, and you should give him a kiss by way of thanks."

"The ear-rings," said the shopwoman, "will be only three louis."

Hereupon the affair took a comic turn; the old woman got into a rage and said,

"How can you be such a cheat? You told me they were only two louis."

"Nay, madam, I asked three."

"That's a lie, and I shall not allow you to rob this gentleman. Niece, put those ear-rings down; let the shopwoman keep them."

So far all was well enough; but the old aunt spoilt everything by saying that if I liked to give her niece the three louis she could get her a pair twice as good at another shop. It was all the same to me, so I smilingly put the three louis in front of the young lady, who still had the ear-rings in her hands. The shop-woman, who was on the look-out, pocketed the money, saying that the bargain was made, that the three louis belonged to her and the ear-rings to the young lady.

"You are a cheat," cried out the enraged old woman.

"And you are an old b——d," answered the shop-woman, "I know you well." A crowd began to gather in front of the shop, hearing the cries of the two harpies. Foreseeing a good deal of unpleasantness, I took the aunt by the arm and led her gently away. The niece, who was quite content with the ear-rings, and did not care whether they cost three louis or two, followed her. We shall hear of them again in due course.

My dear Baret having made me waste a score of louis, which her poor husband would have regretted much more than myself, we got into the carriage again, and I took her to the church door from which we had started. On the way

152

she told me she was coming to stop a few days with me at Little Poland, and that it was her husband who would ask me for the invitation.

"When will he do that?"

"To-morrow, if you go by the shop. Come and buy some stockings; I shall have a bad headache, and Baret will speak to you."

It may be imagined that I took care to call the next day, and as I did not see his wife in the shop I asked in a friendly way after her health.

"She is ill in bed," he replied; "she wants a little country air."

"If you have not fixed for any place, I shall be happy to put you up at Little Poland."

He replied by a smile of delight.

"I will go and urge her to come myself; in the meanwhile, M. Baret, will you pack me up a dozen pairs of stockings?"

I went upstairs and found the invalid in bed, and laughing in spite of her imaginary headache. "The business is done," said I, "you will soon hear of it." As I had said, the husband came upstairs with my stockings and told her that I had been good enough to give her a room in my house. The crafty little creature thanked me, assuring her husband that the fresh air would soon cure her.

"You shall be well looked after," said I, "but you must excuse me if I do not keep you company—I have to attend to my business. M. Baret will be able to come and sleep with you every night, and start early enough in the morning to be in time for the opening of his shop."

After many compliments had been interchanged, Baret decided on having his sister stay in the house while his wife was away, and as I took leave I said that, I should give orders for their reception that very evening, in case I was out when they came.

Next day I stayed out till after midnight, and the cook told me that the wedded couple had made a good supper and had gone to bed. I warned her that I should be dining at home every day, and that I should not see my company.

The following day I was up betimes, and on enquiring if the husband had risen I learnt that he had got up at day-break and would not be back till supper-time. The wife was still asleep. I thought with reason she was not asleep for me, and I went to pay her my first visit. In point of fact she was awake, and I took a foretaste of greater joys by a thousand kisses, which she returned with interest. We jested at the expense of the worthy man who had trusted me with a jewel of which I was about to make such good use, and we congratulated each other on the prospect of a week's mutual pleasures.

"Come, my dear," said I, "get up and put on a few clothes and we will take breakfast in my room."

She did not make an elaborate toilette; a cotton dressing gown, a pretty lace cap, a lawn kerchief, that was all, but how the simple dress was lighted by the roses of her cheeks! We were quick over our breakfast, we were in a hurry, and when we had done I shut the door and we gave ourselves over to the enjoyment of our bliss.

Surprised to find her in the same condition in which I had left her, I told her I had hoped . . . but she, without giving me time to finish the phrase, said,

"My jewel, Baret thinks, or pretends to think, that he has done his duty as a husband; but he is no hand at the business, and I am disposed to put myself in your hands, and then there will be no doubt of my condition."

"We shall thus, my sweet, be doing him a service, and the service shall be well done."

As I said these words I was on the threshold of the temple, and I opened the door in a manner that overthrew all obstacles. A little scream and then several sighs announced the completion of the sacrifice, and, to tell the truth, the altar of love was covered with the blood of the victim. After the necessary ablutions the priest once more began his pious work, while the victim growing bolder so provoked his rage that it was not till the fourth mactation that we rested and put off our joust to another season. We swore a thousand times to love each other and to remain constant, and we may possibly have been sincere, as we were in our ecstasy of pleasure.

We only separated to dress; then after taking a turn in the garden we dined together, sure that in a sumptuous repast, washed down by the choicest wines, we should find strength to reanimate our desires and to lull them to sleep in bliss.

At dessert, as I was pouring champagne into her glass, I asked her how with such a fiery temperament she had managed to preserve her virtue?

"Cupid," said I, "might have gathered the fruit that Hymen could not taste. You are seventeen, and the pear has been ripe for two years at least."

"Very true, but I have never had a lover."

"Never?"

"I have been courted, but to no effect. My heart was ever silent. Possibly my father thought otherwise when I begged him, a month ago, to get me married soon."

"Very likely, but as you were not in love, why were you in such a hurry?"

"I knew that the Duc d'Elbeuf would soon be coming to town, and that if he found me still single he would oblige me to become the wife of a man I detest, who would have me at any price."

"Who is this man for whom you have such an aversion?"

"He is one of the duke's pets, a monster who sleeps with his master."

"Really! I did not know the duke had such tastes."

"Oh yes; he is eighty-four, and he thinks himself a woman; he says he must have a husband."

"That is very funny. And is this aspirant to your hand a handsome man?"

"I think him horrible; but everybody else thinks he is a fine man."

The charming Baret spent a week with me, and each day we renewed the combat in which we were always conquerors and always conquered. I have seen few women as pretty and seductive, and none whose skin was more exquisitely soft and fair. Her breath was aromatic, and this made her kisses most sweet. Her neck was exquisitely shaped, and the two globes, tipped with coral, were as hard as marble. The exquisite curves of her figure would have defied the skill of the ablest painter. I experienced an ineffable joy in contemplating her, and in the midst of my happiness I called myself unhappy because I could not satisfy all the desires which her charms aroused in me. The frieze which crowned her columns was composed of links of pale gold of the utmost fineness, and my fingers strove in vain to give them another direction to that which nature had given them. She could easily have been taught those lively yet graceful movements which double the pleasure; nature had done her part in that direction, and I do not think a more expert mistress in the art of love could be found.

Each of us looked forward to the day of her departure with equal grief, and our only consolation lay in the hope of meeting again, and often. Three days after she went away, I went to see her, more in love than ever, and I gave her two notes of five thousand francs apiece. Her husband might have his suspicions, but he was too happy at being enabled to pay his debts and to keep his shop open to say anything unpleasant. Many husbands besides himself think themselves lucky to have such productive wives.

In the beginning of November I sold shares for fifty thousand francs to a man named Gamier, living in the Rue du Mail, giving up to him a third part of the materials in my warehouse, and accepting a manager chosen by him and paid by the company. Three days after signing the deed I received the money; but in the night the doctor, my warehouseman, emptied the till and absconded. I have always thought that this robbery could not have been effected without the connivance of the painter. This loss was a serious blow to me, as my affairs were getting into an embroiled condition; and, for a finishing touch to my misfortunes, Gamier had me served with a summons to repay him the fifty thousand francs. My answer was that I was not liable, that his manager had been appointed, the agreement and sale of the shares was valid, and that he being one of the company would have to share in the loss. As he persisted in his claim, I was advised to go to law, but Gamier declared the agreement null and void, accusing me in an indirect manner of having appropriated the money which I had said was stolen. I would willingly have given him a good thrashing, but he was an old man, and that course would not have mended matters, so I kept my temper. The merchant who had given surety for the doctor was not to be found; he had become bankrupt. Garnier had all my stock seized, and sequestrated my horses, carriages, and all my private property.

While these troubles were harassing me, I dismissed all my work-girls, who had always been a great expense, and replaced them with workmen and some of my servants. The painter still retained his position, which was an assured one, as he always paid himself out of the sales.

My attorney was an honest man—a rare bird amongst lawyers—but my counsel, who kept telling me that the case would soon be decided, was a rascal. While the decision was pending, Garnier served me with a writ to pay the sum claimed. I took it to my counsel, who promised to appeal the same day, which he did not do, while he appropriated to his own use the money assigned by me for the costs of an action which, if there had been justice in France, I should certainly have gained. Two other summonses were issued against me, and before I knew what was going on a warrant was issued for my arrest. I was seized at eight o'clock in the morning, as I was driving along the Rue St. Denis. The sergeant of police sat beside me, a second got up beside the coachman, and a third stationed himself at the back of the coach, and in this state we drove to Fort l'Eveque.

As soon as the police had handed me over to the gaoler, he informed me that by payment of the fifty thousand francs, or by giving good bail, I might instantly regain my freedom.

"For the moment," said I, "I can neither command money nor bail."

"Very good, then you will stay in prison."

The gaoler took me to a decent-looking room, and I told him I had only been served with one writ.

"Very likely," answered he, "it often happens like that; but it is rather difficult to prove."

"Bring me writing materials, and have a trusty messenger at my disposal."

I wrote to my counsel, my attorney, to Madame d'Urfe, and to all my friends, including my brother, who was just married. The attorney called immediately, but the barrister contented himself with writing to the effect that as he had put in an appeal my seizure was illegal, and that damages might be recovered. He ended by begging me to give him a free hand, and to have patience for a few days.

Manon Baletti sent her brother with her diamond earrings. Madame du Rumain dispatched her barrister—a man of rare honesty—to me, and wrote a friendly note in which she said that if I wanted five hundred louis I should have them to-morrow. My brother neither wrote nor came to see me. As to dear Madame d'Urfe she sent to say that she would expect me at dinner. I thought she had gone mad, as I could not think she was making fun of me.

At eleven o'clock my room was full of people. Poor Baret had come weeping, and offering me all his shop held. I was touched by the worthy man's kindness. At last I was told that a lady in a coach wanted to see me. I waited, but nobody came. In my impatience I called the turnkey, who told me that, after questioning the clerk of the prison, she had gone away again. From the description I was given I had no difficulty in identifying the lady with Madame d'Urfe.

To find myself deprived of my liberty was a disagreeable shock to me. I thought of The Leads, and though my present situation was not to be compared with that, I cursed my fate as I foresaw that my imprisonment would damage my reputation. I had thirty thousand francs in hard cash and jewels to more than double that amount, but I could not decide on making such a sacrifice, in spite of the advice given by Madame du Rumain's barrister, who would have me got out of prison at any cost.

"All you have to do," said the barrister, "is to deposit half the sum demanded which I will give to the clerk of the court, and in a short time I can promise a decision in your favour and the restoration of your money."

We were discussing the matter, when the gaoler entered, and said, very politely,

"Sir, you are a free man again, and a lady is waiting for you at the door in her carriage."

I called Le Duc, my man, and told him to go and see who the lady was. He returned with the information that it was Madame d'Urfe. I made my bow to everybody, and after four very disagreeable hours of imprisonment, I found myself free again and sitting in a splendid coach.

Madame d'Urfe received me with dignified kindness, and a judge who was in the carriage apologized for his country, where strangers were exposed to such insults. I thanked Madame d'Urfe in a few words, telling her that I was glad to become her debtor, but that it was Garnier who benefited by her generosity. She replied with a pleasant smile that she was not so sure of that, and that we would talk it over at dinner. She wanted me to go and walk in the Tuileries and the Palais Royal, to convince people that the report of my imprisonment had been false. I thought the advice excellent, and as I set out I promised to be with her at two o'clock.

After skewing myself at the two principal walks of Paris, amusing myself by the astonishment depicted on certain faces well known to me, I went and returned the ear-rings to my dear Manon, who gave an astonished but a happy cry when she saw me. I thanked her tenderly for the proof she had given me of her attachment, and said that I had been arrested by a plot for which I would make the plotters pay dear. After promising to spend the evening with them I went to Madame d'Urfe's.

This good lady, whose foible is well known to my readers, made me laugh when she said that her genius had told her that I had got myself arrested to be talked about, for reasons which were known only to myself.

"As soon as I was informed of your arrest," said she, "I went to the Fort l'Eveque, and on learning from the clerk what the affair was about, I deposited bonds to bail you out. If you are not in a position to have justice done you, Gamier will have to reckon with me before he takes the money I have deposited. But your first step should be to commence a criminal prosecution against your counsel, who has not only failed to put in your appeal but has robbed and deceived you."

I left her in the evening, assuring her that in a few days her bail should be returned to her; and went to the French and Italian plays in succession, taking care to render myself conspicuous that my reappearance might be complete. Afterwards I went to sup with Manon Baletti, who was too happy to have had an opportunity of spewing her affection for me; and her joy was full when I told her that I was going to give up business, for she thought that my seraglio was the only obstacle to my marriage with her.

The next day was passed with Madame du Rumain. I felt that my obligations to her were great, while she, in the goodness of her heart, was persuaded that she could make no adequate return to me for the oracles with which I furnished her, and by following which she was safely guided through the perplexities of life. I cannot understand how she, whose wit was keen, and whose judgment on other subjects was of the soundest kind, could be liable to such folly. I was sorry when I reflected that I could not undeceive her, and glad when I reflected that to this deceit of mine the kindness she had shewn me was chiefly due.

My imprisonment disgusted me with Paris, and made me conceive a hatred of the law, which I feel now. I found myself entangled in a double maze of knavery—Garnier was my foe, and so was my own counsel. Every time I went to plead, to spend my money amongst lawyers, and to waste the time better given to pleasure, I felt as if I was going to execution. In this perturbed kind of life, so contrary to my inclinations, I resolved to set to work in earnest to make my fortune, so that I might become independent and free to enjoy life according to my tastes. I decided in the first place that I would cut myself free of all that bound me to Paris, make a second journey into Holland to replenish my purse and invest my money in a yearly income for two lives, and from thenceforth live free from care. The two lives were those of my wife and myself; my wife would be Manon Baletti, and when I told her my plans she would have thought them delightful if I had begun by marrying her.

The first thing I did was to give up Little Poland. I then drew the twenty-four thousand francs which were my surety for keeping a lottery office in the Rue St. Denis. Thus I got rid of my ridiculous office of lottery receiver, and after getting my clerk married I handed over the office to him; in short, I made his fortune. A friend of his wife's was his surety; such things often happen.

I did not like to leave Madame d'Urfe involved in a troublesome suit with Gamier, so I went to Versailles to see the Abbe de la Ville, a great friend of his, and begged him to induce Gamier to make a composition.

The abbe saw that his friend was in the wrong, and so was all the more willing to help me; and a few days afterwards he wrote to me to go and see him, assuring me that I should find him inclined to arrange matters in a friendly manner.

Gamier was at Ruelle, where he had a house which cost him four hundred thousand francs—a fine estate for a man who had made his money as an army contractor during the last war. He was rich, but he was so unfortunate as to be still fond of women at the age of seventy, while his impotence debarred him from the proper enjoyment of their society. I found him in company with three young ladies, all of whom were pretty, and (as I heard afterwards) of good families; but they were poor, and their necessities forced them to submit to a disgusting intercourse with the old profligate. I stayed to dinner and admired the propriety and modesty of their behaviour in spite of the humiliation which accompanies poverty. After dinner, Gamier went to sleep, and left me to entertain these girls whom I would willingly have rescued from their unfortunate situation if I had been able. After Gamier woke, we went into his study to talk over our business.

At first he maintained his claim tenaciously, and seemed unwilling to yield an inch; but when I told him that I was leaving Paris in a few days, he saw that as he could not keep me, Madame d'Urfe might take the suit over and carry it on to infinity, and that he might lose it at last. That made him think it over, and he asked me to stay in his house for the night. The next day, after breakfast, he said,—

"I have made up my mind: I will have twenty-five thousand francs, or keep the matter before the courts till my dying day."

I answered that he would find the sum in the hands of Madame d'Urfe's solicitor, and that he could receive it as soon as he had given replevy on the bail at the Fort l'Eveque.

I could not persuade Madame d'Urfe that I had acted wisely in coming to an arrangement till I had told her that my genius had commanded me not to leave Paris before my affairs were settled, so that no one might be able to accuse me of having gone away to avoid creditors whose claims I could not satisfy.

Three or four days afterwards I went to take leave of M. de Choiseul, who promised to instruct M. d'Afri to aid me in negotiating a loan at five per cent. either with the States-General or a private company.

"You can tell everyone," said he, "that peace is certain to be made in the course of the winter, and I will take care that you shall have what is due to you on your return to France."

M. de Choiseul deceived me, for he knew very well that peace would not be made; but I had no definite project, and I repented of having given M. de Boulogne my confidence, and also of having done anything for the Government, the reward of which was not immediate and certain.

I sold my horses, my carriages, my furniture; I went bail for my brother who had contracted debts he was sure of paying, as he had several pictures on the easel which he had been ordered to paint by some of his rich and noble patrons. I took leave of Manon, whom I left in floods of tears, though I swore with the utmost sincerity to come back soon and marry her.

At last all my preparations were finished, and I left Paris with a hundred thousand francs in bills of exchange and jewels to the same amount. I was alone in my post-chaise, Le Duc preceding me on horseback, which the rascal preferred to being shut up in a carriage.

This Le Duc of mine was a Spaniard, aged eighteen, a sharp fellow, whom I valued highly, especially because he did my hair better than anyone else. I never refused him a pleasure which a little money would buy. Besides him I had a good Swiss servant, who served as my courier.

It was the 1st of December, 1759, and the air was frosty, but I was fortified against the inclemency of the season. I was able to read comfortably, and I took Helvetius's "Esprit," which I had never had time to read before. After perusing it I was equally astonished at the sensation it created and at the stupidity of the High Court which condemned it. Of course that exalted body was largely influenced by the king and the clergy, and between them all no effort was spared to ruin Helvetius, a good-hearted man with more wit than his book. I saw nothing novel either in the historical part relating to the morals of nations (in which Helvetius dismisses us as triflers), or in the position that morality is dependent on the reason. All that he says has been said over and over again, and

Blaise Pascal went much farther, but he wrote more skilfully and better in every way than Helvetius, who, wishing to remain in France, was obliged to retract. He preferred a quiet life to his honour and his philosophy. His wife had a nobler soul than he, as she wanted to sell all they had, and to take refuge in Holland rather than submit to the shame of a recantation. Perhaps Helvetius would have followed the noble advice of his wife if he had foreseen that this monstrous recantation would make his book into a fraud; for he had to confess that he had written without due reflection, that he was more in jest than earnest, and that his arguments were mere sophisms. But many men of keen intellects had not waited for him to recant before exposing this wretched system of his. And admitting that whatever man does is done for his own interest, does it follow that gratitude is a folly, and virtue and vice identical? Are a villain and a man of honour to be weighed in the same balance? If such a dreadful system were not absurd, virtue would be mere hypocrisy; and if by any possibility it were true, it ought to be proscribed by general consent, since it would lead to general ruin and corruption.

It might have been proved to Helvetius that the propositions that the first motive is always self-interest, and that we should always consult our own interest first, are fallacious. It is a strange thing that so virtuous a man would not admit the existence of virtue. It is an amusing suggestion that he only published his book out of modesty, but that would have contradicted his own system. But if it were so, was it well done to render himself contemptible to escape the imputation of pride? Modesty is only a virtue when it is natural; if it is put on, or merely the result of training, it is detestable. The great d'Alembert was the most truly modest man I have ever seen.

When I got to Brussels, where I spent two days, I went to the "Hotel de l'Imperatrice," and chance sent Mdlle. X. C. V. and Farsetti in my way, but I pretended not to see them. From Brussels I went straight to the Hague, and got out at the "Prince of Orange." On my asking the host who sat down at his table, he told me his company consisted of general officers of the Hanoverian army, same English ladies, and a Prince Piccolomini and his wife; and this made me make up my mind to join this illustrious assemblage.

I was unknown to all, and keeping my eyes about me I gave my chief attention to the observation of the supposed Italian princess, who was pretty enough, and more especially of her husband whom I seemed to recognize. In the course of conversation I heard some talk of the celebrated St. Germain, and it seemed that he was stopping in the same hotel.

I had returned to my room, and was thinking of going to bed, when Prince Piccolomini entered, and embraced me as an old friend.

"A look in your face," said he, "tells me that the recognition has been mutual. I knew you directly in spite of the sixteen years that have passed since we saw each other at Vicenza. To-morrow you can tell everybody that we are friends, and that though I am not a prince I am really a count; here is my passport from the King of Naples, pray read it."

During this rapid monologue I could not get in a single word, and on attentively scanning his features I could only recollect that I had seen him before, but when or where or how I knew not. I opened the passport and read the name of Ruggero di Rocco, Count Piccolomini. That was enough; I remembered an individual of that name who was a fencing-master in Vicenza, and on looking at him again his aspect, though much changed left no doubt as to the identity of the swordsman and the count.

"I congratulate you," said I, "on your change of employment, your new business is doubtless much better than the old."

"I taught fencing," he replied, "to save myself from dying of hunger, for my father was so hard a man that he would not give me the wherewithal to live, and I disguised my name so as not to disgrace it. On my father's death I succeeded to the property, and at Rome I married the lady you have seen."

"You had good taste, for she's a pretty woman."

"She is generally thought so, and it was a love match on my side."

He ended by asking me to come and see him in his room the next day, after dinner, telling me that I should find good company and a bank at faro, which he kept himself. He added, without ceremony, that if I liked we could go half shares, and that I should find it profitable. I thanked him, and promised to pay him a visit.

I went abroad at an early hour next morning, and after having spent some time with the Jew, Boaz, and having given a polite refusal to his offer of a bed, I went to pay my respects to M. d'Afri, who since the death of the Princess of Orange, the Regent of the Low Countries, was generally known as His Most Christian Majesty's ambassador. He gave me an excellent reception, but he said that if I had returned to Holland hoping to do business on behalf of the Government I should waste my time, since the action of the comptroller-general had lowered the credit of the nation, which was thought to be on the verge of bankruptcy.

"This M. Silhouette," said he, "has served the king very badly. It is all very well to say that payments are only suspended for a year, but it is not believed."

He then asked me if I knew a certain Comte de St. Germain, who had lately arrived at the Hague.

"He has not called on me," said the ambassador, "though he says he is commissioned by the king to negotiate a loan of a hundred millions. When I am asked about him, I am obliged to say that I know nothing about him, for fear of compromising myself. Such a reply, as you can understand, is not likely to increase his chance of success, but that is his fault and not mine. Why has he not brought me a letter from the Duc de Choiseul or the Marquise de Pompadour? I take him to be an impostor, but I shall know something more about him in the course of ten days."

I told him, in my turn, all I knew of this truly eccentric individual. He was not a little surprised to hear that the king had given him an apartment at Chambord, but when I told him that the count professed to be able to make diamonds he laughed and said that in that case he would no doubt make the hundred millions. Just as I was leaving, M. d'Afri asked me to dine with him on the following day.

On returning to the hotel I called on the Comte de St. Germain.

"You have anticipated me," said he, on seeing me enter, "I intended to have called on you. I suppose, my dear Casanova, that you have come to try what you can do for our Court, but you will find your task a difficult one, as the Exchange is highly offended at the late doings of that fool Silhouette. All the same I hope I shall be able to get my hundred millions. I have passed my word to my friend, Louis XV. (I may call him so), and I can't disappoint him; the business will be done in the next three or four weeks."

"I should think M. d'Afri might assist you."

"I do not require his assistance. Probably I shall not even call upon him, as he might say he helped me. No, I shall have all the trouble, and I mean to have all the glory, too."

"I presume you will be going to Court, where the Duke of Brunswick may be of service to you?"

"Why should I go to Court? As for the Duke of Brunswick, I do not care to know him. All I have got to do is to go to Amsterdam, where my credit is sufficiently good for anything. I am fond of the King of France; there's not a better man in the kingdom."

"Well, come and dine at the high table, the company is of the best and will please you."

"You know I never eat; moreover, I never sit down at a table where I may meet persons who are unknown to me."

"Then, my lord, farewell; we shall see each other again at Amsterdam."

I went down to the dining-room, where, while dinner was being served, I conversed with some officers. They asked me if I knew Prince Piccolomini, to which I answered that he was not a prince but a count, and that it was many years since I had seen him.

When the count and his fair wife (who only spoke Italian) came down, I shewed them some polite attentions, and we then sat down to dinner.

EPISODE 13 — HOLLAND AND GERMANY

CHAPTER X

Portrait of the Pretended Countess Piccolomini—Quarrel and Duel—Esther and Her Father, M. D'O.—Esther Still Taken with the Cabala—Piccolomini Forges a Bill of Exchange: Results I Am Fleeced, and in Danger of Being Assassinated—Debauch with the Two Paduan Girls—I Reveal A Great Secret To Esther—I Bate the Rascally St. Germain; His Flight—Manon Baletti Proves Faithless to Me; Her Letter Announcing Her Marriage: My Despair—Esther Spends a Day With Me—My Portrait and My Letters to Manon Get Into Esther's Hands—I Pass a Day with Her—We Talk of Marrying Each Other

The so-called Countess Piccolomini was a fine example of the adventurers. She was young, tall, well-made, had eyes full of fire, and skin of a dazzling whiteness; not, however, that natural whiteness which delights those who know the value of a satin skin and rose petals, but rather that artificial fairness which is commonly to be seen at Rome on the faces of courtezans, and which disgusts those who know how it is produced. She had also splendid teeth, glorious hair as black as jet, and arched eyebrows like ebony. To these advantages she added attractive manners, and there was something intelligent about the way she spoke; but through all I saw the adventuress peeping out, which made me detest her.

As she did not speak anything but Italian the countess had to play the part of a mute at table, except where an English officer named Walpole was concerned, who, finding her to his taste, set himself to amuse her. I felt friendly disposed towards this Englishman, though my feelings were certainly not the result of sympathy. If I had been blind or deaf Sir James Walpole would have been totally indifferent to me, as what I felt for him was the result of my observation.

Although I did not care for the countess, for all that I went up to her room after dinner with the greater part of the guests. The count arranged a game of whist, and Walpole played at primero with the countess, who cheated him in a masterly manner; but though he saw it he laughed and paid, because it suited his purpose to do so. When he had lost fifty Louis he called quarter, and the countess asked him to take her to the theatre. This was what the good-natured Englishman wanted; and he and the countess went off, leaving the husband playing whist.

I, too, went to the play, and as chance would have it my neighbour in the pit was Count Tot, brother to the count famous for his stay in Constantinople. We had some conversation together, and he told me he had been obliged to leave France on account of a duel which he had had with a man who had jested with him for not being present at the battle of Minden, saying that he had absented himself in view of the battle. The count had proved his courage with the sword on the other's body—a rough kind of argument which was fashionable then as now. He told me he had no money, and I immediately put my purse at his service; but, as the saying goes, a kindness is never thrown away, and five years later he did the same by me at St. Petersburg. Between the acts he happened to notice the Countess Piccolomini, and asked me if I knew her husband. "I know him very slightly," I answered, "but we happen to be staying at the same hotel."

"He's a regular black sheep," said the count, "and his wife's no better than he."

It seemed that they had already won a reputation in the town.

After the play I went back to the hotel by myself, and the head-waiter told me that Piccolomini had set out hot-foot with his servant, his only luggage being a light portmanteau. He did not know the reason of this sudden departure, but a minute afterwards the countess came in, and her maid having whispered something to her she told me that the count had gone away because he had fought a duel but that often happened. She asked me to sup with her and Walpole, and her appetite did not seem to suffer from the absence of her spouse.

Just as we were finishing supper, an Englishman, who had been of the whist party, came up and told Walpole that the Italian had been caught cheating and had given the lie to their fellow Englishman, who had detected him, and that they had gone out together. An hour afterwards the Englishman returned with two wounds, one on the fore-arm and one on the shoulder. It was a trifling affair altogether.

Next day, after I had had dinner with the Comte d'Afri, I found a letter from Piccolomini, with an enclosure addressed to the countess, waiting for me at the inn. He begged me to give his wife the letter, which would inform her of his plans, and then to bring her to the Ville de Lyon at Amsterdam, where he was staying. He wanted to know how the Englishman whom he had wounded was getting on.

The duty struck me as an amusing one, and I should have laughed with all my heart if I had felt the least desire to profit by the confidence he was pleased to place in me. Nevertheless I went up to the countess, whom I found sitting up in bed playing with Walpole. She read the letter, told me that she could not start till the day following, and informed me what time she would go, as if it had been all settled; but I smiled sardonically, and told her that my business kept me at the Hague, and that I could not possibly escort her. When Walpole heard me say this he offered to be my substitute, to which she agreed. They set out the day following, intending to lie at Leyden.

Two days after their departure, I was sitting down to dinner with the usual company, increased by two Frenchmen who had just come. After the soup one of them said, coolly,

"The famous Casanova is now in Holland."

"Is he?" said the other, "I shall be glad to see him, and ask for an explanation which he will not like."

I looked at the man, and feeling certain that I had never seen him before I began to get enraged; but I merely asked the fellow if he knew Casanova.

"I'll ought to know him," said he, in that self-satisfied tone which is always so unpleasant.

"Nay, sir, you are mistaken; I am Casanova."

Without losing his self-possession, he replied, insolently,

"You are really very much mistaken if you think you are the only Casanova in the world."

It was a sharp answer, and put me in the wrong. I bit my lips and held my tongue, but I was grievously offended, and determined to make him find the Casanova who was in Holland, and from whom he was going to extract an unpleasant explanation, in myself. In the meanwhile I bore as well as I could the poor figure he must be cutting before the officers at table, who, after hearing the insolence of this young blockhead, might take me for a coward. He, the insolent fellow, had no scruple in abusing the triumph his answer had given him, and talked away in the random fashion. At last he forgot himself so far as to ask from what country I came.

"I am a Venetian, sir," I replied.

"Ah! then you are a good friend to France, as your republic is under French protection."

At these words my ill-temper boiled aver, and, in the tone of voice one uses to put down a puppy, I replied that the Republic of Venice was strong enough to do without the protection of France or of any other power, and that during the thirteen centuries of its existence it had had many friends and allies but no protectors. "Perhaps," I ended, "you will reply by begging my pardon for not knowing that these was only one Venice in the world."

I had no sooner said this than a burst of laughter from the whole table set me right again. The young blockhead seemed taken aback and in his turn bit his lips, but his evil genius made him, strike in again at dessert. As usual the conversation went from one subject to another, and we began to talk about the Duke of Albermarle. The Englishmen spoke in his favour, and said that if he had been alive there would have been no war between England and France; they were probably right, but even if the duke had lived war might have broken out, as the two nations in question have never yet succeeded in understanding that it is for both their interests to live at peace together. Another Englishman praised Lolotte, his mistress. I said I had seen that charming woman at the Duchess of Fulvi's, and that no one deserved better to become the Countess of Eronville. The Count of Eronville, a lieutenant-general and a man of letters, had just married her.

I had scarcely finished what I had to say when Master Blockhead said, with a laugh, that he knew Lolotte to be a good sort of girl, as he had slept with her at Paris. I could restrain myself no longer; my indignation and rage consumed me. I took up my plate, and made as if I would throw it at his head, saying at the same time, "You infernal liar!" He got up, and stood with his back to the fire, but I could see by his sword-knot that he was a soldier.

Everybody pretended not to hear anything of this, and the conversation went on for some time on indifferent subjects; and at last they all rose from their seats and left the room.

My enemy said to his companion that they would see one another again after the play, and remained by the fire, with his elbow resting on the chimney-piece. I remained at table till the company had all left the room, and when we were alone together I got up and looked him straight in the face, and went out, walking towards Sheveningue, sure that he would follow me if he were a man of any mettle. When I had got to some distance from the hotel I looked round, and saw that he was following me at a distance of fifty paces.

When I got to the wood I stopped at a suitable place, and stood awaiting my antagonist. He was ten paces off when he drew his sword, and I had plenty of time to draw mine though he came on fast. The fight did not last long, for as soon as he was near enough I gave him a thrust which has never failed me, and sent him back quicker than he came. He was wounded in the chest above the right breast, but as my sword was flat and the opening large enough the wound bled easily. I lowered my sword and ran up to him, but I could do nothing; he said that we should meet again at Amsterdam, if I was going there, and that he would have his revenge. I saw him again five or six years afterwards at Warsaw, and then I did him a kindness. I heard afterwards that his name was Varnier, but I do not know whether he was identical with the president of the National Convention under the infamous Robespierre.

I did not return to the hotel till after the play, and I then heard that the Frenchman, after having the surgeon with him for an hour, had set out for Rotterdam with his friend. We had a pleasant supper and talked cheerfully together without a word being said about the duel, with the exception that an English lady said, I forget in what connection, that a man of honour should never risk sitting down to dinner at an hotel unless he felt inclined, if necessary, to fight. The remark was very true at that time, when one had to draw the sword for an idle word, and to expose one's self to the consequences of a duel, or else be pointed at, even by the ladies, with the finger of scorn.

I had nothing more to keep me at the Hague, and I set out next morning before day-break for Amsterdam. On the way I stopped for dinner and recognized Sir James Walpole, who told me that he had started from Amsterdam the evening before, an hour after giving the countess into her husband's charge. He said that he had got very tired of her, as he had nothing more to get from a woman who gave more than one asked, if one's purse-strings were opened wide enough. I got to Amsterdam about midnight and took up my abode at "The Old Bible." The neighbourhood of Esther had awakened my love for that charming girl, and I was so impatient to see her that I could not sleep.

I went out about ten o'clock and called on M. d'O, who welcomed me in the friendliest manner and reproached me for not having alighted at his house. When he heard that I had given up business he congratulated me on not having removed it into Holland, as I should have been ruined. I did not tell him that I had nearly come to that in France, as I considered such a piece of information would not assist my designs. He complained bitterly of the bad faith of the French Government, which had involved him in considerable losses; and then he asked me to come and see Esther.

I was too impatient to embrace her to stay to be asked twice; I ran to greet her. As soon as she saw me she gave a cry of surprise and delight, and threw herself in my arms, where I received her with fondness equal to her own. I found her grown and improved; she looked lovely. We had scarcely sat down when she told me that she had become as skilled in the cabala as myself.

"It makes my life happy," said she, "for it gives me a power over my father, and assures me that he will never marry me to anyone but the man of my choice."

"I am delighted that you extract the only good that can proceed from this idle science, namely, the power to guide persons devoid of strength of will. But your father must think that I taught you the secret?"

"Yes, he does; and he said, one day, that he would forgive me any sacrifices I might have made to obtain this precious secret from you."

"He goes a little further than we did, my dearest Esther."

"Yes, and I told him that I had gained it from you without any sacrifice, and that now I was a true Pythoness without having to endure the torments of the tripod; and I am sure that the replies you gave were invented by yourself."

"But if that were so how could I have known where the pocket-book was, or whether the ship was safe?"

"You saw the portfolio yourself and threw it where it was discovered, and as for the vessel you spoke at random; but as you are an honest man, confess that you were afraid of the results. I am never so bold as that, and when my father asks me questions of that kind, my replies are more obscure than a sibyl's. I don't wish him to lose confidence in my oracle, nor do I wish him to be able to reproach me with a loss that would injure my own interests."

"If your mistake makes you happy I shall leave you in it. You are really a woman of extraordinary talents—, you are quite unique."

"I don't want your compliments," said she, in a rather vexed manner, "I want a sincere avowal of the truth."

"I don't think I can go as far as that."

At these words, which I pronounced in a serious way, Esther went into a reverie, but I was not going to lose the superiority I had over her, and racked my brains to find some convincing prediction the oracle might make to her, and while I was doing so dinner was announced.

There were four of us at table, and I concluded that the fourth of the party must be in love with Esther, as he kept his eyes on her the whole time. He was her father's favourite clerk, and no doubt her father would have been glad if she had fallen in love with him, but I soon saw that she was not likely to do so. Esther was silent all through dinner, and we did not mention the cabala till the clerk was gone.

"Is it possible," said M. d'O, "for my daughter to obtain the answers of the oracle without your having taught her?"

"I always thought such a thing impossible till to-day," I answered, "but Esther has convinced me that I was mistaken. I can teach the secret to no one without losing it myself, for the oath I swore to the sage who taught me forbids me to impart it to another under pain of forfeiture. But as your daughter has taken no such oath, having acquired it herself, she may be for all I know at perfect liberty to communicate the secret to anyone."

Esther, who was as keen as a razor, took care to say that the same oath that I had taken had been imposed on her by the oracle, and that she could not communicate the cabalistic secret to anyone without the permission of her genius, under pain of losing it herself.

I read her inmost thoughts, and was rejoiced to see that her mind was calmed. She had reason to be grateful to me, whether I had lied or not, for I had given her a power over her father which a father's kindness could not have assured; but she perceived that what I had said about her oracular abilities had been dictated merely by politeness, and she waited till we were alone to make me confess as much.

Her worthy father, who believed entirely in the infallibility of our oracles, had the curiosity to put the same question to both of us, to see if we should agree in the answer. Esther was delighted with the idea, as she suspected that the one answer would flatly contradict the other, and M. d'O having written his question on two sheets of paper gave them to us. Esther went up to her own room for the operation, and I questioned the oracle on the table at which we had had dinner, in the presence of the father. Esther was quick, as she came down before I had extracted from the pyramid the letters which were to compose my reply, but as I knew what to say as soon as I saw her father read the answer she gave him I was not long in finishing what I had to do.

M. d'O——— asked if he should try to get rid of the French securities he held in spite of the loss he would incur by selling out.

Esther's oracle replied,

"You must sow plentifully before you reap. Pluck not up the vine before the season of the vintage, for your vine is planted in a fruitful soil."

Mine ran as follows:—

"If you sell out you will repent, for there will be a new comptroller-general, who will pay all claims before another year has elapsed."

Esther's answer was conceived in the sibylline style, and I admired the readiness of her wit; but mine went right to the point, and the worthy man embraced us joyfully, and, taking his hat and stick, said that since our replies agreed he would run the risk of losing three million francs and make a profit of five or six hundred thousand in the course of the year. His daughter began to recant, and would have warned him against the danger, but he, who was as firm as a Mussulman, kissed her again, saying,

"The oracle is not wont to lie, and even if it does deceive me this time it will only be a fourth part of my fortune that I shall lose."

When Esther and I were alone I began to compliment her, much to her delight, on the cleverness of her answer, the elegance of her style, and her boldness, for she could not be as well acquainted with French affairs as I was.

"I am much obliged to you," said she, "for having confirmed my reply, but confess that you lied to please me."

"I confess, since that will please you, and I will even tell you that you have nothing more to learn."

"You are a cruel man! But how could you reply that there would be another comptroller-general in a year's time, and run the risk of compromising the oracle? I never dare to say things like that; I love the oracle too well to expose it to shame and confusion.".

"That shews that I do not invent the answers; but since the oracle has pronounced it I am willing to bet that Silhouette will be dismissed."

"Your obstinacy drives me to despair, for I shall not rest till I know that I am as much a master of the cabala as you are, and yet you will not confess that you invent the answers yourself. For charity's sake do something to convince me of the contrary."

"I will think it over."

I passed the whole day with this delightful girl, whose amiable disposition and great wealth would have made me a happy man if it were not for my master-passion, the love of independence, and my aversion to make up my mind to live for the rest of my days in Holland.

In the course of my life I have often observed that the happiest hours are often the heralds of misfortune. The very next day my evil genius took me to the Ville de Lyon. This was the inn where Piccolomini and his wife were staying, and I found them there in the midst of a horde of cheats and sharpers, like themselves. As soon as the good people heard my name they rushed forward, some to greet me, and others to have a closer look at me, as if I were some strange wild beast. Amongst those present were a Chevalier de Sabi, who wore the uniform of a Polish major, and protested he had known me at Dresden; a Baron de Wiedan, claiming Bohemia as his fatherland, who greeted me by saying that his friend the Comte St. Germain had arrived at the Etoile d'Orient, and had been enquiring after me; an attenuated-looking bravo who was introduced to me as the Chevalier de la Perine, whom I recognized at the first glance as the fellow called Talvis, who had robbed the Prince-Bishop of Presburg, who had lent me a hundred Louis the same day, and with whom I had fought a duel at Paris. Finally, there was an Italian named Neri, who looked like a blacksmith minus his honesty, and said that he remembered seeing me one evening at the casino. I recollected having seen him at the place where I met the wretched Lucie.

In the midst of this band of cut-purses I saw the so-called wife of the pretended Chevalier de Sabi, a pretty woman from Saxony, who, speaking Italian indifferently well, was paying her addresses to the Countess Piccolomini.

I bit my lips with anger to find myself in such honourable company, but putting a good face on a bad game I greeted everybody politely, and then drawing a roll of a hundred Louis from my pocket I presented them to Master Perine Talvis, telling him I was glad to be able to return them to him with my best thanks.

My politeness did not meet with much of a reception, for the impudent scoundrel answered me, as he pocketed the money, that he remembered having lent it me at Presburg, but he also remembered a more important matter.

"And pray what is that?" said I, in a dry and half-disdainful tone.

"You owe me a revenge at the sword's point, as you know right well. Here is the mark of the gash you gave me seven years ago."

So saying, the wretched little man opened his shirt and shewed the small round scar. This scene, which belonged more to farce than comedy, seemed to have struck all tongues with paralysis.

"Anywhere else than in Holland, where important and delicate business debars me from fighting, I shall be glad to meet you and mark you again, if you still desire to cross swords with me; but while I am here I must beg you not to disturb me. All the same, you may as well know that I never go out without a couple of friends in my pockets, and that if you attack me I shall blow your brains out in self-defence."

"My revenge must be with crossed swords," said he. "However, I will let you finish your business."

"You will do wisely."

Piccolomini, who had been casting a hungry eye upon my hundred louis, proposed immediately afterwards a bank at faro, and began to deal. Prudence would have restrained me from playing in such company, but the dictates of prudence were overcome by my desire to get back the hundred louis which I had given Talvis, so I cut in. I had a run of bad luck and lost a hundred ducats, but, as usual, my loss only excited me. I wished to regain what I had lost, so I stayed to supper, and afterwards, with better luck, won back my money. I was content to stop at this, and to let the money I had paid to Talvis go, so I asked Piccolomini to pay me, which he did with a bill of exchange on an Amsterdam bank drawn by a firm in Middlesburg. At first I made some difficulty in taking it, on the pretext that it would be difficult to negotiate, but he promised to let me have the money next day, and I had to give in.

I made haste to leave this cut-throat place, after refusing to lend Talvis a hundred Louis, which he wanted to borrow of me on the strength of the revenge I owed him. He was in a bad humour, both on this account and because he had lost the hundred Louis I had paid him, and he allowed himself to use abusive language, which I treated with contempt. I went to bed, promising myself never to set foot in such a place again.

The next morning, however, I went out with the intention of calling on Piccolomini to get the bill of exchange cashed, but on my way I happened to go into a coffee-house and to meet Rigerboos, Therese's friend, whose acquaintance the reader has already made. After greeting each other, and talking about Therese, who was now in London and doing well, I skewed him my bill, telling him the circumstances under which I had it. He looked at it closely, and said,

"It's a forgery, and the original from which it was copied was honoured yesterday."

He saw that I could scarcely believe it, and told me to come with him to be convinced of the truth of what he said.

He took me to a merchant of his acquaintance, who skewed me the genuine bill, which he had cashed the day before for an individual who was unknown to him. In my indignation I begged Rigerboos to come with me to Piccolomini, telling him that he might cash it without remark, and that otherwise he would witness what happened.

We arrived at the count's and were politely received, the count asking me to give him the bill and he would send it to the bank to be cashed, but Rigerboos broke in by saying that it would be dishonoured, as it was a mere copy of a bill which had been cashed the evening before.

Piccolomini pretended to be greatly astonished, and said that, "though he could not believe it, he would look into the matter."

"You may look into it when you please," said I, "but in the mean time I should be obliged by your giving me five hundred florins."

"You know me, sir," said he, raising his voice, "I guarantee to pay you, and that ought to be enough."

"No doubt it would be enough, if I chose; but I want my money."

At this his wife came in and began to take her part in the dispute, and on the arrival of the count's man, a very cut-threat, Rigerboos took hold of me by the arm and drew me forcibly away. "Follow me," said he, when we were outside, "and let me see to this business myself." He took me to a fine-looking man, who turned out to be the lieutenant of police, and after he had heard the case he told me to give him the bill of exchange and to say where I was going to dine. I told him I should be at M. d'O 's, and saying that would do he went off. I thanked Rigerboos, and went to Esther, who reproached me tenderly for not having been to see her the evening before. That flattered me, and I thought her a really charming girl.

"I must take care," said I, "not to see you every day, for your eyes have a sway over me that I shall not be able to resist much longer."

"I shall believe as much of that as I choose, but, by-the-by, have you thought of any way of convincing me?"

"What do you want to be convinced about?"

"If it be true that there is in your cabala an intelligence distinct from your own you ought to be able to find some way of proving it to me."

"That is a happy thought; I will think it over."

At that moment her father came in from the Exchange, and we sat dawn to dinner.

We were at dessert when a police official brought me five hundred florins, for which I gave him a receipt.

When he had gone I told my entertainers what had happened the evening before and in the morning, and the fair Esther reproached me for preferring such bad company to her. "By way of punishment," said she, "I hope you will come with me to the theatre this evening, though they are going to give a Dutch play, of which you will not understand a word."

"I shall be near you, and that is enough for me:"

In fact, I did not comprehend a word of the actors' gibberish, and was terribly bored, as Esther preserved a solemn and serious silence the whole time.

As we were coming from the theatre she told me all about the piece with charming grace and wonderful memory; she seemed to wish to give me some pleasure in return for the tedium to which she had condemned me. When we got home we had supper, and that evening, Heaven be thanked! I heard nothing more about the cabala. Before we parted, Esther and her father made me promise to dine with them every day, and to let them know if anything prevented my coming.

Next morning, about eight o'clock, while I was still dressing, I suddenly saw Piccolomini standing before me, and as he had not sent in his name I began to feel suspicious. I rang the bell for my faithful Spaniard, who came in directly.

"I want to speak to you privately," said he, "tell that fellow to go out."

"He can stay," I answered, "he does not know a word of Italian." Le Duc, of course, knew Italian perfectly well.

"Yesterday, about noon," he began, "two men came into my room. They were accompanied by the innkeeper, who served as interpreter. One of the men asked me if I felt inclined to cash there and then a forged bill of exchange, which I had given the night before, and which he held in his hands. As I gave no reply, he told me that there was no time for consideration or argument; I must say yes or no there and then, for such were their instructions from the chief of police. I had no choice in the matter, so I paid the five hundred florins, but I did not get back the bill, and the man told me I could not have it unless I told the police the name of the person from whom I got it, as, in the interests of commerce, the forger must be prosecuted. My reply was that I could not possibly tell them what they wanted, as I had got it of a stranger who had come into my room while I was holding a small bank of faro, to pass the time.

"I told him that after this person (who I had thought introduced by someone in the company) had gone, I found to my surprise that nobody knew him; and I added that if I had been aware of this I would not only have refused the bill but would not have allowed him to play. Thereupon the second policeman said that I had better find out who this person was, or else I should be considered as the forger and prosecuted accordingly; after this threat they went out.

"In the afternoon my wife called on the chief of police and was politely received, but after hearing what she had to say he informed her that she must find out the forger, since M. Casanova's honour might be endangered by the banker taking proceedings against him, in which case he would have to prosecute me.

"You see in what a difficult position we are placed, and I think you ought to try to help us. You have got your money and you are not without friends. Get their influence exerted in the matter, and we shall hear no more about it. Your interests as well as mine are concerned."

"Except as a witness of the fact," I answered, "I can have nothing to do with this affair. You agree that I received the bill from you, since you cashed it; that is enough for me. I should be glad to be of service to you, but I really don't see what I can do. The best advice I can give you is to make a sacrifice of the rascally sharper who gave you the forged bill, and if you can't do that I would counsel you to disappear, and the sooner the better, or else you may come to the galleys, or worse."

He got into a rage at this, and turning his back on me went out, saying I should be sorry for what I had said.

My Spaniard followed him down the stair and came back to tell me that the signor had gone off threatening vengeance, and that, in his opinion, I would do well to be on my guard.

"All right," said I, "say no more about it."

All the same I was really very grateful for his advice, and I gave the matter a good deal of thought.

I dressed myself and went to see Esther, whom I had to convince of the divinity of my oracle, a different task with one whose own wits had told her so much concerning my methods. This was the problem she gave me to solve,

"Your oracle must tell me something which I, and only I, know."

Feeling that it would be impossible to fulfil these conditions, I told her that the oracle might reveal some secret she might not care to have disclosed.

"That is impossible," she answered, "as the secret will be known only to myself."

"But, if the oracle replies I shall know the answer as well as you, and it may be something you would not like me to know."

"There is no such thing, and, even if there were, if the oracle is not your own brain you can always find out anything you want to know."

"But there is some limit to the powers of the oracle."

"You are making idle excuses; either prove that I am mistaken in my ideas or acknowledge that my oracle is as good as yours."

This was pushing me hard, and I was on the point of declaring myself conquered when a bright idea struck me.

In the midst of the dimple which added such a charm to her chin Esther had a little dark mole, garnished with three or four extremely fine hairs. These moles, which we call in Italian 'neo, nei', and which are usually an improvement to the prettiest face, when they occur on the face, the neck, the arms, or the hands, are duplicated on the corresponding parts of the body. I concluded, therefore, that Esther had a mole like that on her chin in a certain place which a virtuous girl does not shew; and innocent as she was I suspected that she herself did not know of this second mole's existence. "I shall astonish her," I said to myself, "and establish my superiority in a manner which will put the idea of having equal

skill to mine out of her head for good." Then with the solemn and far-away look
of a seer I made my pyramid and extracted these words from it,

"Fair and discreet Esther, no one knows that at the entrance of the temple
of love you have a mole precisely like that which appears on your chin."

While I was working at my calculations, Esther was leaning over me and
following every movement. As she really knew as much about the cabala as I did
she did not want it to be explained to her, but translated the numbers into letters
as I wrote them down. As soon as I had extracted all the combinations of
numbers from the pyramid she said, quietly, that as I did not want to know the
answer, she would be much obliged if I would let her translate the cypher.

"With pleasure," I replied. "And I shall do so all the more willingly as I shall
thereby save your delicacy from sharing with me a secret which may or may not
be agreeable. I promise you not to try to find it out. It is enough for me to see
you convinced."

"I shall be convinced when I have verified the truth of the reply."

"Are you persuaded, dearest Esther, that I have had nothing to do with
framing this answer?"

"I shall be quite sure of it if it has spoken the truth, and if so the oracle will
have conquered, for the matter is so secret a one that even I do not know of it.
You need not know yourself, as it is only a trifle which would not interest you;
but it will be enough to convince me that the answers of your oracle are dictated
by an intelligence which has nothing in common with yours."

There was so much candour and frankness in what she said that a feeling of
shame replaced the desire of deceiving her, and I shed some tears, which Esther
could only interpret favourably to me. Nevertheless, they were tears of remorse,
and now, as I write after such a lapse of years, I still regret having deceived one
so worthy of my esteem and love. Even then I reproached myself, but a pitiable
feeling of shame would not let me tell the truth; but I hated myself for thus
leading astray one whose esteem I desired to gain.

In the mean time I was not absolutely sure that I had hit the mark, for in
nature, like everything else, every law has its exceptions, and I might possibly
have dug a pitfall for myself. On the other hand, if I were right, Esther would no
doubt be convinced for the moment, but her belief would speedily disappear if
she chanced to discover that the correspondence of moles on the human body
was a necessary law of nature. In that case I could only anticipate her scorn. But
however I might tremble I had carried the deception too far, and could not draw
back.

I left Esther to call on Rigerboos, whom I thanked for his offices on my
behalf with the chief of the police. He told me that I had nothing to fear from
Piccolomini in Holland, but all the same he advised me not to go about without
pistols. "I am on the eve of embarking for Batavia," said he, "in a vessel which I
have laden with the ruins of my fortune. In the state my affairs are in I thought
this the best plan. I have not insured the cargo, so as not diminish my profits,
which will be considerable if I succeed. If the ship is taken or wrecked I shall
take care not to survive its loss; and after all I shall not lose much."

Poor Riberboos said all this as if he were jesting, but despair had no doubt a good deal to do with his resolve, since it is only in great misery that we despise both life and fortune. The charming Therese Trenti, whom Rigerboos always spoke of as Our Lady, had contributed to his ruin in no small degree. She was then in London, where, by her own account, she was doing well. She had exchanged the name of Trenti for that of Cornelis, or Cornely, which, as I found out afterwards, was Rigerboo's real name. We spent an hour in writing to this curious woman, as we desired to take advantage of the circumstance that a man whom Rigerboos desired to commend to her was shortly going to England. When we had finished we went sleighing on the Amstel, which had been frozen over for several days. This diversion, of which the Dutch are very fond, is, to my thinking, the dullest imaginable, for an objectless journey is no pleasure to me. After we were well frozen we went to eat oysters, with Sillery, to warm ourselves again, and after that we went from one casino to another, not intending to commit any debauchery, but for want of something better to do; but it seemed decreed that whenever I preferred any amusement of this kind to the charms of Esther's society I should come to grief.

I do not know how it happened, but as we were going into one of these casinos Rigerboos called me loudly by my name, and at that instant a woman, such as one usually finds in these places, came forward and began to gaze at me. Although the room was ill enough lighted I saw it was the wretched Lucie, whom I had met a year before without her recognizing me. I turned away, pretending not to know her, for the sight of her was disagreeable to me, but in a sad voice she called me by my name, congratulating me on my prosperity and bewailing her own wretchedness. I saw that I could neither avoid her nor repulse her without inhumanity, so I called to Rigerboos to come upstairs and the girl would divert us by recounting the history of her life.

Strictly speaking, Lucie had not become ugly; one could still see that she had been a beautiful woman; but for all that her appearance inspired me with terror and disgust. Since the days when I had known her at Pasean, nineteen years of misery, profligacy, and shame had made her the most debased, the vilest creature that can be imagined. She told us her story at great length; the pith of it might be expressed in six lines.

The footman who had seduced her had taken her to Trieste to lie in, and the scoundrel lived on the sale of her charms for five or six months, and then a sea captain, who had taken a fancy to her, took her to Zante with the footman, who passed for her husband.

At Zante the footman turned soldier, and deserted the army four years after. She was left alone and continued living on the wages of prostitution for six years; but the goods she had to offer lowering in value, and her customers being of the inferior kind, she set out for England with a young Greek girl, whom an English officer of marines treated as his wife, and whom he abandoned in the streets of London when he got tired of her. After living for two or three years in the vilest haunts in London, Lucie came to Holland, where, not being able to sell her own person any longer, she became a procuress—a natural ending to her career. Lucie was only thirty-three, but she was the wreck of a woman, and women are always as old as they look.

While she told her history she emptied two bottles of Burgundy I had ordered, and which neither I nor my friend touched. Finally, she told us she was now supported by two pretty girls whom she kept, and who had to give her the half of what they got.

Rigerboos asked her, jokingly, if the girls were at the casino.

"No," said she, "they are not here, and shall never come here, for they are ladies of high birth, and their uncle, who looks after their interests, is a Venetian gentleman."

At this I could not keep back my laughter, but Lucie, without losing countenance, told me that she could only repeat the account they had given of themselves, that if we wanted to be convinced we had only to go and see them at a house she rented fifty paces off, and that we need not be afraid of being disturbed if we went, as their uncle lived in a different part of the town.

"Oh, indeed!" said I, "he does not live with his highborn nieces, then?"

"No, he only comes to dinner to hear how business has been going, and to take all the money from them."

"Come along," said Rigerboos, "we will go and see them."

As I was desirous of seeing and addressing the noble Venetian ladies of so honourable a profession, I told Lucie to take us to the house. I knew very well that the girls were impostors, and their gentleman-uncle a blackguard; but the die was cast.

We found them to be young and pretty. Lucie introduced me as a Venetian, and they were beside themselves with joy to have someone to whom they could talk. I found out directly that they came from Padua, not Venice, as they spoke the Paduan dialect, which I knew very well. I told them so, and they confessed it was the truth. I asked the name of their uncle, but they said they could not tell me.

"We can get on without knowing," said Rigerboos, catching hold of the one he liked best. Lucie brought in some ham, oysters, a pie, and a good many bottles of wine, and then left us.

I was not in the humour for wantonness, but Rigerboos was disposed to be merry; his sweetheart was at first inclined to be prudish on his taking liberties with her, but as I began to follow his example the ladies relaxed their severity; we went first to one and then the other, and before long they were both in the state of Eve before she used the fig-leaf.

After passing an hour in these lascivious combats we gave each of the girls four ducats, paid for the provisions we had consumed, and sent six Louis to Lucie. We then left them, I going to bed cross with myself for having engaged in such brutal pleasures.

Next morning I awoke late and in a bad humour, partly from the debauch of the night before (for profligacy depresses as well as degrades the mind) and partly from the thought that I had neglected Esther, who had unquestionably been grieved by my absence. I felt that I must hasten to reassure her, feeling certain that I should find some excuses to make, and that they would be well received. I rang for Le Duc, put on my dressing-gown, and sent him for my coffee. He had scarcely left the room when the door opened and I saw Perine and the fellow named Wiedan, whom I had seen at Piccolomini's, and who styled himself a friend of St. Germain. I was sitting on my bed, putting on my stockings. My apartments consisted of three fine rooms, but they were at the back of the house, and all the noise I could have made would not have been heard. The bell was on the other side of the room; Le Duc would be gone fully ten minutes, and I was in imminent danger of being assassinated without the possibility of self-defence.

The above thoughts flashed through my head with lightning speed, and all that I could do was to keep calm and say,

"Well, gentlemen, what can I do for you?" Wiedan took upon himself to answer me.

"Count Piccolomini has found himself forced to declare that he received the forged bill from us, in order that he may escape from the difficult position in which your denunciation placed him. He has warned us that he is going to do so, and we must escape forthwith if we want to avoid prosecution. We have not a penny; we are desperate men."

"Well, gentlemen, what have I to do with that?"

"Give us four hundred florins immediately; we do not want more, but we must have that much, and now. If you refuse we will take to flight with everything of yours that we can lay our hands on; and our arguments are these."

With this, each man drew a pistol from his pocket and aimed it at my head.

"You need not have recourse to violence," said I, "it can only be fatal to you. Stay, here are a hundred ducats more than you asked. Begone, and I wish you a pleasant journey, but I would not be here when my servant comes back if I were you."

Wiedan took the roll of money with a trembling hand and put it in his pocket without examining it; but Perine came up, and praising my noble generosity, would have put his arms around my neck and kissed me. I repulsed him, but without rudeness, and they went their ways, leaving me very glad to have rid myself of them at so cheap a rate.

As soon as I was out of this snare I rang my bell, not to have them followed but that I might get dressed as quickly as possible. I did not say a word to Le Duc about what had happened, I was silent even to my landlord; and, after I had sent my Spaniard to M. d'O to excuse my dining there that day, I went to the chief of police, but had to wait two hours before I could see him. As soon as the worthy man had heard my account of my misfortune he said he would do his best to catch the two rascals, but he did not conceal from me his fears that it was already too late.

I took the opportunity of telling him of Piccolomini's visit to me, his claims and threats. He thanked me for doing so, and promised to see to it; but he advised me for the future to be on my guard and ready to defend myself in case

I was attacked before he could place my enemies in a place where they could do me no harm.

I hastened home again, as I felt ill. An acid taste in my mouth skewed me how all these shocks had upset me; but I knew what to do. I took a strong glass of lemonade, which made me bring up a good deal of bile, and I then felt much better.

Towards evening I went to see Esther, and found her looking serious and rather vexed; but as soon as she saw how pale I was her face lighted up, and she asked me, in a voice of tenderest interest, if I had been ill. I told her I had been out of sorts, that I had taken some medicine, and that I now felt better.

"You will see my appetite at supper," added I, to calm her fears, "I have had nothing to eat since dinner yesterday."

This was really the truth, as I had only eaten a few oysters with the Paduan girls.

She could scarcely contain her joy at my recovery, and bade me kiss her, with which request I complied gladly, all unworthy though I felt of so great a favour.

"I am going to tell you an important piece of news," said she, "and that is that I am sure that you do not invent the answers to your oracle, or at least that you only do so when you choose. The reply you procured me was wonderful—nay, divine, for it told me of a secret unknown to all, even to myself. You may imagine my surprise when I convinced myself, with no little trouble of the truth of the answer.

"You possess a treasure, your oracle is infallible; but surely it can never lie, and my oracle tells me that you love me. It makes me glad to know that, for you are the man of my heart. But I want you to give me an exemplary proof of your love, and if you do love me you will not hesitate to do so. Stay, read the reply you got me; I am sure you do not know what it says; then I will tell you how you can make me quite happy."

I pretended to read, and kissed the words which declared I loved her. "I am delighted," said I, "that the oracle has convinced you so easily, but I must be excused if I say that I believe you knew as much long ago." She replied, blushing, that if it were possible to chew me the object in question I should not wonder at her ignorance. Then, coming to the proof of my love, she told me that she wanted me to communicate the secret to her. "You love me," said she, "and you ought to make no difficulty in assuring the bliss of a girl who will be your wife, and in your power. My father will agree to our marriage, and when I become your wife I will do whatever you please. We will even go and live in another country if that would add to your happiness. But you must teach me how to obtain the answer to any question without inventing it myself."

I took Esther's hands in mine; she inspired me with the tenderest feelings, and I kissed her hands with respectful fervour, saying, "You know, Esther, dear, that my word is passed at Paris. Certainly, Manon is not to be compared to you; but for all that I gave my promise to her poor mother, and I must keep it."

A sigh escaped from Esther, and her head fell upon her breast: but what could I do? I could not teach her any other way of consulting the oracle than the method she understood as well as I: my superiority over her only consisting in my greater craft and more extensive experience.

Early one morning, two or three days later, a man was announced as wanting to see me. He called himself an officer, but his name was perfectly unknown to me. I sent down to say that I could not see him, and as soon as my Spaniard went out I locked my door. What had happened already had made me suspicious, and I did not care to see any more gentlemen alone. The two scoundrels who had robbed me had eluded all the snares of the police, and Piccolomini was not to be found; but I knew a good many of the gang were still in Amsterdam, and I thought it well to be on my guard.

Some time after, Le Duc came in with a letter written in bad Italian, saying that it had been given him by an officer who was waiting for an answer. I opened it, and recognized the name I had heard a short while ago. The writer said we knew each other, but that he could only give his true name with his own lips, and that he had important information to give me.

I told Le Duc to shew him in, and to stay by the door. I saw enter a well-made man of about forty, dressed in the uniform of an officer of I do not know what army, and bearing on his countenance all the marks of an escaped gallows'-bird.

"What can I do for you, sir?" said I, as soon as he entered.

"Sir, we knew each other at Cerigo, sixteen or seventeen years ago, and I am delighted to have an opportunity of renewing the acquaintance."

I knew that I had spent but a few minutes at Cerigo, on my way to Constantinople, and concluded that my visitor must be one of the unfortunate wretches to whom I gave alms.

"Are you the man," I said, "who told me that you were the son of a Count Peccini, of Padua, although there is no such count in Padua at all?"

"I congratulate you on your excellent memory," said he, coolly, "I am that very individual."

"Well, what do you want with me now?"

"I can't divulge my business in the presence of your servant."

"My servant does not understand Italian, so you can speak out; however, if you like, I will send him away."

I ordered Le Duc to stay in the ante-chamber, and when he had left the room my Paduan count told me that I had been with his nieces, and had treated them as if they were courtezans, and that he was come to demand satisfaction.

I was tired of being cheated, and I took hold of my pistols and pointed them at him, bidding him be gone instantly. Le Duc came in and the third robber took himself off, muttering that "a time would come."

I was placed in a disagreeable position; if I wanted to prosecute, I should have to tell the whole story to the police. I thought of my honour and determined to be silent, and the only person to whom I mentioned the matter was Rigerboos, who not being in the same position as myself took his measures, the result of which was that Lucie had to send her high-born dames about their business. But the wretched woman came to me to say that this misfortune had plunged her into the deepest distress, so I made her a present of a few ducats, and she went away somewhat consoled. I begged her not to call on me again.

Everything I did when I was away from Esther seemed to turn out ill, and I felt that if I wanted to be happy I should do well to keep near her; but my destiny, or rather my inconstancy, drew me away.

Three days afterwards, the villainous Major Sabi called on me to warn me to be on my guard, as, according to his account, a Venetian officer I had insulted and refused to give satisfaction to had vowed vengeance against me.

"Then," said I, "I shall have him arrested as an escaped galley slave, in which character I have given him alms, and for wearing without the right to do so the uniform of an officer, thereby disgracing the whole army. And pray what outrage can I have committed against girls who live in a brothel, and whom I have paid according to their deserts?"

"If what you say is true you are quite right, but this poor devil is in a desperate situation; he wants to leave the country, and does not possess a single florin. I advise you to give him an alms once more, and you will have done with him. Two score florins will not make you any the poorer, and will rid you of a villainous enemy."

"A most villainous one, I think." At last I agreed to give him the forty florins, and I handed them to him in a coffee-house where the major told me I should find him. The reader will see how I met this blackguard four months later.

Now, when all these troubles have been long over and I can think over them calmly, reflecting on the annoyances I experienced at Amsterdam, where I might have been so happy, I am forced to admit that we ourselves are the authors of almost all our woes and griefs, of which we so unreasonably complain. If I could live my life over again, should I be wiser? Perhaps; but then I should not be myself.

M. d'O—— asked me to sup with him at the Burgomasters' Lodge, and this was a great distinction, for, contrary to the rules of Freemasonry, no one but the twenty-four members who compose the lodge is admitted, and these twenty-four masons were the richest men on the Exchange.

"I have told them that you are coming," said M. d'O——, "and to welcome you more honourably the lodge will be opened in French." In short, these gentlemen gave me the most distinguished reception, and I had the fortune to make myself so agreeable to them that I was unanimously chosen an honorary member during the time I should stay at Amsterdam. As we were going away, M. d'O—— told me that I had supped with a company which represented a capital of three hundred millions.

Next day the worthy Dutchman begged me to oblige him by answering a question to which his daughter's oracle had replied in a very obscure manner. Esther encouraged me, and I asked what the question was. It ran as follows:

"I wish to know whether the individual who desires me and my company to transact a matter of the greatest importance is really a friend of the King of France?"

It was not difficult for me to divine that the Comte de St. Germain was meant. M. d'O was not aware that I knew him, and I had not forgotten what M. d'Afri had told me.

"Here's a fine opportunity," thought I, "for covering my oracle with glory, and giving my fair Esther something to think about."

I set to work, and after erecting my pyramid and placing above the four keys the letters O, S, A, D, the better to impose on Esther, I extracted the reply, beginning with the fourth key, D. The oracle ran as follows:

"The friend disavows. The order is signed. They grant. They refuse. All vanishes. Delay."

I pretended to think the reply a very obscure one, but Esther gave a cry of astonishment and declared that it gave a lot of information in an extraordinary style. M. d'O———, in an ecstasy of delight, exclaimed,

"The reply is clear enough for me. The oracle is divine; the word 'delay' is addressed to me. You and my daughter are clever enough in making the oracle speak, but I am more skilled than you in the interpretation thereof. I shall prevent the thing going any further. The project is no less a one than to lend a hundred millions, taking in pledge the diamonds of the French crown. The king wishes the loan to be concluded without the interference of his ministers and without their even knowing anything about it. I entreat you not to mention the matter to anyone."

He then went out.

"Now," said Esther, when we were by ourselves, "I am quite sure that that reply came from another intelligence than yours. In the name of all you hold sacred, tell me the meaning of those four letters, and why you usually omit them."

"I omit them, dearest Esther, because experience has taught me that in ordinary cases they are unnecessary; but while I was making the pyramid the command came to me to set them down, and I thought it well to obey."

"What do they mean?"

"They are the initial letters of the holy names of the cardinal intelligences of the four quarters of the world."

"I may not tell you, but whoever deals with the oracle should know them."

"Ah! do not deceive me; I trust in you, and it would be worse than murder to abuse so simple a faith as mine."

"I am not deceiving you, dearest Esther."

"But if you were to teach me the cabala, you would impart to me these holy names?"

"Certainly, but I cannot reveal them except to my successor. If I violate this command I should lose my knowledge; and this condition is well calculated to insure secrecy, is it not?"

"It is, indeed. Unhappy that I am, your successor will be, of course, Manon."

"No, Manon is not fitted intellectually for such knowledge as this."

"But you should fix on someone, for you are mortal after all. If you like, my father would give you the half of his immense fortune without your marrying me."

"Esther! what is it that you have said? Do you think that to possess you would be a disagreeable condition in my eyes?"

After a happy day—I think I may call it the happiest of my life—I left the too charming Esther, and went home towards the evening.

Three or four days after, M. d'O—— came into Esther's room, where he found us both calculating pyramids. I was teaching her to double, to triple, and to quadruple the cabalistic combinations. M. d'O—— strode into the room in a great hurry, striking his breast in a sort of ecstasy. We were surprised and almost frightened to see him so strangely excited, and rose to meet him, but he running up to us almost forced us to embrace him, which we did willingly.

"But what is the matter, papa dear?" said Esther, "you surprise me more than I can say."

"Sit down beside me, my dear children, and listen to your father and your best friend. I have just received a letter from one of the secretaries of their high mightinesses informing me that the French ambassador has demanded, in the name of the king his master, that the Comte St. Germain should be delivered over, and that the Dutch authorities have answered that His Most Christian Majesty's requests shall be carried out as soon as the person of the count can be secured. In consequence of this the police, knowing that the Comte St. Germain was staying at the Etoile d'Orient, sent to arrest him at midnight, but the bird had flown. The landlord declared that the count had posted off at nightfall, taking the way to Nimeguen. He has been followed, but there are small hopes of catching him up.

"It is not known how he can have discovered that a warrant existed against him, or how he continued to evade arrest."

"It is not known;" went an M. d'O——, laughing, "but everyone guesses that M. Calcoen, the same that wrote to me, let this friend of the French king's know that he would be wanted at midnight, and that if he did not get the key of the fields he would be arrested. He is not so foolish as to despise a piece of advice like that. The Dutch Government has expressed its sorrow to M. d'Afri that his excellence did not demand the arrest of St. Germain sooner, and the ambassador will not be astonished at this reply, as it is like many others given on similar occasions.

"The wisdom of the oracle has been verified, and I congratulate myself on having seized its meaning, for we were on the point of giving him a hundred thousand florins on account, which he said he must have immediately. He gave us in pledge the finest of the crown diamonds, and this we still retain. But we will return it to him an demand, unless it is claimed by the ambassador. I have never seen a finer stone.

"And now, my children, you see what I owe to the oracle. On the Exchange the whole company can do nothing but express their gratitude to me. I am regarded as the most prudent and most farseeing man in Holland. To you, my dear children, I owe this honour, but I wear my peacock's feathers without scruple.

"My dear Casanova, you will dine with us, I hope. After dinner I shall beg you to enquire of your inscrutable intelligence whether we ought to declare ourselves in possession of the splendid diamond, or to observe secrecy till it is reclaimed."

After this discourse papa embraced us once more and left us.

"Sweetheart," said Esther, throwing her arms round my neck, "you have an opportunity for giving me a strong proof of your friendship. It will cost you nothing, but it will cover me with honour and happiness."

"Command me, and it shall be done. You cannot think that I would refuse you a favour which is to cost me nothing, when I should deem myself happy to shed my blood for your sake."

"My father wishes you to tell him after dinner whether it will be better to declare that they have the diamond or to keep silence till it is claimed. When he asks you a second time, tell him to seek the answer of me, and offer to consult the oracle also, in case my answer may be too obscure. Then perform the operation, and I will make my father love me all the better, when he sees that my knowledge is equal to yours."

"Dearest one, would I not do for thee a task a thousand times more difficult than this to prove my love and my devotion? Let us set to work. Do you write the question, set up the pyramids, and inscribe with your own hand the all-powerful initials. Good. Now begin to extract the answer by means of the divine key. Never was a cleverer pupil!"

When all this had been done, I suggested the additions and subtractions I wanted made, and she was quite astonished to read the following reply: "Silence necessary. Without silence, general derision. Diamond valueless; mere paste."

I thought she would have gone wild with delight. She laughed and laughed again.

"What an amazing reply!" said she. "The diamond is false, and it is I who am about to reveal their folly to them. I shall inform my father of this important secret. It is too much, it overwhelms me; I can scarcely contain myself for joy! How much I owe you, you wonderful and delightful man! They will verify the truth of the oracle immediately, and when it is found that the famous diamond is but glittering paste the company will adore my father, for it will feel that but for him it would have been covered with shame, by avowing itself the dupe of a sharper. Will you leave the pyramid with me?"

"Certainly; but it will not teach you anything you do not know." The father came in again and we had dinner, and after the dessert, when the worthy d 'O—— learnt from his daughter's oracle that the stone was false, the scene became a truly comical one. He burst into exclamations of astonishment, declared the thing impossible, incredible, and at last begged me to ask the same question, as he was quite sure that his daughter was mistaken, or rather that the oracle was deluding her.

I set to work, and was not long in obtaining my answer. When he saw that it was to the same effect as Esther's, though differently expressed, he had no longer any doubts as to his daughter's skill, and hastened to go and test the pretended diamond, and to advise his associates to say nothing about the matter after they had received proofs of the worthlessness of the stone. This advice was, as it happened, useless; for though the persons concerned said nothing, everybody knew about it, and people said, with their usual malice, that the dupes had been duped most thoroughly, and that St. Germain had pocketed the hundred thousand florins; but this was not the case.

Esther was very proud of her success, but instead of being satisfied with what she had done, she desired more fervently every day to possess the science in its entirety, as she supposed I possessed it.

It soon became known that St. Germain had gone by Emden and had embarked for England, where he had arrived in safety. In due time we shall hear some further details concerning this celebrated impostor; and in the meanwhile I must relate a catastrophe of another kind, which was near to have made me die the death of a fool.

It was Christmas Day. I had got up early in the morning in better spirits than usual. The old women tell you that always presages misfortune, but I was as far then as I am now from making my happiness into an omen of grief. But this time chance made the foolish belief of good effect. I received a letter and a large packet from Paris; they came from Manon. I opened the letter and I thought I should have died of grief when I read,—

"Be wise, and receive the news I give you calmly. The packet contains your portrait and all the letters you have written to me. Return me my portrait, and if you have kept my letters be kind enough to burn them. I rely on your honour. Think of me no more. Duty bids me do all I can to forget you, for at this hour to-morrow I shall become the wife of M. Blondel of the Royal Academy, architect to the king. Please do not seem as if you knew me if we chance to meet on your return to Paris."

This letter struck me dumb with astonishment, and for more than two hours after I read it I was, as it were, bereft of my senses. I sent word to M. d'O——that, not feeling well, I was going to keep my room all day. When I felt a little better I opened the packet. The first thing to fall out was my portrait. I looked at it, and such was the perturbation of my mind, that, though the miniature really represented me as of a cheerful and animated expression, I thought I beheld a dreadful and a threatening visage. I went to my desk and wrote and tore up a score of letters in which I overwhelmed the faithless one with threats and reproaches.

I could bear no more; the forces of nature were exhausted, and I was obliged to lie down and take a little broth, and court that sleep which refused to come. A thousand designs came to my disordered imagination. I rejected them one by one, only to devise new ones. I would slay this Blondel, who had carried off a woman who was mine and mine only; who was all but my wife. Her treachery should be punished by her losing the object for whom she had deserted me. I accused her father, I cursed her brother for having left me in ignorance of the insult which had so traitorously been put upon me.

I spent the day and night in these delirious thoughts, and in the morning, feeling worse than ever, I sent to M. d'O—— to say that I could not possibly leave my room. Then I began to read and re-read the letters I had written to Manon, calling upon her name in a sort of frenzy; and again set myself to write to her without finishing a single letter. The emptiness of my stomach and the shock I had undergone began to stupefy me, and for a few moments I forgot my anguish only to re-awaken to acuter pains soon after.

About three o'clock, the worthy M. d'O—— came to invite me to go with him to the Hague, where the chief masons of Holland met on the day following to keep the Feast of St. John, but when he saw my condition he did not press me to come.

"What is the matter with you, my dear Casanova?" said he.

"I have had a great grief, but let us say no more about it."

He begged me to come and see Esther, and left me looking almost as downcast as I was. However, the next morning Esther anticipated my visit, for at nine o'clock she and her governess came into the room. The sight of her did me good. She was astonished to see me so undone and cast down, and asked me what was the grief of which I had spoken to her father, and which had proved too strong for my philosophy.

"Sit down beside me, Esther dear, and allow me to make a mystery of what has affected me so grievously. Time, the mighty healer, and still more your company, will effect a cure which I should in vain seek by appealing to my reason. Whilst we talk of other things I shall not feel the misfortune which gnaws at my heart."

"Well, get up, dress yourself, and come and spend the day with me, and I will do my best to make you forget your sorrow."

"I feel very weak; for the last three days I have only taken a little broth and chocolate."

At these words her face fell, and she began to weep.

After a moment's silence she went to my desk, took a pen, and wrote a few lines, which she brought to me. They were,—

"Dear, if a large sum of money, beyond what my father owes you, can remove or even soothe your grief I can be your doctor, and you ought to know that your accepting my treatment would make me happy."

I took her hands and kissed them affectionately, saying,—

"No, dear Esther, generous Esther, it is not money I want, for if I did I would ask you and your father as a friend: what I want, and what no one can give me, is a resolute mind, and determination to act for the best."

"Ask advice of your oracle."

I could not help laughing.

"Why do you laugh?" said she, "if I am not mistaken, the oracle must know a remedy for your woes."

"I laughed, dearest, because I felt inclined to tell you to consult the oracle this time. As for me I will have nothing to do with it, lest the cure be worse than the disease."

"But you need not follow your advice unless you like it."

"No, one is free to act as one thinks fit; but not to follow the advice of the oracle would be a contempt of the intelligence which directs it."

Esther could say no more, and stood silent for several minutes, and then said that if I like she would stay with me for the rest of the day. The joy which illumined my countenance was manifest, and I said that if she would stay to dinner I would get up, and no doubt her presence would give me an appetite. "Ah!" said she, "I will make you the dish you are so fond of." She ordered the sedan-chairs to be sent back, and went to my landlady to order an appetising repast, and to procure the chafing-dish and the spirits of wine she required for her own cooking.

Esther was an angel, a treasure, who consented to become mine if I would communicate to her a science which did not exist. I felt that I was looking forward to spending a happy day; this shewed me that I could forget Manon, and I was delighted with the idea. I got out of bed, and when Esther came back and found me on my feet she gave a skip of pleasure. "Now," said she, "you must oblige me by dressing, and doing your hair as if you were going to a ball."

"That," I answered, "is a funny idea, but as it pleases you it pleases me."

I rang for Le Duc, and told him I wanted to have my hair done, and to be dressed as if I were going to a ball. "Choose the dress that suits me best."

"No," said Esther, "I will choose it myself."

Le Duc opened my trunk, and leaving her to rummage in it he came to shave me, and to do my hair. Esther, delighted with her task, called in the assistance of her governess. She put on my bed a lace shirt, and the suit she found most to her taste. Then coming close, as if to see whether Le Duc was dressing my hair properly, she said,

"A little broth would do you good; send for a dish, it will give you an appetite for dinner."

I thought her advice dictated by the tenderest care, and I determined to benefit by it. So great was the influence of this charming girl over me, that, little by little, instead of loving Manon, I hated her. That gave me courage, and completed my cure. At the present time I can see that Manon was very wise in accepting Blondel's offer, and that my love for self and not my love for her was wounded.

I was in my servant's hands, my face turned away towards the fire, so that I could not see Esther, but only divert myself with the idea that she was inspecting my belongings, when all at once she presented herself with a melancholy air, holding Mamon's fatal letter in her hand.

"Am I to blame," said she, timidly, "for having discovered the cause of your sorrow?"

I felt rather taken aback, but looking kindly at her, I said,

"No, no, my dear Esther; pity your friend, and say no more about it."

"Then I may read all the letters?"

"Yes, dearest, if it will amuse you."

All the letters of the faithless Manon Baletti to me, with mine to her, were together on my table. I pointed them out to Esther, who begun to read them quite eagerly.

When I was dressed, as if for some Court holiday, Le Duc went out and left us by ourselves, for the worthy governess, who was working at her lace by the window, looked at her lace, and nothing else. Esther said that nothing had ever amused her so much as those letters.

"Those cursed epistles, which please you so well, will be the death of me."

"Death? Oh, no! I will cure you, I hope."

"I hope so, too; but after dinner you must help me to burn them all from first to last."

"Burn them! No; make me a present of them. I promise to keep them carefully all my days."

"They are yours, Esther. I will send them to you to-morrow."

These letters were more than two hundred in number, and the shortest were four pages in length. She was enchanted to find herself the possessor of the letters, and she said she would make them into a parcel and take them away herself.

"Shall you send back the portrait to your faithless mistress?" said she.

"I don't know what to do with it."

"Send it back to her; she is not worthy of your honouring her by keeping it. I am sure that your oracle would give you the same advice. Where is the portrait? Will you shew it me?"

I had the portrait in the interior of a gold snuff-box, but I had never shewn it to Esther for fear she should think Manon handsomer than herself, and conclude that I only shewd it her out of vanity; but as she now asked to see it I opened the box where it was and gave it her.

Any other woman besides Esther would have pronounced Manon downright ugly, or have endeavored at the least to find some fault with her, but Esther pronounced her to be very beautiful, and only said it was a great pity so fair a body contained so vile a soul.

The sight of Manon's portrait made Esther ask to see all the other portraits which Madame Manzoni had sent me from Venice. There were naked figures amongst them, but Esther was too pure a spirit to put on the hateful affectations of the prude, to whom everything natural is an abomination. O-Murphy pleased her very much, and her history, which I related, struck her as very curious. The portrait of the fair nun, M—— M——, first in the habit of her order and afterwards naked, made her laugh, but I would not tell Esther her story, in spite of the lively desire she displayed to hear it.

At dinner-time a delicate repast was brought to us, and we spent two delightful hours in the pleasures of a conversation and the table. I seemed to have passed from death to life, and Esther was delighted to have been my physician. Before we rose from table I had declared my intention of sending

Manon's portrait to her husband on the day following, but her good nature found a way of dissuading me from doing so without much difficulty.

Some time after, while we were talking in front of the fire, she took a piece of paper, set up the pyramids, and inscribed the four keys O, S, A, D. She asked if I should send the portrait to the husband, or whether it would not be more generous to return it to the faithless Manon. Whilst she was calculating she said over and over again, with a smile, "I have not made up the answer." I pretend to believe her, and we laughed like two augurs meeting each other alone. At last the reply came that I ought to return the portrait, but to the giver, since to send it to the husband would be an act unworthy of a man of honour.

I praised the wisdom of the oracle, and kissed the Pythoness a score of times, promising that the cabala should be obeyed implicitly, adding that she had no need of being taught the science since she knew it as well as the inventor.

I spoke the truth, but Esther laughed, and, fearing lest I should really think so, took pains to assure me of the contrary.

It is thus that love takes his pleasure, thus his growth increases, and thus that he so soon becomes a giant in strength.

"Shall I be impertinent," said Esther, "if I ask you where your portrait is? Manon says in her letter that she is sending it back; but I don't see it anywhere."

"In my first paroxysm of rage, I threw it down; I don't know in what direction. What was thus despised by her cannot be of much value to me."

"Let us look for it; I should like to see it."

We soon found it on my table, in the midst of a of books; Esther said it was a speaking likeness.

"I would give it you if such a present were worthy of you."

"Ah! you could not give me anything I would value more."

"Will you deign to accept it, Esther, though it has been possessed by another?"

"It will be all the dearer to me."

At last she had to leave me, after a day which might be called delightful if happiness consists of calm and mutual joys without the tumultuous raptures of passion. She went away at ten, after I had promised to spend the whole of the next day with her.

After an unbroken sleep of nine hours' duration I got up refreshed and feeling once more in perfect health, and I went to see Esther immediately. I found she was still abed and asleep, but her governess went and roused her in spite of my request that her repose should be respected.

She received me with a sweet smile as she sat up in bed, and shewd me my voluminous correspondence with Manon on her night-table, saying that she had been reading it till two o'clock in the morning.

Her appearance was ravishing. A pretty cambric night-cap, tied with a light-blue ribbon and ornamented with lace, set off the beauties of her face; and a light shawl of Indian muslin, which she had hastily thrown on, veiled rather than concealed her snowy breast, which would have shamed the works of Praxiteles. She allowed me to take a hundred kisses on her rosy lips—ardent kisses which the sight of such charms made yet more ardent; but her hands forbade my approach to those two spheres I so longed to touch.

I sat down by her and told her that her charms of body and mind would make a man forget all the Manons that ever were.

"Is your Marion fair to see all over?" said she.

"I really can't say, for, not being her husband, I never had an opportunity of investigating the matter."

"Your discretion is worthy of all praise," she said, with a smile, "such conduct becomes a man of delicate feeling."

"I was told by her nurse that she was perfect in all respects, and that no mote or blemish relieved the pure whiteness of her skin."

"You must have a different notion of me?"

"Yes, Esther, as the oracle revealed to me the great secret you desired to know. Nevertheless, I should find you perfect in all your parts."

Hereupon I was guilty of a stupidity which turned to my confusion. I said,

"If I became your husband, I could easily refrain from touching you there."

"I suppose you think," said she, blushing, and evidently a little vexed, "that if you touched it your desires might be lessened?"

This question probed me to the core and covered me with shame. I burst into tears, and begged her pardon in so truly repentant a voice that sympathy made her mingle her tears with mine. The incident only increased our intimacy, for, as I kissed her tears away, the same desires consumed us, and if the voice of prudence had not intervened, doubtless all would have been over. As it was, we had but a foretaste and an earnest of that bliss which it was in our power to procure. Three hours seemed to us as many minutes. She begged me to go into her sitting-room while she dressed, and we then went down and dined with the wretched secretary, who adored her, whom she did not love, and who must have borne small love to me, seeing how high I stood in her graces.

We passed the rest of the day together in that confidential talk which is usual when the foundations of the most intimate friendship have been laid between two persons of opposite sex, who believe themselves created for each other. Our flames burnt as brightly, but with more restraint, in the dining-room as in the bedroom. In the very air of the bedroom of a woman one loves there is something so balmy and voluptuous that the lover, asked to choose between this garden of delights and Paradise, would not for one moment hesitate in his choice.

We parted with hearts full of happiness, saying to each other, "Till tomorrow."

I was truly in love with Esther, for my sentiment for her was composed of sweeter, calmer, and more lively feelings than mere sensual love, which is ever stormy and violent. I felt sure I could persuade her to marry me without my first teaching her what could not be taught. I was sorry I had not let her think herself as clever as myself in the cabala, and I feared it would be impossible to undeceive her without exciting her to anger, which would cast out love.

Nevertheless, Esther was the only woman who would make me forget Manon, whom I began to think unworthy of all I had proposed doing for her.

M. d'O—— came back and I went to dine with him. He was pleased to hear that his daughter had effected a complete cure by spending a day with me. When we were alone he told me that he had heard at the Hague that the Comte St. Germain had the art of making diamonds which only differed from the real ones in weight, and which, according to him, would make his fortune. M. d'O—— would have been amused if I had told him all I knew about this charlatan.

Next day I took Esther to the concert, and while we were there she told me that on the day following she would not leave her room, so that we could talk about getting married without fear of interruption. This was the last day of the year 1759.

CHAPTER XI

I Undeceive Esther—I set out for Germany—Adventure Near Cologne—The Burgomaster's Wife; My Conquest of Her—Ball at Bonn—Welcome From the Elector of Cologne—Breakfast at Bruhl—First Intimacy—I sup Without Being Asked at General Kettler's I am Happy—I Leave Cologne—The Toscani —The Jewel—My Arrival at Stuttgart

The appointment which Esther had made with me would probably have serious results; and I felt it due to my honour not to deceive her any longer, even were it to cost me my happiness; however, I had some hope that all would turn out well.

I found her in bed, and she told me that she intended to stop there throughout the day. I approved, for in bed I thought her ravishing.

"We will set to work," said she; and her governess set a little table by her bed, and she gave me a piece of paper covered with questions tending to convince me that before I married her I should communicate to her my supposed science. All these questions were artfully conceived, all were so worded as to force the oracle to order me to satisfy her, or to definitely forbid my doing so. I saw the snare, and all my thoughts were how to avoid it, though I pretended to be merely considering the questions. I could not make the oracle speak to please Esther, and I could still less make it pronounce a positive prohibition, as I feared that she would resent such an answer bitterly and revenge herself on me. Nevertheless, I had to assume an indifferent air, and I got myself out of the difficulty by equivocal answers, till the good-humoured papa came to summon me to dinner.

He allowed his daughter to stay in bed on the condition that she was to do no more work, as he was afraid that by applying herself so intently she would increase her headache. She promised, much to my delight, that he should be obeyed, but on my return from dinner I found her asleep, and sitting at her bedside I let her sleep on.

When she awoke she said she would like to read a little; and as if by inspiration, I chanced to take up Coiardeau's 'Heroides', and we inflamed each other by reading the letters of Heloise and Abelard. The ardours thus aroused passed into our talk and we began to discuss the secret which the oracle had revealed.

"But, Esther dear," said I, "did not the oracle reveal a circumstance of which you knew perfectly well before?"

"No, sweetheart, the secret was perfectly unknown to me and would have continued unknown."

"Then you have never been curious enough to inspect your own person?"

"However curious I may have been, nature placed that mole in such a position as to escape any but the most minute search."

"You have never felt it, then?"

"It is too small to be felt."

"I don't believe it."

She allowed my hand to wander indiscreetly, and my happy fingers felt all the precincts of the temple of love. This was enough to fire the chastest disposition. I could not find the object of my research, and, not wishing to stop short at so vain an enjoyment, I was allowed to convince myself with my eyes that it actually existed. There, however, her concessions stopped short, and I had to content myself by kissing again and again all those parts which modesty no longer denied to my gaze.

Satiated with bliss, though I had not attained to the utmost of enjoyment, which she wisely denied me, after two hours had been devoted to those pastimes which lead to nothing, I resolved to tell her the whole truth and to shew her how I had abused her trust in me, though I feared that her anger would be roused.

Esther, who had a large share of intelligence (indeed if she had had less I could not have deceived her so well), listened to me without interrupting me and without any signs of anger or astonishment. At last, when I had brought my long and sincere confession to an end, she said,

"I know your love for me is as great as mine for you; and if I am certain that what you have just said cannot possibly be true, I am forced to conclude that if you do not communicate to me all the secrets of your science it is because to do so is not in your power. Let us love one another till death, and say no more about this matter."

After a moment's silence, she went on,—

"If love has taken away from you the courage of sincerity I forgive you, but I am sorry for you. You have given me too positive proof of the reality of your science to be able to shake my belief. You could never have found out a thing of which I myself was ignorant, and of which no mortal man could know."

"And if I shew you, Esther dear, that I knew you had this mole, that I had good reasons for supposing you to be ignorant of it, will your belief be shaken then?"

"You knew it? How could you have seen it? It's incredible!"

"I will tell you all."

I then explained to her the theory of the correspondence of moles on the various parts of the human body, and to convince her I ended by saying that her governess who had a large mark on her right cheek ought to have one very like it on her left thigh. At this she burst into laughter, and said, "I will find out, but after all you have told me I can only admire you the more for knowing what no one else does."

"Do you really think, Esther, that I am the sole possessor of this science? Undeceive yourself. All who have studied anatomy, physiology, and astrology, know of it."

"Then I beg you to get me, by to-morrow—yes, tomorrow—all the books which will teach me secrets of that nature. I long to be able to astonish the ignorant with my cabala, which I see requires a mixture of knowledge and imposition. I wish to devote myself entirely to this study. We can love each other to the death, but we can do that without getting married."

I re-entered my lodging in a peaceful and happy frame of mind; an enormous weight seemed taken off my spirits. Next morning I purchased such volumes as I judged would instruct and amuse her at the same time, and went to present them to her. She was most pleased with my Conis, as she found in it the character of truth. As she wished to shine by her answers through the oracle it was necessary for her to have an extensive knowledge of science, and I put her on the way.

About that time I conceived the idea of making a short tour in Germany before returning to Paris, and Esther encouraged me to do so, after I had promised that she should see me again before the end of the year. This promise was sincerely, given; and though from that day to this I have not beheld the face of that charming and remarkable woman, I cannot reproach myself with having deceived her wilfully, for subsequent events prevented me from keeping my word.

I wrote to M. d'Afri requesting him to procure me a passport through the empire, where the French and other belligerent powers were then campaigning. He answered very politely that I had no need of a passport, but that if I wished to have one he would send it me forthwith. I was content with this letter and put it among my papers, and at Cologne it got me a better reception than all the passports in the world.

I made M. d'O—— the depositary of the various moneys I had in different banking houses, and the worthy man, who was a true friend to me, gave me a bill of exchange on a dozen of the chief houses in Germany.

When my affairs were all in order I started in my post-chaise, with the sum of nearly a hundred thousand Dutch florins to my credit, some valuable jewels, and a well-stocked wardrobe. I sent my Swiss servant back to Paris, keeping only my faithful Spaniard, who on this occasion travelled with me, seated behind my chaise.

Thus ends the history of my second visit to Holland, where I did nothing to augment my fortune. I had some unpleasant experiences there for which I had my own imprudence to thank, but after the lapse of so many years I feel that these mishaps were more than compensated by the charms of Esther's society.

I only stopped one day at Utrecht, and two days after I reached Cologne at noon, without accident, but not without danger, for at a distance of half a league from the town five deserters, three on the right hand and two on the left, levelled their pistols at me, with the words, "Your money or your life." However, I covered the postillion with my own pistol, threatening to fire if he did not drive on, and the robbers discharged their weapons at the carriage, not having enough spirit to shoot the postillion.

If I had been like the English, who carry a light purse for the benefit of the highwaymen, I would have thrown it to these poor wretches; but, as it was, I risked my life rather than be robbed. My Spaniard was quite astonished not to have been struck by any of the balls which whistled past his ears.

The French were in winter quarters at Cologne, and I put up at the "Soleil d'Or." As I was going in, the first person I met was the Comte de Lastic, Madame d'Urfe's nephew, who greeted me with the utmost politeness, and offered to take me to M. de Torci, who was in command. I accepted, and this gentleman was quite satisfied with the letter M. d'Afri had written me. I told him what had happened to me as I was coming into Cologne, and he congratulated me on the happy issue of the affair, but with a soldier's freedom blamed the use I had made of my courage.

"You played high," said he, "to save your money, but you might have lost a limb, and nothing would have made up for that."

I answered that to make light of a danger often diminished it. We laughed at this, and he said that if I was going to make any stay in Cologne I should probably have the pleasure of seeing the highwaymen hanged.

"I intend to go to-morrow," said I, "and if anything could keep me at Cologne it would certainly not be the prospect of being present at an execution, as such sights are not at all to my taste."

I had to accept M. de Lastic's invitation to dinner, and he persuaded me to go with himself and his friend, M. de Flavacour, an officer of high rank, and an agreeable man, to the theatre. As I felt sure that I should be introduced to ladies, and wished to make something of a figure, I spent an hour in dressing.

I found myself in a box opposite to a pretty woman, who looked at me again and again through her opera-glass. That was enough to rouse my curiosity, and I begged M. de Lastic to introduce me; which he did with the best grace imaginable. He first presented me to Count Kettler, lieutenant-general in the Austrian army, and on the general staff of the French army—just as the French General Montacet was on the staff of the Austrian army. I was then presented to the lady whose beauty had attracted my attention the moment I entered my box. She greeted me graciously, and asked me questions about Paris and Brussels, where she had been educated, without appearing to pay any attention to my replies, but gazing at my lace and jewellery.

While we were talking of indifferent matters, like new acquaintances, she suddenly but politely asked me if I intended to make a long stay in Cologne.

"I think of crossing the Rhine to-morrow," I answered, "and shall probably dine at Bonn."

This reply, which was given as indifferently as her question, appeared to vex her; and I thought her vexation a good omen. General Kettler then rose, saying,—

"I am sure, sir, that this lady will persuade you to delay your departure—at least, I hope so, that I may bane the pleasure of seeing more of your company."

I bowed and he went out with Lastic, leaving me alone with this ravishing beauty. She was the burgomaster's wife, and the general was nearly always with her.

"Is the count right," said she, pleasantly, "in attributing such power to me?"

"I think so, indeed," I answered, "but he may possibly be wrong in thinking you care to exercise it."

"Very good! We must catch him, then, if only as the punishment of his indiscretion. Stay."

I was so astonished at this speech that I looked quite foolish and had to collect my senses. I thought the word indiscretion sublime, punishment exquisite, and catching admirable; and still more the idea of catching him by means of me. I thought it would be a mistake to enquire any further, and putting on an expression of resignation and gratitude I lowered my lips and kissed her hand with a mixture of respect and sentiment, which, without exactly imparting my feelings for her, let her know that they might be softened without much difficulty.

"Then you will stay, sir! It is really very kind of you, for if you went off to-morrow people might say that you only came here to shew your disdain for us. Tomorrow the general gives a ball, and I hope you will be one of the party."

"Can I hope to dance with you all the evening?"

"I promise to dance with nobody but you, till you get tired of me."

"Then we shall dance together through all the ball."

"Where did you get that pomade which perfumes the air? I smelt it as soon as you came into the box."

"It came from Florence, and if you do not like it you shall not be troubled with it any more."

"Oh! but I do like it. I should like some of it myself."

"And I shall be only too happy if you will permit me to send you a little to-morrow."

Just then the door of the box opened and the entrance of the general prevented her from replying. I was just going, when the count said:

"I am sure madame has prevailed on you to stay, and to come to my ball and supper to-morrow?"

"She has led me to anticipate that you would do me that honour, and she promises to dance the quadrilles with me. How can one resist entreaty from such lips?"

"Quite so, and I am obliged to her for having kept you with us. I hope to see you to-morrow."

I went out of the box in love, and almost happy in anticipation. The pomade was a present from Esther, and it was the first time I had used it. The box contained twenty-four pots of beautiful china. The next day I put twelve into an elegant casket, which I wrapped up in oil-cloth and sent to her without a note.

I spent the morning by going over Cologne with a guide; I visited all the marvels of the place, and laughed with all my heart to see the horse Bayard, of whom Ariosto has sung, ridden by the four sons of Aimon, or Amone, father of Bradamante the Invincible, and Ricciardetto the Fortunate.

I dined with M. de Castries, and everybody was surprised that the general had asked me himself to the ball, as his jealousy was known, while the lady was supposed only to suffer his attentions through a feeling of vanity. The dear general was well advanced in years, far from good-looking, and as his mental qualities by no means compensated for his lack of physical ones he was by no means an object to inspire love. In spite of his jealousy, he had to appear pleased that I sat next the fair at supper, and that I spent the night in dancing with her or talking to her. It was a happy night for me, and I re-entered my lodging no longer thinking of leaving Cologne. In a moment of ecstasy, emboldened by the turn the conversation had taken, I had dared to tell her that if she would meet me alone I would stay in Cologne till the end of the carnival. "And what would you say," she asked, "if I give my promise, and do not keep it?"

"I should bemoan my lot, without accusing you; I should say to myself that you had found it impossible to keep your word."

"You are very good; you must stay with us."

The day after the ball I went to pay her my first visit. She made me welcome, and introduced me to her worthy husband, who, though neither young nor handsome, was extremely good-hearted. After I had been there an hour, we heard the general's carriage coming, and she said to me:

"If he asks you whether you are going to the Elector's ball at Bonn, say yes!"

The general came in, and after the usual compliments had been passed I withdrew.

I did not know by whom the ball was to be given, or when it was to take place, but scenting pleasure from afar off I hastened to make enquiries about it, and heard that all the good families in Cologne were going. It was a masked ball, and consequently open to all. I decided then that I would go; indeed I concluded that I had had orders to that effect, and at all events my lady would be there, and I might hope for a happy meeting with her. But as I wished to keep up my incognito as much as possible, I resolved to reply to all who asked me that important business would prevent my being present.

It fell out that the general asked me this very question in the presence of the lady, and without regard to the orders I had received from her I replied that my health would forbid my having that pleasure.

"You are very wise, sir," said the general, "all the pleasures on earth should be sacrificed when it is a question of one's health."

I think so, too, now, but I thought differently then.

On the day of the ball, towards the evening, I set out in a post-chaise, disguised so that not a soul in Cologne could have recognized me, and provided with a box containing two dominoes; and on my arrival at Bonn I took a room and put on one of the dominoes, locking up the other in the box; and I then had myself carried to the ball in a sedan-chair.

I got in easily and unperceived, and recognized all the ladies of Cologne without their masks, and my mistress sitting at a faro-table risking a ducat. I was glad to see in the banker, Count Verita of Verona, whom I had known in Bavaria. He was in the Elector's service. His small bank did not contain more than five or six ducats, and the punters, men and women, were not more than twelve. I took up a position by my mistress, and the banker asked me to cut. I excused myself with a gesture, and my neighbour cut without being asked. I put ten ducats on a single card, and lost four times running; I played at the second deal, and experienced the same fate. At the third deal nobody would cut, and the general, who was standing by but not playing, agreed to do so. I fancied his cutting would be lucky, and I put fifty ducats on one card. I won. I went 'paroli', and at the second deal I broke the bank. Everybody was curious about me; I was stared at and followed, but seizing a favourable opportunity I made my escape.

I went to my room, took out my money, changed my costume, and returned to the ball. I saw the table occupied by new gamesters, and another banker who seemed to have a good deal of gold, but not caring to play any more I had not brought much money with me. I mingled in all the groups in the ballroom, and on all sides I heard expressions of curiosity about the mask who broke the first bank.

I did not care to satisfy the general curiosity, but made my way from one side of the room to the other till I found the object of my search talking to Count Verita, and as I drew near I found out that they were talking of me. The count was saying that the Elector had been asking who had broken the bank, and that General Kettler had expressed his opinion that it was a Venetian who had been in Cologne for the last week. My mistress answered that she did not think I was there, as she had heard me say that the state of my health would keep me at home.

"I know Casanova," said the count, "and if he be at Bonn the Elector shall hear of it, and he shan't go off without my seeing him." I saw that I might easily be discovered after the ball, but I defied the keenest eyes to penetrate beneath my present disguise. I should have, no doubt, remained unknown, but when the quadrilles were being arranged I took my place in one, without reflecting that I should have to take off my mask.

As soon as my mistress saw me she told me she had been deceived, as she would have wagered that I was the masker who broke Count Verita's bank. I told her I had only just come.

At the end of the dance the count spied me out and said, "My dear fellow-countryman, I am sure you are the man who broke my bank; I congratulate you."

"I should congratulate myself if I were the fortunate individual."

"I am sure that it was you."

I left him laughing, and after having taken some refreshments I continued dancing. Two hours afterwards the count saw me again and said,—

"You changed your domino in such a room, in such a house. The Elector knows all about it, and as a punishment for this deceit he has ordered me to tell you that you are not to leave Bonn to-morrow."

"Is he going to arrest me, then?"

"Why not, if you refuse his invitation to dinner tomorrow?"

"Tell his highness that his commands shall be obeyed. Will you present me to him now?"

"He has left the ball, but wait on me to-morrow at noon." So saying, he gave me his hand and went away.

I took care to keep the appointment on the day following, but when I was presented I was in some confusion, as the Elector was surrounded by five or six courtiers, and never having seen him I looked in vain for an ecclesiastic. He saw my embarrassment and hastened to put an end to it, saying, in bad Venetian, "I am wearing the costume of Grand Master of the Teutonic Order to-day." In spite of his costume I made the usual genuflexion, and when I would have kissed his hand he would not allow it, but shook mine in an affectionate manner. "I was at Venice," said he, "when you were under the Leads, and my nephew, the Elector of Bavaria, told me that after your fortunate escape you stayed some time at Munich; if you had come to Cologne I should have kept you. I hope that after dinner you will be kind enough to tell us the story of your escape, that you will stay to supper, and will join in a little masquerade with which we propose to amuse ourselves."

I promised to tell my tale if he thought it would not weary him, warning him that it would take two hours. "One could never have too much of a good thing," he was kind enough to say; and I made him laugh by my account of the conversation between the Duc de Choiseul and myself.

At dinner the prince spoke to me in Venetian, and was pleased to be most gracious towards me. He was a man of a jovial and easy-going disposition, and with his look of health one would not have prophesied so soon an end as came to him. He died the year following.

As soon as we rose from table he begged me to begin my story, and for two hours I had the pleasure of keeping this most brilliant company amused.

My readers know the history; its interest lies in the dramatic nature of the details, but it is impossible to communicate the fire of a well-told story to an account in writing.

The Elector's little bail was very pleasant. We were all dressed as peasants, and the costumes were taken from a special wardrobe of the prince's. It would have been ridiculous to choose any other dresses, as the Elector wore one of the same kind himself. General Kettler was the best disguised of us all; he looked the rustic to the life. My mistress was ravishing. We only danced quadrilles and German dances. There were only four or five ladies of the highest rank; all the others, who were more or less pretty, were favourites of the prince, all his days a great lover of the fair sex. Two of these ladies danced the Forlana, and the Elector was much amused in making me dance it also. I have already said that the Forlana is a Venetian dance, and one of the most energetic kind imaginable. It is danced by a lady and gentleman opposite to one another, and as the two ladies relieved one another they were almost the death of me. One has to be strong to dance twelve turns, and after the thirteenth I felt I could do no more, and begged for mercy.

Soon after we danced another dance, where each gentleman kisses a lady. I was not too shy, and each time I continued to kiss my mistress with considerable ardour, which made the peasant-elector burst with laughter and the peasant-general burst with rage.

In a lull between the dances, this charming and original woman found means to tell me in private that all the Cologne ladies would leave at noon on the next day, and that I would increase my popularity by inviting them all to breakfast at Bruhl.

"Send each one a note with the name of her cavalier, and trust in Count Verita to do everything for the best; you need only tell him that you wish to give an entertainment similar to that given two years ago by the Prince de Deux-Ponts. Lose no time. You will have a score of guests; mind you let them know the hour of the repast. Take care, too, that your invitations are sent round by nine o'clock in the morning."

All these instructions were uttered with lightning speed, and I, enchanted with the power my mistress thought she possessed over me, thought only of obeying, without reflecting whether I owed her obedience. Bruhl, breakfast, a score of people like the Prince Deux-Ponts, invitations to the ladies, Count Verita; I knew as much as she could have told me if she had taken an hour.

I left the room in my peasant's dress, and begged a page to take me to Count Verita, who began to laugh on seeing my attire. I told my business with the importance of an ambassador, and this made him in a still better humour.

"It can all easily be arranged," said he, "I have only to write to the steward, and I will do so immediately. But how much do you want to spend?"

"As much as possible."

"As little as possible, I suppose you mean."

"Not at all; I want to treat my guests with magnificence."

"All the same you must fix on a sum, as I know whom I've got to deal with."

"Well, well! two-three hundred ducats; will that do?"

"Two hundred; the Prince de Deux-Ponts did not spend more."

He began to write, and gave me his word that everything should be in readiness. I left him and addressing myself to a sharp Italian page said that I would give two ducats to the valet who would furnish me with the names of the Cologne ladies who were in Bonn, and of the gentlemen who had accompanied them. I got what I wanted in less than half an hour, and before leaving the ball I told my mistress that all should be done according to her desires.

I wrote eighteen notes before I went to bed, and in the morning a confidential servant had delivered them before nine o'clock.

At nine o'clock I went to take leave of Count Verita, who gave me, on behalf of the Elector, a superb gold snuff-box with his portrait set in diamonds. I was very sensible of this mark of kindness, and I wished to go and thank his serene highness before my departure, but my friendly fellow-countryman told me that I might put off doing so till I passed through Bonn on my way to Frankfort.

Breakfast was ordered for one o'clock. At noon I had arrived at Bruhl, a country house of the Elector's, with nothing remarkable about it save its furniture. In this it is a poor copy of the Trianon. In a fine hall I found a table laid for twenty-four persons, arranged with silver gilt plates, damask linen, and exquisite china, while the sideboard was adorned with an immense quantity of silver and silvergilt plate. At one end of the room were two other tables laden with sweets and the choicest wines procurable. I announced myself as the host, and the cook told me I should be perfectly satisfied.

"The collation," said he, "will be composed of only twenty-four dishes, but in addition there will be twenty-four dishes of English oysters and a splendid dessert."

I saw a great number of servants, and told him that they would not be necessary, but he said they were, as the guests' servants could not be admitted.

I received all my guests at the door, confining my compliments to begging their pardons for having been so bold as to procure myself this great honour.

The breakfast was served at one exactly, and I had the pleasure of enjoying the astonishment in my mistress's eyes when she saw that I had treated them as well as a prince of the empire. She was aware that everybody knew her to be the chief object of this lavish outlay, but she was delighted to see that I did not pay her any attentions which were at all invidious. The table was seated for twenty-four, and though I had only asked eighteen people every place was occupied. Three couples, therefore, had come without being asked; but that pleased me all the more. Like a courtly cavalier I would not sit down, but waited on the ladies, going from one to the other, eating the dainty bits they gave me, and seeing that all had what they wanted.

By the time the oysters were done twenty bottles of champagne had been emptied, so that when the actual breakfast commenced everybody began to talk at once. The meal might easily have passed for a splendid dinner, and I was glad to see that not a drop of water was drunk, for the Champagne, Tokay, Rhine wine, Madeira, Malaga, Cyprus, Alicante, and Cape wine would not allow it.

Before dessert was brought on an enormous dish of truffles was placed on the table. I advised my guests to take Maraschino with it, and those ladies who appreciated the liqueur drank it as if it had been water. The dessert was really sumptuous. In it were displayed the portraits of all the monarchs of Europe. Everyone complimented the cook on his achievement, and he, his vanity being tickled and wishing to appear good-natured, said that none of it would spoil in the pocket, and accordingly everybody took as much as they chose.

General Kettler, who, in spite of his jealousy and the part he saw me play, had no suspicion of the real origin of the banquet, said,

"I will wager that this is the Elector's doing. His highness has desired to preserve his incognito, and M. Casanova has played his part to admiration."

This remark set all the company in a roar.

"General," said I, "if the Elector had given me such an order, I should, of course, have obeyed him, but I should have felt it a humiliating part to play. His highness, however, has deigned to do me a far greater honour; look here." So saying, I shewed him the gold snuff-box, which made the tour of the table two or three times over.

When we had finished, we rose from table, astonished to find we had been engaged for three hours in a pleasurable occupation, which all would willingly have prolonged; but at last we had to part, and after many compliments they all went upon their way, in order to be in time for the theatre. As well pleased as my guests, I left twenty ducats with the steward, for the servants, and promised him to let Count Verita know of my satisfaction in writing.

I arrived at Cologne in time for the French play, and as I had no carriage I went to the theatre in a sedan chair. As soon as I got into the house, I saw the Comte de Lastic alone with my fair one. I thought this a good omen, and I went to them directly. As soon as she saw me, she said with a melancholy air that the general had got so ill that he had been obliged to go to bed. Soon after, M. de Lastic left us, and dropping her assumed melancholy she made me, with the utmost grace, a thousand compliments, which compensated me for the expenses of my breakfast a hundred times over.

"The general," said she, "had too much to drink; he is an envious devil, and has discovered that it is not seemly of you to treat us as if you were a prince. I told him that, on the contrary, you had treated us as if we were princes, waiting on us with your napkin on your arm. He thereupon found fault with me for degrading you."

"Why do you not send him about his business? So rude a fellow is not worthy of serving so famous a beauty."

"It's too late. A woman whom you don't know would get possession of him. I should be obliged to conceal my feelings, and that would vex me."

"I understand—I understand. Would that I were a great prince! In the mean time, let me tell you that my sickness is greater than Kettler's."

"You are joking, I hope."

"Nay, not at all; I am speaking seriously, for the kisses I was so happy to snatch from you at the ball have inflamed my blood, and if you have not enough kindness to cure me in the only possible way I shall leave Cologne with a life-long grief."

"Put off your departure: why should you desire to go to Stuttgart so earnestly? I think of you, believe me, and I do not wish to deceive you; but it is hard to find an opportunity."

"If you had not the general's carriage waiting for you to-night, and I had mine, I could take you home with perfect propriety."

"Hush! As you have not your carriage, it is my part to take you home. It is a splendid idea, that we must so contrive it that it may not seem to be a concerted plan. You must give me your arm to my carriage, and I shall then ask you where your carriage is; you will answer that you have not got one. I shall ask you to come into mine, and I will drop you at your hotel. It will only give us a couple of minutes, but that is something till we are more fortunate."

I replied to her only by a look which expressed the intoxication of my spirits at the prospect of so great bliss.

Although the play was quite a short one, it seemed to me to last for ever. At last the curtain fell, and we went downstairs. When we got to the portico she asked me the questions we had agreed upon, and when I told her I had not got a carriage, she said, "I am going to the general's to ask after his health; if it will not take you too much out of your way, I can leave you at your lodging as we come back."

It was a grand idea. We should pass the entire length of the ill-paved town twice, and thus we secured a little more time. Unfortunately, the carriage was a chariot, and as we were going the moon shone directly on us. On that occasion the planet was certainly not entitled to the appellation of the lovers' friend. We did all we could, but that was almost nothing, and I found the attempt a desperate one, though my lovely partner endeavoured to help me as much as possible. To add to our discomforts, the inquisitive and impudent coachman kept turning his head round, which forced us to moderate the energy of our movements. The sentry at the general's door told our coachman that his excellency could see no one, and we joyfully turned towards my hotel, and now that the moon was behind us and the man's curiosity less inconvenient, we got on a little better, or rather not so badly as before, but the horses seemed to me to fly rather than gallop; however, feeling that it would be well to have the coachman on my side in case of another opportunity, I gave him a ducat as I got down.

I entered the hotel feeling vexed and unhappy, though more in love than ever, for my fair one had convinced me that she was no passive mistress, but could experience pleasure as well as give it. That being the case I resolved not to leave Cologne before we had drained the cup of pleasure together, and that, it seemed to me, could not take place till the general was out of the way.

Next day, at noon, I went to the general's house to write down my name, but I found he was receiving visitors and I went in. I made the general an appropriate compliment, to which the rude Austrian only replied by a cold inclination of the head. He was surrounded by a good many officers, and after four minutes I made a general bow and went out. The boor kept his room for three days, and as my mistress did not come to the theatre I had not the pleasure of seeing her.

On the last day of the carnival Kettler asked a good many people to a ball and supper. On my going to pay my court to my mistress in her box at the theatre, and being left for a moment alone with her, she asked me if I were invited to the general's supper. I answered in the negative.

"What!" said she, in an imperious and indignant voice, "he has not asked you? You must go, for all that."

"Consider what you say," said I, gently, "I will do anything to please you but that."

"I know all you can urge; nevertheless, you must go. I should feel insulted if you were not at that supper. If you love me you will give me this proof of your affection and (I think I may say) esteem."

"You ask me thus? Then I will go. But are you aware that you are exposing me to the danger of losing my life or taking his? for I am not the man to pass over an affront."

"I know all you can say," said she. "I have your honour at heart as much as mine, or perhaps more so, but nothing will happen to you; I will answer for everything. You must go, and you must give me your promise now, for I am resolved if you do not go, neither will I, but we must never see each other more."

"Then you may reckon upon me."

At that moment M. de Castries came in, and I left the box and went to the pit, where I passed two anxious hours in reflecting on the possible consequences of the strange step this woman would have me take. Nevertheless, such was the sway of her beauty aver my soul, I determined to abide by my promise and to carry the matter through, and to put myself in the wrong as little as possible. I went to the general's at the end of the play, and only found five or six people there. I went up to a canoness who was very fond of Italian poetry, and had no trouble in engaging her in an interesting discussion. In half an hour the room was full, my mistress coming in last on the general's arm. I was taken up with the canoness and did not stir, and consequently Kettler did not notice me, while the lady in great delight at seeing me left him no time to examine his guests, and he was soon talking to some people at the other end of the room. In a quarter of an hour afterwards supper was announced. The canoness rose, took my arm, and we seated ourselves at table together, still talking about Italian literature. Then came the catastrophe. When all the places had been taken one gentleman was left standing, there being no place for him. "How can that have happened?" said the general, raising his voice, and while the servants were bringing another chair and arranging another place he passed his guests in review. All the while I pretended not to notice what was going on, but when he came to me he said loudly,

"Sir, I did not ask you to come."

"That is quite true, general," I said, respectfully, "but I thought, no doubt correctly, that the omission was due to forgetfulness, and I thought myself obliged all the same to come and pay my court to your excellency."

Without a pause I renewed my conversation with the canoness, not so much as looking around. A dreadful silence reigned for four or five minutes, but the canoness began to utter witticisms which I took up and communicated to my neighbours, so that in a short time the whole table was in good spirits except the general, who preserved a sulky silence. This did not much matter to me, but my vanity was concerned in smoothing him down, and I watched for my opportunity.

M. de Castries was praising the dauphin, and his brothers, the Comte de Lusace and the Duc de Courlande, were mentioned; this led the conversation up to Prince Biron, formerly a duke, who was in Siberia, and his personal qualities were discussed, one of the guests having said that his chiefest merit was to have pleased the Empress Anne. I begged his pardon, saying,—

"His greatest merit was to have served faithfully the last Duke Kettler; who if it had not been for the courage of him who is now so unfortunate, would have lost all his belongings in the war. It was Duke Kettler who so heroically sent him to the Court of St. Petersburg, but Biron never asked for the duchy. An earldom would have satisfied him, as he recognized the rights of the younger branch of the Kettler family, which would be reigning now if it were not for the empress's whim: nothing would satisfy her but to confer a dukedom on the favourite."

The general, whose face had cleared while I was speaking, said, in the most polite manner of which he was capable, that I was a person of remarkable information, adding regretfully,—

"Yes, if it were not for that whim I should be reigning now."

After this modest remark he burst into a fit of laughter and sent me down a bottle of the best Rhine wine, and addressed his conversation to me till the supper was over. I quietly enjoyed the turn things had taken, but still more the pleasure I saw expressed in the beautiful eyes of my mistress.

Dancing went on all night, and I did not leave my canoness, who was a delightful woman and danced admirably. With my lady I only danced one minuet. Towards the end of the ball the general, to finish up with a piece of awkwardness, asked me if I was going soon. I replied that I did not think of leaving Cologne till after the grand review.

I went to bed full of joy at having given the burgomaster's wife such a signal proof of my love, and full of gratitude to fortune who had helped me so in dealing with my doltish general, for God knows what I should have done if he had forgotten himself so far as to tell me to leave the table! The next time I saw the fair she told me she had felt a mortal pang of fear shoot through her when the general said he had not asked me.

"I am quite sure," said she, "that he would have gone further, if your grand answer had not stopped his mouth; but if he had said another word, my mind was made up."

"To do what?"

"I should have risen from the table and taken your arm, and we should have gone out together. M. de Castries has told me that he would have done the same, and I believe all the ladies whom you asked to breakfast would have followed our example."

"But the affair would not have stopped then, for I should certainly have demanded immediate satisfaction, and if he had refused it I should have struck him with the flat of my sword."

"I know that, but pray forget that it was I who exposed you to this danger. For my part, I shall never forget what I owe to you, and I will try to convince you of my gratitude."

Two days later, on hearing that she was indisposed, I went to call on her at eleven o'clock, at which time I was sure the general would not be there. She received me in her husband's room, and he, in the friendliest manner possible, asked me if I had come to dine with them. I hastened to thank him for his invitation, which I accepted with pleasure, and I enjoyed this dinner better than Kettler's supper. The burgomaster was a fine-looking man, pleasant-mannered and intelligent, and a lover of peace and quietness. His wife, whom he adored, ought to have loved him, since he was by no means one of those husbands whose motto is, "Displease whom you like, so long as you please me."

On her husband's going out for a short time, she shewed me over the house.

"Here is our bedroom," said she; "and this is the closet in which I sleep for five or six nights in every month. Here is a church which we may look upon as our private chapel, as we hear mass from those two grated windows. On Sundays we go down this stair and enter the church by a door, the key to which is always in my keeping." It was the second Saturday in Lent; we had an excellent fasting dinner, but I did not for once pay much attention to eating. To see this young and beautiful woman surrounded by her children, adored by her family, seemed to me a beautiful sight. I left them at an early hour to write to Esther, whom I did not neglect, all occupied as I was with this new flame.

Next day I went to hear mass at the little church next to the burgomaster's house. I was well cloaked so as not to attract attention. I saw my fair one going out wearing a capuchin, and followed by her family. I noted the little door which was so recessed in the wall that it would have escaped the notice of anyone who was unaware of its existence; it opened, I saw, towards the staircase.

The devil, who, as everybody knows, has more power in a church than anywhere else, put into my head the idea of enjoying my mistress by means of the door and stair. I told her my plan the next day at the theatre.

"I have thought of it as well as you," said she, laughing, "and I will give you the necessary instructions in writing; you will find them in the first gazette I send you."

We could not continue this pleasant interview, as my mistress had with her a lady from Aix-la-Chapelle, who was staying with her for a few days. And indeed the box was full of company.

I had not long to wait, for next day she gave me back the gazette openly, telling me that she had not found anything to interest her in it. I knew that it would be exceedingly interesting to me. Her note was as follows:

"The design which love inspired is subject not to difficulty but uncertainty. The wife only sleeps in the closet when her husband asks her—an event which only occurs at certain periods, and the separation does not last for more than a few days. This period is not far off, but long custom has made it impossible for the wife to impose on her husband. It will, therefore, be necessary to wait. Love will warn you when the hour of bliss has come. The plan will be to hide in the church; and there must be no thought of seducing the door-keeper, for though poor he is too stupid to be bribed, and would betray the secret. The only way will be to hide so as to elude his watchfulness. He shuts the church at noon on working days; on feast days he shuts it at evening, and he always opens it again at dawn. When the time comes, all that need be done is to give the door a gentle push-it will not be locked. As the closet which is to be the scene of the blissful combat is only separated from the room by a partition, there must be no spitting, coughing, nor nose-blowing: it would be fatal. The escape will be a matter of no difficulty; one can go down to the church, and go out as soon as it is opened. Since the beadle has seen nobody in the evening, it is not likely that he will see more in the morning."

I kissed again and again this charming letter, which I thought shewed great power of mental combination, and I went next day to see how the coast lay: this was the first thing to be done. There was a chair in the church in which I should never have been seen, but the stair was on the sacristy side, and that was always locked up. I decided on occupying the confessional, which was close to the door. I could creep into the space beneath the confessor's seat, but it was so small that I doubted my ability to stay there after the door was shut. I waited till noon to make the attempt, and as soon as the church was empty I took up my position. I had to roll myself up into a ball, and even then I was so badly concealed by the folding door that anyone happening to pass by at two paces distance might easily have seen me. However I did not care for that, for in adventures of that nature one must leave a great deal to fortune. Determined to run all risks I went home highly pleased with my observations. I put everything I had determined down in writing, and sent it to her box at the theatre, enclosed in an old gazette.

A week after she asked the general in my presence if her husband could do anything for him at Aix-la-Chapelle, where he was going on the morrow, with the intention of returning in three days. That was enough for me, but a glance from her added meaning to her words. I was all the more glad as I had a slight cold, and the next day being a feast day I could take up my position at night fall, and thus avoid a painful vigil of several hours' duration.

I curled myself up in the confessional at four o'clock, hiding myself as best I could, and commending myself to the care of all the saints. At five o'clock the beadle made his usual tour of inspection, went out and locked the door. As soon as I heard the noise of the key I came out of my narrow cell and sat down on a bench facing the windows. Soon after my mistress's shadow appeared on the grated panes, and I knew she had seen me.

I sat on the bench for a quarter of an hour and then pushed open the little door and entered. I shut it and sat down on the lowest step of the stair, and spent there five hours which would probably have not been unpleasant ones if I had not been dreadfully tormented by the rats running to and fro close to me. Nature has given me a great dislike to this animal, which is comparatively harmless; but the smell of rats always sickens me.

At last I heard the clock strike ten, the hour of bliss, and I saw the form of my beloved holding a candle, and I was then freed from my painful position. If my readers have been in such a situation they can imagine the pleasures of that happy night, but they cannot divine the minute circumstances; for if I was an expert my partner had an inexhaustible store of contrivances for augmenting the bliss of that sweet employment. She had taken care to get me a little collation, which looked delicious, but which I could not touch, my appetite lying in another quarter.

For seven hours, which I thought all too short, we enjoyed one another, not resting, except for talk, which served to heighten our pleasure.

The burgomaster was not the man for an ardent passion, but his strength of constitution enabled him to do his duty to his wife every night without failing, but, whether from regard to his health or from a religious scruple, he suspended his rights every month while the moon exercised hers, and to put himself out of temptation he made his wife sleep apart. But for once in a way, the lady was not in the position of a divorcee.

Exhausted, but not satiated with pleasure, I left her at day-break, assuring her that when we met again she would find me the same; and with that I went to hide in the confessional, fearing lest the growing light might betray me to the beadle. However, I got away without any difficulty, and passed nearly the whole day in bed, having my dinner served to me in my room. In the evening I went to the theatre, to have the pleasure of seeing the beloved object of whom my love and constancy had made me the possessor.

At the end of a fortnight she sent me a note in which she told me that she would sleep by herself on the night following. It was a ferial day, and I therefore went to the church at eleven in the morning after making an enormous breakfast. I hid myself as before, and the beadle locked me in without making any discovery.

I had a wait of ten hours, and the reflection that I should have to spend the time partly in the church and partly on the dark and rat-haunted staircase, without being able to take a pinch of snuff for fear of being obliged to blow my nose, did not tend to enliven the prospect; however, the hope of the great reward made it easy to be borne. But at one o'clock I heard a slight noise, and looking up saw a hand appear through the grated window, and a paper drop on the floor of the church. I ran to pick it up, while my heart beat fast, for my first idea was that some obstacle had occurred which would compel me to pass the night on a bench in the church. I opened it, and what was my joy to read as follows:

"The door is open, and you will be more comfortable on the staircase, where you will find a light, a little dinner, and some books, than in the church. The seat is not very easy, but I have done my best to remedy the discomfort with a cushion. Trust me, the time will seem as long to me as to you, but be patient. I have told the general that I do not feel very well, and shall not go out to-day. May God keep you from coughing, especially during the night, for on the least noise we should be undone."

What stratagems are inspired by love! I opened the door directly, and found a nicely-laid meal, dainty viands, delicious wine, coffee, a chafing dish, lemons, spirits of wine, sugar, and rum to make some punch if I liked. With these comforts and some books, I could wait well enough; but I was astonished at the dexterity of my charming mistress in doing all this without the knowledge of anybody in the house.

I spent three hours in reading, and three more in eating, and making coffee and punch, and then I went to sleep. At ten o'clock my darling came and awoke me. This second night was delicious, but not so much so as the former, as we could not see each other, and the violence of our ecstatic combats was restrained by the vicinity of the good husband. We slept part of the time, and early in the morning I had to make good my retreat. Thus ended my amour with this lady. The general went to Westphalia, and she was soon to go into the country. I thus made my preparations for leaving Cologne, promising to come and see her the year following, which promise however I was precluded, as the reader will see, from keeping. I took leave of my acquaintance and set out, regretted by all.

The stay of two months and a half which I made in Cologne did not diminish my monetary resources, although I lost whenever I was persuaded to play. However, my winnings at Bonn made up all deficiencies, and my banker, M. Franck, complained that I had not made any use of him. However, I was obliged to be prudent so that those persons who spied into my actions might find nothing reprehensible.

I left Cologne about the middle of March, and I stopped at Bonn, to present my respects to the Elector, but he was away. I dined with Count Verita and the Abbe Scampar, a favourite of the Elector's. After dinner the count gave me a letter of introduction to a canoness at Coblentz, of whom he spoke in very high terms. That obliged me to stop at Coblentz; but when I got down at the inn, I found that the canoness was at Manheim, while in her stead I encountered an actress named Toscani, who was going to Stuttgart with her young and pretty daughter. She was on her way from Paris, where her daughter had been learning character-dancing with the famous Vestris. I had known her at Paris, but had not seen much of her, though I had given her a little spaniel dog, which was the joy of her daughter. This daughter was a perfect jewel, who had very little difficulty in persuading me to come with them to Stuttgart, where I expected, for other reasons, to have a very pleasant stay. The mother was impatient to know what the duke would think of her daughter, for she had destined her from her childhood to serve the pleasures of this voluptuous prince, who, though he had a titular mistress, was fond of experimenting with all the ballet-girls who took his fancy.

We made up a little supper-party, and it may be guessed that two of us belonging to the boards the conversation was not exactly a course in moral theology. The Toscani told me that her daughter was a neophyte, and that she had made up her mind not to let the duke touch her till he had dismissed his reigning mistress, whose place she was designed to take. The mistress in question was a dancer named Gardella, daughter of a Venetian boatman, whose name has been mentioned in my first volume—in fine, she was the wife of Michel d'Agata, whom I found at Munich fleeing from the terrible Leads, where I myself languished for so long.

As I seemed to doubt the mother's assertion, and threw out some rather broad hints to the effect that I believed that the first bloom had been plucked at Paris, and that the Duke of Wurtemburg would only have the second, their vanity was touched; and on my proposing to verify the matter with my own eyes it was solemnly agreed that this ceremony should take place the next day. They kept their promise, and I was pleasantly engaged for two hours the next morning, and was at last obliged to extinguish in the mother the flames her daughter had kindled in my breast.

Although the Toscani was young enough, she would have found me ice if her daughter had been able to satisfy my desires, but she did not trust me well enough to leave us alone together. As it was she was well satisfied.

I resolved, then, on going to Stuttgart in company with the two nymphs, and I expected to see there the Binetti, who was always an enthusiastic admirer of mine. This actress was the daughter of a Roman boatman. I had helped her to get on the boards the same year that Madame de Valmarana had married her to a French dancer named Binet, whose name she had Italianized by the addition of one syllable, like those who ennoble themselves by adding another syllable to their names. I also expected to see the Gardella, young Baletti, of whom I was very fond, his young wife the Vulcani, and several other of my old friends, who I thought would combine to make my stay at Stuttgart a very pleasant one. But it will be seen that it is a risky thing to reckon without one's host. At the last posting station I bid adieu to my two friends, and went to the "Bear."

CHAPTER XII

Gardella Portrait of The Duke of Wurtemburg—My Dinner with Gardella, And its Consequences—Unfortunate Meeting I Play and Lose Four Thousand Louis—Lawsuit—Lucky Flight—My Arrival at Zurich—Church Consecrated By Jesus Christ Himself

At that period the Court of the Duke of Wurtemburg was the most brilliant in Europe. The heavy subsidies paid by France for quartering ten thousand men upon him furnished him with the means for indulging in luxury and debauchery. The army in question was a fine body of men, but during the war it was distinguished only by its blunders.

The duke was sumptuous in his tastes, which were for splendid palaces, hunting establishments on a large scale, enormous stables—in short, every whim imaginable; but his chief expense was the large salaries he paid his theatre, and, above all, his mistresses. He had a French play, an Italian opera, grand and comic, and twenty Italian dancers, all of whom had been principal dancers in Italian theatres. His director of ballets was Novers, and sometimes five hundred dancers appeared at once. A clever machinist and the best scene painters did their best to make the audience believe in magic. All the ballet-girls were pretty, and all of them boasted of having been enjoyed at least once by my lord. The chief of them was a Venetian, daughter of a gondolier named Gardella. She was brought up by the senator Malipiero, whom my readers know for his good offices towards myself, who had her taught for the theatre, and gave her a dancing-master. I found her at Munich, after my flight from The Leads, married to Michel Agata. The duke took a fancy to her, and asked her husband, who was only too happy to agree, to yield her; but he was satisfied with her charms in a year, and put her on the retired list with the title of madame.

This honour had made all the other ballet-girls jealous, and they all thought themselves as fit as she to be taken to the duke's titular mistress, especially as she only enjoyed the honour without the pleasure. They all intrigued to procure her dismissal, but the Venetian lady succeeded in holding her ground against all cabals.

Far from reproaching the duke for this incorrigible infidelity, she encouraged him in it, and was very glad to be left to herself, as she cared nothing for him. Her chief pleasure was to have the ballet-girls who aspired to the honours of the handkerchief come to her to solicit her good offices. She always received them politely, gave them her advice, and bade them do their best to please the prince. In his turn the duke thought himself bound to shew his gratitude for her good nature, and gave her in public all the honours which could be given to a princess.

I was not long in finding out that the duke's chief desire was to be talked about. He would have liked people to say that there was not a prince in Europe to compare with him for wit, taste, genius, in the invention of pleasures, and statesman-like capacities; he would fain be regarded as a Hercules in the pleasures of Bacchus and Venus, and none the less an Aristides in governing his people. He dismissed without pity an attendant who failed to wake him after he had been forced to yield to sleep for three or four hours, but he did not care how roughly he was awakened.

It has happened that after having given his highness a large cup of coffee, the servant has been obliged to throw him into a bath of cold water, where the duke had to choose between awaking or drowning.

As soon as he was dressed the duke would assemble his council and dispatch whatever business was on hand, and then he would give audience to whoever cared to come into his presence. Nothing could be more comic than the audiences he gave to his poorer subjects. Often there came to him dull peasants and workmen of the lowest class; the poor duke would sweat and rage to make them hear reason, in which he was sometimes unsuccessful, and his petitioners would go away terrified, desperate, and furious. As to the pretty country maidens, he examined into their complaints in private, and though he seldom did anything for them they went away consoled.

The subsidies which the French Crown was foolish enough to pay him for a perfectly useless service did not suffice for his extravagant expenses. He loaded his subjects with taxes till the patient people could bear it no longer, and some years after had recourse to the Diet of Wetzlar, which obliged him to change his system. He was foolish enough to wish to imitate the King of Prussia, while that monarch made fun of the duke, and called him his ape. His wife was the daughter of the Margrave of Bayreuth, the prettiest and most accomplished princess in all Germany. When I had come to Stuttgart she was no longer there; she had taken refuge with her father, on account of a disgraceful affront which had been offered her by her unworthy husband. It is incorrect to say that this princess fled from her husband because of his infidelities.

After I had dined by myself, I dressed and went to the opera provided gratis by the duke in the fine theatre he had built. The prince was in the front of the orchestra, surrounded by his brilliant Court. I sat in a box on the first tier, delighted to be able to hear so well the music of the famous Jumella, who was in the duke's service. In my ignorance of the etiquette of small German Courts I happened to applaud a solo, which had been exquisitely sung by a castrato whose name I have forgotten, and directly afterwards an individual came into my box and addressed me in a rude manner. However, I knew no German, and could only answer by 'nich verstand'—"I don't understand."

He went out, and soon after an official came in, who told me, in good French, that when the sovereign was present all applause was forbidden.

"Very good, sir. Then I will go away and come again when the sovereign is not here, as when an air pleases me I always applaud."

After this reply I called for my carriage, but just as I was getting into it the same official came and told me that the duke wanted to speak to me. I accordingly followed him to the presence.

"You are M. Casanova, are you?" said the duke.

"Yes, my lord."

"Where do you come from?"

"From Cologne."

"Is this the first time you have been to Stuttgart?"

"Yes, my lord."

"Do you think of staying long?"

"For five or six days, if your highness will allow me."

"Certainly, you may stay as long as you like, and you may clap when you please."

"I shall profit by your permission, my lord."

"Good."

I sat down again, and the whole audience settled down to the play. Soon after, an actor sung an air which the duke applauded, and of course all the courtiers, but not caring much for the song I sat still—everyone to his taste. After the ballet the duke went to the favourite's box, kissed her hand, and left the theatre. An official, who was sitting by me and did not know that I was acquainted with the Gardella, told me that as I had had the honour of speaking to the prince I might obtain the honour of kissing his favourite's hand.

I felt a strong inclination to laugh, but I restrained myself; and a sudden and very irrational impulse made me say that she was a relation of mine. The words had no sooner escaped me than I bit my lip, for this stupid lie could only do me harm, but it was decreed that I should do nothing at Stuttgart but commit blunders. The officer, who seemed astonished at my reply, bowed and went to the favourite's box to inform her of my presence. The Gardelia looked in my direction and beckoned to me with her fan, and I hastened to comply with the invitation, laughing inwardly at the part I was going to play. As soon as I came in she graciously gave me her hand, which I kissed, calling her my cousin.

"Did you tell the duke you were my cousin?" said she.

"No," I replied.

"Very good, then I will do so myself; come and dine with me to-morrow."

She then left the house, and I went to visit the ballet-girls, who were undressing: The Binetti, who was one of the oldest of my acquaintances, was in an ecstasy of joy at seeing me, and asked me to dine with her every day. Cartz, the violin, who had been with me in the orchestra at St. Samuel's, introduced me to his pretty daughter, saying,

"She is not made for the duke's eyes to gaze on, and he shall never have her."

The good man was no prophet, as the duke got possession of her a short time after. She presented him with two babies, but these pledges of affection could not fix the inconstant prince. Nevertheless, she was a girl of the most captivating kind, for to the most perfect beauty she added grace, wit, goodness, and kindness, which won everyone's heart. But the duke was satiated, and his only pleasure lay in novelty.

After her I saw the Vulcani, whom I had known at Dresden, and who suddenly presented her husband to me. He threw his arms round my neck. He was Baletti, brother of my faithless one, a young man of great talent of whom I was very fond.

I was surrounded by all these friends, when the officer whom I had so foolishly told that I was related to the Gardella came in and began to tell the story. The Binetti, after hearing it, said to him,

"It's a lie."

"But my dear," said I to her, "you can't be better informed on the subject than I am." She replied by laughing, but Cartz said, very wittily,

"As Gardella is only a boatman's daughter, like Binetti, the latter thinks, and very rightly, that you ought to have given her the refusal of your cousinship."

Next day I had a pleasant dinner with the favourite, though she told me that, not having seen the duke, she could not tell me how he would take my pleasantry, which her mother resented very much. This mother of hers, a woman of the lowest birth, had become very proud since her daughter was a prince's mistress, and thought my relationship a blot on their escutcheon. She had the impudence to tell me that her relations had never been players, without reflecting that it must be worse to descend to this estate than to rise from it, if it were dishonourable. I ought to have pitied her, but not being of a forbearing nature I retorted by asking if her sister was still alive, a question which made her frown and to which she gave no answer. The sister I spoke of was a fat blind woman, who begged on a bridge in Venice.

After having spent a pleasant day with the favourite, who was the oldest of my theatrical friends, I left her, promising to come to breakfast the next day; but as I was going out the porter bade me not to put my feet there again, but would not say on whose authority he gave me this polite order. It would have been wiser to hold my tongue, as this stroke must have come from the mother; or, perhaps, from the daughter, whose vanity I had wounded: she was a good-enough actress to conceal her anger.

I was angry with myself, and went away in an ill humour; I was humiliated to see myself treated in such a manner by a wretched wanton of an actress; though if I had been more discreet I could have got a welcome in the best society. If I had not promised to dine with Binetti the next day I should have posted off forthwith, and I should thus have escaped all the misadventures which befell me in that wretched town.

The Binetti lived in the house of her lover, the Austrian ambassador, and the part of the house she occupied adjoined the town wall. As will be seen; this detail is an important one. I dined alone with my good fellow-countrywoman, and if I had felt myself capable of love at that period all my old affection would have resumed its sway over me, as her beauty was undiminished, and she had more tact and knowledge of the world than when I knew her formerly.

The Austrian ambassador was a good-natured, easygoing, and generous man; as for her husband he was not worthy of her, and she never saw him. I spent a pleasant day with her, talking of our old friends, and as I had nothing to keep me in Wurtemburg I decided to leave in two days, as I had promised the Toscani and her daughter to go with them on the next day to Louisbourg. We were to start at five in the morning, but the following adventure befell me:—

As I was leaving Binetti's house I was greeted very courteously by three officers whom I had become acquainted with at the coffee house, and I walked along the promenade with them.

"We are going," said one of them, "to visit certain ladies of easy virtue; we shall be glad to have you of our company."

"I only speak a few words of German," I answered, "and if I join you I shall be bored."

"Ah! but the ladies are Italians," they exclaimed, "nothing could suit you better."

I did not at all like following them, but my evil genius led me in that wretched town from one blunder to another, and so I went in spite of myself.

We turned back into the town, and I let myself be led up to the third floor of an ill-looking house, and in the meanest of rooms I saw the pretended nieces of Peccini. A moment after Peccini appeared, and had the impudence to throw his arms around my neck, calling me his best friend. His nieces overwhelmed me with caresses, and seemed to confirm the idea that we were old friends. I did nothing and held my tongue.

The officers prepared for a debauch; I did not imitate their example, but this made no difference to them. I saw into what an evil place I had been decoyed, but a false shame prevented me from leaving the house without ceremony. I was wrong, but I determined to be more prudent for the future.

Before long a pot-house supper was served, of which I did not partake; but not wishing to seem bad company I drank two or three small glasses of Hungarian wine. After supper, which did not last very long, cards were produced, and one of the officers held a bank at faro. I punted and lost the fifty or sixty Louis I had about me. I felt that I was drunk, my head was reeling, and I would have gladly given over playing and gone away, but I have never been so possessed as on that day, either from false shame or from the effects of the drugged wine they gave me. My noble officers seemed vexed that I had lost, and would give me my revenge. They made me hold a bank of a hundred Louis in fish, which they counted out to me. I did so, and lost. I made a bank again, and again I lost. My inflamed understanding, my increasing drunkenness, and my anger, deprived me of all sense, and I kept increasing my bank, losing all the time, till at midnight my good rascals declared they would play no more. They made a calculation, and declared that I had lost nearly a hundred thousand francs. So great was my intoxication, although I had had no more wine, that they were obliged to send for a sedan chair to take me to my inn. While my servant was undressing me he discovered that I had neither my watches nor my gold snuff-boy.

"Don't forget to wake me at four in the morning," said I. Therewith I went to bed and enjoyed a calm and refreshing sleep.

While I was dressing next morning I found a hundred Louis in my pocket, at which I was much astonished, for my dizziness of brain being over now, I remembered that I had not this money about me the evening before; but my mind was taken up with the pleasure party, and I put off thinking of this incident and of my enormous losses till afterwards. I went to the Toscani and we set out for Louisbourg, where we had a capital dinner, and my spirits ran so high that my companions could never have guessed the misfortune that had just befallen me. We went back to Stuttgart in the evening.

When I got home my Spaniard told me that they knew nothing about my watches and snuff-box at the house where I had been the evening before, and that the three officers had come to call on me, but not finding me at home they had told him to warn me that they would breakfast with me on the following morning. They kept the appointment.

"Gentlemen," said I, as soon as they came in, "I have lost a sum which I cannot pay, and which I certainly should not have lost without the drugged wine you gave me. You have taken me to a den of infamy, where I was shamefully robbed of jewellery to the value of more than three hundred Louis. I complain of no one, since I have only my own folly to complain of. If I had been wiser all this would not have happened to me."

They exclaimed loudly at this speech, and tried to play the part of men of honour. They spoke in vain, as I had made up my mind to pay nothing.

Whilst we were in the thick of the fight, and were beginning to get angry over it, Baletti, Toscani, and Binetti came in, and heard the discussion. I then had breakfast brought in, and after we had finished my friends left me.

When we were once more alone, one of the rascals addressed me as follows:

"We are too honest, sir, to take advantage of your position. You have been unfortunate, but all men are sometimes unfortunate, and we ask nothing better than a mutual accommodation. We will take over all your properties; jewels, diamonds, arms, and carriage, and have them valued; and if the sum realized does not cover your debt we will take your acceptance, payable at date, and remain good friends."

"Sir, I do not wish for the friendship of robbers, and I will not play a single farthing."

At this they tried threats, but I kept cool and said,—

"Gentlemen, your menaces will not intimidate me, and, as far as I can see, you have only two ways of getting paid; either by way of the law, in which case I do not think I shall find it difficult to get a barrister to take up my case, or, secondly, you can pay yourselves on my body, honourably, with sword in hand."

As I had expected, they replied that if I wished they would do me the honour of killing me after I had paid them. They went off cursing, telling me that I would be sorry for what I had said.

Soon after I went out and spent the day with the Toscani in gaiety which, situated as I was, was not far off madness. At the time I placed it to the daughter's charms, and to the need my spirits were in of recovering their elasticity.

However, the mother having witnessed the rage of the three robbers was the first to urge me to fortify myself against their villainy by an appeal to the law.

"If you give them the start," said she, "they may possibly gain a great advantage over you in spite of the right being on your side."

And whilst I toyed with her charming daughter, she sent for a barrister. After hearing my case the counsel told me that my best way would be to tell the whole story to the sovereign as soon as possible.

"They took you to the house of ill-fame; they poured out the drugged wine which deprived you of your reason; they made you play in spite of their prince's prohibition (for gaming is strictly forbidden); in this company you were robbed of your jewels after they had made you lose an enormous sum. It's a hanging matter, and the duke's interest will be to do you justice, for an act of scoundrelism like this committed by his officers would dishonour him all over Europe."

I felt some repugnance to this course, for though the duke was a shameless libertine I did not like telling him such a disgraceful story. However, the case was a serious one, and after giving it due reflection I determined to wait on the dike on the following morning.

"As the duke gives audience to the first comer," I said to myself, "why should I not have as good a reception as a labouring man?" In this way I concluded that it would be no use to write to him, and I was on my way to the Court, when, at about twenty paces from the gate of the castle, I met my three gentlemen who accosted me rudely and said I had better make up my mind to pay, or else they would play the devil with me.

I was going on without paying any attention to them, when I felt myself rudely seized by the right arm. A natural impulse of self-defence made me put my hand to my sword, and I drew it in a manner that shewed I was in earnest. The officer of the guard came running up, and I complained that the three were assaulting me and endeavouring to hinder my approach to the prince. On enquiry being made, the sentry and the numerous persons who were present declared that I had only drawn in self-defence, so the officer decided that I had perfect liberty to enter the castle.

I was allowed to penetrate to the last antechamber without any obstacle being raised. Here I addressed myself to the chamberlain, demanding an audience with the sovereign, and he assured me that I should be introduced into the presence. But directly afterwards the impudent scoundrel who had taken hold of my arm came up and began to speak to the chamberlain in German. He said his say without my being able to contradict him, and his representations were doubtless not in my favour. Very possibly, too, the chamberlain was one of the gang, and I went from Herod to Pilate. An hour went by without my being able to see the prince, and then the chamberlain, who had assured me that I should have an audience, came and told me that I might go home, as the duke had heard all the circumstances of the case, and would no doubt see that justice was done me.

I saw at once that I should get no justice at all, and as I was walking away I thought how best I could get out of the difficulty. On my way I met Binetti, who knew how I was placed, and he asked me to come and dine with him, assuring me that the Austrian ambassador would take me under his protection, and that he would save me from the violent measures which the rascals no doubt intended to take, in spite of the chamberlain's assurances. I accepted the invitation, and Binetti's charming wife, taking the affair to heart, did not lose a moment in informing her lover, the ambassador, of all the circumstances.

This diplomatist came into the room with her, and after hearing all the details from my lips he said that in all probability the duke knew nothing about it.

"Write a brief account of the business," said he, "and I will lay it before the sovereign, who will no doubt see justice done."

I went to Binetti's desk, and as soon as I had written down my true relation I gave it, unsealed, to the ambassador, who assured me that it should be in the duke's hands in the course of an hour.

At dinner my country-woman assured me again that her lover should protect me, and we spent the day pleasantly enough; but towards evening my Spaniard came and assured me that if I returned to the inn I should be arrested, "for," said he, "an officer came to see you, and finding you were out he took up his position at the street door and has two soldiers standing at the foot of the staircase."

The Binetti said, "You must not go to the inn; stay here, where you have nothing to fear. Send for what you want, and we will wait and see what happens." I then gave orders to my Spaniard to go and fetch the belongings which were absolutely necessary to me.

At midnight the ambassador came in; we were still up, and he seemed pleased that his mistress had sheltered me. He assured me that my plea had been laid before the sovereign, but during the three days I was in the house I heard no more about it.

On the fourth day, whilst I was pondering as to how I should act, the ambassador received a letter from a minister requesting him, on behalf of the sovereign, to dismiss me from his house, as I had a suit pending with certain officers of his highness, and whilst I was with the ambassador justice could not take its course. The ambassador gave me the letter, and I saw that the minister promised that strict justice should be done me. There was no help for it; I had to make up my mind to return to my inn, but the Binetti was so enraged that she began to scold her lover, at which he laughed, saying, with perfect truth, that he could not keep me there in defiance of the prince.

I re-entered the inn without meeting anyone, but when I had had my dinner and was just going to see my counsel an officer served me with a summons, which was interpreted to me by my landlord, which ordered me to appear forthwith before the notary appointed to take my deposition. I went to him with the officer of the court, and spent two hours with the notary, who wrote down my deposition in German while I gave it in Latin. When it was done he told me to sign my name; to which I answered that I must decline to sign a document I did not understand. He insisted on my doing it, but I was immovable. He then got in a rage and said I ought to be ashamed of myself for suspecting a notary's honour. I replied calmly that I had no doubts as to his honour, but that I acted from principle, and that as I did not understand what he had written I refused to sign it. I left him, and was accompanied by the officer to my own counsel, who said I had done quite right, and promised to call on me the next day to receive my power of attorney.

"And when I have done that," he said, "your business will be mine."

I was comforted by this man, who inspired me with confidence, and went back to the hotel, where I made a good supper and went tranquilly to sleep. Next morning, however, when I awoke, my Spaniard announced an officer who had followed him, and told me in good French that I must not be astonished to find myself a prisoner in my room, for being a stranger and engaged in a suit at law it was only right that the opposite party should be assured that I would not escape before judgment was given. He asked very politely for my sword, and to my great regret I was compelled to give it him. The hilt was of steel, exquisitely chased; it was a present from Madame d'Urfe, and was worth at least fifty louis.

I wrote a note to my counsel to tell him what had happened; he came to see me and assured me that I should only be under arrest for a few days.

As I was obliged to keep my room, I let my friends know of my confinement, and I received visits from dancers and ballet-girls, who were the only decent people I was acquainted with in that wretched Stuttgart, where I had better never have set foot. My situation was not pleasant to contemplate: I had been drugged, cheated, robbed, abused, imprisoned, threatened with a mulct of a hundred thousand francs, which would have stripped me to my shirt, as nobody knew the contents of my pocket-book. I could think of nothing else. I had written to Madame the Gardella, but to no purpose, as I got no answer. All the consolation I got was from Binetti, Toscani, and Baletti, who dined or supped with me every day. The three rascals came to see me one by one, and each tried to get me to give him money unknown to the other two, and each promised that if I would do that, he would get me out of the difficulty. Each would have been content with three or four hundred louis, but even if I had given that sum to one of them I had no guarantee that the others would desist from their persecution. Indeed, if I had done so I should have given some ground to their pretensions, and bad would have been made worse. My answer was that they wearied me, and that I should be glad if they would desist from visiting me.

On the fifth day of my arrest the duke left for Frankfort; and the same day Binetti came and told me from her lover that the duke had promised the officers not to interfere, and that I was therefore in danger of an iniquitous sentence. His advice was to neglect no means of getting out of the difficulty, to sacrifice all my property, diamonds, and jewellery, and thus to obtain a release from my enemies. The Binetti, like a wise woman, disliked this counsel, and I relished it still less, but she had to perform her commission.

I had jewellery and lace to the value of more than a hundred thousand francs, but I could not resolve to make the sacrifice. I did not know which way to turn or where to go, and while I was in this state of mind my barrister came in. He spoke as follows:

"Sir, all my endeavors on your behalf have been unsuccessful. There is a party against you which seems to have support in some high quarter, and which silences the voice of justice. It is my duty to warn you that unless you find some way of arranging matters with these rascals you are a ruined man. The judgment given by the police magistrate, a rascal like the rest of them, is of a summary character, for as a stranger you will not be allowed to have recourse to the delays of the law. You would require bail to do that. They have managed to procure witnesses who swear that you are a professional gamester, that it was you who seduced the three officers into the house of your countryman Peccini, that it is not true that your wine was drugged that you did not lose your watches nor your snuff-box, for, they say, these articles will be found in your mails when your goods are sold. For that you will only have to wait till to-morrow or the day after, and do not think that I am deceiving you in any particular, or you will be sorry for it. They will come here and empty your mails, boxes, and pockets, a list will be made, and they will be sold by auction the same day. If the sum realized is greater than the debt the surplus will go in costs, and you may depend upon it that a very small sum will be returned to you; but if, on the other hand, the sum is not sufficient to pay everything, including the debt, costs, expenses of the auction, etc., you will be enrolled as a common soldier in the forces of His Most Serene Highness. I heard it said to the officer, who is your greatest creditor, that the four Louis enlistment money would be taken into account, and that the duke would be glad to get hold of such a fine man."

The barrister left me without my noticing him. I was so petrified by what he had said. I was in such a state of collapse that in less than an hour all the liquids in my body must have escaped. I, a common soldier in the army of a petty sovereign like the duke, who only existed by the horrible traffic in human flesh which he carried on after the manner of the Elector of Hesse. I, despoiled by those knaves, the victim of an iniquitous sentence. Never! I would endeavour to hit upon some plan to gain time.

I began by writing to my chief creditor that I had decided to come to an agreement with them, but I wished them all to wait upon my notary, with witnesses, to put a formal close to the action and render me a free man again.

I calculated that one of them was sure to be on duty on the morrow, and thus I should gain a day at any rate. In the mean time I hoped to discover some way of escape.

I next wrote to the head of the police, whom I styled "your excellency" and "my lord," begging him to vouchsafe his all-powerful protection. I told him that I had resolved on selling all my property to put an end to the suit which threatened to overwhelm me, and I begged him to suspend the proceedings, the cost of which could only add to my difficulties. I also asked him to send me a trustworthy man to value my effects as soon as I had come to an agreement with my creditors, with whom I begged for his good offices. When I had done I sent my Spaniard to deliver the letters.

The officer to whom I had written, who pretended that I was his debtor to the amount of two thousand Louis, came to see me after dinner. I was in bed;

and I told him I thought I had fever. He began to offer his sympathy, and, genuine or not, I was pleased with it. He told me he had just had some conversation with the chief of the police, who had shewn him my letter.

"You are very wise," said he, "in consenting to a composition, but we need not all three be present. I have full powers from the other two, and that will be sufficient for the notary:"

"I am in bad enough case," I replied, "for you to grant me the favour of seeing you all together; I cannot think you will refuse me."

"Well, well, you shall be satisfied, but if you are in a hurry to leave Stuttgart I must warn you that we cannot come before Monday, for we are on duty for the next four days."

"I am sorry to hear it, but I will wait. Give me your word of honour that all proceedings shall be suspended in the mean time."

"Certainly; here is my hand, and you may reckon on me. In my turn I have a favour to ask. I like your post-chaise; will you let me have it for what it cost you?"

"With pleasure."

"Be kind enough to call the landlord, and tell him in my presence that the carriage belongs to me."

I had the landlord upstairs and did as the rascal had asked me, but mine host told him that he could dispose of it after he had paid for it, and with that he turned his back on him and left the room.

"I am certain of having the chaise," said the officer, laughing. He then embraced me, and went away.

I had derived so much pleasure from my talk with him that I felt quite another man. I had four days before me; it was a rare piece of good luck.

Some hours after, an honest-looking fellow who spoke Italian well came to tell me, from the chief of police, that my creditors would meet on the ensuing Monday, and that he himself was appointed to value my goods. He advised me to make it a condition of the agreement that my goods should not be sold by auction, and that my creditors should consider his valuation as final and binding. He told me that I should congratulate myself if I followed his advice.

I told him that I would not forget his services, and begged him to examine my mails and my jewel-box. He examined everything and told me that my lace alone was worth twenty thousand francs. "In all," he added, "your goods are worth more than a hundred thousand francs, but I promise to tell your adversaries another story, Thus, if you can persuade them to take half their debt, you will get off with half your effects."

"In that ease," I said, "you shall have fifty louis, and here are six as an earnest."

"I am grateful to you, and you can count upon my devotion. The whole town and the duke as well know your creditors to be knaves, but they have their reasons for refusing to see their conduct in its true light."

I breathed again, and now all my thoughts were concentrated on making my escape with all I possessed, my poor chaise excepted. I had a difficult task before me, but not so difficult a one as my flight from The Leads, and the recollection of my great escape gave me fresh courage.

My first step was to ask Toscani, Baletti, and the dancer Binetti to supper, as I had measures to concert with these friends of mine, whom I could rely on, and who had nothing to fear from the resentment of three rascals.

After we had had a good supper I told them how the affair stood, and that I was determined to escape, and to carry my goods with me. "And now," I said, "I want your advice."

After a brief silence Binetti said if I could get to his house I could lower myself down from a window, and once on the ground I should be outside the town walls and at a distance of a hundred paces from the high road, by which I could travel post and be out of the duke's dominions by daybreak. Thereupon Baletti opened the window and found that it would be impossible to escape that way, on account of a wooden roof above a shop. I looked out also, and seeing that he was right I said that I should no doubt hit on some way of making my escape from the inn, but what troubled me chiefly was my luggage. The Toscani then said:—

"You will have to abandon your mails, which you could not take off without attracting attention, and you must send all your effects to my house. I engage to deliver safely whatever you may put in my care. I will take away your effects under my clothes in several journeys, and I can begin to-night."

Baletti thought this idea a good one, and said that to do it the quicker his wife would come and help. We fixed on this plan, and I promised Binetti to be with him at midnight on Sunday, even if I had to stab the sentry, who was at my door all day, but who went away at night after locking me in. Baletti said he would provide me with a faithful servant, and a post-chaise with swift horses, which would take my effects in other mails. To make the best use of the time, the Toscani began to load herself, putting two of my suits of clothes under her dress. For the next few days my friends served me so well that, at midnight on Saturday, my mails and my dressing case were empty; I kept back all the jewellery intending to carry it in my pocket.

On Sunday, the Toscani brought me the keys of the two mails, in which she had put my goods; and Baletti came also to tell me that all the necessary measures had been taken, and that I should find a post-chaise, under the charge of his servant, waiting for me on the high road. So far good, and the reader shall now hear how I contrived to escape from my inn.

The sentry confined himself to a small ante-chamber, where he walked up and down, without ever coming into my room, except at my invitation. As soon as he heard that I had gone to bed he locked the door, and went off till the next day. He used to sup on a little table in a corner of the ante-room; his food being sent out by me. Profiting by my knowledge of his habits, I gave my Spaniard the following instructions:

"After supper, instead of going to bed, I shall hold myself in readiness for leaving my room, and I shall leave it when I see the light extinguished in the ante-room, while I shall take care that my candle be so placed as not to shew any light outside, or to reflect my shadow. Once out of my room, I shall have no difficulty in reaching the stairs, and my escape will be accomplished. I shall go to Binetti's, leave the town by his house, and wait for you at Furstenburg. No one can hinder you from joining me in the course of a day or two. So when you see me ready in my room, and this will be whilst the sentry is having his supper, put out the candle on the table: you can easily manage to do so whilst snuffing it. You will then take it to re-light it, and I shall seize that moment to get off in the darkness. When you conclude that I have got out of the ante-room, you can come back to the soldier with the lighted candle, and you can help him to finish his bottle. By that time I shall be safe, and when you tell him I have gone to bed he will come to the door, wish me good night, and after locking the door and putting the key in his pocket he will go away with you. It is not likely that he will come in and speak to me when he hears I have gone to bed."

Nevertheless, as he might possibly take it into his head to come into the room, I carefully arranged a wig-block in a night-cap on the pillow, and huddled up the coverlet so as to deceive a casual glance.

All my plans were successful, as I heard afterwards from my Spaniard. Whilst he was drinking with the sentry I was getting on my great coat, girding on my hanger (I had no longer a sword), and putting my loaded pistols in my pocket. As soon as the darkness told me that Le Duc had put out the candle I went out softly, and reached the staircase without making the least noise. Once there the rest was easy, for the stair led into the passage, and the passage to the main door, which was always open till nearly midnight.

I stepped out along the street, and at a quarter to twelve I got to Binetti's, and found his wife looking out for me at the window. When I was in the room, whence I intended to escape, we lost no time. I threw my overcoat to Baletti, who was standing in the ditch below, up to the knees in mud, and binding a strong cord round my waist I embraced the Binetti and Baletti's wife, who lowered me down as gently as possible. Baletti received me in his arms, I cut the cord, and after taking my great coat I followed his footsteps. We strode through the mud, and going along a hedge we reached the high road in a state of exhaustion, although it was not more than a hundred paces as the crow flies from where we stood to the house. At a little distance off, beside a small wayside inn, we found the postchaise in which sat Baletti's servant. He got out, telling us that the postillion had just gone into the inn to have a glass of beer and light his pipe. I took the good servant's place, and gave him a reward, and begged them both to be gone, saying I would manage all the rest myself.

It was April and, 1760—my birthday—and a remarkable period in my career, although my whole life has been filled with adventures, good or bad.

I had been in the carriage for two or three minutes when the postillion came and asked me if we had much longer to wait. He thought he was speaking to the same person that he had left in the chaise, and I did not undeceive him. "Drive on," I answered, "and make one stage of it from here to Tubingen, without changing horses at Waldenbach." He followed my instructions, and we went along at a good pace, but I had a strong inclination to laugh at the face he made when he saw me at Tubingen. Baletti's servant was a youth, and slightly built; I was tall, and quite a man. He opened his eyes to their utmost width, and told me I was not the same gentleman that was in the carriage when he started. "You're drunk," said I, putting in his hand four times what he was accustomed to get, and the poor devil did not say a word. Who has not experienced the persuasive influence of money? I went on my journey, and did not stop till I reached Furstenburg, where I was quite safe.

I had eaten nothing on the way, and by the time I got to the inn I was dying of hunger. I had a good supper brought to me, and then I went to bed and slept well. As soon as I awoke I wrote to my three rascals. I promised to wait ten days for them at the place from which I dated the letter, and I challenged them to a duel a l'outrance, swearing that I would publish their cowardice all over Europe if they refused to measure swords with me. I next wrote to the Toscani, to Baletti, and to the good-natured mistress of the Austrian ambassador, commending Le Duc to their care, and thanking them for their friendly help.

The three rascals did not come, but the landlord's two daughters, both of them pretty, made me pass the three days very agreeably.

On the fourth day, towards noon, I had the pleasure of seeing my faithful Spaniard riding into the town carrying his portmanteau on his saddle.

"Sir," said he, "all Stuttgart knows you to be here, and I fear, lest the three officers who were too cowardly to accept your challenge may have you assassinated. If you are wise you will set out for Switzerland forthwith."

"That's cowardly, my lad," said I. "Don't be afraid about me, but tell me all that happened after my escape."

"As soon as you were gone, sir, I carried out your instructions, and helped the poor devil of a sentry to empty his bottle, though he would have willingly dispensed with my assistance in the matter; I then told him you had gone to bed, and he locked the door as usual, and went away after shaking me by the hand. After he had gone I went to bed. Next morning the worthy man was at his post by nine o'clock, and at ten the three officers came, and on my telling them that you were still asleep they went away, bidding me come to a coffee-house, and summon them when you got up. As they waited and waited to no purpose, they came again at noon, and told the soldier to open the door. What followed amused me, though I was in some danger in the midst of the rascals.

"They went in, and taking the wig-block for your head they came up to the bed and politely wished you good morning. You took no notice, so one of them proceeded to give you a gentle shake, and the bauble fell and rolled along the floor. I roared with laughter at the sight of their amazement.

"'You laugh, do you, rascal? Tell us where your master is.' And to give emphasis to their words they accompanied them with some strokes of the cane.

"I was not going to stand this sort of thing, so I told them, with an oath, that if they did not stop I should defend myself, adding that I was not my master's keeper, and advising them to ask the sentry.

"The sentry on his part swore by all the saints that you must have escaped by the window, but in spite of this a corporal was summoned, and the poor man was sent to prison.

"The clamour that was going on brought up the landlord, who opened your mails, and on finding them empty said that he would be well enough paid by your postchaise, replying only with a grin to the officer who pretended you had given it him.

"In the midst of the tumult a superior officer came up, who decided that you must have escaped through the window, and ordered the sentry to be set at liberty on the spot. Then came my turn, for, as I kept on laughing and answered all questions by 'I don't know,' these gentleman had me taken to prison, telling me I should stay there till I informed them where you, or at least your effects, could be found.

"The next day one of them came to the prison, and told me that unless I confessed I should undoubtedly be sent to the galleys.

"'On the faith of a Spaniard,' I answered, I know nothing, but if I did it would be all the same to you, for no one can make an honest servant betray his master.

"At this the rascal told the turnkey to give me a taste of the lash, and after this had been done I was set at liberty.

"My back was somewhat scarified, but I had the proud consciousness of having done my duty, and I went back and slept at the inn, where they were glad to see me. Next morning everyone knew you were here and had sent a challenge to the three sharpers, but the universal opinion was that they were too knowing to risk their lives by meeting you. Nevertheless, Madame Baletti told me to beg you to leave Furstenburg, as they might very likely have you assassinated. The landlord sold your chaise and your mails to the Austrian ambassador, who, they say, let you escape from a window in the apartment occupied by his mistress. No one offered to prevent me coming here.

"Three hours after Le Duc's arrival I took post and went to Schaffhaus, and from there to Zurich, with hired horses, as there are no posts in Switzerland. At Zurich I put up at the 'Sward,' an excellent inn.

"After supper, powdering over my arrival in Zurich where I had dropped from the clouds as it were, I began, to reflect seriously upon my present situation and the events of my past life. I recalled my misfortunes and scrutinized my conduct; and was not long in concluding that all I had suffered was through my own fault, and that when fortune would have crowned me with happiness I had persistently trifled that happiness away. I had just succeeded in escaping from a trap where I might have perished, or at least have been overwhelmed with shame, and I shuddered at the thought. I resolved to be no more fortune's plaything, but to escape entirely from her hands. I calculated my assets and found I was possessed of a hundred thousand crowns. 'With that,' said I, 'I can live secure amidst the changes and chances of this life, and I shall at last experience true happiness.'"

I went to bed pondering over these fancies, and my sleep was full of happy dreams. I saw myself dwelling in a retired spot amidst peace and plenty. I thought I was surrounded on all sides by a fair expanse of country which belonged to me, where I enjoyed that freedom the world cannot give. My dreams had all the force of reality, till a sudden awakening at day-break came to give them the lie. But the imaginary bliss I had enjoyed had so taken my fancy that I could not rest till I realized it. I arose, dressed myself hastily, and went out, fasting, without knowing where I was going.

I walked on and on, absorbed in contemplation, and did not really awake till I found myself in a ravine between two lofty mountains. Stepping forward I reached a valley surrounded by mountains on all sides, and in the distance a fine church, attached to a pile of buildings, magnificently situated. I guessed it to be a monastery, and I made my way towards it.

The church door was open, and I went in and was amazed at the rich marbles and the beauty of the altars; and, after hearing the last mass, I went to the sacristy and found myself in a crowd of Benedictines.

The abbot, whom I recognized by his cross, came towards me and asked if I wished to see the church and monastery. I replied that I should be delighted, and he, with two other brethren, offered to shew me all. I saw their rich ornaments, chasubles embroidered with gold and pearls, the sacred vessels adorned with diamonds and other precious stones, a rich balustrade, etc.

As I understood German very imperfectly and the Swiss dialect (which is hard to acquire and bears the same relation to German that Genoese has to Italian) not at all, I began to speak Latin, and asked the abbot if the church had been built for long. Thereupon the very reverend father entered into a long history, which would have made me repent my inquisitiveness if he had not finished by saying that the church was consecrated by Jesus Christ Himself. This was carrying its foundation rather far back, and no doubt my face expressed some surprise, for to convince me of the truth of the story the abbot bade me follow him into the church, and there on a piece of marble pavement he shewed me the imprint of the foot of Jesus, which He had left there at the moment of the consecration, to convince the infidels and to save the bishop the trouble of consecrating the church.

The abbot had had this divinely revealed to him in a dream, and going into the church to verify the vision he saw the print of the Divine Foot, and gave thanks to the Lord.

EPISODE 14 — SWITZERLAND

CHAPTER XIII

I Resolve to Become a Monk—I go to Confession—Delay of a Fortnight—
Giustiniani, the Apostle Capuchin—I Alter my Mind; My Reasons—My Pranks
at the Inn—I Dine With the Abbot

The cool way in which the abbot told these cock-and-bull stories gave me an
inclination to laughter, which the holiness of the place and the laws of politeness
had much difficulty in restraining. All the same I listened with such an attentive
air that his reverence was delighted with me and asked where I was staying.

"Nowhere," said I; "I came from Zurich on foot, and my first visit was to
your church."

I do not know whether I pronounced these words with an air of
compunction, but the abbot joined his hands and lifted them to heaven, as if to
thank God for touching my heart and bringing me there to lay down the burden
of my sins. I have no doubt that these were his thoughts, as I have always had
the look of a great sinner.

The abbot said it was near noon and that he hoped I would do him the
honour of dining with him, and I accepted with pleasure, for I had had nothing
to eat and I knew that there is usually good cheer in such places. I did not know
where I was and I did not care to ask, being willing to leave him under the
impression that I was a pilgrim come to expiate my sins.

On our way from the church the abbot told me that his monks were fasting,
but that we should eat meat in virtue of a dispensation he had received from
Benedict XIV., which allowed him to eat meat all the year round with his guests.
I replied that I would join him all the more willingly as the Holy Father had
given me a similar dispensation. This seemed to excite his curiosity about myself,
and when we got to his room, which did not look the cell of a penitent, he
hastened to shew me the brief, which he had framed and glazed and hung up
opposite the table so that the curious and scrupulous might have it in full view.

As the table was only laid for two, a servant in full livery came in and
brought another cover; and the humble abbot then told me that he usually had
his chancellor with him at dinner, "for," said he, "I have a chancery, since as
abbot of Our Lady of Einsiedel I am a prince of the Holy Roman Empire."

This was a relief to me, as I now knew where I was, and I no longer ran the
risk of shewing my ignorance in the course of conversation.

This monastery (of which I had heard before) was the Loretto of the
Mountains, and was famous for the number of pilgrims who resorted to it.

In the course of dinner the prince—abbot asked me where I came from, if I
were married, if I intended to make a tour of Switzerland, adding that he should
be glad to give me letters of introduction. I replied that I was a Venetian, a
bachelor, and that I should be glad to accept the letters of introduction he had

kindly offered me, after I had had a private conference with him, in which I desired to take his advice on my conscience.

Thus, without premeditation, and scarcely knowing what I was saying, I engaged to confess to the abbot.

This was my way. Whenever I obeyed a spontaneous impulse, whenever I did anything of a sudden, I thought I was following the laws of my destiny, and yielding to a supreme will. When I had thus plainly intimated to him that he was to be my confessor, he felt obliged to speak with religious fervour, and his discourses seemed tolerable enough during a delicate and appetising repast, for we had snipe and woodcock; which made me exclaim,—

"What! game like that at this time of year?"

"It's a secret," said he, with a pleased smile, "which I shall be glad to communicate to you."

The abbot was a man of taste, for though he affected sobriety he had the choicest wines and the most delicious dishes on the table. A splendid salmon-trout was brought, which made him smile with pleasure, and seasoning the good fare with a jest, he said in Latin that we must taste it as it was fish, and that it was right to fast a little.

While he was talking the abbot kept a keen eye on me, and as my fine dress made him feel certain that I had nothing to ask of him he spoke at ease.

When dinner was over the chancellor bowed respectfully and went out. Soon after the abbot took me over the monastery, including the library, which contained a portrait of the Elector of Cologne in semi-ecclesiastical costume. I told him that the portrait was a good though ugly likeness, and drew out of my pocket the gold snuffbox the prince had given me, telling him that it was a speaking likeness. He looked at it with interest, and thought his highness had done well to be taken in the dress of a grand-master. But I perceived that the elegance of the snuff-box did no harm to the opinion the abbot had conceived of me. As for the library, if I had been alone it would have made me weep. It contained nothing under the size of folio, the newest books were a hundred years old, and the subject-matter of all these huge books was solely theology and controversy. There were Bibles, commentators, the Fathers, works on canon law in German, volumes of annals, and Hoffman's dictionary.

"I suppose your monks have private libraries of their own," I said, "which contain accounts of travels, with historical and scientific works."

"Not at all," he replied; "my monks are honest folk, who are content to do their duty, and to live in peace and sweet ignorance."

I do not know what happened to me at that moment, but a strange whim came into my head—I would be a monk, too. I said nothing about it at the moment, but I begged the abbot to take me to his private chamber.

"I wish to make a general confession of all my sins," said I, "that I may obtain the benefit of absolution, and receive the Holy Eucharist on the morrow."

He made no answer, but led the way to a pretty little room, and without requiring me to kneel down said he was ready to hear me.

I sat down before him and for three consecutive hours I narrated scandalous histories unnumerable, which, however, I told simply and not spicily, since I felt ascetically disposed and obliged myself to speak with a contrition I did not feel, for when I recounted my follies I was very far from finding the remembrance of them disagreeable.

In spite of that, the serene or reverend abbot believed, at all events, in my attrition, for he told me that since by the appointed means I had once more placed myself in a state of grace, contrition would be perfected in me.

According to the good abbot, and still more according to me, without grace contrition is impossible.

After he had pronounced the sacramental words which take away the sins of men, he advised me to retire to the chamber he had appointed for me, to pass the rest of the day in prayer, and to go to bed at an early hour, but he added that I could have supper if I was accustomed to that meal. He told me that I might communicate at the first mass next morning, and with that we parted.

I obeyed with a docility which has puzzled me ever since, but at the time I thought nothing of it. I was left alone in a room which I did not even examine, and there I pondered over the idea which had come into my head before making my confession; and I quite made up my mind that chance, or rather my good genius, had led me to that spot, where happiness awaited me, and where I might shelter all my days from the tempests of the world.

"Whether I stay here," said I, "depends on myself alone, as I am sure the abbot will not refuse me the cowl if I give him ten thousand crowns for my support."

All that was needed to secure my happiness seemed a library of my own choosing, and I did not doubt but that the abbot would let me have what books I pleased if I promised to leave them to the monastery after my death.

As to the society of the monks, the discord, envy, and all the bickerings inseparable from such a mode of life, I thought I had nothing to pass in that way, since I had no ambitions which could rouse the jealousy of the other monks. Nevertheless, despite my fascination, I foresaw the possibility of repentance, and I shuddered at the thought, but I had a cure for that also.

"When I ask for the habit," I said, "I will also ask that my novitiate be extended for ten years, and if repentance do not come in ten years it will not come at all. I shall declare that I do not wish for any cure or any ecclesiastical dignity. All I want is peace and leave to follow my own tastes, without scandalising anyone." I thought: I could easily remove any objections which might be made to the long term of my novitiate, by agreeing, in case I changed my mind, to forfeit the ten thousand crowns which I would pay in advance.

I put down this fine idea in writing before I went to bed; and in the morning, finding myself unshaken in my resolve, after I had communicated I gave my plan to the abbot, who was taking chocolate in his room.

He immediately read my plan, and without saying anything put it on the table, and after breakfast he walked up and down the room and read it again, and finally told me that he would give me an answer after dinner.

I waited till night with the impatience of a child who has been promised toys on its birthday—so completely and suddenly can an infatuation change one's nature. We had as good a dinner as on the day before, and when we had risen from the table the good abbot said,

"My carriage is at the door to take you to Zurich. Go, and let me have a fortnight to think it over. I will bring my answer in person. In the meanwhile here are two sealed letters, which please deliver yourself."

I replied that I would obey his instructions and that I would wait for him at the "Sword," in the hope that he would deign to grant my wishes. I took his hand, which he allowed me to kiss, and I then set out for Zurich.

As soon as my Spaniard saw me the rascal began to laugh. I guessed what he was thinking, and asked him what he was laughing at.

"I am amazed to see that no sooner do you arrive in Switzerland than you contrive to find some amusement which keeps you away for two whole days."

"Ah, I see; go and tell the landlord that I shall want the use of a good carriage for the next fortnight, and also a guide on whom I can rely."

My landlord, whose name was Ote, had been a captain, and was thought a great deal of at Zurich. He told me that all the carriages in the neighbourhood were uncovered. I said they would do, as there was nothing better to be had, and he informed me I could trust the servant he would provide me with.

Next morning I took the abbot's letters. One was for M. Orelli and the other for a M. Pestalozzi, neither of whom I found at home; but in the afternoon they both called on me, asked me to dinner, and made me promise to come with them the same evening to a concert. This is the only species of entertainment allowed at Zurich, and only members of the musical society can be present, with the exception of strangers, who have to be introduced by a member, and are then admitted on the payment of a crown. The two gentlemen both spoke in very high terms of the Abbot of Einsiedel.

I thought the concert a bad one, and got bored at it. The men sat on the right hand and the women on the left. I was vexed with this arrangement, for in spite of my recent conversation I saw three or four ladies who pleased me, and whose eyes wandered a good deal in my direction. I should have liked to make love to them, to make the best of my time before I became a monk.

When the concert was over, men and women went out together, and the two citizens presented me to their wives and daughters, who looked pleasant, and were amongst those I had noticed.

Courtesy is necessarily cut short in the street, and, after I had thanked the two gentlemen, I went home to the "Sword."

Next day I dined with M. Orelli, and I had an opportunity for doing justice to his daughter's amiability without being able to let her perceive how she had impressed me. The day after, I played the same part with M. Pestalozzi, although his charming daughter was pretty enough to excite my gallantry. But to my own great astonishment I was a mirror of discretion, and in four days that was my character all over the town. I was quite astonished to find myself accosted in quite a respectful manner, to which I was not accustomed; but in the pious state of mind I was in, this confirmed me in the belief that my idea of taking the cowl had been a Divine inspiration. Nevertheless, I felt listless and weary, but I looked upon that as the inevitable consequence of so complete a change of life, and thought it would disappear when I grew more accustomed to goodness.

In order to put myself, as soon as possible, on an equality with my future brethren, I passed three hours every morning in learning German. My master was an extraordinary man, a native of Genoa, and an apostate Capuchin. His name was Giustiniani. The poor man, to whom I gave six francs every morning, looked upon me as an angel from heaven, although I, with the enthusiasm of a devotee, took him for a devil of hell, for he lost no opportunity of throwing a stone at the religious orders. Those orders which had the highest reputation, were, according to him, the worst of all, since they led more people astray. He styled monks in general as a vile rabble, the curse of the human race.

"But," said I to him one day, "you will confess that Our Lady of Einsiedel . . ."

"What!" replied the Genoese, without letting me finish my remark, "do you think I should make an exception in favour of a set of forty ignorant, lazy, vicious, idle, hypocritical scoundrels who live bad lives under the cloak of humility, and eat up the houses of the poor simpletons who provide for them, when they ought to be earning their own bread?"

"But how about his reverend highness the abbot?"

"A stuck-up peasant who plays the part of a prince, and is fool enough to think himself one."

"But he is a prince."

"As much a prince as I am. I look upon him as a mere buffoon."

"What has he done to you?"

"Nothing; but he is a monk."

"He is a friend of mine."

"I cannot retract what I have said, but I beg your pardon."

This Giustiniani had a great influence upon me, although I did not know it, for I thought my vocation was sure. But my idea of becoming a monk at Einsiedel came to an end as follows:

The day before the abbot was coming to see me, at about six o'clock in the evening, I was sitting at my window, which looked out on the bridge, and gazing at the passers-by, when all at once a carriage and four came up at a good pace and stopped at the inn. There was no footman on it, and consequently the waiter came out and opened the door, and I saw four well-dressed women leave the carriage. In the first three I saw nothing noticeable, but the fourth, who was dressed in a riding-habit, struck me at once with her elegance and beauty. She was a brunette with fine and well-set eyes, arched eyebrows, and a complexion in which the hues of the lily and the rose were mingled. Her bonnet was of blue satin with a silver fillet, which gave her an air I could not resist. I stretched out from the window as far as I could, and she lifted her eyes and looked at me as if I had bade her do so. My position obliged me to look at her for half a minute; too much for a modest woman, and more than was required to set me all ablaze.

I ran and took up my position at the window of my ante-chamber, which commanded a view of the staircase, and before long I saw her running by to rejoin her three companions. When she got opposite to my window she chanced to turn in that direction, and on seeing me cried out as if she had seen a ghost; but she soon recollected herself and ran away, laughing like a madcap, and rejoined the other ladies who were already in their room.

Reader, put yourself in my place, and tell me how I could have avoided this meeting. And you who would bury yourselves in monastic shades, persevere, if you can, after you have seen what I saw at Zurich on April 23rd.

I was in such a state of excitement that I had to lie down on my bed. After resting a few minutes, I got up and almost unconsciously went towards the passage window and saw the waiter coming out of the ladies' room.

"Waiter," said I, "I will take supper in the dining-room with everybody else."

"If you want to see those ladies, that won't do, as they have ordered their supper to be brought up to them. They want to go to bed in good time as they are to leave at day-break."

"Where are they going?"

"To Our Lady of Einsiedel to pay their vows."

"Where do they come from?"

"From Soleure."

"What are their names?"

"I don't know."

I went to lie down again, and thought how I could approach the fair one of my thoughts. Should I go to Einsiedel, too? But what could I do when I got there? These ladies are going to make their confessions; I could not get into the confessional. What kind of a figure should I cut among the monks? And if I were to meet the abbot on the way, how could I help returning with him? If I had had a trusty friend I would have arranged an ambuscade and carried off my charmer. It would have been an easy task, as she had nobody to defend her. What if I were to pluck up my heart and beg them to let me sup in their company? I was afraid of the three devotees; I should meet with a refusal. I judged that my charmer's devotion was more a matter of form than any thing else, as her physiognomy declared her to be a lover of pleasure, and I had long been accustomed to read womens' characters by the play of their features.

I did not know which way to turn, when a happy idea came into my head. I went to the passage window and stayed there till the waiter went by. I had him into the room, and began my discourse by sliding a piece of gold into his hand. I then asked him to lend me his green apron, as I wished to wait upon the ladies at supper.

"What are you laughing at?"

"At your taking such a fancy, sir, though I think I know why."

"You are a sharp fellow."

"Yes, sir, as sharp as most of them; I will get you a new apron. The pretty one asked me who you were."

"What did you tell her?"

"I said you were an Italian; that's all."

"If you will hold your tongue I will double that piece of gold."

"I have asked your Spaniard to help me, sir, as I am single-handed, and supper has to be served at the same time both upstairs and downstairs."

"Very good; but the rascal mustn't come into the room or he would be sure to laugh. Let him go to the kitchen, bring up the dishes, and leave them outside the door."

The waiter went out, and returned soon after with the apron and Le Duc, to whom I explained in all seriousness what he had to do. He laughed like a madman, but assured me he would follow my directions. I procured a carving-knife, tied my hair in a queue, took off my coat, and put on the apron over my scarlet waistcoat ornamented with gold lace. I then looked at myself in the glass, and thought my appearance mean enough for the modest part I was about to play. I was delighted at the prospect, and thought to myself that as the ladies came from Soleure they would speak French.

Le Duc came to tell me that the waiter was going upstairs. I went into the ladies' room and said, "Supper is about to be served, ladies."

"Make haste about it, then," said the ugliest of them, "as we have got to rise before day-break."

I placed the chairs round the table and glanced at my fair one, who looked petrified. The waiter came in, and I helped him to put the dishes on the table, and he then said to me, "Do you stay here, as I have to go downstairs."

I took a plate and stood behind a chair facing the lady, and without appearing to look at her I saw her perfectly, or rather I saw nothing else. She was astonished the others did not give me a glance, and they could not have pleased me better. After the soup I hurried to change her plate, and then did the same office for the rest: they helped themselves to the boiled beef.

While they were eating, I took a boiled capon and cut it up in a masterly manner.

"We have a waiter who knows his work," said the lady of my thoughts.

"Have you been long at this inn?"

"Only a few weeks, madam."

"You wait very well."

"Madam is very good."

I had tucked in my superb ruffles of English point lace, but my frilled shirt front of the same material protruded slightly through my vest, which I had not buttoned carefully. She saw it, and said, "Come here a moment."

"What does madam require?"

"Let me see it. What beautiful lace!"

"So I have been told, madam, but it is very old. An Italian gentleman who was staying here made me a present of it."

"You have ruffles of the same kind, I suppose?"

"Yes, madam;" and so saying I stretched out my hand, unbuttoning my waistcoat. She gently drew out the ruffle, and seemed to place herself in a position to intoxicate me with the sight of her charms, although she was tightly laced. What an ecstatic moment! I knew she had recognized me, and the thought that I could not carry the masquerade beyond a certain point was a veritable torment to me.

When she had looked a long time, one of the others said,

"You are certainly very curious, my dear, one would think you had never seen lace before."

At this she blushed.

When the supper was done, the three ugly ladies each went apart to undress, while I took away the dishes, and my heroine began to write. I confess that I was almost infatuated enough to think that she was writing to me; however, I had too high an opinion of her to entertain the idea.

As soon as I had taken away the dishes, I stood by the door in the respectful manner becoming the occasion.

"What are you waiting for?" she said.

"For your orders, madam."

"Thank you, I don't want anything."

"Your boots, madam, you will like them removed before you retire."

"True, but still I don't like to give you so much trouble."

"I am here to attend on you, madam."

So saying, I knelt on one knee before her, and slowly unplaced her boots while she continued writing. I went farther; I unbuckled her garters, delighting in the contemplation and still more in the touch of her delicately-shaped legs, but too soon for me she turned her head, and said,

"That will do, thank you. I did not notice that you were giving yourself so much trouble. We shall see you to-morrow evening."

"Then you will sup here, ladies?"

"Certainly."

I took her boots away, and asked if I should lock the door.

"No, my good fellow," said she, in the voice of a syren, "leave the key inside."

Le Duc took the charmer's boots from me, and said, laughing,—

"She has caught you."

"What?"

"I saw it all, sir, you played your part as well as any actor in Paris; and I am certain that she will give you a louis to-morrow, but if you don't hand it over to me I will blow on the whole thing."

"That's enough, you rascal; get me my supper as quickly as possible."

Such are the pleasures which old age no longer allows me to enjoy, except in my memory. There are monsters who preach repentance, and philosophers who treat all pleasures as vanity. Let them talk on. Repentance only befits crimes, and pleasures are realities, though all too fleeting.

A happy dream made me pass the night with the fair lady; doubtless it was a delusion, but a delusion full of bliss. What would I not give now for such dreams, which made my nights so sweet!

Next morning at day-break I was at her door with her boots in my hand just as their coachman came to call them. I asked them, as a matter of form, if they would have breakfast, and they replied merrily that they had made too good a supper to have any appetite at such an early hour. I went out of the room to give them time to dress, but the door was half open, and I saw reflected in the glass the snow-white bosom of my fair one; it was an intoxicating sight. When she had laced herself and put on her dress she called for her boots. I asked if I should put them on, to which she consented with a good grace, and as she had green velvet breeches, she seemed to consider herself as almost a man. And, after all, a waiter is not worth putting one's self out about. All the worst for him if he dare conceive any hopes from the trifling concessions he receives. His punishment will be severe, for who would have thought he could have presumed so far? As for me, I am now, sad to say, grown old, and enjoy some few privileges of this description, which I relish, though despising myself, and still more those who thus indulge me.

After she had gone I went to sleep again, hoping to see her in the evening. When I awoke I heard that the abbot of Einsiedel was at Zurich, and my landlord told me that his reverend highness would dine with me in my room. I told him that I wished to treat the abbot well, and that he must set the best dinner he could for us.

At noon the worthy prelate was shewn up to my room, and began by complimenting me on the good reputation I had at Zurich, saying that this made him believe that my vocation was a real one.

"The following distich," he added, "should now become your motto: "Inveni portum. Spes et fortuna valete; Nil mihi vobiscum est: ludite nuns alios."

"That is a translation of two verses from Euripides," I answered; "but, my lord, they will not serve me, as I have changed my mind since yesterday."

"I congratulate you," said he, "and I hope you will accomplish all your desires. I may tell you confidentially that it is much easier to save one's soul in the world where one can do good to one's neighbours, than in the convent, where a man does no good to himself nor to anyone else."

This was not speaking like the hypocrite Guistiniani had described to me; on the contrary, it was the language of a good and sensible man.

We had a princely dinner, as my landlord had made each of the three courses a work of art. The repast was enlivened by an interesting conversation, to which wit and humour were not lacking. After coffee I thanked the abbot with the greatest respect, and accompanied him to his carriage, where the reverend father reiterated his offers of serving me, and thus, well pleased with one another, we parted.

The presence and the conversation of this worthy priest had not for a moment distracted my thoughts from the pleasing object with which they were occupied. So soon as the abbot had gone, I went to the bridge to await the blessed angel, who seemed to have been sent from Soleure with the express purpose of delivering me from the temptation to become a monk, which the devil had put into my heart. Standing on the bridge I built many a fine castle in

Spain, and about six in the evening I had the pleasure of seeing my fair traveller once more. I hid myself so as to see without being seen. I was greatly surprised to see them all four looking towards my window. Their curiosity shewed me that the lady had told them of the secret, and with my astonishment there was some admixture of anger. This was only natural, as I not only saw myself deprived of the hope of making any further advances, but I felt that I could no longer play my part of waiter with any confidence. In spite of my love for the lady I would not for the world become the laughing-stock of her three plain companions. If I had interested her in my favour, she would certainly not have divulged my secret, and I saw in her doing so proof positive that she did not want the jest to go any further, or rather of her want of that spirit so necessary to ensure the success of an intrigue. If the three companions of my charmer had had anything attractive about them, I might possibly have persevered and defied misfortune; but in the same measure as beauty cheers my heart, ugliness depresses it. Anticipating the melancholy which I foresaw would result from this disappointment, I went out with the idea of amusing myself, and happening to meet Giustiniani I told him of my misfortune, saying that I should not be sorry to make up for it by a couple of hours of the society of some mercenary beauty.

"I will take you to a house," said he, "where you will find what you want. Go up to the second floor and you will be well received by an old woman, if you whisper my name to her. I dare not accompany you, as I am well known in the town and it might get me into trouble with the police, who are ridiculously strict in these matters. Indeed I advise you to take care that nobody sees you going in."

I followed the ex-Capuchin's advice and waited for the dusk of the evening. I had a good reception, but the supper was poor, and the hours that I spent with two young girls of the working class were tedious. They were pretty enough, but my head was full of my perfidious charmer, and besides, despite their neatness and prettiness, they were wanting in that grace which adds so many charms to pleasure. The liberality of my payment, to which they were not accustomed, captivated the old woman, who said she would get me all the best stuff in the town; but she warned me to take care that nobody saw me going into her house.

When I got back Le Duc told me that I had been wise to slip away, as my masquerade had become generally known, and the whole house, including the landlord, had been eagerly waiting to see me play the part of waiter. "I took your place," he added. "The lady who has taken your fancy is Madame——, and I must confess she is vastly fine."

"Did she ask where the other waiter was?"

"No, but the other ladies asked what had become of you several times."

"And Madame said nothing?"

"She didn't open her mouth, but looked sad and seemed to care for nothing, till I said you were away because you were ill."

"That was stupid of you. Why did you say that?"

"I had to say something."

"True. Did you untie her shoe?"

"No; she did not want me to do so."

"Good. Who told you her name?"

"Her coachman. She is just married to a man older than herself."

I went to bed, but could only think of the indiscretion and sadness of my fair lady. I could not reconcile the two traits in her character. Next day, knowing that she would be starting early, I posted myself at the window to see her get into the carriage, but I took care to arrange the curtain in such a way that I could not be seen. Madame was the last to get in, and pretending that she wanted to see if it rained, she took off her bonnet and lifted her head. Drawing the curtain with one hand, and taking off my cap with the other, I wafted her a kiss with the tips of my fingers. In her turn she bowed graciously, returning my kiss with a good-natured smile.

CHAPTER XIV

I Leave Zurich—Comic Adventure at Baden—Soleure—M. De Chavigni—M. and Madame * * * I Act in a Play—I Counterfeit Sickness to Attain Happiness

M. Mote, my landlord, introduced his two sons to me. He had brought them up like young princes. In Switzerland, an inn-keeper is not always a man of no account. There are many who are as much respected as people of far higher rank are in other countries. But each country has its own manners. My landlord did the honours of the table, and thought it no degradation to make his guests pay for the meal. He was right; the only really degrading thing in the world is vice. A Swiss landlord only takes the chief place at table to see that everyone is properly attended to. If he have a son, he does not sit down with his father, but waits on the guests, with napkin in hand. At Schaffhaus, my landlord's son, who was a captain in the Imperial army, stood behind my chair and changed my plate, while his father sat at the head of the table. Anywhere else the son would have been waited on, but in his father's house he thought, and rightly, that it was an honour to wait.

Such are Swiss customs, of which persons of superficial understanding very foolishly make a jest. All the same, the vaunted honour and loyalty of the Swiss do not prevent them from fleecing strangers, at least as much as the Dutch, but the greenhorns who let themselves be cheated, learn thereby that it is well to bargain before-hand, and then they treat one well and charge reasonably. In this way, when I was at Bale, I baffled the celebrated Imhoff, the landlord of the "Three Kings."

M. Ote complimented me on my waiter's disguise, and said he was sorry not to have seen me officiating, nevertheless, he said he thought I was wise not to repeat the jest. He thanked me for the honour I had done his house, and begged me to do him the additional favour of dining at his table some day before I left. I answered that I would dine with him with pleasure that very day. I did so, and was treated like a prince.

The reader will have guessed that the last look my charmer gave me had not extinguished the fire which the first sight of her had kindled in my breast. It had rather increased my flame by giving me hopes of being better acquainted with her; in short, it inspired me with the idea of going to Soleure in order to give a happy ending to the adventure. I took a letter of credit on Geneva, and wrote to Madame d'Urfe, begging her to give me a written introduction, couched in strong terms to M. de Chavigni, the French ambassador, telling her that the interests of our order were highly involved in my knowing this diplomatist, and requesting her to address letters to me at the post office at Soleure. I also wrote to the Duke of Wurtemburg, but had no answer from him, and indeed he must have found my epistle very unpleasant reading.

I visited the old woman whom Giustiniani had told me of several times before I left Zurich, and although I ought to have been well satisfied as far as physical beauty was concerned, my enjoyment was very limited, as the nymphs I wooed only spoke Swiss dialect—a rugged corruption of German. I have always found that love without speech gives little enjoyment, and I cannot imagine a more unsatisfactory mistress than a mute, were she as lovely as Venus herself.

I had scarcely left Zurich when I was obliged to stop at Baden to have the carriage M. Ote had got me mended. I might have started again at eleven, but on hearing that a young Polish lady on her way to Our Lady of Einseidel was to dine at the common table, I decided to wait; but I had my trouble for nothing, as she turned out to be quite unworthy of the delay.

After dinner, while my horses were being put in, the host's daughter, a pretty girl enough, came into the room and made me waltz with her; it chanced to be a Sunday. All at once her father came in, and the girl fled.

"Sir," said the rascal, "you are condemned to pay a fine of one louis."

"Why?"

"For having danced on a holy day."

"Get out; I won't pay."

"You will pay, though," said he, shewing me a great parchment covered with writing I did not understand.

"I will appeal."

"To whom, sir?"

"To the judge of the place."

He left the room, and in a quarter of an hour I was told that the judge was waiting for me in an adjoining chamber. I thought to myself that the judges were very polite in that part of the world, but when I got into the room I saw the rascally host buried in a wig and gown.

"Sir," said he, "I am the judge."

"Judge and plaintiff too, as far as I can see."

He wrote in his book, confirming the sentence, and mulcting me in six francs for the costs of the case.

"But if your daughter had not tempted me." said I, "I should not have danced; she is therefore as guilty as I."

"Very true, sir; here is a Louis for her." So saying he took a Louis out of his pocket, put it into a desk beside him, and said; "Now yours."

I began to laugh, paid my fine, and put off my departure till the morrow.

As I was going to Lucerne I saw the apostolic nuncio (who invited me to dinner), and at Fribourg Comte d'Afri's young and charming wife; but at ten leagues from Soleure I was a witness of the following curious circumstances.

I was stopping the night in a village, and had made friends with the surgeon, whom I had found at the inn, and while supper, which he was to share with me, was getting ready, we walked about the village together. It was in the dusk of the evening, and at a distance of a hundred paces I saw a man climbing up the wall of a house, and finally vanishing through a window on the first floor.

"That's a robber," said I, pointing him out to the surgeon. He laughed and said,—

"The custom may astonish you, but it is a common one in many parts of Switzerland. The man you have just seen is a young lover who is going to pass the night with his future bride. Next morning he will leave more ardent than before, as she will not allow him to go too far. If she was weak enough to yield to his desires he would probably decline to marry her, and she would find it difficult to get married at all."

At Soleure I found a letter from Madame d'Urfe, with an enclosure from the Duc de Choiseul to the ambassador, M. de Chavigni. It was sealed, but the duke's name was written below the address.

I made a Court toilet, took a coach, and went to call on the ambassador. His excellency was not at home, so I left my card and the letter. It was a feast-day, and I went to high mass, not so much, I confess, to seek for God as for my charmer, but she was not there. After service I walked around the town, and on my return found an officer who asked me to dinner at the ambassador's.

Madame d'Urfe said that on the receipt of my letter she had gone straightway to Versailles, and that with the help of Madame de Grammont she had got me an introduction of the kind I wanted. This was good news for me, as I desired to cut an imposing figure at Soleure. I had plenty of money, and I knew that this magic metal glittered in the eyes of all. M. de Chavigni had been ambassador at Venice thirty years before, and I knew a number of anecdotes about his adventures there, and I was eager to see what I could make out of him.

I went to his house at the time appointed, and found all his servants in full livery, which I looked upon as a happy omen. My name was not announced, and I remarked that when I came in both sides of the door were opened for me by the page. A fine old man came forward to meet me, and paying me many well-turned compliments introduced me to those present. Then, with the delicate tact of the courtier, pretending not to recollect my name, he drew the Duc de Choiseul's letter from his pocket, and read aloud the paragraph in which the minister desired him to treat me with the utmost consideration. He made me sit on an easy chair at his right hand, and asked me questions to which I could only answer that I was travelling for my pleasure, and that I considered the Swiss nation to be in many respects superior to all other nations whatsoever.

Dinner was served, and his excellency set me on his right hand in a position of equal honour to his own. We were sixteen in company, and behind every chair stood a magnificent lackey in the ambassador's livery. In the course of conversation I got an opportunity of telling the ambassador that he was still spoken of at Venice with the utmost affection.

"I shall always remember," he said, "the kindness with which the Venetians treated me; but tell me, I beg, the names of those gentlemen who still remember me; they must be quite old now."

This was what I was waiting for. M. de Malipiero had told me of certain events which had happened during the regency, and M. de Bragadin had informed me of the ambassador's amours with the celebrated Stringhetta.

His excellency's fare was perfect, but in the pleasure of conversing I forgot that of eating. I told all my anecdotes so racily that his features expressed the pleasure I was affording him, and when we rose from the table he shook me by the hand, and told me he had not had so agreeable a dinner since he had been at Soleure.

"The recollection of my Venetian gallantries," said the worthy old man, "makes me recall many a happy moment; I feel quite young again."

He embraced me, and bade me consider myself as one of his family during my stay at Soleure.

After dinner he talked a good deal about Venice, praising the Government, and saying that there was not a town in the world where a man could fare better, provided he took care to get good oil and foreign wines. About five o'clock he asked me to come for a drive with him, getting into the carriage first to give me the best place.

We got out at a pretty country house where ices were served to us. On our way back he said that he had a large party every evening, and that he hoped I would do him the honour to be present whenever it suited my inclinations, assuring me that he would do his best to amuse me. I was impatient to take part in the assembly, as I felt certain I should see my charmer there. It was a vain hope, however, for I saw several ladies, some old and ugly, some passable, but not one pretty.

Cards were produced, and I soon found myself at a table with a young lady of fair complexion and a plain-looking woman well advanced in years, who seemed, however, not to be destitute of wit. Though I was looed I played on, and I lost five or six hundred fish without opening my lips. When it came to a profit and loss account, the plain woman told me I owed three louis.

"Three louis, madam."

"Yes, sir; we have been playing at two sous the fish. You thought, perhaps, we were playing for farthings."

"On the contrary, I thought it was for francs, as I never play lower." She did not answer this boast of mine, but she seemed annoyed. On rejoining the company after this wearisome game, I proceeded to scrutinize all the ladies present rapidly but keenly, but I could not see her for whom I looked, and was on the point of leaving, when I happened to notice two ladies who were looking at me attentively. I recognized them directly. They were two of my fair one's companions, whom I had had the honour of waiting on at Zurich. I hurried off, pretending not to recognize them.

Next day, a gentleman in the ambassador's suite came to tell me that his excellency was going to call on me. I told him that I would not go out till I had the honour of receiving his master, and I conceived the idea of questioning him concerning that which lay next to my heart. However, he spared me the trouble, as the reader will see for himself.

I gave M. de Chavigni the best reception I could, and after we had discussed the weather he told me, with a smile, that he had the most ridiculous affair to broach to me, begging me to credit him when he said that he did not believe it for a moment.

"Proceed, my lord."

"Two ladies who saw you at my house yesterday told me in confidence, after you had gone, that I should do well to be on my guard, as you were the waiter in an inn at Zurich where they had stayed. They added that they had seen the other waiter by the Aar, and that in all probability you had run away from the inn together; God alone knows why! They said, furthermore, that you slipped away from my house yesterday as soon as you saw them. I told them that even if you were not the bearer of a letter from his grace the Duc de Choiseul I should have been convinced that they were mistaken, and that they should dine with you to-day, if they would accept my invitation. I also hinted that you might have merely disguised yourself as a waiter in the hopes of winning some favours from them, but they rejected the hypothesis as absurd, and said that you could carve a capon and change a plate dexterously enough, but were only a common waiter for all that, adding that with my permission they would compliment you on your skill to-day.

"'Do so, by all means, ladies,' said I, 'M. Casanova and myself will be highly amused.' And now do you mind telling me whether there be any foundation of truth in the whole story?"

"Certainly, my lord, I will tell you all without reserve, but in confidence, as this ridiculous report may injure the honour of one who is dear to me, and whom I would not injure for the world."

"It is true, then? I am quite interested to hear all about it."

"It is true to a certain extent; I hope you don't take me for the real waiter at the 'Sword.'"

"Certainly not, but I supposed you played the part of waiter?"

"Exactly. Did they tell you that they were four in company."

"Ah, I have got it! Pretty Madame was one of the party. That explains the riddle; now I understand everything. But you were quite right in saying that discretion was needful; she has a perfectly blameless reputation."

"Ah! I did not know that. What happened was quite innocent, but it might be so garbled in the telling as to become prejudicial to the honour of a lady whose beauty struck me with admiration."

I told him all the details of the case, adding that I had only come to Soleure in the hopes of succeeding in my suit.

"If that prove an impossibility," said I, "I shall leave Soleure in three or four days; but I will first turn the three ugly companions of my charmer into ridicule. They might have had sense enough to guess that the waiter's apron was only a disguise. They can only pretend to be ignorant of the fact in the hope of getting some advantage over me, and injuring their friend, who was ill advised to let them into the secret."

"Softly, softly, you go too fast and remind me of my own young days. Permit me to embrace you, your story has delighted me. You shall not go away, you shall stay here and court your charmer. To-day you can turn two mischievous women into ridicule, but do it in an easy way. The thing is so straightforward that M.——— will be the first to laugh at it. His wife cannot be ignorant of your love for her, and I know enough of women to pronounce that your disguise cannot have displeased her. She does know of your love?"

"Undoubtedly."

He went away laughing, and at the door of his coach embraced me for the third time.

I could not doubt that my charmer had told the whole story to her three friends as they were returning from Einsiedel to Zurich, and this made the part they had played all the more ill-natured; but I felt that it was to my interest to let their malice pass for wit.

I went to the ambassador's at half-past one, and after making my bow to him I proceeded to greet the company, and saw the two ladies. Thereupon, with a frank and generous air, I went up to the more malicious-looking of the two (she was lame, which may have made me think her more ill-looking) and asked if she recognized me.

"You confess, then, that you are the waiter at the 'Sword'?"

"Well, not quite that, madam, but I confess that I was the waiter for an hour, and that you cruelly disdained to address a single word to me, though I was only a waiter, because I longed for the bliss of seeing you. But I hope I shall be a little more fortunate here, and that you will allow me to pay you my respectful homage."

"This is very wonderful! You played your part so well that the sharpest eye would have been deceived. Now we shall see if you play your new part as well. If you do me the honour to call on me I will give you a good welcome."

After these complimentary speeches, the story became public property, and the whole table was amusing itself with it, when I had the happiness of seeing M.—— and Madame coming into the room.

"There is the good-natured waiter," said she to her husband.

The worthy man stepped forward, and politely thanked me for having done his wife the honour of taking off her boots.

This told me that she had concealed nothing, and I was glad. Dinner was served, M. de Chavigni made my charmer sit at his right hand, and I was placed between my two calumniators. I was obliged to hide my game, so, although I disliked them intensely, I made love to them, hardly raising my eyes to glance at Madame, who looked ravishing. I did not find her husband either as old or as jealous as I had expected. The ambassador asked him and his wife to stay the evening to an impromptu ball, and then said, that in order for me to be able to tell the Duc de Choiseul that I was well amused at Soleure, he would be delighted to have a play, if Madame would act the fair 'Ecossaise' again. She said she should be delighted, but two more actors were wanted.

"That is all right," said the kind old gentleman, "I will play Montrose."

"And I, Murray," I remarked.

My lame friend, angry at this arrangement, which only left her the very bad part of Lady Alton, could not help lancing a shaft at me.

"Oh! why isn't there a waiter's part in the play?" said she, "you would play it so well."

"That is well said, but I hope you will teach me to play Murray even better."

Next morning, I got the words of my part, and the ambassador told me that the ball would be given in my honour. After dinner I went to my inn, and after making an elaborate toilette I returned to the brilliant company.

The ambassador begged me to open the ball, and introduced me to the highest born but not the most beautiful lady in the place. I then danced with all the ladies present until the good-natured old man got me the object of my vows as a partner in the quadrilles, which he did so easily that no one could have made any remark. "Lord Murray," said he, "must dance with no one but Lindane."

At the first pause I took the opportunity of saying that I had only come to Soleure for her sake, that it was for her sake that I had disguised myself at Zurich, and that I hoped she would permit me to pay my addresses to her.

"I cannot invite you to my house," said she, "for certain sufficient reasons; but if you will stay here some time we shall be able to see each other. But I entreat you not to shew me any marked attention in public, for there are those who will spy upon our actions, and it is not pleasant to be talked about."

I was quite satisfied with this, and told her that I would do all in my power to please her, and that the most prying eyes should have nothing to fix on. I felt that the pleasure I looked forward to would be rendered all the sweeter by a tincture of mystery.

I had proclaimed myself as a novice in the mimic art, and had entreated my lame friend to be kind enough to instruct me. I therefore went to her in the morning, but she could only flatter herself that hers was a reflected light, as I had opportunities for paying my court to my charmer in her house, and however great her vanity may have been, she must have had some suspicions of the truth.

This woman was a widow, aged between thirty and forty years, of a jaundiced complexion, and a piercing and malicious aspect. In her efforts to hide the inequality of her legs, she walked with a stiff and awkward air; and, wishing to be thought a wit, she increased her natural dullness by a ceaseless flow of small talk. I persisted in behaving towards her with a great air of respect, and one day she said that, having seen me in the disguise of a waiter, she would not have thought I was a man of a timid nature.

"In what respect do you think me timid?" said I; to which she gave me no answer, but I knew perfectly well what she meant. I was tired of my part, and I had determined to play it no more when we had acted L'Ecossaise.

All the best people at Soleure were present at our first performance. The lame lady was delighted with the horror inspired by her acting; but she might credit a great deal of it to her appearance. M. de Chavigni drew forth the tears of the audience, his acting was said to be better than the great Voltaire's. As for me, I remember how near I was to fainting when, in the third scene of the fifth act, Lindane said to me,

"What! You! You dare to love me?"

She pronounced these words with such fiery scorn that all the spectators applauded vehemently. I was almost put out of countenance, for I thought I detected in her voice an insult to my honour. However, I collected myself in the minute's respite which the loud applause gave me, and I replied,—

"Yes; I adore you! How should I not?"

So pathetically and tenderly did I pronounce these words that the hall rang again with the applause, and the encores from four hundred throats made me repeat the words which, indeed, came from my heart.

In spite of the pleasure we had given to the audience, we judged ourselves not perfect in our parts, and M. de Chavigni advised us to put off our second performance for a couple of days.

"We will have a rehearsal to-morrow at my country house," said he, "and I beg the favour of all your companies to dinner there."

However, we all made each other compliments on our acting. My lame friend told me I had played well, but not so well as in the part of waiter, which really suited me admirably. This sarcasm got the laugh on her side, but I returned it by telling her that my performance was a work of art, while her playing of Lady Alton was pure nature. M. de Chavigni told Madame that the spectators were wrong to applaud when she expressed her wonder at my loving her, since she had spoken the words disdainfully; and it was impossible that Lindane could have despised Murray. The ambassador called for me the next day in his carriage, and when we reached his country-house we found all the actors assembled there. His excellency addressed himself in the first place to M.——, telling him he thought his business was as good as done, and that they would talk about it after dinner. We sat down to table, and afterwards rehearsed the piece without any need of the prompter's assistance.

Towards evening the ambassador told the company that he would expect them to supper that evening at Soleure, and everyone left with the exception of the ambassador, myself, and M.—— and Madame——. Just as we were going I had an agreeable surprise.

"Will you come with me," said the Ambassador to M.——, "we can talk the matter over at our ease? M. Casanova will have the honour of keeping your wife company in your carriage."

I gave the fair lady my hand respectfully, and she took it with an air of indifference, but as I was helping her in she pressed my hand with all her might. The reader can imagine how that pressure made my blood circulate like fire in my veins.

Thus we were seated side by side, our knees pressed tenderly against each other. Half an hour seemed like a minute, but it must not be thought that we wasted the time. Our lips were glued together, and were not set apart till we came within ten paces of the ambassador's house, which I could have wished at ten leagues distance. She was the first to get down, and I was alarmed to see the violent blush which overspread her whole face. Such redness looked unnatural; it might betray us; our spring of happiness would soon be dry. The watchful eye of the envious Alton would be fixed upon us, and not in vain; her triumph would outweigh her humiliation. I was at my wits' end.

Love and luck, which have so favoured me throughout the course of my life, came to my aid. I had about me a small box containing hellebore. I opened it as if by instinct, and invited her to take a small pinch. She did so, and I followed her example; but the dose was too strong, and as we were going up the stairs we began to sneeze, and for the next quarter of an hour we continued sneezing. People were obliged to attribute her high colour to the sneezing, or at least no one could give voice to any other suppositions. When the sneezing fit was over, this woman, who was as clever as she was pretty, said her headache was gone, but she would take care another time not to take so strong a dose. I looked out of the corner of my eye at the malicious widow, who said nothing but seemed deep in thought.

This piece of good luck decided me on staying at Soleure till my love was crowned with success, and I determined to take a country house. I shall not have much opinion of my readers if they find themselves in my position—rich, young, independent, full of fire, and having only pleasure to seek for—and do not follow my example. A perfect beauty was before me with whom I was madly in love, and who, I was sure, shared that love. I had plenty of money, and I was my own master. I thought this a much better plan than turning monk, and I was above caring "what people would say." As soon as the ambassador had returned, which he always did at an early hour on account of his advanced age, I left the company and went to see him in his private room. In truth I felt I must give him that confidence which he had so well deserved.

As soon as he saw me he said,—

"Well, well, did you profit by the interview I got you?"

I embraced him, and said,—

"I may hope for everything."

When I was telling him about the hellebore he was lavish in his compliments on my presence of mind, for, as he said, such an unusual colour would have made people think there had been some kind of a combat—a supposition which would not have tended towards my success. After I had told him all, I imparted my plan.

"I shall do nothing in a hurry," said I, "as I have to take care that the lady's honour does not suffer, and I trust to time to see the accomplishment of my wishes. I shall want a pretty country house, a good carriage, two lackeys, a good cook, and a housekeeper. All that I leave to your excellency, as I look upon you as my refuge and guardian angel."

"To-morrow, without fail, I will see what I can do, and I have good hopes of doing you a considerable service and of rendering you well content with the attractions of Soleure."

Next day our rehearsal went off admirably, and the day after the ambassador spoke to me as follows:

"So far as I can see, what you are aiming at in this intrigue is the satisfying of your desires without doing any harm to the lady's reputation. I think I know the nature of your love for her well enough to say that if she told you that your leaving Soleure was necessary to her peace of mind you would leave her at once.

You see that I have sounded you well enough to be a competent adviser in this delicate and important affair, to which the most famous events in the annals of diplomacy are not to be compared."

"Your excellency does not do sufficient justice to a career which has gained you such distinction."

"That's because I am an old man, my dear fellow, and have shaken off the rust and dust of prejudices, and am able to see things as they really are, and appreciate them at their true value. But let us return to your love-affair. If you wish to keep it in the dark, you must avoid with the greatest care any action which may awaken suspicion in the minds of people who do not believe that anything is indifferent. The most malicious and censorious will not be able to get anything but the merest chance out of the interview I procured you today, and the accident of the sneezing bout, defy the most ill-natured to draw any deductions; for an eager lover does not begin his suit by sending the beloved one into convulsions. Nobody can guess that your hellebore was used to conceal the blush that your caresses occasioned, since it does not often happen that an amorous combat leaves such traces; and how can you be expected to have foreseen the lady's blushes, and to have provided yourself with a specific against them? In short, the events of to-day will not disclose your secret. M.—— who, although he wishes to pass for a man devoid of jealousy, is a little jealous; M.—— himself cannot have seen anything out of the common in my asking him to return with me, as I had business of importance with him, and he has certainly no reasons for supposing that I should be likely to help you to intrigue with his wife. Furthermore, the laws of politeness would have forbidden me, under any circumstances, offering the lady the place I offered him, and as he prides himself on his politeness he can raise no possible objection to the arrangement which was made. To be sure I am old and you are young—a distinction not unimportant in a husband's eyes." After this exordium, added the good-natured ambassador, with a laugh, "an exordium which I have delivered in the official style of a secretary of state, let us see where we are. Two things are necessary for you to obtain your wished-for bliss. The first thing, which concerns you more particularly, is to make M.—— your friend, and to conceal from him that you have conceived a passion for his wife, and here I will aid you to the best of my ability. The second point concerns the lady's honour; all your relations with her must appear open and above-board. Consider yourself under my protection; you must not even take a country house before we have found out some plan for throwing dust into the eyes of the observant. However, you need not be anxious; I have hit upon a plan.

"You must pretend to be taken ill, but your illness must be of such a kind that your doctor will be obliged to take your word for the symptoms. Luckily, I know a doctor whose sole idea is to order country air for all complaints. This physician, who is about as clever as his brethren, and kills or cures as well as any of them, will come and feel my pulse one of these days. You must take his advice, and for a couple of louis he will write you a prescription with country air as the chief item. He will then inform everybody that your case is serious, but that he will answer for your cure."

"What is his name?"

"Doctor Herrenschwand."

"What is he doing here? I knew him at Paris; he was Madame du Rumain's doctor."

"That is his brother. Now find out some polite complaint, which will do you credit with the public. It will be easy enough to find a house, and I will get you an excellent cook to make your gruel and beef-tea."

The choice of a complaint cost me some thought; I had to give it a good deal of attention. The same evening I managed to communicate my plan to Madame who approved of it. I begged her to think of some way of writing to me, and she said she would.

"My husband," said she, "has a very high opinion of you. He has taken no offence at our coming in the same carriage. But tell me, was it an accident or design that made M. de Chavigni take my husband and leave us together?"

"It was the result of design, dearest." She raised her beautiful eyes and bit her lips. "Are you sorry it was so?"

"Alas! no."

In three or four days, on the day on which we were going to act L'Ecossaise, the doctor came to dine with the ambassador and stayed till the evening to see the play. At dessert he complimented me on my good health, on which I took the opportunity, and told him that appearances were deceitful, and that I should be glad to consult him the next day. No doubt he was delighted to be deceived in his estimate of my health, and he said he should be glad if he could be of any service. He called on me at the hour agreed upon, and I told him such symptoms as my fancy dictated; amongst other things, that I was subject to certain nocturnal irritations which made me extremely weak, especially in the reins.

"Quite so, quite so; it's a troublesome thing, but we will see what can be done. My first remedy, which you may possibly not care much for, is for you to pass six weeks in the country, where you will not see those objects which impress your brain, acting on the seventh pair of nerves, and causing that lumbar discharge which no doubt leaves you in a very depressed state."

"Yes, it certainly does."

"Quite so, quite so. My next remedy is cold bathing."

"Are the baths far from here?"

"They are wherever you like. I will write you a prescription, and the druggist will make it up."

I thanked him, and after he had pouched the double-louis I slipped politely into his hand, he went away assuring me that I should soon experience an improvement in my health. By the evening the whole town knew that I was ill and had to go into the country. M. de Chavigni said pleasantly at dinner to the doctor, that he should have forbidden me all feminine visitors; and my lame friend, refining on the idea, added that I should above all be debarred access to certain portraits, of which I had a box-full. I laughed approvingly, and begged M. de Chavigni, in the presence of the company, to help me to find a pretty house and a good cook, as I did not intend to take my meals alone.

I was tired of playing a wearisome part, and had left off going to see my lame friend, but she soon reproached me for my inconstancy, telling me that I had made a tool of her. "I know all," said this malicious woman, "and I will be avenged."

"You cannot be avenged for nothing," said I, "for I have never done you an injury. However, if you intend to have me assassinated, I shall apply for police protection."

"We don't assassinate here," said she, savagely. "We are not Italians."

I was delighted to be relieved from the burden of her society, and henceforth Madame was the sole object of my thoughts. M. de Chavigni, who seemed to delight in serving me, made her husband believe that I was the only person who could get the Duc de Choiseul to pardon a cousin of his who was in the guards, and had had the misfortune to kill his man in a duel. "This," said the kindly old gentleman, "is the best way possible of gaining the friendship of your rival. Do you think you can manage it?"

"I am not positive of success."

"Perhaps I have gone a little too far; but I told him that by means of your acquaintance with the Duchesse de Grammont you could do anything with the minister."

"I must make you a true prophet; I will do all I can."

The consequence was that M.—— informed me of the facts in the ambassador's presence, and brought me all the papers relative to the case.

I spent the night in writing to the Duchesse de Grammont. I made my letter as pathetic as possible, with a view to touching her heart, and then her father's; and I then wrote to the worthy Madame d'Urfe telling her that the well-being of the sublime order of the Rosy Cross was concerned in the pardon of a Swiss officer, who had been obliged to leave the kingdom on account of a duel in which the order was highly concerned.

In the morning, after resting for an hour, I went to the ambassador, and shewed him the letter I had written to the duchess. He thought it excellently expressed, and advised me to skew it to M.—— I found him with his night-cap on; he was extremely grateful for the interest I took in a matter which was so near to his heart. He told me that his wife had not yet risen, and asked me to wait and take breakfast with her. I should have much liked to accept the invitation, but I begged him to make my excuses to his lady for my absence, on the pretence that I had to finish my letters, and hand them to the courier who was just leaving. I hoped in this way to scatter any jealousy that might be hovering in his brain, by the slight importance I attached to a meeting with his wife.

I went to dine with M. de Chavigni, who thought my conduct had been very politic, and said that he was certain that henceforth M.—— would be my best friend. He then skewed me a letter from Voltaire thanking him for playing

Montrose in his Ecossaise; and another from the Marquis de Chauvelin, who was then at Delices with the philosopher of Ferney. He promised to come and see him after he had been to Turin, where he had been appointed ambassador.

CHAPTER XV

My Country House—Madame Dubois—Malicious Trick Played on Me by My Lame Enemy—My Vexation

There was a reception and a supper at the Court, as they styled the hotel of M. de Chavigni, or rather of the ambassador of the King of France in Switzerland. As I came in I saw my charmer sitting apart reading a letter. I accosted her, apologizing for not having stayed to breakfast, but she said I had done quite right, adding that if I had not chosen a country house she hoped I would take one her husband would probably mention to me that evening. She could not say any more, as she was called away to a game at quadrille. For my part I did not play, but wandered from one table to another.

At supper everybody talked to me about my health, and my approaching stay in the country. This gave M.——— an opportunity to mention a delightful house near the Aar; "but," he added, "it is not to be let for less than six months."

"If I like it," I replied, "and am free to leave it when I please, I will willingly pay the six months' rent in advance."

"There is a fine hall in it."

"All the better; I will give a ball as evidence of my gratitude to the people of Soleure for the kind welcome I have received from them."

"Would you like to come and see it to-morrow?"

"With pleasure."

"Very good, then I will call for you at eight o'clock, if that hour will suit you."

"I shall expect you."

When I got back to my lodging I ordered a travelling carriage and four, and the next morning, before eight o'clock, I called for M. who was ready, and seemed flattered at my anticipating him.

"I made my wife promise to come with us; but she is a sluggard, who prefers her bed to the fresh air."

In less than an hour we reached our journey's end, and I found the house a beautiful one and large enough to lodge the whole court of a prince of the Holy Roman Empire. Besides the hall, which I thought magnificent, I noted with great pleasure a closet arranged as a boudoir, and covered with the most exquisite pictures. A fine garden, fountains, baths, several well-furnished rooms, a good kitchen—in a word, everything pleased me, and I begged M.——— to arrange for me to take up my abode there in two days' time.

When we got back to Soleure, Madame told me how pleased she was that I liked the house; and seizing the opportunity, I said that I hoped they would often do me the honour of dining with me. They promised they would do so. I drew from my pocket a packet containing a hundred louis, which I gave M.——— to pay the rent. I then embraced him, and after imprinting a respectful kiss on the hand of his fair mate I went to M. de Chavigni, who approved of my having taken the house as it pleased my lady, and asked me if it was true that I was going to give a ball.

"Yes, if I see any prospect of its being a brilliant one, and if I have your approbation."

"You need have no doubts on that point, my dear fellow, and whatever you can't find in the shops come to me for. Come, I see you are going to spend a little money. It is a good plan, and overcomes many difficulties. In the meanwhile you shall have two footmen, an excellent cook, a housekeeper, and whatever other servants you require. The head of my household will pay them, and you can settle with him afterwards, he is a trustworthy man. I will come now and then and take a spoonful of soup with you, and you shall reward me for what services I may have done you by telling me how things are getting on. I have a great esteem for your charming friend, her discretion is beyond her years, and the pledges of love you will obtain of her will doubtless increase your passion and your esteem. Is she aware that I know all?"

"She knows that we are firm friends, and she is glad of it, as she is sure that you will be discreet."

"She may count on my discretion. She is really a delicious woman; I should have been tempted to seduce her myself thirty years ago."

A druggist, whom the doctor had recommended to me, set out the same day to get ready the baths which were to cure me of my imaginary complaint, and in two days I went myself, after having given Le Duc orders to bring my baggage on.

I was extremely surprised, on entering the apartment I was to occupy, to see a pretty young woman who came up to me in a modest way to kiss my hand. I stopped her doing so, and my astonished air made her blush.

"Do you belong to the household?" I said.

"The ambassador's steward has engaged me as your housekeeper."

"Pardon my surprise. Take me to my room."

She obeyed, and sitting down on the couch I begged her to sit beside me.

"That is an honour," said she, in the most polite and modest way, "I cannot allow myself. I am only your servant."

"Very good, but when I am alone I hope you will consent to take your meals with me, as I don't like eating by myself."

"I will do so, sir."

"Where is your room?"

"This is the one the steward assigned to me, but you have only to speak if you wish me to sleep in another."

"Not at all; it will do very well."

Her room was just behind the recess in which my bed stood. I went in with her and was astonished to see a great display of dresses, and in an adjoining closet all the array of the toilette, linen in abundance, and a good stock of shoes and embroidered slippers. Dumb with surprise I looked at her, and was thoroughly satisfied with what I saw. Nevertheless I determined to subject her to a close examination, as I thought her manners too interesting and her linen too extensive for her to be a mere servant. All at once I was struck with the idea that it might be a trick of the ambassador's, for a fine woman, well educated, and aged twenty-four or at the most twenty-five years, seemed to me more fitted to be my mistress than my housekeeper. I therefore asked her if she knew the ambassador, and what wages she was to receive. She replied that she only knew M. de Chavigni by sight, and that the steward had promised her two louis a month and her meals in her own room.

"Where do you come from? What's your name?"

"I come from Lyons; I am a widow, and my name is Dubois."

"I am delighted to have you in my service. I shall see you again."

She then left me, and I could not help thinking her a very interesting woman, as her speech was as dignified as her appearance. I went down to the kitchen and found the cook, an honest-looking fellow, who told me his name was Rosier. I had known his brother in the service of the French ambassador at Venice. He told me that supper would be ready at nine o'clock.

"I never eat by myself," said I.

"So I hear, sir; and I will serve supper accordingly."

"What are your wages?"

"Four louis a month."

I then went to see the rest of my people. I found two sharp-looking footmen, and the first of them told me he would see I had what wine I wanted. Then I inspected my bath, which seemed convenient. An apothecary was preparing certain matters for my imaginary cure. Finally, I took a walk round my garden, and before going in I went into the gate-keeper's, where I found a numerous family, and some girls who were not to be despised. I was delighted to hear everybody speak French, and I talked with them some time.

When I got back to my room, I found Le Duc occupied in unpacking my mails; and telling him to give my linen to Madame Dubois, I went into a pretty cabinet adjoining, where there was a desk and all materials necessary for writing. This closet had only one window facing north, but it commanded a view capable of inspiring the finest thoughts. I was amusing myself with the contemplation of this sublime prospect, when I heard a knock at my door. It was my pretty housekeeper, who wore a modest and pleasant expression, and did not in the least resemble a person who bears a complaint.

"What can I do for you, madam?"

"I hope you will be good enough to order your man to be polite to me?"

"Certainly; how has he failed in politeness?"

"He might possibly tell you in no respect. He wanted to kiss me, and as I refused he thought himself justified in being rather insolent."

"How?"

"By laughing at me. You will pardon me, sir, but I do not like people who make game."

"You are right; they are sure to be either silly or malicious. Make yourself easy; Le Duc shall understand that you are to be treated with respect. You will please sup with me."

Le Duc came in soon after, and I told him to behave respectfully towards Madame Dubois.

"She's a sly cat," said the rascal; "she wouldn't let me kiss her."

"I am afraid you are a bad fellow."

"Is she your servant or your mistress?"

"She might be my wife."

"Oh! well, that's different. That will do; Madame Dubois shall have all respect, and I will try my luck somewhere else."

I had a delicious supper. I was contented with my cook, my butler, my housekeeper, and even with my Spaniard, who waited capitally at table.

After supper I sent out Le Duc and the other servant, and as soon as I was alone with my too lovely housekeeper, who had behaved at table like a woman of the world, I begged her to tell me her history.

"My history, sir, is short enough, and not very interesting. I was—born at Lyons, and my relations took me to Lausanne, as I have been told, for I was too young at the time to remember anything about it. My father, who was in the service of Madame d'Ermance, left me an orphan when I was fourteen. Madame d'Ermance was fond of me, and knowing that my mother's means were small she took me to live with her. I had attained my seventeenth year when I entered the service of Lady Montagu as lady's maid, and some time after I was married to Dubois, an old servant of the house. We went to England, and three years after my marriage I lost my husband. The climate of England affected my lungs, and I was obliged to beg my lady to allow me to leave her service. The worthy lady saw how weak I was, and paid the expenses of my journey and loaded me with rich presents. I returned to my mother at Lausanne, where my health soon returned, and I went into the service of an English lady who was very fond of me, and would have taken me with her to Italy if she had not conceived some suspicions about the young Duke of Rosebury, with whom she was in love, and whom she thought in love with me. She suspected me, but wrongfully, of being her rival in secret. She sent me away, after giving me rich presents, and saying how sorry she was she could not keep me. I went back to my mother, and for two years I have lived with the toil of my hands. Four days ago M. Lebel, the ambassador's steward, asked me if I would enter the service of an Italian gentleman as housekeeper. I agreed, in the hope of seeing Italy, and this hope is the cause of my stupidity. In short: here I am."

"What stupidity are you referring to?"

"The stupidity of having entered your service before I knew you."

"I like your freedom. You would not have come, then, if you had not known me?"

"Certainly not, for no lady will ever take me after having been with you."

"Why not? may I ask."

"Well, sir; do you think you are the kind of man to have a house-keeper like myself without the public believing my situation to be of quite a different nature?"

"No, you are too pretty, and I don't look like a fossil, certainly; but after all, what matter does it make?"

"It is all very well for you to make light of it, and if I were in your place I would do the same; but how am I, who am a woman and not in an independent position, to set myself above the rules and regulations of society?"

"You mean, Madame Dubois, that you would very much like to go back to Lausanne?"

"Not exactly, as that would not be just to you."

"How so?"

"People would be sure to say that either your words or your deeds were too free, and you might possibly pass a rather uncharitable judgment on me."

"What judgment could I pass on you?"

"You might think I wanted to impose on you."

"That might be, as I should be very much hurt by so sudden and uncalled-for a departure. All the same I am sorry for you, as with your ideas you can neither go nor stay with any satisfaction. Nevertheless, you must do one or the other."

"I have made up my mind. I shall stay, and I am almost certain I shall not regret it."

"I am glad to hear that, but there is one point to which I wish to call your attention."

"What is that?"

"I will tell you. Let us have no melancholy and no scruples."

"You shall not see me melancholy, I promise you; but kindly explain what you mean by the word 'scruples.'"

"Certainly. In its ordinary acceptation, the word 'scruple' signifies a malicious and superstitious whim, which pronounces an action which may be innocent to be guilty."

"When a course of action seems doubtful to me, I never look upon the worst side of it. Besides, it is my duty to look after myself and not other people."

"I see you have read a good deal."

"Reading is my greatest luxury. Without books I should find life unbearable."

"Have you any books?"

"A good many. Do you understand English?"

"Not a word."

"I am sorry for that, as the English books would amuse you."

"I do not care for romances."

"Nor do I. But you don't think that there are only romances in English, do you? I like that. Why do you take me for such a lover of the romantic, pray?"

"I like that, too. That pretty outburst is quite to my taste, and I am delighted to be the first to make you laugh."

"Pardon me if I laugh, but . . ."

"But me no buts, my dear; laugh away just as you like, you will find that the best way to get over me. I really think, though, that you put your services at too cheap a rate."

"That makes me laugh again, as it is for you to increase my wages if you like."

"I shall take care that it is done."

I rose from table, not taken, but surprised, with this young woman, who seemed to be getting on my blind side. She reasoned well, and in this first interview she had made a deep impression on me. She was young, pretty, elegant, intellectual, and of distinguished manners; I could not guess what would be the end of our connection. I longed to speak to M. Lebel, to thank him for getting me such a marvel, and still more, to ask him some questions about her.

After the supper had been taken away, she came to ask if I would have my hair put in curl papers.

"It's Le Duc's business," I answered, "but if you like, it shall be yours for the future."

She acquitted herself like an expert.

"I see," said I, "that you are going to serve me as you served Lady Montagu."

"Not altogether; but as you do not like melancholy, allow me to ask a favour."

"Do so, my dear."

"Please do not ask me to give you your bath."

"Upon my honour, I did not think of doing so. It would be scandalous. That's Le Duc's business."

"Pardon me, and allow me to ask another favour."

"Tell me everything you want."

"Allow me to have one of the door-keeper's daughters to sleep with me."

"If it had come into my head, I would have proposed it to you. Is she in your room now?"

"No."

"Go and call her, then."

"Let us leave that till to-morrow, as if I went at this time of night it might make people talk."

"I see you have a store of discretion, and you may be sure I will not deprive you of any of it."

She helped me to undress, and must have found me very modest, but I must say it was not from virtue. My heart was engaged elsewhere, and Madame Dubois had impressed me; I was possibly duped by her, but I did not trouble myself to think whether I was or not. I rang for Le Duc in the morning, and on coming in he said he had not expected the honour.

"You're a rascal," I said, "get two cups of chocolate ready directly after I have had my bath."

After I had taken my first cold bath, which I greatly enjoyed, I went to bed again. Madame Dubois came in smiling, dressed in a style of careless elegance.

"You look in good spirits."

"I am, because I am happy with you. I have had a good night, and there is now in my room a girl as lovely as an angel, who is to sleep with me."

"Call her in."

She called her, and a monster of ugliness entered, who made me turn my head away.

"You haven't given yourself a rival certainly, my dear, but if she suits you it is all right. You shall have your breakfast with me, and I hope you will take chocolate with me every morning."

"I shall be delighted, as I am very fond of it."

I had a pleasant afternoon. M. de Chavigni spent several hours with me. He was pleased with everything, and above all with my fair housekeeper, of whom Lebel had said nothing to him.

"She will be an excellent cure for your love for Madame," said he.

"There you are wrong," I answered, "she might make me fall in love with her without any diminution of my affection for my charmer."

Next day, just as I was sitting down to table with my housekeeper, I saw a carriage coming into the courtyard, and my detestable lame widow getting out of it. I was terribly put out, but the rules of politeness compelled me to go and receive her.

"I was far from anticipating that you would do me so great an honour, madam."

"I daresay; I have come to dine with you, and to ask you to do me a favour."

"Come in, then, dinner is just being served. I beg to introduce Madame Dubois to you."

I turned towards my charming housekeeper, and told her that the lady would dine with us.

Madame Dubois, in the character of mistress of the house, did the honours admirably, and my lame friend, in spite of her pride, was very polite to her. I did not speak a dozen words during the meal, and paid no sort of attention to the detestable creature; but I was anxious to know what she could want me to do for her. As soon as Madame Dubois had left the room she told me straight out that she had come to ask me to let her have a couple of rooms in my house for three weeks or a month at the most.

I was astonished at such a piece of impudence, and told her she asked more than I was at liberty to give.

"You can't refuse me, as everybody knows I have come on purpose to ask you."

"Then everybody must know that I have refused you. I want to be alone—absolutely alone, without any kind of restriction on my liberty. The least suspicion of company would bore me."

"I shall not bore you in any way, and you will be at perfect liberty to ignore my presence. I shall not be offended if you don't enquire after me, and I shall not ask after you—even if you are ill. I shall have my meals served to me by my own servant, and I shall take care not to walk in the garden unless I am perfectly certain you are not there. You must allow that if you have any claims to politeness you cannot refuse me."

"If you were acquainted with the most ordinary rules of politeness, madam, you would not persist in a request to which I have formally declined to accede."

She did not answer, but my words had evidently produced no effect. I was choking with rage. I strode up and down the room, and felt inclined to send her away by force as a madwoman. However, I reflected that she had relations in a good position whom I might offend if I treated her roughly, and that I might make an enemy capable of exacting a terrible revenge; and, finally, that Madame might disapprove of my using violence to this hideous harpy....

"Well, madam," said I, "you shall have the apartment you have solicited with so much importunity, and an hour after you come in I shall be on my way back to Soleure."

"I accept the apartment, and I shall occupy it the day after to-morrow. As for your threat of returning to Soleure, it is an idle one, as you would thereby make yourself the laughing-stock of the whole town."

With this final impertinence she rose and went away, without taking any further notice of me. I let her go without moving from my seat. I was stupefied. I repented of having given in; such impudence was unparalleled. I called myself a fool, and vowed I deserved to be publicly hooted. I ought to have taken the whole thing as a jest; to have contrived to get her out of the house on some pretext, and then to have sent her about her business as a madwoman, calling all my servants as witnesses.

My dear Dubois came in, and I told my tale. She was thunderstruck.

"I can hardly credit her requesting, or your granting, such a thing," said she, "unless you have some motives of your own."

I saw the force of her argument, and not wishing to make a confidante of her I held my tongue, and went out to work off my bile.

I came in tired, after taking a stiff walk. I took supper with Madame Dubois, and we sat at table till midnight. Her conversation pleased me more and more; her mind was well-furnished, her speech elegant, and she told her stories and cracked her jokes with charming grace. She was devoid of prejudices, but by no means devoid of principle. Her discretion was rather the result of system than of virtue; but if she had not a virtuous spirit, her system would not have shielded her from the storms of passion or the seductions of vice.

My encounter with the impudent widow had so affected me that I could not resist going at an early hour on the following day to communicate it to M. de Chavigni. I warned Madame Dubois that if I were not back by dinner-time she was not to wait for me.

M. de Chavigni had been told by my enemy that she was going to pay me a visit, but he roared with laughter on hearing the steps she had taken to gain her ends.

"Your excellency may find it very funny," said I, "but I don't."

"So I see; but take my advice, and be the first to laugh at the adventure. Behave as if you were unaware of her presence, and that will be a sufficient punishment for her. People will soon say she is smitten with you, and that you disdain her love. Go and tell the story to M.——, and stay without ceremony to dinner. I have spoken to Lebel about your pretty housekeeper: the worthy man had no malicious intent in sending her to you. He happened to be going to Lausanne, and just before, I had told him to find you a good housekeeper; thinking it over on his way, he remembered his friend Madame Dubois, and the matter was thus arranged without malice or pretense. She is a regular find, a perfect jewel for you, and if you get taken with her I don't think she will allow you to languish for long."

"I don't know, she seems to be a woman of principle."

"I shouldn't have thought you would be taken in by that sort of thing. I will ask you both to give me a dinner to-morrow, and shall be glad to hear her chatter."

M—— welcomed me most kindly, and congratulated me on my conquest, which would make my country house a paradise. I joined in the jest, of course, with the more ease that his charming wife, though I could see that she suspected the truth, added her congratulations to those of her husband; but I soon changed the course of their friendly mirth by telling them the circumstances of the case. They were indignant enough then, and the husband said that if she had really quartered herself on me in that fashion, all I had to do was to get an injunction from the courts forbidding her to put her foot within my doors.

"I don't want to do that," said I, "as besides publicly disgracing her I should be skewing my own weakness, and proclaiming that I was not the master in my own house, and that I could not prevent her establishing herself with me."

"I think so, too," said the wife, "and I am glad you gave way to her. That shews how polite you are, and I shall go and call on her to congratulate her on the welcome she got, as she told me that her plans had succeeded."

Here the matter ended, and I accepted their invitation to dine with them. I behaved as a friend, but with that subtle politeness which takes away all ground for suspicion; accordingly, the husband felt no alarm. My charmer found the opportunity to tell me that I had done wisely in yielding to the ill-timed demand of that harpy, and that as soon as M. de Chauvelin, whom they were expecting, had gone away again, I could ask her husband to spend a few days with me, and that she would doubtless come too.

"Your door-keeper's wife," she added, "was my nurse. I have been kind to her, and when necessary I can write to you by her without running any risk."

After calling on two Italian Jesuits who were passing through Soleure, and inviting them to dine with me on the following day, I returned home where the good Dubois amused me till midnight by philosophical discussions. She admired Locke; and maintained that the faculty of thought was not a proof of the existence of spirit in us, as it was in the power of God to endow matter with the capacity for thought; I was unable to controvert this position. She made me laugh by saying that there was a great difference between thinking and reasoning, and I had the courage to say,—

"I think you would reason well if you let yourself be persuaded to sleep with me, and you think you reason well in refusing to be so persuaded."

"Trust me, sir," said she; "there is as much difference between the reasoning powers of men and women as there is between their physical characteristics."

Next morning at nine o'clock we were taking our chocolate, when my enemy arrived. I heard her carriage, but I did not take the slightest notice. The villainous woman sent away the carriage and installed herself in her room with her maid.

I had sent Le Duc to Soleure for my letters, so I was obliged to beg my housekeeper to do my hair; and she did it admirably, as I told her we should have the ambassador and the two Jesuits to dinner. I thanked her, and kissed her for the first time on the cheek, as she would not allow me to touch her beautiful lips. I felt that we were fast falling in love with one another, but we continued to keep ourselves under control, a task which was much easier for her than for me, as she was helped by that spirit of coquetry natural to the fair sex, which often has greater power over them than love itself.

M. de Chavigni came at two; I had consulted him before asking the Jesuits, and had sent my carriage for them. While we were waiting for these gentlemen we took a turn in the garden, and M. de Chavigni begged my fair housekeeper to join us as soon as she had discharged certain petty duties in which she was then engaged.

M. de Chavigni was one of those men who were sent by France to such powers as she wished to cajole and to win over to her interests. M. de l'Hopital, who knew how to gain the heart of Elizabeth Petrovna, was another; the Duc de Nivernois, who did what he liked with the Court of St. James's in 1762, is a third instance.

Madame Dubois came out to us in due course, and entertained us very agreeably; and M. de Chavigni told me that he considered she had all the qualities which would make a man happy. At dinner she enchanted him and captivated the two Jesuits by her delicate and subtle wit. In the evening this delightful old nobleman told me he had spent a most pleasant day, and after asking me to dine at his house while M. de Chauvelin was there, he left me with an effusive embrace.

M. de Chauvelin, whom I had the honour to know at Versailles, at M. de Choiseul's, was an extremely pleasant man. He arrived at Soleure in the course of two days, and M. de Chavigni having advised me of his presence I hastened to pay my court to him. He remembered me, and introduced me to his wife, whom I had not the honour of knowing. As chance placed me next to my charmer at table, my spirits rose, and my numerous jests and stories put everybody in a good temper. On M. de Chauvelin remarking that he knew some pleasant histories of which I was the hero, M. de Chavigni told him that he did not know the best of all, and recounted to him my adventure at Zurich. M. de Chauvelin then told Madame that to serve her he would willingly transform himself into a footman, on which M.—— joined in and said that I had a finer taste for beauty, as she, for whose sake I had made myself into a waiter, was at that moment a guest of mine in my country house."

"Ah, indeed!" said M. de Chauvelin, "then we must come and see your quarters, M. Casanova."

I was going to reply, when M. de Chavigni anticipated me by saying,

"Yes, indeed! and I hope he will lend me his beautiful hall to give you a ball next Sunday."

In this manner the good-natured courtier prevented me from promising to give a ball myself, and relieved me of my foolish boast, which I should have been wrong in carrying out, as it would have been an encroachment on his privilege as ambassador of entertaining these distinguished strangers during the five or six days they might stay at Soleure. Besides, if I had kept to my word, it would have involved me in a considerable expense, which would not have helped me in my suit.

The conversation turning on Voltaire, the Ecossaise was mentioned, and the acting of my neighbour was highly commended in words that made her blush and shine in her beauty like a star, whereat her praises were renewed.

After dinner the ambassador invited us to his ball on the day after the morrow, and I went home more deeply in love than ever with my dear charmer, whom Heaven had designed to inflict on me the greatest grief I have had in my life, as the reader shall see.

I found that my housekeeper had gone to bed, and I was glad of it, for the presence of my fair one had excited my passions to such an extent that my reason might have failed to keep me within the bounds of respect. Next morning she found me sad, and rallied me in such a way that I soon recovered my spirits. While we were taking our chocolate the lame creature's maid brought me a note, and I sent her away, telling her that I would send the answer by my own servant. This curious letter ran as follows:

"The ambassador has asked me to his ball on Sunday. I answered that I was not well, but if I found myself better in the evening I would come. I think that as I am staying in your house I ought to be introduced by you or stay away altogether. So if you do not wish to oblige me by taking me, I must beg of you to tell the ambassador that I am ill. Pardon me if I have taken the liberty of infringing our agreement in this peculiar instance, but it is a question of keeping up some sort of appearance in public."

"Not so," I cried, mad with rage; and taking my pen I wrote thus:

"I think your idea is a beautiful one, madam. You will have to be ill, as I mean to keep to the conditions you made yourself, and to enjoy full liberty in all things, and I shall therefore deny myself the honour of taking you to the ball which the ambassador is to give in my hall."

I read her insolent letter and my reply to my housekeeper, who thought the answer just what she deserved. I then sent it to her.

I passed the next two days quietly and agreeably without going out or seeing any visitors, but the society of Madame Dubois was all-sufficient for me. Early on Sunday morning the ambassador's people came to make the necessary preparations for the ball and supper. Lebel came to pay me his respects while I was at table. I made him sit down, while I thanked him for procuring me a housekeeper who was all perfection.

Lebel was a fine man, middle-aged, witty, and an excellent steward, though perfectly honest.

"Which of you two," said he to me, "is the most taken in?"

"We are equally pleased with each other," answered my charming housekeeper.

To my great delight the first pair to appear were M.——— and Madame. She was extremely polite to Madame Dubois, and did not shew the slightest astonishment when I introduced her as my housekeeper. She told me that I must take her to see her lame friend, and to my great disgust I had to go. We were received with a show of great friendship, and she went out with us into the garden, taking M.———'s arm, while his wife leant amorously on mine.

When we had made a few turns of the garden, Madame begged me to take her to her nurse. As her husband was close by, I said,—

"Who is your nurse?"

"Your door-keeper's wife," said her husband, "we will wait for you in this lady's apartment."

"Tell me, sweetheart," said she on the way, "does not your pretty housekeeper sleep with you?"

"I swear she does not; I can only love you."

"I would like to believe you, but I find it hard to do so; however, if you are speaking the truth it is wrong of you to keep her in the house, as nobody will believe in your innocence."

"It is enough for me that you believe in it. I admire her, and at any other time I expect we could not sleep under the same roof without sleeping in the same bed; but now that you rule my heart I am not capable of a passion for her."

"I am delighted to hear it; but I think she is very pretty."

We went in to see her nurse, who called her "my child," and kissed her again and again, and then left us alone to prepare some lemonade for us. As soon as we found ourselves alone our mouths were glued together, and my hands touched a thousand beauties, covered only by a dress of light sarcenet; but I could not enjoy her charms without this cruel robe, which was all the worse because it did not conceal the loveliness beneath it. I am sure that the good nurse would have kept us waiting a long time if she had known how we longed to be left alone for a few moments longer; but, alas! the celerity with which she made those two glasses of lemonade was unexampled.

"It was made beforehand, was it?" said I, when I saw her coming in.

"Not at all, sir; but I am a quick hand."

"You are, indeed."

These words made my charmer go off into a peal of laughter, which she accompanied with a significant glance in my direction. As we were going away she said that as things seemed to be against us we must wait till her husband came to spend a few days with me.

My terrible enemy gave us some sweets, which she praised very highly, and above all some quince marmalade, which she insisted on our testing. We begged to be excused, and Madame pressed my foot with hers. When we had got away she told me I had been very wise not to touch anything, as the widow was suspected of having poisoned her husband.

The ball, the supper, the refreshments, and the guests were all of the most exquisite and agreeable kind. I only danced one minuet with Madame de Chauvelin, nearly all my evening being taken up with talking to her husband. I made him a present of my translation of his poem on the seven deadly sins, which he received with much pleasure.

"I intend," said I, "to pay you a visit at Turin."

"Are you going to bring your housekeeper with you?"

"No."

"You are wrong, for she is a delightful person."

Everybody spoke of my dear Dubois in the same way. She had a perfect knowledge of the rules of good breeding, and she knew how to make herself respected without being guilty of the slightest presumption. In vain she was urged to dance, and she afterwards told me that if she had yielded she would have become an object of hatred to all the ladies. She knew that she could dance exquisitely.

M. de Chauvelin went away in two days, and towards the end of the week I heard from Madame d'Urfe, who told me that she had spent two days at Versailles in furtherance of my desires. She sent me a copy of the letters of pardon signed by the king in favour of the relation of M.——, assuring me that the original had been sent to the colonel of his regiment, where he would be reinstated in the rank which he held before the duel.

I had my horses put into my carriage, and hastened to carry this good news to M. de Chavigni. I was wild with joy, and I did not conceal it from the ambassador, who congratulated me, since M.—— having obtained by me, without the expenditure of a penny, a favour which would have cost him dear if he had succeeded in purchasing it, would henceforth be only too happy to treat me with the utmost confidence.

To make the matter still more important, I begged my noble friend to announce the pardon to M.—— in person, and he immediately wrote a note to that gentleman requesting his presence.

As soon as he made his appearance, the ambassador handed him the copy of the pardon, telling him that he owed it all to me. The worthy man was in an ecstasy, and asked what he owed me.

"Nothing, sir, unless you will give me your friendship, which I value more than all the gold in the world; and if you would give me a proof of your friendship, come and spend a few days with me; I am positively dying of loneliness. The matter I have done for you is a mere trifle; you see how quickly it has been arranged."

"A mere trifle! I have devoted a year's labour to it; I have moved heaven and earth without succeeding, and in a fortnight you have accomplished it. Sir, you may dispose of my life."

"Embrace me, and come and see me. I am the happiest of men when I am enabled to serve persons of your merit."

"I will go and tell the good news to my wife, who will love you as well as I do."

"Yes, do so," said the ambassador, "and bring her to dinner here to-morrow."

When we were alone together, the Marquis de Chavigni, an old courtier and a wit, began to make some very philosophical reflections on the state of a court where nothing can be said to be easy or difficult per se, as the one at a moment's notice may become the other; a court where justice often pleads in vain, while interest or even importunity get a ready hearing. He had known Madame d'Urfe, had even paid his court to her at the period when she was secretly beloved by the regent. He it was who had given her the name of Egeria, because she said she had a genius who directed her and passed the nights with her when she slept by herself. The ambassador then spoke of M.———, who had undoubtedly become a very great friend of mine.

"The only way to blind a jealous husband," said he, "is to make him your friend, for friendship will rarely admit jealousy."

The next day at dinner, at the ambassador's, Madame gave me a thousand proofs of grateful friendship, which my heart interpreted as pledges of love. The husband and wife promised to pay me a three days' visit in the following week at my country house.

They kept their word without giving me any further warning, but I was not taken by surprise as I had made all preparations for their reception.

My heart leapt with joy on seeing my charmer getting down from the carriage, but my joy was not unalloyed, as the husband told me that they must absolutely return on the fourth day, and the wife insisted on the horrible widow being present at all our conversation.

I took my guests to the suite of rooms I had prepared for them, and which I judged most suitable for my designs. It was on the ground floor, opposite to my room. The bedroom had a recess with two beds, separated by a partition through which one passed by a door. I had the key to all the doors, and the maid would sleep in a closet beyond the ante-chamber.

In obedience to my divinity's commands we went and called on the widow, who gave us a cordial welcome; but under the pretext of leaving us in freedom refused to be of our company during the three days. However, she gave in when I told her that our agreement was only in force when I was alone.

My dear Dubois, with her knowledge of the rules of society, did not need a hint to have her supper in her room, and we had an exquisite meal as I had given orders that the fare should be of the best. After supper I took my guests to their apartment, and felt obliged to do the same by the widow. She wanted me to assist at her toilet, but I excused myself with a bow. She said, maliciously, that after all the pains I had taken I deserved to be successful. I gave her no answer.

Next morning, as we were walking in the garden, I warned my charmer that I had all the keys of the house, and that I could introduce myself into her room at any moment.

"I am waiting," said she, "for my husband's embraces, which he has prefaced with caresses, as is usual with him. We must therefore wait till the night after next, which will take away all risk, as I have never known him to embrace me for two nights in succession."

About noon we had a visit from M. de Chavigni, who came to ask for dinner, and made a great to-do when he heard that my housekeeper dined in her room. The ladies said he was quite right, so we all went and made her sit down at table with us. She must have been flattered, and the incident evidently increased her good humour, as she amused us by her wit and her piquant stories about Lady Montagu. When we had risen from table Madame said to me,—

"You really must be in love with that young woman; she is ravishing."

"If I could pass two hours in your company to-night, I would prove to you that I am yours alone."

"It is still out of the question, as my husband has ascertained that the moon changes to-day."

"He has to ask leave of the moon, has he, before discharging so sweet a duty?"

"Exactly. According to his system of astrology, it is the only way to keep his health and to have the son that Heaven wills to grant him, and indeed without aid from above it is hardly likely that his wishes will be accomplished."

"I hope to be the instrument of Heaven," said I, laughing.

"I only hope you may."

Thus I was obliged to wait. Next morning, as we were walking in the garden, she said to me,—

"The sacrifice to the moon has been performed, and to make sure I will cause him to renew his caresses tonight as soon as we go to bed; and after that he is certain to sleep soundly. You can come at an hour after midnight; love will await you."

Certain of my bliss, I gave myself up to the joy that such a certainty kindles in a fiery heart. It was the only night remaining, as M.—— had decided that on the next day they would return to Soleure.

After supper I took the ladies to their apartments, and on returning told my housekeeper that I had a good deal of writing to do, and that she should go to bed.

Just before one o'clock I left my room, and the night being a dark one I had to feel my way half round my house, and to my surprise found the door open; but I did not pay any attention to this circumstance. I opened the door of the second ante-chamber, and the moment I shut it again a hand seized mine, whilst another closed my lips. I only heard a whispered "hush!" which bade me silent. A sofa was at hand; we made it our altar of sacrifice, and in a moment I was within the temple of love. It was summer time and I had only two hours before me, so I did not lose a moment, and thinking I held between my arms the woman I had so long sighed for I renewed again and again the pledges of my ardent love. In the fulness of my bliss I thought her not awaiting me in her bed an admirable idea, as the noise of our kisses and the liveliness of our motions might have awakened the troublesome husband. Her tender ecstasies equalled mine, and increased my bliss by making me believe (oh, fatal error!) that of all my conquests this was the one of which I had most reason to boast.

To my great grief the clock warned me that it was time for me to be gone. I covered her with the tenderest kisses, and returning to my room, in the greatest gladness, I resigned myself to sleep.

I was roused at nine o'clock by M.——, who seemed in a happy frame of mind, and shewed me a letter he had just received, in which his relative thanked me for restoring him to his regiment. In this letter, which was dictated by gratitude, he spoke of me as if I had been a divinity.

"I am delighted," I said, "to have been of service to you."

"And I," said he, "am equally pleased to assure you of my gratitude. Come and breakfast with us, my wife is still at her toilette. Come along."

I rose hastily, and just as I was leaving the room I saw the dreadful widow, who seemed full of glee, and said,—

"I thank you, sir; I thank you with all my heart. I beg to leave you at liberty again; I am going back to Soleure."

"Wait for a quarter of an hour, we are going to breakfast with Madame."

"I can't stop a moment, I have just wished her good day, and now I must be gone. Farewell, and remember me."

"Farewell, madam."

She had hardly gone before M.—— asked me if the woman was beside herself.

"One might think so, certainly," I replied, "for she has received nothing but politeness at my hands, and I think she might have waited to go back with you in the evening."

We went to breakfast and to discuss this abrupt leave-taking, and afterwards we took a turn in the garden where we found Madame Dubois. M.—— took possession of her; and as I thought his wife looking rather downcast I asked her if she had not slept well.

"I did not go to sleep till four o'clock this morning," she replied, "after vainly sitting up in bed waiting for you till that time. What unforeseen accident prevented your coming?"

I could not answer her question. I was petrified. I looked at her fixedly without replying; I could not shake off my astonishment. At last a dreadful suspicion came into my head that I had held within my arms for two hours the horrible monster whom I had foolishly received in my house. I was seized with a terrible tremor, which obliged me to go and take shelter behind the arbour and hide my emotion. I felt as though I should swoon away. I should certainly have fallen if I had not rested my head against a tree.

My first idea had been a fearful thought, which I hastened to repel, that Madame, having enjoyed me, wished to deny all knowledge of the fact—a device which is in the power of any woman who gives up her person in the dark to adopt, as it is impossible to convict her of lying. However, I knew the divine creature I had thought I possessed too well to believe her capable of such base deceit. I felt that she would have been lacking in delicacy, if she had said she had waited for me in vain by way of a jest; as in such a case as this the least doubt is a degradation. I was forced, then, to the conclusion that she had been supplanted by the infernal widow. How had she managed it? How had she ascertained our arrangements? I could not imagine, and I bewildered myself with painful surmises. Reason only comes to the aid of the mind when the confusion produced by painful thoughts has almost vanished. I concluded, then, that I had spent two hours with this abominable monster; and what increased my anguish, and made me loathe and despise myself still more, was that I could not help confessing that I had been perfectly happy. It was an unpardonable mistake, as the two women differed as much as white does from black, and though the darkness forbade my seeing, and the silence my hearing, my sense of touch should have enlightened me—after the first set-to, at all events, but my imagination was in a state of ecstasy. I cursed love, my nature, and above all the inconceivable weakness which had allowed me to receive into my house the serpent that had deprived me of an angel, and made me hate myself at the thought of having defiled myself with her. I resolved to die, after having torn to pieces with my own hands the monster who had made me so unhappy.

While I was strengthening myself in this resolution M.—— came up to me and asked me kindly if I were ill; he was alarmed to see me pale and covered with drops of sweat. "My wife," said the worthy man, "is uneasy about you, and sent me to look after you." I told him I had to leave her on account of a sudden dizziness, but that I began to feel better. "Let us rejoin her." Madame Dubois brought me a flask of strong waters, saying pleasantly that she was sure it was only the sudden departure of the widow that had put me out.

We continued our walk, and when we were far enough from the husband, who was with my housekeeper, I said I had been overcome by what she had said, but that it had doubtless been spoken jestingly.

"I was not jesting at all," said she, with a sigh, "tell me what prevented your coming."

Again I was struck dumb. I could not make up my mind to tell her the story, and I did not know what to say to justify myself. I was silent and confused when my housekeeper's little servant came up and gave me a letter which the wretched widow had sent her by an express. She had opened it, and found an enclosure addressed to me inside. I put it in my pocket, saying I would read it at my leisure. On Madame saying in joke that it was a love-letter, I could not laugh, and made no answer. The servant came to tell us that dinner was served, but I could touch nothing. My abstinence was put down to my being unwell.

I longed to read the letter, but I wished to be alone to do so, and that was a difficult matter to contrive.

Wishing to avoid the game of piquet which formed our usual afternoon's amusement, I took a cup of coffee, and said that I thought the fresh air would do me good. Madame seconded me, and guessing what I wanted she asked me to walk up and down with her in a sheltered alley in the garden. I offered her my arm, her husband offered his to my housekeeper, and we went out.

As soon as my mistress saw that we were free from observation, she spoke as follows,—

"I am sure that you spent the night with that malicious woman, and I am afraid of being compromised in consequence. Tell me everything; confide in me without reserve; 'tis my first intrigue, and if it is to serve as a lesson you should conceal nothing from me. I am sure you loved me once, tell me that you have not become my enemy."

"Good heavens! what are you saying? I your enemy!"

"Then tell me all, and before you read that wretched creature's letter. I adjure you in the name of love to hide nothing from me."

"Well, divine creature, I will do as you bid me. I came to your apartment at one o'clock, and as soon as I was in the second ante-chamber, I was taken by the arm, and a hand was placed upon my lips to impose silence; I thought I held you in my arms, and I laid you gently on the sofa. You must remember that I felt absolutely certain it was you; indeed, I can scarcely doubt it even now. I then passed with you, without a word being spoken, two of the most delicious hours I have ever experienced. Cursed hours! of which the remembrance will torment me for the remainder of my days. I left you at a quarter past three. The rest is known to you."

"Who can have told the monster that you were going to visit me at that hour?"

"I can't make out, and that perplexes me."

"You must confess that I am the most to be pitied of us three, and perhaps, alas! the only one who may have a just title to the name 'wretched.'"

"If you love me, in the name of Heaven do not say that; I have resolved to stab her, and to kill myself after having inflicted on her that punishment she so well deserves."

"Have you considered that the publicity of such an action would render me the most unfortunate of women? Let us be more moderate, sweetheart; you are not to blame for what has happened, and if possible I love you all the more. Give me the letter she has written to you. I will go away from you to read it, and you can read it afterwards, as if we were seen reading it together we should have to explain matters."

"Here it is."

I then rejoined her husband, whom my housekeeper was sending into fits of laughter. The conversation I had just had had calmed me a little, and the trustful way in which she had asked for the letter had done me good. I was in a fever to know the contents, and yet I dreaded to read it, as it could only increase my rage and I was afraid of the results.

Madame rejoined us, and after we had separated again she gave me the letter, telling me to keep it till I was alone. She asked me to give her my word of honour to do nothing without consulting her, and to communicate all my designs to her by means of her nurse.

"We need not fear the harpy saying anything about it," she remarked, "as she would first have to proclaim her own prostitution, and as for us, concealment is the best plan. And I would have you note that the horrible creature gives you a piece of advice you would do well to follow."

What completely tore my heart asunder during this interview was to see great tears—tears of love and grief—falling from her beautiful eyes; though to moderate my anguish she forced a smile. I knew too well the importance she attached to her fair fame not to guess that she was tormented with the idea that the terrible widow knew of the understanding between us, and the thought added fresh poignancy to my sorrow.

This amiable pair left me at seven in the evening, and I thanked the husband in such a manner that he could not doubt my sincerity, and, in truth, I said no more than I felt. There is no reason why the love one feels for a woman should hinder one from being the true friend of her husband—if she have a husband. The contrary view is a hateful prejudice, repugnant both to nature and to philosophy. After I had embraced him I was about to kiss the hand of his charming wife, but he begged me to embrace her too, which I did respectfully but feelingly.

I was impatient to read the terrible letter, and as soon as they were gone I shut myself up in my room to prevent any interruptions. The epistle was as follows:

"I leave your house, sir, well enough pleased, not that I have spent a couple of hours with you, for you are no better than any other man, but that I have revenged myself on the many open marks of contempt you have given me; for your private scorn I care little, and I willingly forgive you. I have avenged myself by unmasking your designs and the hypocrisy of your pretty prude, who will no longer be able to treat me with that irritating air of superiority which she, affecting a virtue which she does not possess, has displayed towards me. I have avenged myself in the fact that she must have been waiting for you all the night, and I would have given worlds to have heard the amusing conversation you must have had when she found out that I had taken for vengeance's sake, and not for love, the enjoyment which was meant for her. I have avenged myself because you can no longer pretend to think her a marvel of beauty, as having mistaken me for her, the difference between us must needs be slight; but I have done you a service, too, as the thought of what has happened should cure you of your passion. You will no longer adore her before all other women who are just as good as she. Thus I have disabused you, and you ought to feel grateful to me; but I dispense you from all gratitude, and do not care if you choose to hate me, provided your hatred leaves me in peace; but if I find your conduct objectionable in the future, I warn you that I will tell all, since I do not care for my own fame as I am a widow and mistress of my own actions. I need no man's favour, and care not what men may say of me. Your mistress, on the other hand, is in quite a different position.

"And here I will give you a piece of advice, which should convince you of my generosity. For the last ten years I have been troubled with a little ailment which has resisted all attempts at treatment. You exerted yourself to such an extent to prove how well you loved me that you must have caught the complaint. I advise you, then, to put yourself under treatment at once to weaken the force of the virus; but above all do not communicate it to your mistress, who might chance to hand it on to her husband and possibly to others, which would make a wretched woman of her, to my grief and sorrow, since she has never done me any harm. I felt certain that you two would deceive the worthy husband, and I wished to have proof; thus I made you take me in, and the position of the apartment you gave them was enough to remove all doubts; still I wanted to have proof positive. I had no need of any help to arrive at my ends, and I found it a pleasant joke to keep you in the dark. After passing two nights on the sofa all for nothing, I resolved on passing the third night there, and my perseverance was crowned with success. No one saw me, and my maid even is ignorant of my nocturnal wanderings, though in any case she is accustomed to observe silence. You are, then, at perfect liberty to bury the story in oblivion, and I advise you to do so.

"If you want a doctor, tell him to keep his counsel, for people at Soleure know of my little indisposition, and they might say you caught it from me, and this would do us both harm."

Her impudence struck me so gigantic in its dimensions that I almost laughed. I was perfectly aware that after the way I had treated her she must hate me, but I should not have thought she would have carried her perverse hatred so far. She had communicated to me an infectious disease, though I did not so far feel any symptoms; however, they would no doubt appear, and I sadly thought I should have to go away to be cured, to avoid the gossip of malicious wits. I gave myself up to reflection, and after two hours' thought I wisely resolved to hold my tongue, but to be revenged when the opportunity presented itself.

I had eaten nothing at dinner, and needed a good supper to make me sleep. I sat down to table with my housekeeper, but, like a man ashamed of himself, I dared not look her in the face.

CHAPTER XVI

Continuation of the Preceding Chapter—I Leave Soleure

When the servants had gone away and left us alone, it would have looked strange if we had remained as dumb as two posts; but in my state of mind I did not feel myself capable of breaking the silence. My dear Dubois, who began to love me because I made her happy, felt my melancholy react on herself, and tried to make me talk.

"Your sadness," said she, "is not like you; it frightens me. You may console yourself by telling me of your troubles, but do not imagine that my curiosity springs from any unworthy motive, I only want to be of service to you. You may rely on my being perfectly discreet; and to encourage you to speak freely, and to give you that trust in me which I think I deserve, I will tell you what I know and what I have learnt about yourself. My knowledge has not been obtained by any unworthy stratagems, or by a curiosity in affairs which do not concern me."

"I am pleased with what you say, my dear housekeeper. I see you are my friend, and I am grateful to you. Tell me all you know about the matter which is now troubling me, and conceal nothing."

"Very good. You are the lover and the beloved of Madame——. The widow whom you have treated badly has played you some trick which has involved you with your mistress, and then the wretched woman has 477 left your house with the most unpardonable rudeness this tortures you. You fear some disastrous consequences from which you cannot escape, your heart and mind are at war, and there is a struggle in your breast between passion and sentiment. Perhaps I am wrong, but yesterday you seemed to me happy and to-day miserable. I pity you, because you have inspired me with the tenderest feelings of friendship. I did my best to-day to converse with the husband that you might be free to talk to the wife, who seems to me well worthy of your love."

"All that you have said is true. Your friendship is dear to me, and I have a high opinion of your intellectual powers. The widow is a monster who has made me wretched in return for my contempt, and I cannot revenge myself on her. Honour will not allow me to tell you any more, and indeed it would be impossible for you or any one else to alleviate the grief that overwhelms me. It may possibly be my death, but in the mean time, my dear Dubois, I entreat you to continue your friendship towards me, and to treat me with entire candour. I shall always attend to what you say, and thus you will be of the greatest service to me. I shall not be ungrateful."

I spent a weary night as I had expected, for anger, the mother of vengeance, always made me sleepless, while sudden happiness had sometimes the same effect.

I rang for Le Duc early in the morning, but, instead of him, Madame Dubois's ugly little attendant came, and told me that my man was ill, and that the housekeeper would bring me my chocolate. She came in directly after, and I had no sooner swallowed the chocolate than I was seized with a violent attack of sickness, the effect of anger, which at its height may kill the man who cannot satisfy it. My concentrated rage called for vengeance on the dreadful widow, the chocolate came on the top of the anger, and if it had not been rejected I should have been killed; as it was I was quite exhausted. Looking at my housekeeper I saw she was in tears, and asked her why she wept.

"Good heavens! Do you think I have a heart of stone?"

"Calm yourself; I see you pity me. Leave me, and I hope I shall be able to get some sleep."

I went to sleep soon after, and I did not wake till I had slept for seven hours. I felt restored to life. I rang the bell, my housekeeper came in, and told me the surgeon of the place had called. She looked very melancholy, but on seeing my more cheerful aspect I saw gladness reappearing on her pretty face.

"We will dine together, dearest," said I, "but tell the surgeon to come in. I want to know what he has to say to me."

The worthy man entered, and after looking carefully round the room to see that we were alone, he came up to me, and whispered in my ear that Le Duc had a malady of a shameful character.

I burst out laughing, as I had been expecting some terrible news.

"My dear doctor," said I, "do all you can to cure him, and I will pay you handsomely, but next time don't look so doleful when you have anything to tell me. How old are you?"

"Nearly eighty."

"May God help you!"

I was all the more ready to sympathize with my poor Spaniard, as I expected to find myself in a like case.

What a fellow-feeling there is between the unfortunate! The poor man will seek in vain for true compassion at the rich man's doors; what he receives is a sacrifice to ostentation and not true benevolence; and the man in sorrow should not look for pity from one to whom sorrow is unknown, if there be such a person on the earth.

My housekeeper came in to dress me, and asked me what had been the doctor's business.

"He must have said something amusing to make you laugh."

"Yes, and I should like to tell you what it was; but before I do so I must ask you if you know what the venereal disease is?"

"Yes, I do; Lady Montagu's footman died of it while I was with her."

"Very good, but you should pretend not to know what it is, and imitate other ladies who assume an ignorance which well becomes them. Poor Le Duc has got this disease."

"Poor fellow, I am sorry for him! Were you laughing at that?"

"No; it was the air of mystery assumed by the old doctor which amused me."

"I too have a confidence to make, and when you have heard it you must either forgive me or send me away directly."

"Here is another bother. What the devil can you have done? Quick! tell me."

"Sir, I have robbed you!"

"What robbed me? When? How? Can you return me what you have taken? I should not have thought you capable of such a thing. I never forgive a robber or a liar."

"You are too hasty, sir. I am sure you will forgive me, as I robbed you only half an hour ago, and I am now going to return to you the theft."

"You are a singular woman, my dear. Come, I will vouchsafe full forgiveness, but restore immediately what you have taken."

"This is what I stole."

"What! that monster's letter? Did you read it?"

"Yes, of course, for otherwise I should not have committed a theft, should I?"

"You have robbed me my secret, then, and that is a thing you cannot give me back. You have done very wrong."

"I confess I have. My theft is all the greater in that I cannot make restoration. Nevertheless, I promise never to speak a word of it all my life, and that ought to gain me my pardon. Give it me quickly."

"You are a little witch. I forgive you, and here is the pledge of my mercy." So saying I fastened my lips on hers.

"I don't doubt the validity of your pardon; you have signed with a double and a triple seal."

"Yes; but for the future do not read, or so much as touch, any of my papers, as I am the depositary of secrets of which I am not free to dispose."

"Very good; but what shall I do when I find papers on the ground, as that letter was?"

"You must pick them up, but not read them."

"I promise to do so."

"Very well, my dear; but you must forget the horrors you have read."

"Listen to me. Allow me to remember what I have read; perhaps you may be the gainer. Let us talk over this affair, which has made my hair stand on end. This monster of immodesty has given you two mortal blows—one in the body and one in the soul; but that is not the worst, as she thinks that Madame's honour is in her keeping. This, in my thinking, is the worst of all; for, in spite of the affront, your mutual love might continue, and the disease which the infamous creature has communicated to you would pass off; but if the malicious woman carries out her threats, the honour of your charming mistress is gone beyond return. Do not try to make me forget the matter, then, but let us talk it over and see what can be done."

I thought I was dreaming when I heard a young woman in her position reasoning with more acuteness than Minerva displays in her colloquies with Telemachus. She had captured not only my esteem but my respect.

"Yes, my dear," I answered, "let us think over some plan for delivering a woman who deserves the respect of all good men from this imminent danger; and the very thought that we have some chance of success makes me indebted to you. Let us think of it and talk of it from noon to night. Think kindly of Madame——, pardon her first slip, protect her honour, and have pity on my distress. From henceforth call me no more your master but your friend. I will be your friend till death; I swear it to you. What you say is full of wisdom; my heart is yours. Embrace me."

"No, no, that is not necessary; we are young people, and we might perhaps allow ourselves to go astray. I only wish for your friendship; but I do not want you to give it to me for nothing. I wish to deserve it by giving you solid proofs of my friendship for you. In the meanwhile I will tell them to serve dinner, and I hope that after you have eaten something you will be quite well."

I was astonished at her sagacity. It might all be calculated artifice, and her aim might be to seduce me, but I did not trouble myself about that. I found myself almost in love with her, and like to be the dupe of her principles, which would have made themselves felt, even if she had openly shared my love. I decided that I would add no fuel to my flames, and felt certain that they would go out of their own accord. By leaving my love thus desolate it would die of exhaustion. I argued like a fool. I forgot that it is not possible to stop at friendship with a pretty woman whom one sees constantly, and especially when one suspects her of being in love herself. At its height friendship becomes love, and the palliative one is forced to apply to soothe it for a moment only increases its intensity. Such was the experience of Anacreon with Smerdis, and Cleobulus with Badyllus. A Platonist who pretends that one is able to live with a young woman of whom one is fond, without becoming more than her friend, is a visionary who knows not what he says. My housekeeper was too young, too pretty, and above all too pleasant, she had too keen a wit, for me not to be captivated by all these qualities conjoined; I was bound to become her lover.

We dined quietly together without saying anything about the affair we had at heart, for nothing is more imprudent or more dangerous than to speak in the presence of servants, who out of maliciousness or ignorance put the worst construction on what they hear; add or diminish, and think themselves privileged to divulge their master's secrets, especially as they know them without having been entrusted with them.

As soon as we were alone, my dear Dubois asked me if I had sufficient proof of Le Duc's fidelity.

"Well, my dear, he is a rascal and a profligate, full of impudence, sharp-witted, ignorant, a fearful liar, and nobody but myself has any power over him. However, he has one good quality, and that is blind obedience to my orders. He defies the stick, and he would defy the gallows if it were far enough off. When I have to ford a river on my travels, he strips off his clothes without my telling him, and jumps in to see if I can across in safety."

"That will do; he is just what we want under the circumstances. I will begin by assuring you, my dear friend, as you will have me style you thus, that Madame's honour is perfectly safe. Follow my advice, and if the detestable widow does not take care she will be the only person put to shame. But we want Le Duc; without him we can do nothing. Above all we must find out how he contracted his disease, as several circumstances might throw obstacles in the way of my design. Go to him at once and find out all particulars, and if he has told any of the servants what is the matter with him. When you have heard what he has to say, warn him to keep the matter quiet."

I made no objection, and without endeavouring to penetrate her design I went to Le Duc. I found him lying on his bed by himself. I sat down beside him with a smile on my face, and promised to have him cured if he would tell me all the circumstances of the case.

"With all my heart, sir, the matter happened like this. The day you sent me to Soleure to get your letters, I got down at a roadside dairy to get a glass of milk. It was served to me by a young wench who caught my fancy, and I gave her a hug; she raised no objection, and in a quarter of an hour she made me what you see."

"Have you told anyone about it?"

"I took good care not to do so, as I should only have got laughed at. The doctor is the only one who knows what is the matter, and he tells me the swelling will be gone down before tomorrow, and I hope I shall be able by that time to wait upon you."

"Very good, but remember to keep your own counsel."

I proceeded to inform my Minerva of our conversation, and she said,—

"Tell me whether the widow could take her oath that she had spent the two hours on the sofa with you."

"No, for she didn't see me, and I did not say a word."

"Very good; then sit down at your desk and write, and tell her she is a liar, as you did not leave your room at all, and that you are making the necessary enquiries in your household to find out who is the wretched person she has unwittingly contaminated. Write at once and send off your letter directly. In an hour and a half's time you can write another letter; or rather you can copy what I am just going to put down."

"My dear, I see your plan; it is an ingenious one, but I have given my word of honour to Madame to take no steps in the matter without first consulting her."

"Then your word of honour must give way to the necessity of saving her honour. Your love retards your steps, but everything depends on our promptitude, and on the interval between the first and second letter. Follow my advice, I beg of you, and you will know the rest from the letter I am going to write for you to copy. Quick I write letter number one."

I did not allow myself to reflect. I was persuaded that no better plan could be found than that of my charming governess, and I proceeded to write the following love-letter to the impudent monster:

"The impudence of your letter is in perfect accord with the three nights you spent in discovering a fact which has no existence save in your own perverse imagination. Know, cursed woman, that I never left my room, and that I have not to deplore the shame of having passed two hours with a being such as you. God knows with whom you did pass them, but I mean to find out if the whole story is not the creation of your devilish brain, and when I do so I will inform you.

"You may thank Heaven that I did not open your letter till after M. and Madame had gone. I received it in their presence, but despising the hand that wrote it I put it in my pocket, little caring what infamous stuff it contained. If I had been curious enough to read it and my guests had seen it, I would have you know that I would have gone in pursuit of you, and at this moment you would have been a corpse. I am quite well, and have no symptoms of any complaint, but I shall not lower myself to convince you of my health, as your eyes would carry contagion as well as your wretched carcase."

I shewed the letter to my dear Dubois, who thought it rather strongly expressed, but approved of it on the whole; I then sent it to the horrible being who had caused me such unhappiness. An hour and a half afterwards I sent her the following letter, which I copied without addition or subtraction:

"A quarter of an hour after I had sent off my letter, the village doctor came to tell me that my man had need of his treatment for a disease of a shameful nature which he had contracted quite recently. I told him to take care of his patient; and when he had gone I went to see the invalid, who confessed, after some pressure, that he had received this pretty present from you. I asked him how he had contrived to obtain access to you, and he said that he saw you going by your self in the dark into the apartment of M.——. Knowing that I had gone to bed, and having no further services to render me, curiosity made him go and see what you were doing there by stealth, as if you had wanted to see the lady, who would be in bed by that time, you would not have gone by the door leading to the garden. He at first thought that you went there with ill-intent, and he waited an hour to see if you stole anything, in which case he would have arrested you; but as you did not come out, and he heard no noise, he resolved to go in after you, and found you had left the door open. He has assured me that he had no intentions in the way of carnal enjoyment, and I can well believe him. He tells me he was on the point of crying for help, when you took hold of him and put your hand over his mouth; but he changed his plans on finding himself drawn gently to a couch and covered with kisses. You plainly took him for somebody else, 'and,' said he, 'I did her a service which she has done ill to recompense in this fashion.' He left you without saying a word as soon as the day began to dawn, his motive being fear of recognition. It is easy to see that you took my servant for myself, for in the night, you know, all cats are grey, and I congratulate you on obtaining an enjoyment you certainly would not have had from me, as I should most surely have recognized you directly from your breath and your aged charms, and I can tell you it would have gone hard with you. Luckily for you and for me, things happened otherwise. I may tell you that the poor fellow is furious, and intends making you a visit, from which course I believe I have no right to dissuade him. I advise you to hear him politely, and to be in a generous mood when he comes, as he is a determined fellow like all Spaniards, and if you do not treat him properly he will publish the matter, and you will have to take the consequences. He will tell you himself what his terms are, and I daresay you will be wise enough to grant them."

An hour after I had sent off this epistle I received a reply to my first letter. She told me that my device was an ingenious one, but that it was no good, as she knew what she was talking about. She defied me to shew her that I was healthy in the course of a few days.

While we were at supper, my dear Dubois tried her utmost to cheer me up, but all to no purpose; I was too much under the influence of strong emotion to yield to her high spirits. We discussed the third step, which would put an apex to the scheme and cover the impudent woman with shame. As I had written the two letters according to my housekeeper's instructions, I determined to follow her advice to the end. She told me what to say to Le Duc in the morning; and she was curious to know what sort of stuff he was made of, she begged me to let her listen behind the curtains of my bed.

Next morning Le Due came in, and I asked if he could ride on horseback to Soleure.

"Yes, sir," he replied, "but the doctor tells me I must begin to bathe to-morrow."

"Very good. As soon as your horse is ready, set out and go to Madame F——, but do not let her know you come from me, or suspect that you are a mere emissary of mine. Say that you want to speak to her. If she refuses to receive you, wait outside in the street; but I fancy she will receive you, and without a witness either. Then say to her, 'You have given me my complaint without having been asked, and I require you to give me sufficient money to get myself cured.' Add that she made you work for two hours in the dark, and that if it had not been for the fatal present she had given to you, you would have said nothing about it; but that finding yourself in such a state (you needn't be ashamed to shew her) she ought not to be astonished at your taking such a course. If she resists, threaten her with the law. That's all you have to do, but don't let my name appear. Return directly without loss of time, that I may know how you have got on."

"That's all very fine, sir, but if this jolly wench has me pitched out of window, I shan't come home quite so speedily."

"Quite so, but you needn't be afraid; I will answer for your safety."

"It's a queer business you are sending me on."

"You are the only man I would trust to do it properly."

"I will do it all right, but I want to ask you one or two essential questions. Has the lady really got the what d'you call it?"

"She has."

"I am sorry for her. But how am I to stick to it that she has peppered me, when I have never spoken to her?"

"Do you usually catch that complaint by speaking, booby?"

"No, but one speaks in order to catch it, or while one is catching it."

"You spent two hours in the dark with her without a word being spoken, and she will see that she gave this fine present to you while she thought she was giving it to another."

"Ah! I begin to see my way, sir. But if we were in the dark, how was I to know it was she I had to do with?

"Thus: you saw her going in by the garden door, and you marked her unobserved. But you may be sure she won't ask you any of these questions."

"I know what to do now. I will start at once, and I am as curious as you to know what her answer will be. But here's another question comes into my head. She may try to strike a bargain over the sum I am to ask for my cure; if so, shall I be content with three hundred francs?"

"That's too much for her, take half."

"But it isn't much for two hours of such pleasure for her and six weeks of such pain for me."

"I will make up the rest to you."

"That's good hearing. She is going to pay for damage she has done. I fancy I see it all, but I shall say nothing. I would bet it is you to whom she has made this fine present, and that you want to pay her out."

"Perhaps so; but keep your own counsel and set out."

"Do you know I think the rascal is unique," said my dear Dubois, emerging from her hiding-place, "I had hard work to keep from laughing when he said that if he were pitched out of the window he would not come back so soon. I am sure he will acquit himself better than ever did diplomatist. When he gets to Soleure the monster will have already dispatched her reply to your second letter. I am curious to see how it will turn out."

"To you, my dear, the honour of this comedy belongs. You have conducted this intrigue like a past master in the craft. It could never be taken for the work of a novice."

"Nevertheless, it is my first and I hope it will be my last intrigue."

"I hope she won't defy me to 'give evidence of my health'."

"You are quite well so far, I think?"

"Yes; and, by the way, it is possible she may only have leucorrhoea. I am longing to see the end of the piece, and to set my mind at rest."

"Will you give Madame an account of our scheme?"

"Yes; but I shall not be able to give you the credit you deserve."

"I only want to have credit in your eyes."

"You cannot doubt that I honour you immensely, and I shall certainly not deprive you of the reward that is your due."

"The only reward I ask for is for you to be perfectly open with me."

"You are very wonderful. Why do you interest yourself so much in my affairs? I don't like to think you are really inquisitive."

"You would be wrong to think that I have a defect which would lower me in my own eyes. Be sure, sir, that I shall only be curious when you are sad."

"But what can have made you feel so generously towards me?"

"Only your honourable conduct towards me."

"You touch me profoundly, and I promise to confide in you for the future."

"You will make me happy."

Le Duc had scarcely gone an hour when a messenger on foot came to bring me a second letter from the widow. He also gave me a small packet, telling me that he had orders to wait for a reply. I sent him down to wait, and I gave the letter to Madame Dubois, that she might see what it contained. While she was reading it I leant upon the window, my heart beating violently.

"Everything is getting on famously," cried my housekeeper. "Here is the letter; read it."

"Whether I am being told the truth, or whether I am the victim of a myth arising from your fertile imagination (for which you are too well known all over Europe), I will regard the whole story as being true, as I am not in a position to disprove it. I am deeply grieved to have injured an innocent man who has never done me any ill, and I will willingly pay the penalty by giving him a sum which will be more than sufficient to cure him of the plague with which I infected him. I beg that you will give him the twenty-five louis I am sending you; they will serve to restore him to health, and to make him forget the bitterness of the pleasure I am so sorry to have procured for him. And now are you sufficiently generous to employ your authority as master to enjoin on your man the most absolute secrecy? I hope so, for you have reason to dread my vengeance otherwise. Consider that, if this affair is allowed to transpire, it will be easy for me to give it a turn which may be far from pleasant to you, and which will force the worthy man you are deceiving to open his eyes; for I have not changed my opinion, as I have too many proofs of your understanding with his wife. As I do not desire that we should meet again, I shall go to Lucerne on the pretext of family concerns. Let me know that you have got this letter."

"I am sorry," I said, "to have sent Le Duc, as the harpy is violent, and I am afraid of something happening to him."

"Don't be afraid," she replied, "nothing will happen, and it is better that they should see each other; it makes it more certain. Send her the money directly; she will have to give it to him herself, and your vengeance will be complete. She will not be able to entertain the slightest suspicion, especially if Le Duc shews her her work, and in two or three hours you will have the pleasure of hearing everything from his lips. You have reason to bless your stars, as the honour of the woman you love is safe. The only thing that can trouble you is the remembrance of the widow's foul embraces, and the certainty that the prostitute has communicated her complaint to you. Nevertheless, I hope it may prove a slight attack and be easily cured. An inveterate leucorrhoea is not exactly a venereal disease, and I have heard people in London say that it was rarely contagious. We ought to be very thankful that she is going to Lucerne. Laugh and be thankful; there is certainly a comic touch in our drama."

"Unfortunately, it is tragi-comic. I know the human heart, and I am sure that I must have forfeited Madame's affections."

"It is true that——; but this is not the time to be thinking of such matters. Quick! write to her briefly and return her the twenty-five Louis."

My reply was as follows:

"Your unworthy suspicions, your abominable design of revenge, and the impudent letter you wrote me, are the only causes of your no doubt bitter repentance. I hope that it will restore peace to your conscience. Our messengers have crossed, through no fault of mine. I send you the twenty-five Louis; you can give them to the man yourself. I could not prevent my servant from paying you a visit, but this time you will not keep him two hours, and you will not find it difficult to appease his anger. I wish you a good journey, and I shall certainly flee all occasions of meeting you, for I always avoid the horrible; and you must know, odious woman, that it isn't everybody who endeavours to ruin the reputation of their friends. If you see the apostolic nuncio at Lucerne, ask him about me, and he will tell you what sort of a reputation I have in Europe. I can assure you that Le Duc has only spoken to me of his misadventure, and that if you treat him well he will be discreet, as he certainly has nothing to boast of. Farewell."

My dear Minerva approved of this letter, and I sent it with the money by the messenger.

"The piece is not yet done," said my housekeeper, "we have three scenes more:"

"What are they?"

"The return of your Spaniard, the appearance of the disease, and the astonishment of Madame when she hears it all."

I counted the moments for Le Duc to return, but in vain; he did not appear. I was in a state of great anxiety, although my dear Dubois kept telling me that the only reason he was away so long was that the widow was out. Some people are so happily constituted that they never admit the possibility of misfortune. I was like that myself till the age of thirty, when I was put under the Leads. Now I am getting into my dotage and look on the dark side of everything. I am invited to a wedding, and see nought but gloom; and witnessing the coronation of Leopold, at Prague, I say to myself, 'Nolo coronari'. Cursed old age, thou art only worthy of dwelling in hell, as others before me have thought also, 'tristisque senectus'.

About half-past nine my housekeeper looked out, and saw Le Duc by the moonlight coming along at a good pace. That news revived me. I had no light in the room, and my housekeeper ran to hide in the recess, for she would not have missed a word of the Spaniard's communication.

"I am dying of hunger," said he, as he came in. "I had to wait for that woman till half-past six. When she came in she found me on the stairs and told me to go about my business, as she had nothing to say to me.

"'That may be, fair lady,' I replied; 'but I have a few words to say to you, and I have been waiting here for a cursed time with that intent.'

"'Wait a minute,' she replied; and then putting into her pocket a packet and a letter which I thought was addressed in your writing, she told me to follow her. As soon as I got to her room, I saw there was no one else present, and I told her that she had infected me, and that I wanted the wherewithal to pay the doctor.

As she said nothing I proceeded to convince her of my infected state, but she turned away her head, and said,—

"'Have you been waiting for me long?

"'Since eleven, without having had a bite or a sup.'

"Thereupon she went out, and after asking the servant, whom I suppose she had sent here, what time he had come back, she returned to me, shut the door, and gave me the packet, telling me that it contained twenty-five Louis for my cure, and that if I valued my life I would keep silence in the matter. I promised to be discreet, and with that I left here, and here I am.

"Does the packet belong to me?"

"Certainly. Have some supper and go to bed."

My dear Dubois came out of her recess and embraced me, and we spent a happy evening. Next morning I noticed the first symptoms of the disease the hateful widow had communicated to me, but in three or four days I found it was of a very harmless character, and a week later I was quite rid of it. My poor Spaniard, on the other hand, was in a pitiable case.

I passed the whole of the next morning in writing to Madame. I told her circumstantially all I had done, in spite of my promise to consult her, and I sent her copies of all the letters to convince her that our enemy had gone to Lucerne with the idea that her vengeance had been only an imaginary one. Thus I shewed her that her honour was perfectly safe. I ended by telling her that I had noticed the first symptoms of the disease, but that I was certain of getting rid of it in a very few days. I sent my letter through her nurse, and in two days' time I had a few lines from her informing me that I should see her in the course of the week in company with her husband and M. de Chavigni.

Unhappy I! I was obliged to renounce all thoughts of love, but my Dubois, who was with me nearly all day on account of Le Duc's illness, began to stand me in good stead. The more I determined to be only a friend to her, the more I was taken with her; and it was in vain that I told myself that from seeing her without any love-making my sentiment for her would die a natural death. I had made her a present of a ring, telling her that whenever she wanted to get rid of it I would give her a hundred louis for it; but this could only happen in time of need—an impossible contingency while she continued with me, and I had no idea of sending her away. She was natural and sincere, endowed with a ready wit and good reasoning powers. She had never been in love, and she had only married to please Lady Montagu. She only wrote to her mother, and to please her I read the letters. They were full of filial piety, and were admirably written.

One day the fancy took me to ask to read the letters her mother wrote in reply. "She never replies," said she, "For an excellent reason, namely, that she cannot write. I thought she was dead when I came back from England, and it was a happy surprise to find her in perfect health when I got to Lausanne."

"Who came with you from England?"

"Nobody."

"I can't credit that. Young, beautiful, well dressed, obliged to associate casually with all kinds of people, young men and profligates (for there are such everywhere), how did you manage to defend yourself?"

"Defend myself? I never needed to do so. The best plan for a young woman is never to stare at any man, to pretend not to hear certain questions and certainly not to answer them, to sleep by herself in a room where there is a lock and key, or with the landlady when possible. When a girl has travelling adventures, one may safely say that she has courted them, for it is easy to be discreet in all countries if one wishes."

She spoke justly. She assured me that she had never had an adventure and had never tripped, as she was fortunate enough not to be of an amorous disposition. Her naive stories, her freedom from prudery, and her sallies full of wit and good sense, amused me from morning till night, and we sometimes thoued each other; this was going rather far, and should have shewn us that we were on the brink of the precipice. She talked with much admiration of the charms of Madame, and shewed the liveliest interest in my stories of amorous adventure. When I got on risky ground, I would make as if I would fain spare her all unseemly details, but she begged me so gracefully to hide nothing, that I found myself obliged to satisfy her; but when my descriptions became so faithful as almost to set us on fire, she would burst into a laugh, put her hand over my mouth, and fly like a hunted gazelle to her room, and then lock herself in. One day I asked her why she did so, and she answered, "To hinder you from coming to ask me for what I could not refuse you at such moments."

The day before that on which M. and Madame and M. de Chavigni came to dine with me, she asked me if I had had any amorous adventures in Holland. I told her about Esther, and when I came to the mole and my inspection of it, my charming curiosity ran to stop my mouth, her sides shaking with laughter. I held her gently to me, and could not help seeking whether she had a mole in the same place, to which she opposed but a feeble resistance. I was prevented by my unfortunate condition from immolating the victim on the altar of love, so we confined ourselves to a make-believe combat which only lasted a minute; however, our eyes took in it, and our excited feelings were by no means appeased. When we had done she said, laughing, but yet discreetly,—

"My dear friend, we are in love with one another; and if we do not take care we shall not long be content with this trifling."

Sighing as she spoke, she wished me good night and went to bed with her ugly little maid. This was the first time we had allowed ourselves to be overcome by the violence of our passion, but the first step was taken. As I retired to rest I felt that I was in love, and foresaw that I should soon be under the rule of my charming housekeeper.

M. and Madame—and M. Chavigni gave us an agreeable surprise, the next day, by coming to dine with us, and we passed the time till dinner by walking in the garden. My dear Dubois did the honours of the table, and I was glad to see that my two male guests were delighted with her, for they did not leave her for a moment during the afternoon, and I was thus enabled to tell my charmer all I had written to her. Nevertheless I took care not to say a word about the share my housekeeper had had in the matter, for my mistress would have been mortified at the thought that her weakness was known to her.

"I was delighted to read your letters," said she, "and to hear that that villainous woman can no longer flatter herself upon having spent two hours with you. But tell me, how can you have actually spent them with her without noticing, in spite of the dark, the difference between her and me? She is much shorter, much thinner, and ten years older. Besides, her breath is disagreeable, and I think you know that I have not that defect. Certainly, you could not see her hair, but you could touch, and yet you noticed nothing! I can scarcely believe it!"

"Unhappily, it is only too true. I was inebriated with love, and thinking only of you, I saw nothing but you."

"I understand how strong the imagination would be at first, but this element should have been much diminished after the first or second assault; and, above all, because she differs from me in a matter which I cannot conceal and she cannot supply."

"You are right—a burst of Venus! When I think that I only touched two dangling flabby breasts, I feel as if I did not deserve to live!"

"And you felt them, and they did not disgust you!"

"Could I be disgusted, could I even reflect, when I felt certain that I held you in my arms, you for whom I would give my life. No, a rough skin, a stinking breath, and a fortification carried with far too much ease; nothing could moderate my amorous fury."

"What do I hear? Accursed and unclean woman, nest of impurities! And could you forgive me all these defects?"

"I repeat, the idea that I possessed you deprived me of my thinking faculties; all seemed to me divine."

"You should have treated me like a common prostitute, you should even have beaten me on finding me such as you describe."

"Ah! now you are unjust!"

"That may be; I am so enraged against that monster that my anger deprives me of reason. But now that she thinks that she had to do with a servant, and after the degrading visit she has had she ought to die of rage and shame. What astonishes me is her believing it, for he is shorter than you by four inches. And how can she imagine that a servant would do it as well as you? It's not likely. I am sure she is in love with him now. Twenty-five louis! He would have been content with ten. What a good thing that the poor fellow's illness happened so conveniently. But I suppose you had to tell him all?"

"Not at all. I gave him to understand that she had made an appointment with me in that room, and that I had really spent two hours with her, not speaking for fear of being heard. Then, thinking over the orders I gave him, he came to the conclusion that on finding myself diseased afterwards I was disgusted, and being able to disavow my presence I had done so for the sake of revenge."

"That's admirable, and the impudence of the Spaniard passes all belief. But her impudence is the most astonishing thing of all. But supposing her illness had been a mere trick to frighten you, what a risk the rascal would have run!"

"I was afraid of that, as I had no symptoms of disease whatever."

"But now you really have it, and all through my fault. I am in despair."

"Be calm, my angel, my disease is of a very trifling nature. I am only taking nitre, and in a week I shall be quite well again. I hope that then . . . ."

"Ah! my dear friend."

"What?"

"Don't let us think of that any more, I beseech you."

"You are disgusted, and not unnaturally; but your love cannot be very strong, Ah! how unhappy I am."

"I am more unhappy than you. I love you, and you would be thankless indeed if you ceased to love me. Let us love each other, but let us not endeavour to give one another proofs of our love. It might be fatal. That accursed widow! She is gone away, and in a fortnight we shall be going also to Bale, where we remain till the end of November."

The die is cast, and I see that I must submit to your decision, or rather to my destiny, for none but fatal events have befallen me since I came to Switzerland. My only consoling thought is that I have made your honour safe."

"You have won my husband's friendship and esteem; we shall always be good friends."

"If you are going I feel that I must go before you. That will tend to convince the wretched author of my woe that there is nothing blame-worthy in my friendship for you."

"You reason like an angel, and you convince me more and more of your love. Where are you going?"

"To Italy; but I shall take Berne and Geneva on my way."

"You will not be coming to Bale, then? I am glad to hear it, in spite of the pleasure it would give me to see you. No doubt your arrival would give a handle for the gossips, and I might suffer by it. But if possible, in the few days you are to remain, shew yourself to be in good spirits, for sadness does not become you."

We rejoined the ambassador and M.—— who had not had time to think about us, as my dear Dubois had kept them amused by her lively conversation. I reproached her for the way in which she husbanded her wit as far as I was concerned, and M. de Chavigni, seizing the opportunity, told us it was because we were in love, and lovers are known to be chary of their words. My housekeeper was not long in finding a repartee, and she again began to entertain the two gentlemen, so that I was enabled to continue my walk with Madame, who said,—

"Your housekeeper, my dear friend, is a masterpiece. Tell me the truth, and I promise to give you a mark of my gratitude that will please you before I go."

"Speak; what do you wish to know?"

"You love her and she loves you in return."

"I think you are right, but so far . . . ."

"I don't want to know any more, for if matters are not yet arranged they soon will be, and so it comes to the same thing. If you had told me you did not love her I should not have believed you, for I can't conceive that a man of your age can live with a woman like that without loving her. She is very pretty and exceedingly intelligent, she has good spirits, talents, an excellent manner, and she speaks exceedingly well: that is enough to charm you, and I expect you will find it difficult to separate from her. Lebel did her a bad turn in sending her to you, as she used to have an excellent reputation, and now she will no longer be able to get a place with ladies in the highest society."

"I shall take her to Berne."

"That is a good idea."

Just as they were going I said that I should soon be coming to Soleure to thank them for the distinguished reception they had given me, as I proposed leaving in a few days. The idea of never seeing Madame again was so painful to me that as soon as I got in I went to bed, and my housekeeper, respecting my melancholy, retired after wishing me good-night.

In two or three days I received a note from my charmer, bidding me call upon them the day following at about ten o'clock, and telling me I was to ask for dinner. I carried out her orders to the letter. M. gave me a most friendly reception, but saying that he was obliged to go into the country and could not be home till one o'clock, he begged me not to be offended if he delivered me over to his wife for the morning. Such is the fate of a miserable husband! His wife was engaged with a young girl at tambour-work; I accepted her company on the condition that she would not allow me to disturb her work.

The girl went away at noon, and soon after we went to enjoy the fresh air outside the house. We sat in a summer-house from which, ourselves unseen, we could see all the carriages that approached the house.

"Why, dearest, did you not procure me the bliss when I was in good health."

"Because at that time my husband suspected that you turned yourself into a waiter for my sake, and that you could not be indifferent towards me. Your discretion has destroyed his suspicions; and also your housekeeper, whom he believes to be your wife, and who has taken his fancy to such an extent, that I believe he would willingly consent to an exchange, for a few days at any rate. Would you agree?"

"Ah! if the exchange could be effected."

Having only an hour before me, and foreseeing that it would be the last I should pass beside her, I threw myself at her feet. She was full of affection, and put no obstacles in the way of my desires, save those which my own feelings dictated, for I loved her too well to consent to injure her health. I did all I could to replace the utmost bliss, but the pleasure she enjoyed doubtless consisted in a great measure in shewing me her superiority to the horrible widow.

When we saw the husband's carriage coming, we rose and took care that the worthy man should not find us in the arbour. He made a thousand excuses for not having returned sooner.

We had an excellent dinner, and at table he talked almost entirely of my housekeeper, and he seemed moved when I said I meant to take her to Lausanne to her mother. I took leave of them at five o'clock with a broken heart, and from there I went to M. de Chavigni and told him all my adventures. He had a right to be told, as he had done all in his power to insure the success of a project which had only failed by an unexampled fatality.

In admiration of my dear Dubois's wit—for I did not conceal the part she played he said that old as he was he should think himself quite happy if he had such a woman with him, and he was much pleased when I told him that I was in love with her. "Don't give yourself the trouble, my dear Casanova, of running from house to house to take leave," said the amiable nobleman. "It can be done just as well at the assembly, and you need not even stay to supper, if you don't want to."

I followed his advice, and thus saw again Madame as I thought, for the last time, but I was wrong; I saw her ten years afterwards; and at the proper time the reader will see where, when, how, and under what circumstances.

Before going away, I followed the ambassador to his room to thank him as he deserved, for his kindness, and to ask him to give me a letter of introduction for Berne, where I thought of staying a fortnight. I also begged him to send Lebel to me that we might settle our accounts. He told me that Lebel should bring me a letter for M. de Muralt, the Mayor of Thun.

When I got home, feeling sad on this, the eve of my leaving a town where I had but trifling victories and heavy losses, I thanked my housekeeper for waiting for me, and to give her a good night I told her that in three days we should set out for Berne, and that my mails must be packed.

Next day, after a somewhat silent breakfast, she said,—

"You will take me with you, won't you?"

"Certainly, if you like me well enough to want to go."

"I would go with you to the end of the world, all the more as you are now sick and sad, and when I saw you first you were blithe and well. If I must leave you, I hope at least to see you happy first."

The doctor came in just then to tell me that my poor Spaniard was so ill that he could not leave his bed.

"I will have him cured at Berne," said I; "tell him that we are going to dine there the day after to-morrow."

"I must tell you, sir, that though it's only a seven leagues' journey, he cannot possibly undertake it as he has lost the use of all his limbs."

"I am sorry to hear that, doctor."

"I dare say, but it's true."

"I must verify the matter with my own eyes;" and so saying I went to see Le Duc.

I found the poor rascal, as the doctor had said, incapable of motion. He had only the use of his tongue and his eyes.

"You are in a pretty state," said I to him.

"I am very ill, sir, though otherwise I feel quite well."

"I expect so, but as it is you can't move, and I want to dine at Berne the day after to-morrow."

"Have me carried there, I shall get cured."

"You are right, I will have you carried in a litter."

"I shall look like a saint out for a walk."

I told one of the servants to look after him, and to see to all that was necessary for our departure. I had him taken to the "Falcon" by two horses who drew his litter.

Lebel came at noon and gave me the letter his master had written for M. de Murat. He brought his receipts and I paid everything without objection, as I found him an entirely honest man, and I had him to dinner with Madame Dubois and myself. I did not feel disposed to talk, and I was glad to see that they got on without me; they talked away admirably and amused me, for Lebel was by no means wanting in wit. He said he was very glad I had given him an opportunity of knowing the housekeeper, as he could not say he had known her before, having only seen her two or three times in passing through Lausanne. On rising from the table he asked my permission to write to her, and she, putting in her voice, called on him not to forget to do so.

Lebel was a good-natured man, of an honest appearance, and approaching his fiftieth year. Just as he was going, without asking my leave, he embraced her in the French fashion, and she seemed not to have the slightest objection.

She told me as soon as he was gone that this worthy man might be useful to her, and that she was delighted to enter into a correspondence with him.

The next day was spent in putting everything in order for our short journey, and Le Duc went off in his litter, intending to rest for the night at four leagues from Soleure. On the day following, after I had remembered the door-keeper, the cook, and the man-servant I was leaving behind, I set out in my carriage with the charming Dubois, and at eleven o'clock I arrived at the inn at Berne, where Le Duc had preceded me by two hours. In the first place, knowing the habits of Swiss innkeepers, I made an agreement with the landlord; and I then told the servant I had kept, who came from Berne, to take care of Le Duc, to put him under good medical superintendence, and to bid the doctor spare nothing to cure him completely.

I dined with my housekeeper in her room, for she had a separate lodging, and after sending my letter to M. de Muralt I went out for a walk.

CHAPTER XVII

Berne—La Mata Madame de la Saone—Sara—My Departure— Arrival at Bale

I reached an elevation from which I could look over a vast stretch of country watered by a little river, and noticing a path leading to a kind of stair, the fancy took me to follow it. I went down about a hundred steps, and found forty small closets which I concluded were bathing machines. While I was looking at the place an honest-looking fellow came up to me, and asked me if I would like a bath. I said I would, and he opened one of the closets, and before long I surrounded by a crowd of young girls.

"Sir," said the man, "they all aspire to the honour of attending you while you bathe; you have only to choose which it shall be. Half-a-crown will pay for the bath, the girl, and your coffee."

As if I were the Grand Turk, I examined the swarm of rustic beauties, and threw my handkerchief at the one I liked the best. We went into a closet, and shutting the door with the most serious air, without even looking at me, she undressed me, and put a cotton cap on my head, and as soon as she saw me in the water she undressed herself as coolly as possible, and without a word came into the bath. Then she rubbed me all over, except in a certain quarter, which I had covered with my hands. When I thought I had been manipulated sufficiently, I asked for coffee. She got out of the bath, opened the door, and after asking for what I wanted got in again without the slightest consciousness.

When the coffee came she got out again to take it, shut the door, and returned to the bath, and held the tray while I was drinking, and when I had finished she remained beside me.

Although I had taken no great notice of her, I could see that she possessed all the qualifications a man could desire in a woman: fine features, lively eyes, a pretty mouth, and an excellent row of teeth, a healthy complexion, a well-rounded bosom a curved back, and all else in the same sort. I certainly thought her hands might have been softer, but their hardness was probably due to hard work. Furthermore, she was only eighteen, and yet I remained cold to all her charms. How was that? That was the question I asked myself; and I think the reason probably was that she was too natural, too devoid of those assumed graces and coquettish airs which women employ with so much art for the seduction of men. We only care for artifice and false show. Perhaps, too, our senses, to be irritated, require woman's charms to be veiled by modesty. But if, accustomed as we are to clothe ourselves, the face is the smallest factor in our perfect happiness, how is it that the face plays the principal part in rendering a man amorous? Why do we take the face as an index of a woman's beauty, and why do we forgive her when the covered parts are not in harmony with her features? Would it not be much more reasonable and sensible to veil the face, and to have the rest of the body naked? Thus when we fall in love with a woman, we should only want, as the crown of our bliss, to see a face answerable to those other charms which had taken our fancy. There can be no doubt that

that would be the better plan, as in that case we should only be seduced by a perfect beauty, and we should grant an easy pardon if at the lifting of the mask we found ugliness instead of loveliness. Under those circumstances an ugly woman, happy in exercising the seductive power of her other charms, would never consent to unveil herself; while the pretty ones would not have to be asked. The plain women would not make us sigh for long; they would be easily subdued on the condition of remaining veiled, and if they did consent to unmask, it would be only after they had practically convinced one that enjoyment is possible without facial beauty. And it is evident and undeniable that inconstancy only proceeds from the variety of features. If a man did not see the face, he would always be constant and always in love with the first woman who had taken his fancy. I know that in the opinion of the foolish all this will seem folly, but I shall not be on the earth to answer their objections.

When I had left the bath, she wiped me with towels, put on my shirt, and then in the same state—that is, quite naked, she did my hair.

While I was dressing she dressed herself too, and having soon finished she came to buckle my shoes. I then gave her half-a-crown for the bath and six francs for herself; she kept the half-crown, but gave me back the six francs with silent contempt. I was mortified; I saw that I had offended her, and that she considered her behaviour entitled her to respect. I went away in a bad enough humour.

After supper I could not help telling my dear Dubois of the adventure I had had in the afternoon, and she made her own comments on the details. "She can't have been pretty," said she, "for if she had been, you would certainly have given way. I should like to see her."

"If you like I will take you there."

"I should be delighted."

"But you will have to dress like a man:"

She rose, went out without a word, and in a quarter of an hour returned in a suit of Le Duc's, but minus the trousers, as she had certain protuberances which would have stood out too much I told her to take a pair of my breeches, and we settled to go to the bath next morning.

She came to wake at six o'clock. She was dressed like a man, and wore a blue overcoat which disguised her shape admirably. I rose and went to La Mata, as the place is called.

Animated by the pleasure the expedition gave her, my dear Dubois looked radiant. Those who saw her must have seen through her disguise, she was so evidently a woman; so she wrapped herself up in her overcoat as well as she could.

As soon as we arrived we saw the master of the baths, who asked me if I wanted a closet for four, and I replied in the affirmative. We were soon surrounded by the girls, and I shewed my housekeeper the one who had not seduced me; she made choice of her, and I having fixed upon a big, determined-looking wench, we shut ourselves up in the bath.

As soon as I was undressed I went into the water with my big attendant. My housekeeper was not so quick; the novelty of the thing astonished her, and her expression told me that she repented of having come; but putting a good face on it, she began to laugh at seeing me rubbed by the feminine grenadier. She had some trouble before she could take off her chemise, but as it is only the first step that costs, she let it fall off, and though she held her two hands before her she dazzled me, in spite of myself, by the beauty of her form. Her attendant prepared to treat her as she had treated me, but she begged to be left alone; and on my following her example she felt obliged to let me look after her.

The two Swiss girls, who had no doubt often been present at a similar situation, began to give us a spectacle which was well known to me, but which was quite strange to my dear Dubois.

These two Bacchantes began to imitate the caresses I lavished on my housekeeper, who was quite astonished at the amorous fury with which my attendant played the part of a man with the other girl. I confess I was a little surprised myself, in spite of the transports which my fair Venetian nun had shewn me six years before in conjunction with C—— C——.

I could not have imagined that anything of the kind could have distracted my attention, holding, as I did, the woman I loved, whose charms were sufficient to captivate all the senses; but the strange strife of the two young Menads took up her attention as well as mine.

"Your attendant," said she, "must be a boy, not a girl."

"But," said I, "you saw her breasts."

"Yes, but she may be a boy all the same."

The big Swiss girl who had heard what we had said turned round and shewed me what I should not have credited. There could be no mistake, however. It was a feminine membrane, but much longer than my little finger, and stiff enough to penetrate. I explained to my dear Dubois what it was, but to convince her I had to make her touch it. The impudent creature pushed her shamelessness so far as to offer to try it on her, and she insisted so passionately that I was obliged to push her away. She then turned to her companion and satiated on her body her fury of lust. In spite of its disgusting nature, the sight irritated us to such a degree that my housekeeper yielded to nature and granted me all I could desire.

This entertainment lasted for two hours, and we returned to the town well pleased with one another. On leaving the bath I gave a Louis to each of the two Bacchantes, and we went away determined to go there no more. It will be understood that after what had happened there could be no further obstacle to the free progress of our love; and accordingly my dear Dubois became my mistress, and we made each other happy during all the time we spent at Berne. I was quite cured of my misadventure with the horrible widow, and I found that if love's pleasures are fleeting so are its pains. I will go farther and maintain that the pleasures are of much longer duration, as they leave memories which can be enjoyed in old age, whereas, if a man does happen to remember the pains, it is so slightly as to have no influence upon his happiness.

At ten o'clock the Mayor of Thun was announced. He was dressed in the French fashion, in black, and had a manner at once graceful and polite that pleased me. He was middle-aged, and enjoyed a considerable position in the Government. He insisted on my reading the letter that M. de Chavigni had written to him on my account. It was so flattering that I told him that if it had not been sealed I should not have had the face to deliver it. He asked me for the next day to a supper composed of men only, and for the day after that, to a supper at which women as well as men would be present. I went with him to the library where we saw M. Felix, an unfrocked monk, more of a scribbler than a scholar, and a young man named Schmidt, who gave good promise, and was already known to advantage in the literary world. I also had the misfortune of meeting here a very learned man of a very wearisome kind; he knew the names of ten thousand shells by heart, and I was obliged to listen to him for two hours, although I was totally ignorant of his science. Amongst other things he told me that the Aar contained gold. I replied that all great rivers contained gold, but he shrugged his shoulders and did not seem convinced.

I dined with M. de Muralt in company with four or five of the most distinguished women in Berne. I liked them very well, and above all Madame de Saconai struck me as particularly amiable and well-educated. I should have paid my addresses to her if I had been staying long in the so-called capital of Switzerland.

The ladies of Berne are well though not extravagantly dressed, as luxury is forbidden by the laws. Their manners are good and they speak French with perfect ease. They enjoy the greatest liberty without abusing it, for in spite of gallantry decency reigns everywhere. The husbands are not jealous, but they require their wives to be home by supper-time.

I spent three weeks in the town, my time being divided between my dear Dubois and an old lady of eighty-five who interested me greatly by her knowledge of chemistry. She had been intimately connected with the celebrated Boerhaave, and she shewed me a plate of gold he had transmuted in her presence from copper. I believed as much as I liked of this, but she assured me that Boerhaave possessed the philosopher's stone, but that he had not discovered the secret of prolonging life many years beyond the century. Boerhaave, however, was not able to apply this knowledge to himself, as he died of a polypus on the heart before he had attained the age of perfect maturity, which Hypocrates fixes at between sixty and seventy years. The four millions he left to his daughter, if they do not prove that he could make gold, certainly prove that he could save it. The worthy old woman told me he had given her a manuscript in which the whole process was explained, but that she found it very obscure.

"You should publish it," said I.

"God forbid!"

"Burn it, then."

"I can't make up my mind to do so."

M. de Muralt took me to see the military evolutions gone through by the citizens of Berne, who are all soldiers, and I asked him the meaning of the bear to be seen above the gate of the town. The German for bear is 'bar', 'bern', and the animal has given its name to the town and canton which rank second in the Republic, although it is in the first place for its wealth and culture. It is a peninsula formed by the Aar, which rises near the Rhine. The mayor spoke to me of the power of the canton, its lordships and bailiwicks, and explained his own powers; he then described the public policy, and told me of the different systems of government which compose the Helvetic Union.

"I understand perfectly well," I said, "that each of the thirteen cantons has its own government."

"I daresay you do," he replied, "but what you don't understand any more than I do is, that there is a canton which has four separate governments."

I had an excellent supper with fourteen or fifteen senators. There were no jokes, no frivolous conversation, and no literature; but law, the commonweal, commerce, political economy, speculation, love of country, and the duty of preferring liberty to life, in abundance.

I felt as if I were in a new element, but I enjoyed the privilege of being a man amidst men who were all in honour to our common humanity. But as the supper went on, these rigid republicans began to expand, the discourse became less measured, there were even some bursts of laughter, owing to the wine. I excited their pity, and though they praised sobriety they thought mine excessive. However, they respected my liberty, and did not oblige me to drink, as the Russians, Swedes, Poles, and most northern peoples do.

We parted at midnight—a very late hour in Switzerland, and as they wished me a good night, each of them made me a sincere offer of his friendship. One of the company at an early period of the supper, before he had begun to get mellow, had condemned the Venetian Republic for banishing the Grisons, but on his intellect being enlightened by Bacchus he made his apologies.

"Every government," said he, "ought to know its own interests better than strangers, and everybody should be allowed to do what he wills with his own."

When I got home I found my housekeeper lying in my bed. I gave her a hundred caresses in witness of my joy, and I assured her practically of my love and gratitude. I considered her as my wife, we cherished each other, and did not allow the thought of separating to enter our minds. When two lovers love each other in all freedom, the idea of parting seems impossible.

Next morning I got a letter from the worthy Madame d'Urfe, who begged me to call on Madame de la Saone, wife of a friend of hers—a lieutenant-general. This lady had come to Berne in the hope of getting cured of a disease which had disfigured her in an incredible manner. Madame de la Saone was immediately introduced to all the best society in the place. She gave a supper every day, only asking men; she had an excellent cook. She had given notice that she would pay no calls, and she was quite right. I hastened to make my bow to her; but, good Heavens! what a terrible and melancholy sight did I behold!

I saw a woman dressed with the utmost elegance, reclining voluptuously upon a couch. As soon as she saw me she arose, gave me a most gracious reception, and going back to her couch invited me to sit beside her. She doubtless noticed my surprise, but being probably accustomed to the impression which the first sight of her created, she talked on in the most friendly manner, and by so doing diminished my aversion.

Her appearance was as follows: Madame de Saone was beautifully dressed, and had the whitest hands and the roundest arms that can be imagined. Her dress, which was cut very low, allowed me to see an exquisite breast of dazzling whiteness, heightened by two rosy buds; her figure was good, and her feet the smallest I have ever seen. All about her inspired love, but when one's eyes turned to her face every other feeling gave way to those of horror and pity. She was fearful. Instead of a face, one saw a blackened and disgusting scab. No feature was distinguishable, and her ugliness was made more conspicuous and dreadful by two fine eyes full of fire, and by a lipless mouth which she kept parted, as if to disclose two rows of teeth of dazzling whiteness. She could not laugh, for the pain caused by the contraction of the muscles would doubtless have drawn tears to her eyes; nevertheless she appeared contented, her conversation was delightful, full of wit and humour, and permeated with the tone of good society. She might be thirty at the most, and she had left three beautiful young children behind in Paris. Her husband was a fine, well-made man, who loved her tenderly, and had never slept apart from her. It is probable that few soldiers have shewn such courage as this, but it is to be supposed that he did not carry his bravery so far as to kiss her, as the very thought made one shudder. A disorder contracted after her first child-bed had left the poor woman in this sad state, and she had borne it for ten years. All the best doctors in France had tried in vain to cure her, and she had come to Berne to put herself into the hands of two well-known physicians who had promised to do so. Every quack makes promises of this sort; their patients are cured or not cured as it happens, and provided that they pay heavily the doctor is ready enough to lay the fault, not on his ignorance, but at the door of his poor deluded patient.

The doctor came while I was with her, and just as her intelligent conversation was making me forget her face. She had already began to take his remedies, which were partly composed of mercury.

"It seems to me," said she, "that the itching has increased since I have taken your medicines."

"It will last," said the son of Æsculapius, "till the end of the cure, and that will take about three months."

"As long as I scratch myself," said she, "I shall be in the same state, and the cure will never be completed."

The doctor replied in an evasive manner. I rose to take my leave, and holding my hand she asked me to supper once for all. I went the same evening; the poor woman took everything and drank some wine, as the doctor had not put her on any diet. I saw that she would never be cured.

Her good temper and her charming conversational powers kept all the company amused. I conceived that it would be possible to get used to her face, and to live with her without being disgusted. In the evening I talked about her to my housekeeper, who said that the beauty of her body and her mental endowments might be sufficient to attract people to her. I agreed, though I felt that I could never become one of her lovers.

Three or four days after, I went to a bookseller's to read the newspaper, and was politely accosted by a fine young man of twenty, who said that Madame de la Saone was sorry not to have seen me again at supper.

"You know the lady?"

"I had the honour to sup at her house with you."

"True; I remember you."

"I get her the books she likes, as I am a bookseller, and not only do I sup with her every evening, but we breakfast together every morning before she gets up."

"I congratulate you. I bet you are in love with her."

"You are pleased to jest, but she is pleasanter than you think."

"I do not jest at all, but I would wager she would not have the courage to push things to an extremity."

"Perhaps you would lose."

"Really? I should be very glad to."

"Let us make a bet."

"How will you convince me I have lost?"

"Let us bet a louis, and you must promise to be discreet."

"Very good."

"Come and sup at her house this evening, and I will tell you something."

"You shall see me there."

When I got home I told my housekeeper what I had heard.

"I am curious to know," said she, "how he will convince you." I promised to tell her, which pleased her very much.

I was exact to my appointment. Madame de la Saone reproached me pleasantly for my absence, and gave me a delicious supper. The young bookseller was there, but as his sweetheart did not speak a word to him he said nothing and passed unnoticed.

After supper we went out together, and he told me on the way that if I liked he would satisfy me the next morning at eight o'clock. "Call here, and the lady's maid will tell you her mistress is not visible, but you have only to say that you will wait, and that you will go into the ante-chamber. This room has a glass door commanding a view of madame's bed, and I will take care to draw back the curtains over the door so that you will be able to see at your ease all that passes between us. When the affair is over I shall go out by another door, she will call her maid, and you will be shewn in. At noon, if you will allow me, I will bring you some books to the 'Falcon,' and if you find that you have lost you shall pay me my louis." I promised to carry out his directions, and we parted.

I was curious to see what would happen, though I by no means regarded it as an impossibility; and on my presenting myself at eight o'clock, the maid let me in as soon as I said that I could wait. I found a corner of the glass door before which there was no curtain, and on applying my eye to the place I saw my young adventurer holding his conquest in his arms on the bed. An enormous nightcap entirely concealed her face—an excellent precaution which favoured the bookseller's enterprise.

When the rascal saw that I had taken up my position, he did not keep me waiting, for, getting up, he presented to my dazzled gaze, not only the secret treasures of his sweetheart, but his own also. He was a small man, but where the lady was most concerned he was a Hercules, and the rogue seemed to make a parade of his proportions as if to excite my jealousy. He turned his victim round so that I should see her under all aspects, and treated her manfully, while she appeared to respond to his ardour with all her might. Phidias could not have modelled his Venus on a finer body; her form was rounded and voluptuous, and as white as Parian marble. I was affected in a lively manner by the spectacle, and re-entered my lodging so inflamed that if my dear Dubois had not been at hand to quench my fire I should have been obliged to have extinguished it in the baths of La Mata.

When I had told her my tale she wanted to know the hero of it, and at noon she had that pleasure. The young bookseller brought me some books I had ordered, and while paying him for them I gave him our bet and a Louis over and above as a mark of my satisfaction at his prowess. He took it with a smile which seemed to shew that he thought I ought to think myself lucky to have lost. My housekeeper looked at him for some time, and asked if he knew her; he said he did not.

"I saw you when you were a child," said she. "You are the son of M. Mignard, minister of the Gospel. You must have been ten when I saw you."

"Possibly, madam."

"You did not care to follow your father's profession, then?"

"No madam, I feel much more inclined to the worship of the creature than to that of the Creator, and I did not think my father's profession would suit me."

"You are right, for a minister of the Gospel ought to be discreet, and discretion is a restraint."

This stroke made him blush, but we did not give him time to lose courage. I asked him to dine with me, and without mentioning the name of Madame de la Saone he told his amorous adventures and numerous anecdotes about the pretty women of Berne.

After he had gone, my housekeeper said that once was quite enough to see a young man of his complexion. I agreed with her, and had no more to do with him; but I heard that Madame de Saone took him to Paris and made his fortune. Many fortunes are made in this manner, and there are some which originated still more nobly. I only returned to Madame de la Saone to take my leave, as I shall shortly relate.

I was happy with my charmer, who told me again and again that with me she lived in bliss. No fears or doubts as to the future troubled her mind; she was certain, as I was, that we should never leave each other; and she told me she would pardon all the infidelities I might be guilty of, provided I made full confession. Hers, indeed, was a disposition with which to live in peace and content, but I was not born to enjoy such happiness.

After we had been a fortnight at Berne, my housekeeper received a letter from Soleure. It came from Lebel. As I saw she read it with great attention, I asked her what it was about.

"Take it and read it," said she; and she sat down in front of me to read my soul by the play of my features.

Lebel asked her, in concise terms, if she would become his wife.

"I have only put off the proposition," said he, "to set my affairs in order, and to see if I could afford to marry you, even if the consent of the ambassador were denied us. I find I am rich enough to live well in Berne or elsewhere without the necessity of my working; however I shall not have to face the alternative, for at the first hint of the matter M. de Chavigni gave his consent with the best grace imaginable."

He went on begging her not to keep him long waiting for a reply, and to tell him in the first place if she consented; in the second, whether she would like to live at Berne and be mistress in her own house, or whether she would prefer to return to Soleure and live with the ambassador, which latter plan might bring them some profit. He ended by declaring that whatever she had would be for her sole use, and that he would give her a dower of a hundred thousand francs. He did not say a word about me.

"Dearest," said I, "you are at perfect liberty to choose your own course, but I cannot contemplate your leaving me without considering myself as the most unhappy of men."

"And if I lose you I should be the most unhappy of women; for if you love me I care not whether we are married or no."

"Very good; but what answer are you going to make."

"You shall see my letter to-morrow. I shall tell him politely but plainly that I love you, that I am yours, that I am happy, and that it is thus impossible for me to accept his flattering propositions. I shall also say that I appreciate his generosity, and that if I were wise I should accept him, but that being the slave of my love for you I can only follow my inclination."

"I think you give an excellent turn to your letter. In refusing such an offer you could not have better reasons than those you give, and it would be absurd to try and persuade him that we are not lovers, as the thing is self-evident. Nevertheless, my darling, the letter saddens me."

"Why, dearest?"

"Because I have not a hundred thousand francs to offer you."

"I despise them; and if you were to offer me such a sum, I should only accept it to lay it at your feet. You are certainly not destined to become miserable, but if that should come to pass, be sure that I should be only too happy to share your misery."

We fell into one another's arms, and love made us taste all its pleasures. Nevertheless, in the midst of bliss, some tinge of sadness gained upon our souls. Languishing love seems to redouble its strength, but it is only in appearance; sadness exhausts love more than enjoyment. Love is a madcap who must be fed on laughter and mirth, otherwise he dies of inanition.

Next day my sweetheart wrote to Lebel in the sense she had decided on, and I felt obliged to write M. de Chavigni a letter in which love, sentiment, and philosophy were mingled. I did not conceal from him that I loved the woman whom Lebel coveted to distraction, but I said that as a man of honour I would rather die than deprive my sweetheart of such solid advantages.

My letter delighted the housekeeper, for she was anxious to know what the ambassador thought of the affair, which needed much reflection.

I got on the same day the letters of introduction I had asked Madame d'Urfe to give me, and I determined, to the joy of my dear Dubois, to set out for Lausanne. But we must hark back a little.

When one is sincerely in love, one thinks the beloved object full of deserts, and the mind, the dupe of the feelings, thinks all the world jealous of its bliss.

A. M. de F——, member of the Council of the Two Hundred, whom I had met at Madame de la Saone's, had become my friend. He came to see me and I introduced him to my dear Dubois, whom he treated with the same distinction he would have used towards my wife. He had presented us to his wife, and had come several times to see us with her and her daughter Sara. Sara was only thirteen, but she was extremely precocious, dark complexioned, and full of wit; she was continually uttering naivetes, of which she understood the whole force, although looking at her face one would have thought her perfectly innocent. She excelled in the art of making her father and mother believe in her innocence, and thus she enjoyed plenty of liberty.

Sara had declared that she was in love with my housekeeper, and as her parents laughed at her she lavished her caresses on my dear Dubois. She often came to breakfast with us, and when she found us in bed she would embrace my sweetheart, whom she called her wife, passing her hand over the coverlet to tickle her, telling her that she was her wife, and that she wanted to have a child. My sweetheart laughed and let her go on.

One day I told her jokingly that she would make me jealous, that I thought she really was a man, and that I was going to make sure. The sly little puss told me that I was making a mistake, but her hand seemed rather to guide mine than to oppose it. That made me curious, and my mind was soon set at rest as to her sex. Perceiving that she had taken me in and got exactly what she wanted, I drew back my hand, and imparted my suspicions to my housekeeper, who said I was right. However, as the little girl had no part in my affections, I did not push the thing any farther.

Two or three days after, this girl came in as I was getting up, and said in her usual simple way,

"Now that you know I am not really a man you can not be jealous or have objection to my taking your place beside my little wife, if she will let me."

My housekeeper, who looked inclined to laugh, said,

"Come along."

In the twinkling of an eye she was undressed and in the arms of her little wife, whom she proceeded to treat as an amorous husband. My sweetheart laughed, and Sara, having contrived in the combat to rid herself of her chemise and the coverlet, displayed herself to me without any veil, while at the same time she shewed me all the beauties of my sweetheart. This sight inflamed me. I shut the door, and made the little hussy witness of my ardour with my sweetheart. Sara looked on attentively, playing the part of astonishment to perfection, and when I had finished she said, with the utmost simplicity,

"Do it again:"

"I can't, my dear; don't you see I am a dead man?"

"That's very funny," she cried; and with the most perfect innocence she came over, and tried to effect my resurrection.

When she had succeeded in placing me in the wished-for condition, she said, "Now go in;" and I should doubtless have obeyed, but my housekeeper said, "No, dearest, since you have effected its resurrection, you must make it die again."

"I should like to," said she, "but I am afraid I have not got enough room;" and so saying she placed herself in a position to shew me that she was speaking the truth, and that if she did not make me die it was not her fault.

Imitating her simplicity I approached her, as if I wished to oblige her, but not to go too far; but not finding any resistance I accomplished the act in all its forms, without her giving the slightest evidence of pain, without any of the accidents of a first trial, but, on the contrary, with all the marks of the utmost enjoyment.

Although I was sure of the contrary, I kept my self-possession enough to tell my housekeeper that Sara had given me what can only be given once, and she pretended to believe me.

When the operation was finished, we had another amusing scene. Sara begged us not to say a word about it to her papa or mamma, as they would be sure to scold her as they had scolded her when she got her ears pierced without asking their leave.

Sara knew that we saw through her feigned simplicity, but she pretended not to do so as it was to her own advantage. Who could have instructed her in the arts of deceit? Nobody; only her natural wit, less rare in childhood than in youth, but always rare and astonishing. Her mother said her simplicities shewed that she would one day be very intelligent, and her father maintained that they were signs of her stupidity. But if Sara had been stupid, our bursts of laughter would have disconcerted her; and she would have died for shame, instead of appearing all the better pleased when her father deplored her stupidity. She would affect astonishment, and by way of curing one sort of stupidity she corroborated it by displaying another. She asked us questions to which we could not reply, and laughed at her instead, although it was evident that before putting such questions she must have reasoned over them. She might have rejoined that the stupidity was on our side, but by so doing she would have betrayed herself.

Lebel did not reply to his sweetheart, but M. de Chavigni wrote me a letter of four pages. He spoke like a philosopher and an experienced man of the world.

He shewed me that if I were an old man like him, and able to insure a happy and independent existence to my sweetheart after my death, I should do well to keep her from all men, especially as there was so perfect a sympathy between us; but that as I was a young man, and did not intend to bind myself to her by the ties of marriage, I should not only consent to a union which seemed for her happiness, but that as a man of honour it was my duty to use my influence with her in favour of the match. "With your experience," said the kind old gentleman, "you ought to know that a time would come when you would regret both having lost this opportunity, for your love is sure to become friendship, and then another love will replace that which you now think as firm as the god Terminus.

"Lebel," he added, "has told me his plans, and far from disapproving, I have encouraged him, for your charming friend won my entire esteem in the five or six times I had the pleasure of seeing her with you. I shall be delighted, therefore, to have her in my house, where I can enjoy her conversation without transgressing the laws of propriety. Nevertheless, you will understand that at my age I have formed no desires, for I could not satisfy them even if their object were propitious." He ended by telling me that Lebel had not fallen in love in a young man's style, that he had reflected on what he was doing, and that he would consequently not hurry her, as she would see in the letter he was going to send her. A marriage ought always to be undertaken in cold blood.

I gave the letter to my housekeeper, who read it attentively, and gave it back to me quite coolly.

"What do you think of his advice, dearest?"

"I think I had better follow it: he says there is no hurry, and delay is all we want. Let us love each other and think only of that. This letter is written with great wisdom, but I cannot imagine our becoming indifferent to each other, though I know such a thing is possible."

"Never indifferent; you make a mistake there."

"Well, friends, then; and that is not much better after being lovers."

"But friendship, dearest, is never indifferent. Love, it is true, may be in its composition. We know it, as it has been thus from the beginning of the world."

"Then the ambassador was right. Repentance might come and torment us when love had been replaced by calmer friendship."

"If you think so, let us marry each other to-morrow, and punish thereby the vices of our human nature."

"Yes, we will marry, but there is no hurry; fearing lest hymen should quicken the departure of love, let us enjoy our happiness while we can."

"You speak admirably, my angel, and deserve the greatest good fortune."

"I wish for no greater than what you procure me."

We went to bed, continuing our discussions, and when we were in each other's arms we made an arrangement which suited us very well.

"Lausanne," said she, "is a little town where you would meet with the warmest hospitality, and during your fortnight's stay you will have nothing to do but to make visits and to go to suppers. I am known to all the nobility, and the Duke of Rosebury, who wearied me with his love-making, is still there. My appearance with you will make everybody talk, and it will be as annoying for you as for me. My mother lives there, too. She would say nothing, but in her heart she would be ill-pleased to see me as the housekeeper of a man like you, for common sense would inform everyone that I was your mistress."

I thought she was right, and that it would be well to respect the rules of society. We decided that she should go to Lausanne by herself and stay with her mother, that in two or three days I should follow her, and should live by myself, as long as I liked, having full liberty to see her at her mother's.

"When you leave Lausanne," said she, "I will rejoin you at Geneva, and then we will travel together where you please and as long as our love lasts."

In two days she started early in the morning, sure of my constancy, and congratulating herself on her discretion. I was sad at her leaving me, but my calls to take leave served to rouse me from my grief. I wished to make M. Haller's acquaintance before I left Switzerland, and the mayor, M. de Muralt, gave me a letter of introduction to him very handsomely expressed. M. de Haller was the bailiff of Roche.

When I called to take leave of Madame de la Saone I found her in bed, and I was obliged to remain by her bedside for a quarter of an hour. She spoke of her disease, and gave the conversation such a turn that she was able with perfect propriety to let me see that the ravages of the disease had not impaired the beauty of her body. The sight convinced me that Mignard had need of less courage than I thought, and I was within an inch of doing her the same service. It was easy enough to look only at her body, and it would have been difficult to behold anything more beautiful.

I know well that prudes and hypocrites, if they ever read these Memoirs, will be scandalized at the poor lady, but in shewing her person so readily she avenged herself on the malady which had disfigured her. Perhaps, too, her goodness of heart and politeness told her what a trial it was to look at her face, and she wished to indemnify the man who disguised his feelings of repugnance by shewing him what gifts nature had given her. I am sure, ladies, that the most prudish—nay, the most virtuous, amongst you, if you were unfortunate enough to be so monstrously deformed in the face, would introduce some fashion which would conceal your ugliness, and display those beauties which custom hides from view. And doubtless Madame de la Saone would have been more chary of her person if she had been able to enchant with her face like you.

The day I left I dined with M——— I———, and was severely taken to task by pretty Sara for having sent her little wife away before me. The reader will see how I met her again at London three years later. Le Duc was still in the doctor's hands, and very weak; but I made him go with me, as I had a good deal of property, and I could not trust it to anybody else.

I left Berne feeling naturally very sad. I had been happy there, and to this day the thought of it is a pleasant one.

I had to consult Dr. Herrenschwand about Madame d'Urfe, so I stopped at Morat, where he lived, and which is only four leagues from Berne. The doctor made me dine with him that I might try the fish of the lake, which I found delicious. I had intended to go on directly after dinner, but I was delayed by a curiosity of which I shall inform the reader.

After I had given the doctor a fee of two Louis for his advice, in writing, on a case of tapeworm, he made me walk with him by the Avanches road, and we went as far as the famous mortuary of Morat.

"This mortuary," said the doctor, "was constructed with part of the bones of the Burgundians, who perished here at the well-known battle lost by Charles the Bold."

The Latin inscription made me laugh.

"This inscription," said I, "contains an insulting jest; it is almost burlesque, for the gravity of an inscription should not allow of laughter."

The doctor, like a patriotic Swiss, would not allow it, but I think it was false shame on his part. The inscription ran as follows, and the impartial reader can judge of its nature:

"Deo. opt. Max. Caroli inclyti et fortisimi Burgundie duds
exercitus Muratum obsidens, ab Helvetiis cesus, hoc sui
monumentum reliquit anno MCDLXXVI."

Till then I had had a great idea of Morat. Its fame of seven centuries, three sieges sustained and repulsed, all had given me a sublime notion of it; I expected to see something and saw nothing.

"Then Morat has been razed to the ground?" said I to the doctor.

"Not at all, it is as it always has been, or nearly so."

I concluded that a man who wants to be well informed should read first and then correct his knowledge by travel. To know ill is worse than not to know at all, and Montaigne says that we ought to know things well.

But it was the following comic adventure which made me spend the night at Morat:

I found at the inn a young maid who spoke a sort of rustic Italian. She struck me by her great likeness to my fair stocking-seller at Paris. She was called Raton, a name which my memory has happily preserved. I offered her six francs for her favours, but she refused the money with a sort of pride, telling me that I had made a mistake and that she was an honest girl.

"It may be so," said I, and I ordered my horses to be put in. When the honest Raton saw me on the point of leaving, she said, with an air that was at once gay and timid, that she wanted two louis, and if I liked to give her them and pass the night with her I should be well content.

"I will stay, but remember to be kind."

"I will."

When everybody had gone to bed, she came into my room with a little frightened manner, calculated to redouble my ardour, but by great good luck, feeling I had a necessity, I took the light and ran to the place where I could satisfy it. While there I amused myself by reading innumerable follies one finds written in such places, and suddenly my eyes lighted on these words:—

"This tenth day of August, 1760, the wretched Raton gave me the what-d'-you-call-it: reader, beware."

I was almost tempted to believe in miracles, for I could not think there were two Ratons in the same house. I returned gaily to my room and found my sweetheart in bed without her chemise. I went to the place beside the bed where she had thrown it down, and as soon as she saw me touching it she begged me in a fright not to do so, as it was not clean. She was right, for it bore numerous marks of the disease which infected her. It may be imagined that my passion cooled, and that I sent her away in a moment; but I felt at the same time the greatest gratitude to what is called chance, for I should have never thought of examining a girl whose face was all lilies and roses, and who could not be more than eighteen.

Next day I went to Roche to see the celebrated Haller.

CHAPTER XVIII

M. Haller—My Stay at Lausanne—Lord Rosebury—The Young Saconai—
Dissertation on Beauty—The Young Theologian

M. Haller was a man six feet high and broad in a proportion; he was a well-
made man, and a physical as well as a mental colossus. He received me
courteously, and when he had read M. de Muralt's letter, he displayed the
greatest politeness, which shews that a good letter of introduction is never out
of place. This learned man displayed to me all the treasures of his knowledge,
replying with exactitude to all my questions, and above all with a rare modesty
which astonished me greatly, for whilst he explained the most difficult questions,
he had the air of a scholar who would fain know; but on the other hand, when
he asked me a scientific question, it was with so delicate an art that I could not
help giving the right answer.

M. de Haller was a great physiologist, a great doctor, and a great anatomist.
He called Morgagni his master, though he had himself made numerous
discoveries relating to the frame of man. While I stayed with him he shewed me
a number of letters from Morgagni and Pontedera, a professor of botany, a
science of which Haller had an extensive knowledge. Hearing me speak of these
learned men whose works I had read at an early age, he complained that
Pontedera's letters were almost illegible and written in extremely obscure Latin.
He shewed me a letter from a Berlin Academician, whose name I have
forgotten, who said that since the king had read his letter he had no more
thoughts of suppressing the Latin language. Haller had written to Frederick the
Great that a monarch who succeeded in the unhappy enterprise of proscribing
the language of Cicero and Virgil from the republic of letters would raise a
deathless monument to his own ignorance. If men of letters require a universal
language to communicate with one another, Latin is certainly the best, for Greek
and Arabic do not adapt themselves in the same way to the genius of modern
civilization.

Haller was a good poet of the Pindaric kind; he was also an excellent
statesman, and had rendered great services to his country. His morals were
irreproachable, and I remember his telling me that the only way to give precepts
was to do so by example. As a good citizen he was an admirable paterfamilias,
for what greater proof could he give of his love of country than by presenting it
with worthy subjects in his children, and such subjects result from a good
education. His wife was still young, and bore on her features the marks of good
nature and discretion. He had a charming daughter of about eighteen; her
appearance was modest, and at table she only opened her mouth to speak in a
low tone to a young man who sat beside her. After dinner, finding myself alone
with M. Haller, I asked him who this young man was. He told me he was his
daughter's tutor.

"A tutor like that and so pretty a pupil might easily become lovers."

"Yes, please God."

This Socratic reply made me see how misplaced my remark had been, and I felt some confusion. Finding a book to my hand I opened it to restore my composure.

It was an octavo volume of his works, and I read in it:

"Utrum memoria post mortem dubito."

"You do not think, then," said I, "that the memory is an essential part of the soul?"

"How is that question to be answered?" M. de Haller replied, cautiously, as he had his reasons for being considered orthodox.

During dinner I asked if M. de Voltaire came often to see him. By way of reply he repeated these lines of the poet:—

"Vetabo qui Cereris sacrum vulgarit arcanum sub usdem sit trabibus."

I spent three days with this celebrated man, but I thought myself obliged to refrain from asking his opinion on any religious questions, although I had a great desire to do so, as it would have pleased me to have had his opinion on that delicate subject; but I believe that in matters of that kind M. Haller judged only by his heart. I told him, however, that I should consider a visit to Voltaire as a great event, and he said I was right. He added, without the slightest bitterness,

"M. de Voltaire is a man who ought to be known, although, in spite of the laws of nature, many persons have found him greater at a distance than close at hand."

M. de Haller kept a good and abundant though plain table; he only drank water. At dessert only he allowed himself a small glass of liqueur drowned in an enormous glass of water. He talked a great deal of Boerhaave, whose favourite pupil he had been. He said that after Hypocrates, Boerhaave was the greatest doctor and the greatest chemist that had ever existed.

"How is it," said I, "that he did not attain mature age?"

"Because there is no cure for death. Boerhaave was born a doctor, as Homer was born a poet; otherwise he would have succumbed at the age of fourteen to a malignant ulcer which had resisted all the best treatment of the day. He cured it himself by rubbing it constantly with salt dissolved in his own urine."

"I have been told that he possessed the philosopher's stone."

"Yes, but I don't believe it."

"Do you think it possible?"

"I have been working for the last thirty years to convince myself of its impossibility; I have not yet done so, but I am sure that no one who does not believe in the possibility of the great work can be a good chemist."

When I left him he begged me to write and tell him what I thought of the great Voltaire, and in, this way our French correspondence began. I possess twenty-two letters from this justly celebrated man; and the last word written six months before, his too, early death. The longer I live the more interest I take in my papers. They are the treasure which attaches me to life and makes death more hateful still.

I had been reading at Berne Rousseau's "Heloise," and I asked M. Haller's opinion of it. He told me that he had once read part of it to oblige a friend, and from this part he could judge of the whole. "It is the worst of all romances, because it is the most eloquently expressed. You will see the country of Vaud, but don't expect to see the originals of the brilliant portraits which Jean Jacques painted. He seems to have thought that lying was allowable in a romance, but he has abused the privilege. Petrarch, was a learned man, and told no lies in speaking of his love for Laura, whom he loved as every man loves the woman with whom he is taken; and if Laura had not contented her illustrious lover, he would not have celebrated her."

Thus Haller spoke to me of Petrarch, mentioning Rousseau with aversion. He disliked his very eloquence, as he said it owed all its merits to antithesis and paradox. Haller was a learned man of the first class, but his knowledge was not employed for the purpose of ostentation, nor in private life, nor when he was in the company of people who did not care for science. No one knew better than he how to accommodate himself to his company he was friendly with everyone, and never gave offence. But what were his qualifications? It would be much easier to say what he had not than what he had. He had no pride, self-sufficiency, nor tone of superiority—in fact, none of those defects which are often the reproach of the learned and the witty.

He was a man of austere virtue, but he took care to hide the austerity under a veil of a real and universal kindness. Undoubtedly he thought little of the ignorant, who talk about everything right or wrong, instead of remaining silent, and have at bottom only contempt for the learned; but he only shewed his contempt by saying nothing. He knew that a despised ignoramus becomes an enemy, and Haller wished to be loved. He neither boasted of nor concealed his knowledge, but let it run like a limpid stream flowing through the meadows. He talked well, but never absorbed the conversation. He never spoke of his works; when someone mentioned them he would turn the conversation as soon as he conveniently could. He was sorry to be obliged to contradict anyone who conversed with him.

When I reached Lausanne I found myself enabled to retain my incognito for a day at any rate. I naturally gave the first place to my affections. I went straight to my sweetheart without needing to ask my way, so well had she indicated the streets through which I had to pass. I found her with her mother, but I was not a little astonished to see Lebel there also. However, my surprise must have passed unnoticed, for my housekeeper, rising from her seat with a cry of joy, threw her arms about my neck, and after having kissed me affectionately presented me to her worthy mother, who welcomed me in the friendliest manner. I asked Lebel after the ambassador, and how long he had been at Lausanne.

He replied, with a polite and respectful air, that his master was quite well, and that he had come to Lausanne on business, and had only been there a few hours; and that, wishing to pay his regards to Madame Dubois's mother, he had been pleasantly surprised to see the daughter there as well.

"You know," he added, "what my intentions are. I have to go back to-morrow, and when you have made up your minds, write to me and I will come and take her to Soleure, where I will marry her."

He could not have spoken more plainly or honourably. I said that I would never oppose the will of my sweetheart, and my Dubois, interrupting me, said in her turn that she would never leave me until I sent her away.

Lebel found these replies too vague, and told me with noble freedom that we must give him a definite reply, since in such cases uncertainty spoils all. At that moment I felt as if I could never agree to his wishes, and I told him that in ten days I would let him know of our resolution, whatever it was. At that he was satisfied, and left us.

After his departure my sweetheart's mother, whose good sense stood her instead of wit, talked to us in a manner that answered our inclinations, for, amorous as we were, we could not bear the idea of parting. I agreed that my housekeeper should wait up for me till midnight, and that we could talk over our reply with our heads on the pillow.

My Dubois had a separate room with a good bed and excellent furniture. She gave me a very good supper, and we spent a delicious night. In the morning we felt more in love than ever, and were not at all disposed to comply with Lebel's wishes. Nevertheless, we had a serious conversation.

The reader will remember that my mistress had promised to pardon my infidelities, provided that I confessed them. I had none to confess, but in the course of conversation I told her about Raton.

"We ought to think ourselves very fortunate," said she, "for if it had not been for chance, we should have been in a fine state now."

"Yes, and I should be in despair."

"I don't doubt it, and you would be all the more wretched as I should never complain to you."

"I only see one way of providing against such a misfortune. When I have been unfaithful to you I will punish myself by depriving myself of the pleasure of giving you proofs of my affection till I am certain that I can do so without danger."

"Ah! you would punish me for your faults, would you? If you love me as I love you, believe me you would find a better remedy than that."

"What is that?"

"You would never be unfaithful to me."

"You are right. I am sorry I was not the first to think of this plan, which I promise to follow for the future."

"Don't make any promises," said she, with a sigh, "it might prove too difficult to keep them."

It is only love which can inspire such conversations, but unfortunately it gains nothing by them.

Next morning, just as I was going out to take my letters, the Baron de Bercei, uncle of my friend Bavois, entered.

"I know," said he, "that my nephew owes his fortune to you; he is just going to be made general, and I and all the family will be enchanted to make your acquaintance. I have come to offer my services, and to beg that you will dine with me to-day, and on any other day you please when you have nothing better to do, and I hope you will always consider yourself of the family.

"At the same time I beg of you not to tell anybody that my nephew has become a Catholic, as according to the prejudices of the country it would be a dishonour which would reflect on the whole family."

I accepted his invitation, and promised to say nothing about the circumstance he had mentioned.

I left my letters of introduction, and I received everywhere a welcome of the most distinguished kind. Madame de Gentil-Langalerie appeared the most amiable of all the ladies I called on, but I had not time to pay my court to one more than another. Every day politeness called me to some dinner, supper, ball, or assembly. I was bored beyond measure, and I felt inclined to say how troublesome it is to have such a welcome. I spent a fortnight in the little town, where everyone prides himself on his liberty, and in all my life I have never experienced such a slavery, for I had not a moment to myself. I was only able to pass one night with my sweetheart, and I longed to set off with her for Geneva. Everybody would give me letters of introduction for M. de Voltaire, and by their eagerness one would have thought the great man beloved, whereas all detested him on account of his sarcastic humour.

"What, ladies!" said I, "is not M. de Voltaire good-natured, polite, and affable to you who have been kind enough to act in his plays with him?"

"Not in the least. When he hears us rehearse he grumbles all the time. We never say a thing to please him: here it is a bad pronunciation, there a tone not sufficiently passionate, sometimes one speaks too softly, sometimes too loudly; and it's worse when we are acting. What a hubbub there is if one add a syllable, or if some carelessness spoil one of his verses. He frightens us. So and so laughed badly; so and so in Alzire had only pretended to weep."

"Does he want you to weep really?"

"Certainly. He will have real tears. He says that if an actor wants to draw tears he must shed them himself."

"I think he is right there; but he should not be so severe with amateurs, above all with charming actresses like you. Such perfection is only to be looked for from professionals, but all authors are the same. They never think that the actor has pronounced the words with the force which the sense, as they see it, requires."

"I told him, one day, that it was not my fault if his lines had not the proper force."

"I am sure he laughed."

"Laughed? No, sneered, for he is a rude and impertinent man."

"But I suppose you overlook all these failings?"

"Not at all; we have sent him about his business."

"Sent him about his business?"

"Yes. He left the house he had rented here, at short notice, and retired to where you will find him now. He never comes to see us now, even if we ask him."

"Oh, you do ask him, though you sent him about his business?"

"We cannot deprive ourselves of the pleasure of admiring his talents, and if we have teased him, that was only from revenge, and to teach him something of the manners of good society."

"You have given a lesson to a great master."

"Yes; but when you see him mention Lausanne, and see what he will say of us. But he will say it laughingly, that's his way."

During my stay I often saw Lord Rosebury, who had vainly courted my charming Dubois. I have never known a young man more disposed to silence. I have been told that he had wit, that he was well educated, and even in high spirits at times, but he could not get over his shyness, which gave him an almost indefinable air of stupidity. At balls, assemblies—in fact, everywhere, his manners consisted of innumerable bows. When one spoke to him, he replied in good French but with the fewest possible words, and his shy manner shewed that every question was a trouble to him. One day when I was dining with him, I asked him some question about his country, which required five or six small phrases by way of answer. He gave me an excellent reply, but blushed all the time like a young girl when she comes out. The celebrated Fox who was then twenty, and was at the same dinner, succeeded in making him laugh, but it was by saying something in English, which I did not understand in the least. Eight months after I saw him again at Turin, he was then amorous of a banker's wife, who was able to untie his tongue.

At Lausanne I saw a young girl of eleven or twelve by whose beauty I was exceedingly struck. She was the daughter of Madame de Saconai, whom I had known at Berne. I do not know her after history, but the impression she made on me has never been effaced. Nothing in nature has ever exercised such a powerful influence over me as a pretty face, even if it be a child's.

The Beautiful, as I have been told, is endowed with this power of attraction; and I would fain believe it, since that which attracts me is necessarily beautiful in my eyes, but is it so in reality? I doubt it, as that which has influenced me has not influenced others. The universal or perfect beauty does not exist, or it does not possess this power. All who have discussed the subject have hesitated to pronounce upon it, which they would not have done if they had kept to the idea of form. According to my ideas, beauty is only form, for that which is not beautiful is that which has no form, and the deformed is the opposite of the 'pulchrum' and 'formosum'.

We are right to seek for the definitions of things, but when we have them to hand in the words; why should we go farther? If the word 'forma' is Latin, we should seek for the Latin meaning and not the French, which, however, often uses 'deforme' or 'difforme' instead of 'laid', ugly, without people's noticing that its opposite should be a word which implies the existence of form; and this can only be beauty. We should note that 'informe' in French as well as in Latin means shapeless, a body without any definite appearance.

We will conclude, then, that it is the beauty of woman which has always exercised an irresistible sway over me, and more especially that beauty which resides in the face. It is there the power lies, and so true is that, that the sphinxes of Rome and Versailles almost make me fall in love with them though, the face excepted, they are deformed in every sense of the word. In looking at the fine proportions of their faces one forgets their deformed bodies. What, then, is beauty? We know not; and when we attempt to define it or to enumerate its qualities we become like Socrates, we hesitate. The only thing that our minds can seize is the effect produced by it, and that which charms, ravishes, and makes me in love, I call beauty. It is something that can be seen with the eyes, and for my eyes I speak. If they had a voice they would speak better than I, but probably in the same sense.

No painter has surpassed Raphael in the beauty of the figures which his divine pencil produced; but if this great painter had been asked what beauty was, he would probably have replied that he could not say, that he knew it by heart, and that he thought he had reproduced it whenever he had seen it, but that he did not know in what it consisted.

"That face pleases me," he would say, "it is therefore beautiful!"

He ought to have thanked God for having given him such an exquisite eye for the beautiful; but 'omne pulchrum difficile'.

The painters of high renown, all those whose works proclaim genius, have excelled in the delineation of the beautiful; but how small is their number compared to the vast craved who have strained every nerve to depict beauty and have only left us mediocrity!

If a painter could be dispensed from making his works beautiful, every man might be an artist; for nothing is easier than to fashion ugliness, and brush and canvas would be as easy to handle as mortar and trowel.

Although portrait-painting is the most important branch of the art, it is to be noted that those who have succeeded in this line are very few. There are three kinds of portraits: ugly likenesses, perfect likenesses, and those which to a perfect likeness add an almost imperceptible character of beauty. The first class is worthy only of contempt and their authors of stoning, for to want of taste and talent they add impertinence, and yet never seem to see their failings. The second class cannot be denied to possess real merit; but the palm belongs to the third, which, unfortunately, are seldom found, and whose authors deserve the large fortunes they amass. Such was the famous Notier, whom I knew in Paris in the year 1750. This great artist was then eighty, and in spite of his great age his talents seemed in all their freshness. He painted a plain woman; it was a speaking likeness, and in spite of that those who only saw the portrait pronounced her to be a handsome woman. Nevertheless, the most minute examination would not have revealed any faithlessness to the original, but some imperceptible touches gave a real but indefinite air of beauty to the whole. Whence does that magic art take its source? One day, when he had been painting the plain-looking

"Mesdames de France," who on the canvas looked like two Aspasias, I asked him the above question. He answered:—

"It is a magic which the god of taste distils from my brains through my brushes. It is the divinity of Beauty whom all the world adores, and which no one can define, since no one knows of what it consists. That canvas shews you what a delicate shade there is between beauty and ugliness; and nevertheless this shade seems an enormous difference to those unacquainted with art."

The Greek painters made Venus, the goddess of beauty, squint-eyed, and this odd idea has been praised by some; but these painters were certainly in the wrong.

Two squinting eyes might be beautiful, but certainly not so beautiful as if they did not squint, for whatever beauty they had could not proceed from their deformity.

After this long digression, with which the reader may not be very well pleased, it is time for me to return to my sweetheart. The tenth day of my visit to Lausanne, I went to sup and sleep with my mistress, and that night was the happiest I remember. In the morning, while we were taking coffee with her mother, I observed that we seemed in no hurry to part. At this, the mother, a woman of few words, took up the discourse in a polite and dignified manner, and told me it was my duty to undeceive Lebel before I left; and at the same time she gave me a letter she had had from him the evening before. The worthy man begged her to remind me that if I could not make up my mind to separate from her daughter before I left Lausanne, it would be much more difficult for me to do so when I was farther off; above all, if, as would probably be the case, she gave me a living pledge of her love. He said that he had no thoughts of drawing back from his word, but he should wish to be able to say that he had taken his wife from her mother's hands.

When I had read the letter aloud, the worthy mother wept, and left us alone. A moment's silence ensued, and with a sigh that shewed what it cost her, my dear Dubois had the courage to tell me that I must instantly write to Lebel to give up all pretensions to her, or to come and take her at once.

"If I write and tell him to think no more of you, I must marry you myself."

"No."

With this no she arose and left me. I thought it over for a quarter of an hour, I weighed the pros and cons and still my love shrank from the sacrifice. At last, on consideration that my housekeeper would never have such a chance again, that I was not sure that I could always make her happy, I resolved to be generous, and determined to write to Lebel that Madame Dubois had decided of her own free will to become his wife, that I had no right to oppose her resolution, and that I would go so far as to congratulate him on a happiness I envied him. I begged him to leave Soleure at once and come and receive her in my presence from the hands of her worthy mother.

I signed the letter and took it to my housekeeper, who was in her mother's room. "Take this letter, dearest, and read it, and if you approve its contents put your signature beside mine." She read it several times, while her good mother wept, and then, with an affectionate and sorrowful air, she took the pen and signed. I begged her mother to find somebody to take the letter to Soleure immediately, before my resolution was weakened by repentance.

The messenger came, and as soon as he had gone, "Farewell," said I, embracing her, with my eyes wet with tears, "farewell, we shall see each other again as soon as Lebel comes."

I went to my inn, a prey to the deepest grief. This sacrifice had given a new impetus to my love for this charming woman, and I felt a sort of spasm, which made me afraid I should get ill. I shut myself up in my room, and I ordered the servants to say I was unwell and could see no one.

In the evening of the fourth day after, Lebel was announced. He embraced me, saying his happiness would be due to me. He then left me, telling me he would expect me at the house of his future bride.

"Excuse me to-day, my dear fellow," said I, "but I will dine with you there to-morrow."

When he had left me, I told Le Duc to make all preparations for our leaving the next day after dinner.

I went out early on the following day to take leave of everybody, and at noon Lebel came to take me to that sad repast, at which, however, I was not so sad as I had feared.

As I was leaving I begged the future Madame Lebel to return me the ring I had given her, and as we had agreed, I presented her with a roll of a hundred Louis, which she took with a melancholy air.

"I should never have sold it," she said, "for I have no need of money."

"In that case I will give it back to you, but promise me never to part with it, and keep the hundred Louis as some small reward of the services you have rendered me."

She shook my hand affectionately, put on my finger her wedding ring, and left me to hide her grief. I wiped my tears away, and said to Lebel,

"You are about to possess yourself of a treasure which I cannot commend too highly. You are a man of honour; you will appreciate her excellent qualities, and you will know how to make her happy. She will love you only, take care of your household, and keep no secrets from you. She is full of wit and spirits, and will easily disperse the slightest shadow of ill humour which may fall on you."

I went in with him to the mother's room to take leave of her, and Madame Dubois begged me to delay my departure and sup once more with her. I told her that my horses were put in and the carriage waiting at my door, and that such a delay would set tongues talking; but that if she liked, she, her future husband and her mother, could come and see me at an inn two leagues off on the Geneva road, where we could stay as long as we liked. Lebel approved of the plan, and my proposition was accepted.

When I got back to my inn I found my carriage ready, and I got in and drove to the meeting-place, and ordered a good supper for four, and an hour later my guests arrived.

The gay and even happy air of the newly betrothed surprised me, but what astonished me more was the easy way with which she threw herself into my arms as soon as she saw me. It put me quite out of countenance, but she had more wit than I. However, I mustered up sufficient strength to follow her cue, but I could not help thinking that if she had really loved me she would not have found it possible to pass thus from love to mere friendship. However, I imitated her, and made no objections to those marks of affection allowed to friendship, which are supposed to have no tincture of love in them.

At supper I thought I saw that Lebel was more delighted at having such a wife than at the prospect of enjoying her and satisfying a strong passion. That calmed me; I could not be jealous of a man like that. I perceived, too, that my sweetheart's high spirits were more feigned than real; she wished to make me share them so as to render our separation less bitter, and to tranquillise her future husband as to the nature of our feelings for one another. And when reason and time had quieted the tempest in my heart, I could not help thinking it very natural that she should be pleased at the prospect of being independent, and of enjoying a fortune.

We made an excellent supper, which we washed down so well that at last the gaiety which had been simulated ended by being real. I looked at the charming Dubois with pleasure; I regarded her as a treasure which had belonged to me, and which after making me happy was with my full consent about to ensure the happiness of another. It seemed to me that I had been magnanimous enough to give her the reward she deserved, like a good Mussulman who gives a favourite slave his freedom in return for his fidelity. Her sallies made me laugh and recalled the happy moments I had passed with her, but the idea of her happiness prevented my regretting having yielded my rights to another.

As Lebel was obliged to return to Lausanne in order to get back to Soleure in two days, we had to part. I embraced him and asked him to continue his friendship towards me, and he promised with great effusion to be my friend till death. As we were going down the stair, my charming friend said, with great candour,

"I am not really gay, but I oblige myself to appear so. I shall not be happy till the scar on my heart has healed. Lebel can only claim my esteem, but I shall be his alone though my love be all for you. When we see each other again, as from what you say I hope we shall, we shall be able to meet as true friends, and perhaps we shall congratulate each other on the wise part we have taken. As for you, though I do not think you will forget me, I am sure that before long some more or less worthy object will replace me and banish your sorrow. I hope it will be so. Be happy. I may be with child; and if it prove to be so, you shall have no cause to complain of my care of your child, which you shall take away when you please. We made an agreement on this point yesterday. We arranged that the marriage should not be consummated for two months; thus we shall be certain whether the child belongs to you or no, and we will let people think that it is the legitimate offspring of our marriage. Lebel conceived this plan that he might have his mind at rest on the supposed force of blood, in which he declares he believes no more than I do. He has promised to love the child as if he were its father. If you write to me, I will keep you acquainted with everything; and if I have the happiness to give you a child, it will be much dearer to me than your ring."

We wept, and Lebel laughed to see us.

I could only reply by pressing her to my breast, and then I gave her over to her future husband, who told me as he got into the carriage that our long talk had pleased him very much.

I went to bed sadly enough. Next morning when I awoke, a pastor of the Church of Geneva came to ask me to give him a place in my carriage. I agreed, and was not sorry I had done so.

This priest was an eloquent man, although a theologian, who answered the most difficult religious questions I could put to him. There was no mystery with him, everything was reason. I have never found a more compliant Christianity than that of this worthy man, whose morals, as I heard afterwards at Geneva, were perfectly pure. But I found out that this kind of Christianity was not peculiar to him, all his fellow-Calvinists thought in the same way.

Wishing to convince him that he was a Calvinist in name only, since he did not believe that Jesus Christ was of the same substance as the Father, he replied that Calvin was only infallible where he spoke 'ex cathedra', but I struck him dumb by quoting the words of the Gospel. He blushed when I reproached him with Calvin's belief that the Pope was the Antichrist of the Apocalypse.

"It will be impossible to destroy this prejudice at Geneva," said he, "till the Government orders the effacement of an inscription on the church door which everybody reads, and which speaks of the head of the Roman Church in this manner."

"The people," he added, "are wholly ignorant; but I have a niece of twenty, who does not belong to the people in this way. I shall have the honour of making you known to her; she is a theologian, and pretty as well."

"I shall be delighted to see her, but God preserve me from arguing with her!"

"She will make you argue, and I can assure you that it will be a pleasure for you!"

"We shall see; but will you give me your address?"

"No sir, but I shall have the honour of conducting you to your inn and acting as your guide."

I got down at Balances, and was well lodged. It was the 20th of August, 1760. On going to the window I noticed a pane of glass on which I read these words, written with the point of a diamond: "You will forget Henriette." In a moment my thoughts flew back to the time in which Henriette had written these words, thirteen years ago, and my hair stood on end. We had been lodged in this room when she separated from me to return to France. I was overwhelmed, and fell on a chair where I abandoned myself to deep thought. Noble Henriette, dear Henriette, whom I had loved so well; where was she now? I had never heard of her; I had never asked anyone about her. Comparing my present and past estates, I was obliged to confess that I was less worthy of possessing her now than then. I could still love, but I was no longer so delicate in my thoughts; I had not those feelings which justify the faults committed by the senses, nor that probity which serves as a contrast to the follies and frailties of man; but, what was worst of all, I was not so strong. Nevertheless, it seemed that the remembrance of Henriette restored me to my pristine vigour. I had no longer my housekeeper; I experienced a great void; and I felt so enthusiastic that if I had known where Henriette was I should have gone to seek her out, despite her prohibition.

Next day, at an early hour, I went to the banker Tronchin, who had all my money. After seeing my account, he gave me a letter of credit on Marseilles, Genoa, Florence and Rome, and I only took twelve thousand francs in cash. I had only fifty thousand crowns, three hundred francs, but that would take me a good way. As soon as I had delivered my letters, I returned to Balances, impatient to see M. de Voltaire.

I found my fellow-traveller in my room. He asked me to dinner, telling me that I should have M. Vilars-Chandieu, who would take me after dinner to M. de Voltaire, who had been expecting me for several days. I followed the worthy man, and found at his house excellent company, and the young theologian whom the uncle did not address till dessert.

I will endeavour to report as faithfully as possible the young woman's conversation.

"What have you been doing this morning, my dear niece?"

"I have been reading St. Augustine, whom I thought absurd, and I think I can refute him very shortly."

"On what point?"

"Concerning the mother of the Saviour."

"What does St. Augustine say?"

"You have no doubt remarked the passage, uncle. He says that the Virgin Mary conceived Jesus Christ through the ears."

"You do not believe that?"

"Certainly not, and for three good reasons. In the first place because God, being immaterial, had no need of a hole to go in or come out by; in the second place, because the ear has no connection with the womb; and in the third place, because Mary, if she had conceived by the ear, would have given birth by the same channel. This would do well enough for the Catholics," said she, giving me a glance, "as then they would be reasonable in calling her a virgin before her conception, during her pregnancy, and after she had given birth to the child."

I was extremely astonished, and my astonishment was shared by the other guests. Divine theology rises above all fleshly considerations, and after what we had heard we had either to allow her this privilege, or to consider the young theologian as a woman without shame. The learned niece did not seem to care what we thought, as she asked for my opinion on the matter.

"If I were a theologian and allowed myself an exact examination into the miracles, it is possible I should be of your opinion; but as this is by no means the case, I must limit myself to condemning St. Augustine for having analysed the mystery of the Annunciation. I may say, however, that if the Virgin had been deaf, St. Augustine would have been guilty of a manifest absurdity, since the Incarnation would have been an impossibility, as in that case the nerves of the ear would have had no sort of communication with the womb, and the process would have been inconceivable; but the Incarnation is a miracle."

She replied with great politeness that I had shown myself a greater theologian than she, and her uncle thanked me for having given her a lesson. He made her discuss various subjects, but she did not shine. Her only subject was the New Testament. I shall have occasion to speak of this young woman when I get back to Geneva.

After dinner we went to see Voltaire, who was just leaving the table as we came in. He was in the middle of a court of gentlemen and ladies, which made my introduction a solemn one; but with this great man solemnity could not fail to be in my favour.

EPISODE 15 — WITH VOLTAIRE

CHAPTER XIX

M. de Voltaire; My Discussions with That Great Man—Ariosto--The Duc de Villars—The Syndic and the Three Girls—Dispute with Voltaire—Aix-en-Savoie—The Marquis Desarmoises

"M. de Voltaire," said I, "this is the happiest moment of my life. I have been your pupil for twenty years, and my heart is full of joy to see my master."

"Honour me with your attendance on my course for twenty years more, and promise me that you will bring me my fees at the end of that time."

"Certainly, if you promise to wait for me."

This Voltairean sally made all present laugh, as was to be expected, for those who laugh keep one party in countenance at the other's expense, and the side which has the laughter is sure to win; this is the rule of good society.

I was not taken by surprise, and waited to have my revenge.

Just then two Englishmen came in and were presented to him.

"These gentlemen are English," said Voltaire; "I wish I were."

I thought the compliment false and out of place; for the gentlemen were obliged to reply out of politeness that they wished they had been French, or if they did not care to tell a lie they would be too confused to tell the truth. I believe every man of honour should put his own nation first.

A moment after, Voltaire turned to me again and said that as I was a Venetian I must know Count Algarotti.

"I know him, but not because I am a Venetian, as seven-eights of my dear countrymen are not even aware of his existence."

"I should have said, as a man of letters."

"I know him from having spent two months with him at Padua, seven years ago, and what particularly attracted my attention was the admiration he professed for M. de Voltaire."

"That is flattering for me, but he has no need of admiring anyone."

"If Algarotti had not begun by admiring others, he would never have made a name for himself. As an admirer of Newton he endeavoured to teach the ladies to discuss the theory of light."

"Has he succeeded?"

"Not as well as M. de Fontenelle in his 'Plurality of Worlds;' however, one may say he has succeeded."

"True. If you see him at Bologna, tell him I am expecting to hear from him about Russia. He can address my letters to my banker, Bianchi, at Milan, and they will be sent on to me."

"I will not fail to do so if I see him."

"I have heard that the Italians do not care for his style."

"No; all that he writes is full of French idioms. His style is wretched."

"But do not these French turns increase the beauty of your language?"

"They make it insufferable, as French would be mixed with Italian or German even though it were written by M. de Voltaire."

"You are right; every language should preserve its purity. Livy has been criticised on this account; his Latin is said to be tainted with patavinity."

"When I began to learn Latin, the Abbe Lazzarini told me he preferred Livy to Sallust."

"The Abbe Lazzarini, author of the tragedy, 'Ulisse il giovine'? You must have been very young; I wish I had known him. But I knew the Abbe Conti well; the same that was Newton's friend, and whose four tragedies contain the whole of Roman history."

"I also knew and admired him. I was young, but I congratulated myself on being admitted into the society of these great men. It seems as if it were yesterday, though it is many years ago; and now in your presence my inferiority does not humiliate me. I wish to be the younger son of all humanity."

"Better so than to be the chief and eldest. May I ask you to what branch of literature you have devoted yourself?"

"To none; but that, perhaps, will come afterwards. In the meantime I read as much as I can, and try to study character on my travels."

"That is the way to become learned, but the book of humanity is too vast. Reading a history is the easier way."

"Yes, if history did not lie. One is not sure of the truth of the facts. It is tiring, while the study of the world is amusing. Horace, whom I know by heart, is my guide-book."

"Algarotti, too, is very fond of Horace. Of course you are fond of poetry?"

"It is my passion."

"Have you made many sonnets?"

"Ten or twelve I like, and two or three thousand which in all probability I have not read twice."

"The Italians are mad after sonnets."

"Yes; if one can call it a madness to desire to put thought into measured harmony. The sonnet is difficult because the thought has to be fitted exactly into the fourteen lines."

"It is Procrustes' bed, and that's the reason you have so few good ones. As for us, we have not one; but that is the fault of our language."

"And of the French genius, which considers that a thought when extended loses all its force."

"And you do not think so?"

"Pardon me, it depends on the kind of thought. A witty saying, for example, will not make a sonnet; in French or Italian it belongs to the domain of epigram."

"What Italian poet do you like best?"

"Ariosto; but I cannot say I love him better than the others, for he is my only love."

"You know the others, though?"

"I think I have read them all, but all their lights pale before Ariosto's. Fifteen years ago I read all you have written against him, and I said that you, would retract when you had read his works."

"I am obliged to you for thinking that I had not read them. As a matter of fact I had done so, but I was young. I knew Italian very imperfectly, and being prejudiced by the learned Italians who adore Tasso I was unfortunate enough to publish a criticism of Ariosto which I thought my own, while it was only the echo of those who had prejudiced me. I adore your Ariosto!"

"Ah! M. de Voltaire, I breathe again. But be good enough to have the work in which you turned this great man into ridicule excommunicated."

"What use would that be? All my books are excommunicated; but I will give you a good proof of my retractation."

I was astonished! The great man began to recite the two fine passages from the thirty-fourth and thirty-fifth cantos, in which the divine poet speaks of the conversation of Astolpho with St. John and he did it without missing a single life or committing the slightest fault against the laws of prosody. He then pointed out the beauties of the passages with his natural insight and with a great man's genius. I could not have had anything better from the lips of the most skilled commentators in Italy. I listened to him with the greatest attention, hardly daring to breath, and waiting for him to make a mistake, but I had my trouble for nothing. I turned to the company crying that I was more than astonished, and that all Italy should know what I had seen. "And I, sir," said the great man, "will let all Europe know of the amends I owe to the greatest genius our continent has produced."

Greedy of the praise which he deserved so well, Voltaire gave me the next day his translation which Ariosto begins thus:

"Quindi avvien the tra principi a signori."

At the end of the recitation which gained the applause of all who heard it, although not one of them knew Italian, Madame Denis, his niece, asked me if I thought the passage her uncle had just recited one of the finest the poet had written.

"Yes, but not the finest."

"It ought to be; for without it Signor Lodovico would not have gained his apotheosis."

"He has been canonised, then? I was not aware of that."

At these words the laugh, headed by Voltaire, went for Madame Denis. Everybody laughed except myself, and I continued to look perfectly serious.

Voltaire was vexed at not seeing me laugh like the rest, and asked me the reason.

"Are you thinking," said he, "of some more than human passage?"

"Yes," I answered.

"What passage is that?"

"The last thirty-six stanzas of the twenty-third canto, where the poet describes in detail how Roland became mad. Since the world has existed no one has discovered the springs of madness, unless Ariosto himself, who became mad in his old age. These stanzas are terrible, and I am sure they must have made you tremble."

"Yes, I remember they render love dreadful. I long to read them again."

"Perhaps the gentleman will be good enough to recite them," said Madame Denis, with a side-glance at her uncle.

"Willingly," said I, "if you will have the goodness to listen to me."

"You have learn them by heart, then, have you?" said Voltaire.

"Yes, it was a pleasure and no trouble. Since I was sixteen, I have read over Ariosto two or three times every year; it is my passion, and the lines naturally become linked in my memory without my having given myself any pains to learn them. I know it all, except his long genealogies and his historical tirades, which fatigue the mind and do not touch the heart. It is only Horace that I know throughout, in spite of the often prosaic style of his epistles, which are certainly far from equalling Boileau's."

"Boileau is often too lengthy; I admire Horace, but as for Ariosto, with his forty long cantos, there is too much of him."

"It is fifty-one cantos, M. de Voltaire."

The great man was silent, but Madame Denis was equal to the occasion.

"Come, come," said she, "let us hear the thirty-six stanzas which earned the author the title of divine, and which are to make us tremble."

I then began, in an assured voice, but not in that monotonous tone adopted by the Italians, with which the French so justly reproach us. The French would be the best reciters if they were not constrained by the rhyme, for they say what they feel better than any other people. They have neither the passionate monotonous tone of my fellow-countrymen, nor the sentimentality of the Germans, nor the fatiguing mannerisms of the English; to every period they give its proper expression, but the recurrence of the same sounds partly spoils their recitation. I recited the fine verses of Ariosto, as if it had been rhythmic prose, animating it by the sound of my voice and the movements of my eyes, and by modulating my intonation according to the sentiments with which I wished to inspire my audience. They saw how hardly I could restrain my tears, and every eye was wet; but when I came to the stanza,

> "Poiche allargare il freno al dolor puote,
> Che resta solo senza altrui rispetto,
> Giu dagli occhi rigando per le gote
> Sparge un fiume de lacrime sul petto,"

my tears coursed down my cheeks to such an extent that everyone began to sob. M. de Voltaire and Madame Denis threw their arms round my neck, but their embraces could not stop me, for Roland, to become mad, had to notice that he was in the same bed in which Angelica had lately been found in the arms of the too fortunate Medor, and I had to reach the next stanza. For my voice of sorrow and wailing I substituted the expression of that terror which arose naturally from the contemplation of his fury, which was in its effects like a tempest, a volcano, or an earthquake.

When I had finished I received with a sad air the congratulations of the audience. Voltaire cried,

"I always said so; the secret of drawing tears is to weep one's self, but they must be real tears, and to shed them the heart must be stirred to its depths. I am obliged to you, sir," he added, embracing me, "and I promise to recite the same stanzas myself to-morrow, and to weep like you."

He kept his word.

"It is astonishing," said Madame Denis, "that intolerant Rome should not have condemned the song of Roland."

"Far from it," said Voltaire, "Leo X. excommunicated whoever should dare to condemn it. The two great families of Este and Medici interested themselves in the poet's favour. Without that protection it is probable that the one line on the donation of Rome by Constantine to Silvester, where the poet speaks 'puzza forte' would have sufficed to put the whole poem under an interdict."

"I believe," said I, "that the line which has excited the most talk is that in which Ariosto throws doubt on the general resurrection. Ariosto," I added, "in speaking of the hermit who would have hindered Rhodomonte from getting possession of Isabella, widow of Zerbin, paints the African, who wearied of the hermit's sermons, seizes him and throws him so far that he dashes him against a rock, against which he remains in a dead swoon, so that 'che al novissimo di forse fia desto'."

This 'forse' which may possibly have only been placed there as a flower of rhetoric or as a word to complete the verse, raised a great uproar, which would doubtless have greatly amused the poet if he had had time!

"It is a pity," said Madame Denis, "that Ariosto was not more careful in these hyperbolical expressions."

"Be quiet, niece, they are full of wit. They are all golden grains, which are dispersed throughout the work in the best taste."

The conversation was then directed towards various topics, and at last we got to the 'Ecossaise' we had played at Soleure.

They knew all about it.

M. de Voltaire said that if I liked to play it at his house he would write to M. de Chavigni to send the Lindane, and that he himself would play Montrose. I excused myself by saying that Madame was at Bale and that I should be obliged to go on my journey the next day. At this he exclaimed loudly, aroused the whole company against me, and said at last that he should consider my visit as an insult unless I spared him a week at least of my society.

"Sir," said I, "I have only come to Geneva to have the honour of seeing you, and now that I have obtained that favour I have nothing more to do."

"Have you come to speak to me, or for me to speak to you?"

"In a measure, of course, to speak to you, but much more for you to speak to me."

"Then stay here three days at least; come to dinner every day, and we will have some conversation."

The invitation was so flattering and pressing that I could not refuse it with a good grace. I therefore accepted, and I then left to go and write.

I had not been back for a quarter of an hour when a syndic of the town, an amiable man, whom I had seen at M. de Voltaire's, and whose name I shall not mention, came and asked me to give him supper. "I was present," said he, "at your argument with the great man, and though I did not open my mouth I should much like to have an hour's talk with you." By way of reply, I embraced him, begging him to excuse my dressing-gown, and telling him that I should be glad if he would spend the whole night with me.

The worthy man spent two hours with me, without saying a word on the subject of literature, but to please me he had no need to talk of books, for he was a disciple of Epicurus and Socrates, and the evening was spent in telling little stories, in bursts of laughter, and in accounts of the various kinds of pleasure obtainable at Geneva. Before leaving me he asked me to come and sup with him on the following evening, promising that boredom should not be of the party.

"I shall wait for you," said I.

"Very good, but don't tell anyone of the party."

I promised to follow his instructions.

Next morning, young Fox came to see me with the two Englishmen I had seen at M. de Voltaire's. They proposed a game of quinze, which I accepted, and after losing fifty louis I left off, and we walked about the town till dinner-time.

We found the Duc de Villars at Delices; he had come there to consult Dr. Tronchin, who had kept him alive for the last ten years.

I was silent during the repast, but at dessert, M. de Voltaire, knowing that I had reasons for not liking the Venetian Government, introduced the subject; but I disappointed him, as I maintained that in no country could a man enjoy more perfect liberty than in Venice.

"Yes," said he, "provided he resigns himself to play the part of a dumb man."

And seeing that I did not care for the subject, he took me by the arm to his garden, of which, he said, he was the creator. The principal walk led to a pretty running stream.

"'Tis the Rhone," said he, "which I send into France."

"It does not cost you much in carriage, at all events," said I.

He smiled pleasantly and shewed me the principal street of Geneva, and Mont Blanc which is the highest point of the Alps.

Bringing back the conversation to Italian literature, he began to talk nonsense with much wit and learning, but always concluding with a false judgment. I let him talk on. He spoke of Homer, Dante, and Petrarch, and everybody knows what he thought of these great geniuses, but he did himself wrong in writing what he thought. I contented myself with saying that if these great men did not merit the esteem of those who studied them; it would at all events be a long time before they had to come down from the high place in which the praise of centuries, had placed them.

The Duc de Villars and the famous Tronchin came and joined us. The doctor, a tall fine man, polite, eloquent without being a conversationalist, a learned physician, a man of wit, a favourite pupil of Boerhaeve, without scientific jargon, or charlatanism, or self-sufficiency, enchanted me. His system of medicine was based on regimen, and to make rules he had to be a man of profound science. I have been assured, but can scarcely believe it, that he cured a consumptive patient of a secret disease by means of the milk of an ass, which he had submitted to thirty strong frictions of mercury by four sturdy porters.

As to Villars he also attracted my attention, but in quite a different way to Tronchin. On examining his face and manner I thought I saw before me a woman of seventy dressed as a man, thin and emaciated, but still proud of her looks, and with claims to past beauty. His cheeks and lips were painted, his eyebrows blackened, and his teeth were false; he wore a huge wig, which, exhaled amber, and at his buttonhole was an enormous bunch of flowers, which touched his chin. He affected a gracious manner, and he spoke so softly that it was often impossible to hear what he said. He was excessively polite and affable, and his manners were those of the Regency. His whole appearance was supremely ridiculous. I was told that in his youth he was a lover of the fair sex, but now that he was no longer good for anything he had modestly made himself into a woman, and had four pretty pets in his employ, who took turns in the disgusting duty of warming his old carcase at night.

Villars was governor of Provence, and had his back eaten up with cancer. In the course of nature he should have been buried ten years ago, but Tronchin kept him alive with his regimen and by feeding the wounds on slices of veal. Without this the cancer would have killed him. His life might well be called an artificial one.

I accompanied M. de Voltaire to his bedroom, where he changed his wig and put on another cap, for he always wore one on account of the rheumatism to which he was subject. I saw on the table the Summa of St. Thomas, and among other Italian poets the 'Secchia Rapita' of Tassoni.

"This," said Voltaire, "is the only tragicomic poem which Italy has. Tassoni was a monk, a wit and a genius as well as a poet."

"I will grant his poetical ability but not his learning, for he ridiculed the system of Copernicus, and said that if his theories were followed astronomers would not be able to calculate lunations or eclipses."

"Where does he make that ridiculous remark?"

"In his academical discourses."

"I have not read them, but I will get them."

He took a pen and noted the name down, and said,—

"But Tassoni has criticised Petrarch very ingeniously."

"Yes, but he has dishonoured taste and literature, like Muratori."

"Here he is. You must allow that his learning is immense."

"Est ubi peccat."

Voltaire opened a door, and I saw a hundred great files full of papers.

"That's my correspondence," said he. "You see before you nearly fifty thousand letters, to which I have replied."

"Have you a copy of your answers?"

"Of a good many of them. That's the business of a servant of mine, who has nothing else to do."

"I know plenty of booksellers who would give a good deal to get hold of your answers.

"Yes; but look out for the booksellers when you publish anything, if you have not yet begun; they are greater robbers than Barabbas."

"I shall not have anything to do with these gentlemen till I am an old man."

"Then they will be the scourge of your old age."

Thereupon I quoted a Macaronic verse by Merlin Coccaeus.

"Where's that from?"

"It's a line from a celebrated poem in twenty-four cantos."

"Celebrated?"

"Yes; and, what is more, worthy of being celebrated; but to appreciate it one must understand the Mantuan dialect."

"I could make it out, if you could get me a copy."

"I shall have the honour of presenting you with one to-morrow."

"You will oblige me extremely."

We had to leave his room and spend two hours in the company, talking over all sorts of things. Voltaire displayed all the resources of his brilliant and fertile wit, and charmed everyone in spite of his sarcastic observations which did not even spare those present, but he had an inimitable manner of lancing a sarcasm without wounding a person's feelings. When the great man accompanied his witticisms with a graceful smile he could always get a laugh.

He kept up a notable establishment and an excellent table, a rare circumstance with his poetic brothers, who are rarely favourites of Plutus as he was. He was then sixty years old, and had a hundred and twenty thousand francs a year. It has been said maliciously that this great man enriched himself by cheating his publishers; whereas the fact was that he fared no better than any other author, and instead of duping them was often their dupe. The Cramers must be excepted, whose fortune he made. Voltaire had other ways of making money than by his pen; and as he was greedy of fame, he often gave his works away on the sole condition that they were to be printed and published. During the short time I was with him, I was a witness of such a generous action; he made a present to his bookseller of the "Princess of Babylon," a charming story which he had written in three days.

My epicurean syndic was exact to his appointment, and took me to a house at a little distance where he introduced me to three young ladies, who, without being precisely beautiful, were certainly ravishing. Two of them were sisters. I had an easy and pleasant welcome, and from their intellectual appearance and gay manners I anticipated a delightful evening, and I was not disappointed. The half hour before supper was passed in conversation, decent but without restraint, and during supper, from the hints the syndic gave me, I guessed what would happen after dessert.

It was a hot evening, and on the pretext of cooling ourselves, we undressed so as to be almost in a state of nature. What an orgy we had! I am sorry I am obliged to draw a veil over the most exciting details. In the midst of our licentious gaiety, whilst we were heated by love, champagne, and a discourse of an exciting nature, I proposed to recite Grecourt's 'Y Gyec'. When I had finished the voluptuous poem, worthy of an abbe's pen, I saw that the eyes of the three beauties were all aflame, and said,—

"Ladies, if you like, I will shew you all three, one after the other, why the sentence, 'Gaudeant bene nati', was uttered"; and without waiting for their reply, I succeeded in making them happy. The syndic was radiant, he was pleased at having given me a present entirely to my taste; and I fancied that the entertainment was not displeasing to the three Graces, who were kept low by the Sybarite, as his powers were almost limited to desires. The girls lavished their thanks on me, while I endeavoured to assure them of my gratitude; but they leapt for joy when they heard the syndic asking me to come next day.

As he was taking me back to my inn I told him how great a pleasure he had given me, and he said he had brought up the three jewels himself.

"You," he added, "are the only man besides myself they know. You shall see them again, but I beg you will take care not to leave anything behind you, for in this town of prejudices that would be a great misfortune for them and for me."

"You are always moderate in your enjoyment, then?" I said to him.

"Unfortunately, that is no merit as far as I am concerned. I was born for the service of love, and Venus has punished me for worshipping her when I was too young."

After a good night's sleep I awoke in an active mood, and began to write a letter to Voltaire in blank verse, which cost me four times the pains that rhymed verses would have done. I sent it to him with the poem of Theophile Falengue, but I made a mistake in doing so, as I might have known he would not care for it; one cannot appreciate what one does not understand. I then went to Mr. Fox, where I found the two Englishmen who offered me my revenge. I lost a hundred Louis, and was glad to see them set out for Lausanne.

The syndic had told me that the three young ladies belonged to respectable families, but were not rich. I puzzled my head to think of some useful present I might make them without offending them, and at last I hit on a plan of the most ridiculous nature, as the reader will see. I went to a jeweller and told him to make me three golden balls, each of two ounces in weight.

At noon I went to M. de Voltaire's. He was not to be seen, but Madame Denis consoled me for his absence. She had wit, learning without pretension, taste, and a great hatred for the King of Prussia, whom she called a villain. She asked about my beautiful housekeeper, and congratulated me on having married her to a respectable man. Although I feel now that she was quite right, I was far from thinking so then; the impression was too fresh on my mind. Madame

Denis begged me to tell her how I had escaped from The Leads, but as the story was rather a long one I promised to satisfy her another time.

M. de Voltaire did not dine with us; he appeared, however, at five o'clock, holding a letter in his hand.

"Do you know," said he, "the Marquis Albergati Capacelli, senator of Bologna, and Count Paradisi?"

"I do not know Paradisi, but I know Albergati by sight and by reputation; he is not a senator, but one of the Forty, who at Bologna are Fifty."

"Dear me! That seems rather a riddle!"

"Do you know him?"

"No, but he has sent me Goldoni's 'Theatre,' the translation of my Tancred, and some Bologna sausages, and he says he will come and see me."

"He will not come; he is not such a fool."

"How a fool? Would there be anything foolish in coming to see me?"

"Certainly not, as far as you are concerned; but very much so far his own sake."

"Would you mind telling me why?"

"He knows what he would lose; for he enjoys the idea you seem to have of him, and if he came you would see his nothingness, and good-bye to the illusion. He is a worthy man with six thousand sequins a year, and a craze for the theatre. He is a good actor enough, and has written several comedies in prose, but they are fit neither for the study nor the stage."

"You certainly give him a coat which does not make him look any bigger."

"I assure you it is not quite small enough."

"But tell me how he can belong to the Forty and the Fifty?"

"Just as at Bale noon is at eleven."

"I understand; just as your Council of Ten is composed of seventeen members."

"Exactly; but the cursed Forty of Bologna are men of another kind."

"Why cursed?"

"Because they are not subject to the fisc, and are thus enabled to commit whatever crimes they like with perfect impunity; all they have got to do is to live outside the state borders on their revenues."

"That is a blessing, and not a curse; but let me return to our subject. I suppose the Marquis Albergati is a man of letters?"

"He writes well enough, but he is fond of the sound of his own voice, his style is prolix, and I don't think he has much brains."

"He is an actor, I think you said?"

"Yes, and a very good one, above all, when he plays the lover's part in one of his own plays."

"Is he a handsome man?"

"Yes, on the stage, but not elsewhere; his face lacks expression."

"But his plays give satisfaction?"

"Not to persons who understand play writing; they would be hissed if they were intelligible."

"And what do you think of Goldoni?"

"I have the highest opinion of him. Goldoni is the Italian Moliere."

"Why does he call himself poet to the Duke of Parma?"

"No doubt to prove that a wit as well as a fool has his weak points; in all probability the duke knows nothing about it. He also calls himself a barrister, though he is such only in his own imagination. Goldoni is a good play writer, and nothing more. Everybody in Venice knows me for his friend, and I can therefore speak of him with authority. He does not shine in society, and in spite of the fine satire of his works he is a man of an extremely gentle disposition."

"So I have been told. He is poor, and wants to leave Venice. The managers of the theatres where they play his pieces will not like that."

"People talked about getting him a pension, but the project has been relegated to the Greek Kalends, as they said that if he had a pension he would write no more."

"Cumae refused to give a pension to Homer, for fear that all the blind men would ask for a pension."

We spent a pleasant day, and he thanked me heartily for the copy of the Macaronicon, which he promised to read. He introduced me to a Jesuit he had in his household, who was called Adam, and he added, after telling me his name, "not the first Adam." I was told afterwards that Voltaire used to play backgammon with him, and when he lost he would throw the dice and the box at his head. If Jesuits were treated like that all the world over, perhaps we should have none but inoffensive Jesuits at last, but that happy time is still far off.

I had scarcely got to my inn in the evening when I received my three golden balls, and as soon as the syndic came we set off to renew our voluptuous orgy. On the way he talked about modesty, and said,—

"That feeling which prevents our shewing those parts which we have been taught to cover from our childhood, may often proceed from virtue, but is weaker than the force of education, as it cannot resist an attack when the attacking party knows what he is about. I think the easiest way to vanquish modesty is to ignore its presence, to turn it into ridicule, to carry it by storm. Victory is certain. The hardihood of the assailer subdues the assailed, who usually only wishes to be conquered, and nearly always thanks you for your victory.

"Clement of Alexandria, a learned man and a philosopher, has remarked that the modesty which appears so deeply rooted in women's hearts really goes no farther than the clothes they wear, and that when these are plucked off no trace of it remains."

We found the three girls lightly clad and sitting on a large sopha, and we sat down opposite to them. Pleasant talk and a thousand amorous kisses occupied the half hour just before supper, and our combat did not begin till we had eaten a delicious repast, washed down with plenty of champagne.

We were sure of not being interrupted by the maid and we put ourselves at our ease, whilst our caresses became more lively and ardent. The syndic, like a careful man, drew a packet of fine French letters from his pocket, and delivered a long eulogium on this admirable preservative from an accident which might give rise to a terrible and fruitless repentance. The ladies knew them, and seemed to have no objection to the precaution; they laughed heartily to see the shape these articles took when they were blown out. But after they had amused themselves thus for some time, I said,

"My dear girls, I care more for your honour than your beauty; but do not think I am going to shut myself in a piece of dead skin to prove that I am alive. Here," I added, drawing out the three golden balls, "is a surer and less disagreeable way of securing you from any unpleasant consequences. After fifteen years' experience I can assure you that with these golden balls you can give and take without running the least risk. For the future you will have no need of those humiliating sheaths. Trust in me and accept this little present from a Venetian who adores you."

"We are very grateful," said the elder of the two sisters, "but how are these pretty balls used?"

"The ball has to be at the rear of the temple of love, whilst the amorous couple are performing the sacrifice. The antipathy communicated to the metal by its being soaked for a certain time in an alkaline solution prevents impregnation."

"But," said the cousin, "one must take great care that the ball is not shaken out by the motion before the end of the sacrifice."

"You needn't be afraid of that if you place yourself in a proper position."

"Let us see how it's done," said the syndic, holding a candle for me to put the ball in place.

The charming cousin had gone too far to turn back; she had to submit to the operation. I placed the ball in such a position that it could not fall out before I was in; however, it fell out towards the end, just as we were separating. The victim perceived that I had taken her in. However, she said nothing, picked up the ball, and challenged the two sisters to submit to the pleasant experiment, to which they lent themselves with the greatest interest; while the syndic, who had no faith in the virtues of the metal, contented himself with looking on. After half an hour's rest I began again, without balls, assuring them that I would be careful, and I kept my word, without depriving them of the pleasure in the slightest degree.

When it was time to part, these girls, who had formerly been scantily provided for, threw their arms round my neck, overwhelmed me with caresses, and declared how much they owed me. The syndic told them that I was going in two days, and suggested that they should make me stay a day longer in Geneva, and I made this sacrifice joyfully. The worthy syndic had an engagement on the following day, and I sorely needed a holiday myself. He took me back to my inn, thanking me almost as heartily as his charming nymphs.

After having enjoyed a calm and refreshing sleep ten hours, I felt myself able to enjoy the delightful society of M. de Voltaire. I went to his house, but I was disappointed in my hopes, as it pleased the great man to be in a fault-finding and sarcastic mood the whole day. He knew I had to leave on the morrow.

He began by thanking me at table for my present of Merlin Coccaeus.

"You certainly gave it me with good intentions," said he, "but I owe you no thanks for praising it so highly, as you made me lose four hours in reading nonsense."

I felt my hair stand on end, but I mastered my emotions, and told him quietly enough that one day, perhaps, he would find himself obliged to praise the poem more highly than I had done. I quoted several instances of the insufficiency of a first perusal.

"That's true," said he; "but as for your Merlin, I will read him no more. I have put him beside Chapelain's 'Pucelle'."

"Which pleases all the critics, in spite of its bad versification, for it is a good poem, and Chapelain was a real poet though he wrote bad verses. I cannot overlook his genius."

My freedom must have shocked him, and I might have guessed it when he told me he had put the 'Macaronicon' beside the 'Pucelle'. I knew that there was a poem of the same title in circulation, which passed for Voltaire's; but I also knew that he disavowed it, and I thought that would make him conceal the vexation my explanation must have caused him. It was not so, however; he contradicted me sharply, and I closed with him.

"Chapelain," said I, "has the merit of having rendered his subject-matter pleasant, without pandering to the tastes of his readers by saying things shocking to modesty and piety. So thinks my master Crebillon:"

"Crebillon! You cite a weighty authority. But how is my friend Crebillon your master, may I ask?"

"He taught me to speak French in less than two years, and as a mark of my gratitude I translated his Radamiste into Italian Alexandrines. I am the first Italian who has dared to use this metre in our language."

"The first? I beg your pardon, as that honour belongs to my friend Pierre Jacques Martelli."

"I am sorry to be obliged to tell you that you are making a mistake."

"Why, I have his works, printed at Bologna, in my room!"

"I don't deny that, I am only talking about the metre used by Martelli. What you are thinking of must be verses of fourteen syllables; without alternative masculine and feminine rhymes. However, I confess that he thinks he has imitated the French Alexandrines, and his preface made me explode with laughter. Did you read it?"

"Read it? I always read prefaces, and Martelli proves there that his verses have the same effect in Italian as our Alexandrine verses have in French."

"Exactly, that's what's so amusing. The worthy man is quite mistaken, and I only ask you to listen to what I have to say on the subject. Your masculine verse has only twelve poetic syllables, and the feminine thirteen. All Martelli's lines have fourteen syllables, except those that finish with a long vowel, which at the end of a line always counts as two syllables. You will observe that the first hemistitch in Martelli always consists of seven syllables, while in French it only has six. Your friend Pierre Jacques was either stone deaf or very hard of hearing."

"Then you have followed our theory of versification rigorously."

"Just so, in spite of the difficulty, as nearly all our words end with a short syllable."

"What reception has been accorded to your innovation?"

"It has not been found pleasing, because nobody knows how to recite my verses; but I hope to triumph when I deliver them myself before our literary clubs."

"Do you remember any of your version of the Radamiste?"

"I remember it all."

"You have a wonderful memory; I should be glad to hear it."

I began to recite the same scene that I had recited to Crebillon ten years before, and I thought M. de Voltaire listened with pleasure.

"It doesn't strike one as at all harsh," said he.

This was the highest praise he would give me. In his turn the great man recited a passage from Tancred which had not as yet been published, and which was afterwards considered, and rightly, as a masterpiece.

We should have got on very well if we had kept to that, but on my quoting a line of Horace to praise one of his pieces, he said that Horace was a great master who had given precepts which would never be out of date. Thereupon I answered that he himself had violated one of them, but that he had violated it grandly.

"Which is that?"

"You do not write, 'Contentus paucis lectoribus'."

"If Horace had had to combat the hydra-headed monster of superstition, he would have written as I have written—for all the world."

"It seems to me that you might spare yourself the trouble of combating what you will never destroy."

"That which I cannot finish others will, and I shall always have the glory of being the first in the field."

"Very good; but supposing you succeed in destroying superstition, what are you going to put in its place?"

"I like that. If I deliver the race of man from a wild beast which is devouring it, am I to be asked what I intend to put in its place?"

"It does not devour it; on the contrary, it is necessary to its existence."

"Necessary to its existence! That is a horrible blasphemy, the falsity of which will be seen in the future. I love the human race; I would fain see men like myself, free and happy, and superstition and freedom cannot go together. Where do you find an enslaved and yet a happy people?"

"You wish, then, to see the people sovereign?"

"God forbid! There must be a sovereign to govern the masses."

"In that case you must have superstition, for without it the masses will never obey a mere man decked with the name of monarch."

"I will have no monarch; the word expresses despotism, which I hate as I do slavery."

"What do you mean, then? If you wish to put the government in the hands of one man, such a man, I maintain, will be a monarch."

"I would have a sovereign ruler of a free people, of which he is the chief by an agreement which binds them both, which would prevent him from becoming a tyrant."

"Addison will tell you that such a sovereign is a sheer impossibility. I agree with Hobbes, of two evils choose the least. A nation without superstition would be a nation of philosophers, and philosophers would never obey. The people will only be happy when they are crushed and down-trodden, and bound in chains."

"This is horrible; and you are of the people yourself. If you have read my works you must have seen how I shew that superstition is the enemy of kings."

"Read your works? I have read and re-read them, especially in places where I have differed from you. Your ruling passion is the love of humanity. 'Est ubi peccas'. This blinds you. Love humanity, but love it as it is. It is not fit to receive the blessings you would lavish on it, and which would only make it more wretched and perverse. Leave men their devouring monster, it is dear to them. I have never laughed so heartily as at Don Quixote assailed by the galley-slaves whom his generosity had set free."

"I am sorry that you have such a bad opinion of your fellow-creatures. And by the way, tell me whether there is freedom in Venice."

"As much as can be expected under an aristocracy. Our liberty is not so great as that which the English enjoy, but we are content."

"Even under The Leads?"

"My imprisonment was certainly despotic; but as I had knowingly abused my liberty I am satisfied that the Government was within its rights in shutting me up without the usual formalities."

"All the same, you made your escape."

"I used my rights as they had used theirs."

"Very good! But as far as I can see, no one in Venice is really free."

"That may be; but you must agree that the essence of freedom consists in thinking you have it."

"I shall not agree to that so easily. You and I see liberty from very different points of view. The aristocrats, the members of the Government even, are not free at Venice; for example, they cannot travel without permission."

"True, but that is a restriction of their own making to preserve their power. Would you say that a Bernese is not free, because he is subject to the sumptuary laws, which he himself had made."

"Well, well, I wish the people made the laws everywhere."

After this lively answer, he abruptly asked me what part I came from.

"From Roche," said I. "I should have been very sorry to leave Switzerland without seeing the famous Haller. In my travels I render homage to my learned contemporaries, and you come the last and best."

"You must have liked Haller."

"I spent three of the happiest days of my life with him."

"I congratulate you. He is a great man and worthy of all honour."

"I think as you do, and I am glad to hear you doing him justice; I am sorry he was not so just towards you."

"Well, you see we may be both of us mistaken."

At this reply, the quickness of which constituted its chief merit, everybody present began to laugh and applaud.

No more was said of literature, and I became a silent actor till M. de Voltaire retired, when I approached Madame Denis, and asked her if she had any commands for me at Rome. I went home well pleased at having compelled the giant of intellect to listen to reason, as I then thought foolishly enough; but there was a rankling feeling left in my heart against him which made me, ten years later, criticise all he had written.

I am sorry now for having done so, though on reading my censures over again I find that in many places I was right. I should have done better, however, to have kept silence, to have respected his genius, and to have suspected my own opinions. I should have considered that if it had not been for those quips and cranks which made me hate him on the third day, I should have thought him wholly sublime. This thought alone should have silenced me, but an angry man always thinks himself right. Posterity on reading my attack will rank me among the Zoyluses, and the humble apology I now make to the great man's shades may not be read.

If we meet in the halls of Pluto, the more peccant parts of our mortal nature purged away, all will be made up; he will receive my heartfelt apologies, and he will be my friend, I his sincere admirer.

I spent part of the night and the whole of the following day in writing down my conversations with Voltaire, and they amounted nearly to a volume, of which I have only given a mere abridgment. Towards the evening my Epicurean syndic called on me, and we went to sup with the three nymphs, and for five hours we indulged in every species of wantonness, in which I had a somewhat fertile imagination. On leaving I promised to call on them again on my return from Rome, and I kept my word. I set out the next day, after dining with the syndic, who accompanied me as far as Anneci, where I spent the night. Next day I dined at Aix, with the intention of lying at Chamberi, but my destiny ordered otherwise.

Aix is a villainous hole where the mineral waters attract people of fashion towards the end of the summer—a circumstance of which I was then ignorant. I dined hastily, wishing to set out immediately for Chamberi, when in the middle of my repast a crowd of fashionable people burst into the room. I looked at them without stirring, replying with an inclination of the head to the bows which some of them made me. I soon discovered from their conversation that they had all come to take the waters. A gentleman of a fine presence came up to me and asked if I were going to Turin; I answered that my way was to Marseilles.

Their dinner was served, and everybody sat down. Among them I noticed several pleasant-looking ladies, with gentlemen who were either their husbands or their lovers. I concluded that I might find some amusement with them, as they all spoke French with that easy tone of good society which is so attractive, and I felt that I should be inclined to stay without much pressing, for that day at all events.

I finished my dinner before the company had come to the end of their first course, and as my coach could not go for another hour I went up to a pretty woman, and complimented her on the good the waters of Aix seemed to have done her, for her appetite made all who looked at her feel hungry.

"I challenge you to prove that you are speaking the truth," said she, with a smile. I sat down next to her, and she gave me a nice piece of the roast which I ate as if I had been fasting.

While I was talking with the lady, and eating the morsels she gave me, I heard a voice saying that I was in the abbe's place, and another voice replying that the abbe had been gone for half an hour.

"Why has he gone?" asked a third, "he said he was going to stay here for another week." At this there was some whispering, but the departure of an abbe had nothing interesting in it for me, and I continued eating and talking. I told Le Duc, who was standing behind my chair, to get me some champagne. I offered the lady some, she accepted, and everyone began to call for champagne. Seeing my neighbour's spirits rising, I proceeded to make love to her, and asked her if she were always as ready to defy those who paid their court to her.

"So many of them," she answered, "are not worthy the trouble."

She was pretty and quick-witted, and I took a fancy to her, and wished for some pretext on which I could put off my departure, and chance came to my aid.

"The place next to you was conveniently empty," said a lady to my neighbour who was drinking with me.

"Very conveniently, for my neighbour wearied me."

"Had he no appetite?" said I.

"Gamesters only have an appetite for money."

"Usually, but your power is extraordinary; for I have never made two dinners on one day before now."

"Only out of pride; as I am sure you will eat no supper."

"Let us make a bet on it."

"We will; we will bet the supper."

"All right."

All the guests began to clap, and my fair neighbour blushed with pleasure. I ordered Le Duc to tell my coachman that I should not be going till the next day.

"It is my business," said the lady, "to order the supper."

"Yes, you are right; for he who pays, orders. My part will be to oppose you to the knife, and if I eat as much as you I shall be the winner."

"Very good."

At the end of dinner, the individual who had addressed me before called for cards, and made a small bank of faro. He put down twenty-five Piedmontese pistoles, and some silver money to amuse the ladies—altogether it amounted nearly to forty louis. I remained a spectator during the first deal, and convinced myself that the banker played very well.

Whilst he was getting ready for the second deal, the lady asked me why I did not play. I whispered to her that she had made me lose my appetite for money. She repaid this compliment with a charming smile.

After this declaration, feeling myself entitled to play, I put down forty louis, and lost them in two deals. I got up, and on the banker saying very politely that he was sorry for my loss, I replied that it was a mere nothing, but that I always made it a rule never to risk a sum of money larger than the bank. Somebody then asked me if I knew a certain Abbe Gilbert.

"I knew a man of that name," said I, "at Paris; he came from Lyons, and owes me a pair of ears, which I mean to cut off his head when I meet him."

My questioner made no reply to this, and everybody remained silent, as if nothing had been said. From this I concluded that the abbe aforesaid must be the same whose place I had occupied at dinner. He had doubtless seen me on my arrival and had taken himself off. This abbe was a rascal who had visited me at Little Poland, to whom I had entrusted a ring which had cost me five thousand florins in Holland; next day the scoundrel had disappeared.

When everybody had left the table, I asked Le Duc if I were well lodged.

"No," said he; "would you like to see your room?"

He took me to a large room, a hundred paces from the inn, whose sole furniture consisted of its four walls, all the other rooms being occupied. I complained vainly to the inn-keeper, who said,

"It's all I can offer you, but I will have a good bed, a table, and chairs taken there."

I had to content myself with it, as there was no choice.

"You will sleep in my room," said I to Le Duc, "take care to provide yourself with a bed, and bring my baggage in."

"What do you think of Gilbert, sir?" said my Spaniard; "I only recognized him just as he was going, and I had a lively desire to take him by the back of his neck."

"You would have done well to have satisfied that desire."

"I will, when I see him again."

As I was leaving my big room, I was accosted politely by a man who said he was glad to be my neighbour, and offered to take me to the fountain if I were going there. I accepted his offer. He was a tall fair man, about fifty years old; he must once have been handsome, but his excessive politeness should have made me suspect him; however, I wanted somebody to talk to, and to give me the various pieces of information I required. On the way he informed me of the condition of the people I had seen, and I learnt that none of them had come to Aix for the sake of the waters.

"I am the only one," said he, "who takes them out of necessity. I am consumptive; I get thinner every day, and if the waters don't do me any good I shall not last much longer."

So all the others have only come here for amusement's sake?"

"And to game, sir, for they are all professional gamesters."

"Are they French?"

"They are all from Piedmont or Savoy; I am the only Frenchman here."

"What part of France do you come from?"

"From Lorraine; my father, who is eighty years old, is the Marquis Desarmoises. He only keeps on living to spite me, for as I married against his wishes he has disinherited me. However, as I am his only son, I shall inherit his property after his death, in spite of him. My house is at Lyons, but I never go there, as I have the misfortune to be in love with my eldest daughter, and my wife watches us so closely as to make my courtship hopeless."

"That is very fine; otherwise, I suppose, your daughter would take pity on her amorous papa?"

"I daresay, for she is very fond of me, and has an excellent heart."

CHAPTER XX

My Adventures at Aix—My Second M. M.—Madame Zeroli

This man, who, though he did not know me, put the utmost confidence in me, so far from thinking he was horrifying me by the confession of such wickedness, probably considered he was doing me a great honour. While I listened to him I reflected that though depraved he might have his good points, and that his weakness might have a pitiable if not a pardonable side. However, wishing to know more of him, I said,—

"In spite of your father's sternness, you live very well."

"On the contrary, I live very ill. I enjoy a pension from the Government, which I surrender to my wife, and as for me I make a livelihood on my travels. I play black gammon and most other games perfectly. I win more often than I lose, and I live on my winnings."

"But is what you have told me about your daughter known to the visitors here?"

"Everybody knows it; why should I hide it? I am a man of honour and injure no one; and, besides, my sword is sharp."

"Quite so; but would you tell me whether you allow your daughter to have a lover?"

"I should have no objection, but my wife is religious."

"Is your daughter pretty?"

"Very; if you are going to Lyons, you can go and see her; I will give you a letter of introduction for her."

"Thank you, but I am going to Italy. Can you tell me the name of the gentleman who kept the bank?"

"That is the famous Parcalier, Marquis de Prie since the death of his father, whom you may have known as ambassador at Venice. The gentleman who asked you if you knew the Abbe Gilbert is the Chevalier Zeroli, husband of the lady you are to sup with. The rest are counts, marquises, and barons of the usual kind, some from Piedmont and some from Savoy. Two or three are merchants' sons, and the ladies are all their friends or relations. They are all professional gamblers and sharp-witted. When a stranger comes here they know how to get over him, and if he plays it is all up with him, for they go together like pickpockets at a fair. They think they have got you, so take care of yourself."

In the evening we returned to the inn, and found all the company playing, and my companion proceeded to play with a Count de Scarnafisch.

The Chevalier Zeroli offered to play faro with me for forty sequins, and I had just lost that sum when supper was served. My loss had not affected my spirits, and the lady finding me at once hungry and gay paid the bet with a good grace. At supper I surprised her in certain side-glances, which warned me that she was going to try to dupe me; I felt myself safe as far as love was concerned, but I had reason to dread fortune, always the friend of those who keep a bank at faro, especially as I had already lost. I should have done well to go, but I had not the strength; all I could do was to promise myself that I would be extremely prudent. Having large sums in paper money and plenty of gold, it was not difficult for me to be careful.

Just after supper the Marquis de Prie made a bank of about three hundred sequins. His staking this paltry sum shewed me that I had much to lose and little to win, as it was evident that he would have made a bank of a thousand sequins if he had had them. I put down fifty Portuguese crowns, and said that as soon as I had lost them I should go to bed. In the middle of the third deal I broke the bank.

"I am good for another two hundred louis," said the marquis.

"I should be glad to continue playing," I replied, "if I had not to go at day-break"; and I thereupon left the room.

Just as I was going to bed, Desarmoises came and asked me to lend him twelve louis. I had expected some such request, and I counted them out to him. He embraced me gratefully, and told me that Madame Zeroli had sworn to make me stay on at least for another day. I smiled and called Le Duc, and asked him if my coachman knew that I was starting early; he replied that he would be at the door by five o'clock.

"Very good," said Desarmoises, "but I will wager that you will not go for all that."

He went out and I went to bed, laughing at his prophecy.

At five o'clock next morning the coachman came to tell me that one of the horses was ill and could not travel. I saw that Desarmoises had had an inkling of some plot, but I only laughed. I sent the man roughly about his business, and told Le Duc to get me post-horses at the inn. The inn-keeper came and told me that there were no horses, and that it would take all the morning to find some, as the Marquis de Prie, who was leaving at one o'clock in the morning, had emptied his stables. I answered that in that case I would dine at Aix, but that I counted on his getting me horses by two o'clock in the afternoon.

I left the room and went to the stable, where I found the coachman weeping over one of his horses stretched out on the straw. I thought it was really an accident, and consoled the poor devil, paying him as if he had done his work, and telling him I should not want him any more. I then went towards the fountain, but the reader will be astonished by a meeting of the most romantic character, but which is yet the strict truth.

At a few paces from the fountain I saw two nuns coming from it. They were veiled, but I concluded from their appearance that one was young and the other old. There was nothing astonishing in such a sight, but their habit attracted my attention, for it was the same as that worn by my dear M—— M——, whom I had seen for the last time on July 24th, 1755, five years before. The look of them was enough, not to make me believe that the young nun was M—— M——, but to excite my curiosity. They were walking towards the country, so I turned to cut them off that I might see them face to face and be seen of them. What was my emotion when I saw the young nun, who, walking in front, and lifting her veil, disclosed the veritable face of M—— M——. I could not doubt that it was she, and I began to walk beside her; but she lowered her veil, and turned to avoid me.

The reasons she might have for such a course passed in a moment through my mind, and I followed her at a distance, and when she had gone about five hundred paces I saw her enter a lonely house of poor appearance that was enough for me. I returned to the fountain to see what I could learn about the nun.

On my way there I lost myself in a maze of conjectures.

"The too charming and hapless M—— M——," said I to myself, "must have left her convent, desperate—nay, mad; for why does she still wear the habit of her order? Perhaps, though, she has got a dispensation to come here for the waters; that must be the reason why she has a nun with her, and why she has not left off her habit. At all events the journey must have been undertaken under false pretences. Has she abandoned herself to some fatal passion, of which the result has been pregnancy? She is doubtless perplexed, and must have been pleased to see me. I will not deceive her expectations; I will do all in my power to convince her that I am worthy of her."

Lost in thought I did not notice I had arrived at the fountain, round which stood the whole host of gamesters. They all crowded round me, and said how charmed they were to see me still there. I asked the Chevalier Zeroli after his wife, and he told me she was still abed, and that it would be a good thing if I would go and make her get up. I was just going when the doctor of the place accosted me, saying, that the waters of the Aix would increase my good health. Full of the one idea, I asked him directly if he were the doctor in attendance on a pretty nun I had seen.

"She takes the waters," he replied, "but she does not speak to anyone."

"Where does she come from?"

"Nobody knows; she lives in a peasant's house."

I left the doctor, and instead of going towards the inn, where the hussy Zeroli was doubtless waiting for me, I made my way towards the peasant's house, which already seemed to me the temple of the most blissful deities, determined to obtain the information I required as prudently as might be. But as if love had favoured my vows, when I was within a hundred paces of the cottage I saw the peasant woman coming out to meet me.

"Sir," said she, accosting me, "the young nun begs you to return this evening at nine o'clock; the lay-sister will be asleep then, and she will be able to speak freely to you."

There could be no more doubt. My heart leapt with joy. I gave the country-woman a louis, and promised to be at the house at nine exactly.

With the certainty of seeing my dear M—— M—— again I returned to the inn, and on ascertaining which was Madame Zeroli's room I entered without ceremony, and told her that her husband had sent me to make her get up.

"I thought you were gone?"

"I am going at two."

I found her still more enticing in bed than at table. I helped her to put on her stays, and the sight of her charms inflamed my ardour, but I experienced more resistance than I had anticipated. I sat down at the foot of the bed, and told her how fervently I loved her, and how unhappy I was at not being able to give her marks of my love before I left.

"But," said she, laughing, "you have only got to stay."

"Give me some hope, and I will stay till to-morrow."

"You are in too much of a hurry, take things more quietly."

I contented myself with the few favours she granted me, pretending as usual only to yield to violence, when I was obliged to restrain myself on the appearance of her husband, who took the precaution of making a noise before he came in. As soon as she saw him, she said, without the slightest perturbation, "I have persuaded the gentleman to stay tell the day after to-morrow."

"I am all the more pleased to hear it, my dear," said the chevalier, "as I owe him his revenge."

With these words he took up a pack of cards, which came as readily to his hands as if they had been placed there on purpose, and seating himself beside his wife, whom he made into the table, he began to deal.

I could not draw back, and as my thoughts were distracted I kept on losing till they came to tell me dinner was ready.

"I have no time to dress," said the lady, "so I will have my dinner in bed, if you gentlemen will keep me company."

How could I refuse? The husband went out to order the dinner, and feeling myself authorized by the loss of twenty Louis, I told the hussy that if she would not give me a plain promise to make me happy that afternoon I should go away when I had had my dinner.

"Breakfast with me to-morrow morning. We shall be alone."

After receiving from her certain earnests of her promise, I promised to stay on.

We dined by her bedside, and I told Le Duc that I should not be going till the afternoon of the next day, which made the husband and wife radiant. When we had done, the lady said she would like to get up; and I went out, promising to return and play piquet with her. I proceeded to reline my purse, and I met Desarmoises, who said,

"I have found out the secret; they gave her coachman two Louis to substitute a sick horse for his own."

"It's a matter of give and take," said I; "I am in love with the chevalier's wife, and I am putting off my departure till I have got all I want out of her."

"I am afraid you will have to pay pretty dearly for your pleasure. However, I will do what I can for your interests."

I thanked him smilingly, and returned to the lady, whom I left at eight o'clock under pretext of a violent headache, after having lost ten louis to her. I reminded her of her promise for next morning at nine o'clock, and I left her in the midst of the company.

It was a fine moonlight night as I walked towards the peasant's house, where I was to see my dear M—— M—— once more. I was impatient to see what the visit, on which the rest of my life might depend, would bring forth.

I had taken the precaution to provide myself with a pair of pistols, and my sword hung at my side, for I was not wholly devoid of suspicion in this place, where there were so many adventurers; but at twenty paces from the cottage I saw the woman coming towards me. She told me that the nun could not come down, so I must be content to enter through the window, by means of a ladder which she had placed there for the purpose. I drew near, and not seeing any light I should not have easily decided on going up, if I had not heard the voice I thought I knew so well, saying, "Fear nothing; come." Besides, the window was not very high up, and there could not be much danger of a trap. I ascended, and thought for certain that I held my dear M—— M—— in my arms, as I covered her face with my ardent kisses.

"Why," said I, in Venetian, "have you not a light? I hope you are going to inform me of an event which seems wonderful to me; quick, dearest, satisfy my impatience."

The reader will guess my surprise when he learns that on hearing her voice close to me I found that she was not M—— M——. She told me that she did not understand Venetian, and that I did not require a light to tell her what M. de Coudert had decided on doing to save her from her peril.

"You surprise me; I do not know M. de Coudert. What! Are you not a Venetian? Are you not the nun I saw this morning?"

"Hapless one! I have made a mistake. I am the nun you saw this morning, but I am French. In the name of God keep my counsel and begone, for I have nothing to say to you! Whisper, for if the lay-sister woke up I should be undone."

"Do not be afraid of my discretion. What deceived me was your exact likeness to a nun of your order who will be always dear to me: and if you had not allowed me to see your features I should not have followed you. Forgive the tenderness I shewed towards you, though you must think me very audacious."

"You astonished me very much, but you did not offend me. I wish I were the nun in whom you are interested. I am on the brink of a fearful precipice."

"If ten louis are any good to you, it will be an honour for me to give you them."

"Thank you, I have no need of money. Allow me to give you back the louis you sent me this morning."

"The louis was for the country-woman. You increase my surprise; pray tell me what is the misfortune under which you labour, for which money can do nothing."

"Perhaps God has sent you to my aid. Maybe you will give me good advice. Listen to what I am about to tell you."

"I am at your service, and I will listen with the greatest attention. Let us sit down."

"I am afraid there is neither seat nor bed."

"Say on, then; we will remain standing."

"I come from Grenoble. I was made to take the veil at Chamberi. Two years after my profession, M. de Coudert found means to see me. I received him in the convent garden, the walls of which he scaled, and at last I was so unfortunate as to become pregnant. The idea of giving birth to a child at the convent was too dreadful—I should have languished till I died in a terrible dungeon—and M. de Coudert thought of a plan for taking me out of the convent. A doctor whom he gained over with a large sum of money declared that I should die unless I came here to take the waters, which he declared were the only cure for my illness. A princess whom M. de Coudert knew was partly admitted to the secret, and she obtained the leave of absence for three months from the Bishop of Chamberi, and the abbess consented to my going.

"I thus hoped to be delivered before the expiration of the three months; but I have assuredly made a mistake, for the time draws to an end and I feel no signs of a speedy delivery. I am obliged to return to the convent, and yet I cannot do so. The lay-sister who is with me is a perfect shrew. She has orders not to let me speak to anybody, and never to let my face be seen. She it was who made me turn when she saw you following us. I lifted my veil for you to see that I was she of whom I thought you were in search, and happily the lay-sister did not notice me. She wants me to return with her to the convent in three days, as she thinks I have an incurable dropsy. She does not allow me to speak to the doctor, whom I might, perhaps, have gained over by telling him the truth. I am only twenty-one, and yet I long for death."

"Do not weep so, dear sister, and tell me how you expect to be delivered here without the lay-sister being aware of it?"

"The worthy woman with whom I am staying is an angel of goodness. I have confided in her, and she promised me that when I felt the pangs coming on she would give that malicious woman a soporific, and thus we should be freed from all fears of her. By virtue of the drug she now sleeps soundly in the room under this garret."

"Why was I not let in by the door?"

"To prevent the woman's brother seeing you; he is a rude boor."

"What made you think that I had anything to do with M. de Coudert?"

"Ten or twelve days ago, I wrote to him and told him of my dreadful position. I painted my situation with such lively colours that I thought he must do all in his power to help me. As the wretched cling to every straw, I thought, when I saw you following me, that you were the deliverer he had sent."

"Are you sure he got your letter?"

"The woman posted it at Anneci."

"You should write to the princess."

"I dare not."

"I will see her myself, and I will see M. de Coudert. In fine, I will move heaven and earth, I will even go to the bishop, to obtain an extension of your leave; for it is out of the question for you to return to the convent in your present situation. You must decide, for I can do nothing without your consent.

Will you trust in me? If so, I will bring you a man's clothes to-morrow and take you to Italy with me, and while I live I swear I will care for you."

For reply, I only heard long-drawn sobs, which distressed me beyond words, for I felt acutely the situation of this poor creature whom Heaven had made to be a mother, and whom the cruelty of her parents had condemned to be a useless nun.

Not knowing what else to say, I took her hand and promised to return the next day and hear her decision, for it was absolutely necessary that she should decide on some plan. I went away by the ladder, and gave a second louis to the worthy woman, telling her that I should be with her on the morrow at the same hour, but that I should like to be able to enter by the door. I begged her to give the lay-sister a stronger dose of opium, so that there should be no fear of her awaking while I talked with the young nun.

I went to bed glad at heart that I had been wrong in thinking that the nun was M——— M———. Nevertheless the great likeness between them made me wish to see her nearer at hand, and I was sure that she would not refuse me the privilege of looking at her the next day. I smiled at the thought of the ardent kisses I had given her, but I felt that I could not leave her to her fate. I was glad to find that I did not need any sensual motive to urge me to a good deed, for as soon as I found that it was not M——— M——— who had received those tender kisses I felt ashamed of having given them. I had not even given her a friendly kiss when I left her.

In the morning Desarmoises came and told me that all the company, not seeing me at supper, had been puzzling itself to find out what had become of me. Madame Zeroli had spoken enthusiastically about me, and had taken the jests of the two other ladies in good part, boasting that she could keep me at Aix as long as she remained there herself. The fact was that I was not amorous but curious where she was concerned, and I should have been sorry to have left the place without obtaining complete possession of her, for once at all events.

I kept my appointment, and entered her room at nine o'clock exactly. I found her dressed, and on my reproaching her she said that it should be of no consequence to me whether she were dressed or undressed. I was angry, and I took my chocolate without so much as speaking to her. When I had finished she offered me my revenge at piquet, but I thanked her and begged to be excused, telling her that in the humour in which she had put me I should prove the better player, and that I did not care to win ladies' money. So saying I rose to leave the room.

"At least be kind enough to take me to the fountain."

"I think not. If you take me for a freshman, you make a mistake, and I don't care to give the impression that I am pleased when I am displeased. You can get whomsoever you please to take you to the fountain, but as for me I must beg to be excused. Farewell, madam."

With these words I went out, paying no attention to her efforts to recall me.

I found the inn-keeper, and told him that I must leave at three o'clock without a fail. The lady, who was at her window, could hear me. I went straight to the fountain where the chevalier asked me what had become of his wife, and I answered that I had left her in her room in perfect health. In half an hour we saw her coming with a stranger, who was welcomed by a certain M. de St. Maurice. Madame Zeroli left him, and tacked herself on to me, as if there had been nothing the matter. I could not repulse her without the most troublesome consequences, but I was very cold. After complaining of my conduct she said that she had only been trying me, that if I really loved her I should put off my departure, and that I should breakfast with her at eight o'clock the next day. I answered coolly that I would think it over. I was serious all dinner-time, and said once or twice that I must go at three o'clock, but as I wanted to find some pretext for staying on account of the nun, I let myself be persuaded into making a bank at faro.

I staked all the gold I had, and I saw every face light up as I put down about four hundred louis in gold, and about six hundred francs in silver. "Gentlemen," said I, "I shall rise at eight o'clock precisely." The stranger said, with a smile, that possibly the bank might not live so long, but I pretended not to understand him. It was just three o'clock. I begged Desarmoises to be my croupier, and I began to deal with due deliberation to eighteen or twenty punters, all professional gamblers. I took a new pack at every deal.

By five o'clock I had lost money. We heard carriage wheels, and they said it was three Englishmen from Geneva, who were changing horses to go on to Chamberi. A moment after they came in, and I bowed. It was Mr. Fox and his two friends, who had played quinze with me. My croupier gave them cards, which they received gladly, and went ten louis, playing on two and three cards, going paroli, seven and the 'va', as well as the 'quinze', so that my bank was in danger of breaking. However, I kept up my face, and even encouraged them to play, for, God being neutral, the chances were in my favour. So it happened, and at the third deal I had cleared the Englishmen out, and their carriage was ready.

While I was shuffling a fresh pack of cards, the youngest of them drew out of his pocket-book a paper which he spewed to his two companions. It was a bill of exchange. "Will you stake the value of this bill on a card, without knowing its value?" said he.

"Yes," I replied, "if you will tell me upon whom it is drawn, and provided that it does not exceed the value of the bank."

After a rapid glance at the pile of gold before me, he said, "The bill is not for so large a sum as your bank, and it is payable at sight by Zappata, of Turin."

I agreed, he cut, and put his money on an ace, the two friends going half shares. I drew and drew and drew, but no ace appeared. I had only a dozen cards left.

"Sir," said I, calmly to the punter, "you can draw back if you like."

"No, go on."

Four cards more, and still no ace; I had only eight cards left.

"My lord," said I, "it's two to one that I do not hold the ace, I repeat you can draw back."

"No, no, you are too generous, go on."

I continued dealing, and won; I put the bill of exchange in my pocket without looking at it. The Englishmen shook me by the hand and went off laughing. I was enjoying the effect this bold stroke had made on the company, when young Fox came in and with a roar of laughter begged me to lend him fifty Louis. I counted them out with the greatest pleasure, and he paid me them back in London three years later.

Everyone was curious to know the value of the bill of exchange, but I was not polite enough to satisfy their curiosity. It was for eight thousand Piedmontese francs, as I saw as soon as I was alone. The Englishmen had brought me good luck, for when they had gone fortune declared for the bank. I rose at eight o'clock, some ladies having won a few louis, all the others were dried up. I had won more than a thousand louis, and I gave twenty-five to Desarmoises, who jumped for joy. I locked up my money, put my pistols in my pocket, and set out towards the meeting-place.

The worthy peasant woman brought me in by the door, telling me that everybody was asleep, and that she had not found it necessary to renew the lay-sister's dose, as she was still asleep.

I was terrified. I went upstairs, and by the light of a single candle I saw the wretched, veiled figure of the nun, extended upon a sack which the peasant woman had placed along the wall instead of a sofa. The candle which lighted this dreary place was fixed in a bottle.

"What have you decided on doing?" said I.

"I have decided on nothing, for an unforeseen incident has confounded us. The lay-sister has been asleep for eighteen hours."

"She will die of convulsions or of an apoplectic fit to-night if you do not call a doctor, who may possibly restore her to life with a dose of castor oil."

"We have thought of that, but we did not dare to take that step for fear of consequences; for whether he restores her or not, he will say that we have poisoned her."

"I pity you, upon my soul! Indeed, I believe that it is too late, and that a doctor could do nothing. One must obey the laws of prudence and let her die. The mischief is done, and I see no remedy."

"At any rate, we ought to think of her soul and send for a priest."

"A priest would do her no good, as she is in a perfect lethargy; her soul is safe enough. Besides, an ignorant priest would find out too much, and would tell the whole story either through malice or stupidity. It will be time to call a priest when she has ceased to breathe. You must tell him that she died very suddenly; you must weep a great deal, and give him a fee, and he will think only of calming your grief, and nothing about the sudden death."

"Then we must let her die?"

"We must leave her to nature."

"If she dies I will send a messenger to the abbess, who will dispatch another lay-sister."

"Yes, and that will give you another ten days. During that time you may be delivered, and you will confess that every cloud has a silver lining. Do not grieve so, but let us endeavour to submit to the will of God. Send for the country-woman, for I must give her some hints as to her conduct in this delicate matter, on which the honour and life of all three may depend. For instance, if it were discovered that I had come here, I might be taken for the poisoner."

The woman came, and I shewed her how necessary it was for her to be prudent and discreet. She understood me perfectly, perceived her own dangerous position, and promised that she would not send for the priest till she was certain of the sister's death. I then made her accept ten louis in case of need.

Seeing herself made rich by my liberality, she kissed my hands, knelt down, and bursting into tears promised to follow my advice carefully. When she had left us, the nun began to weep bitterly, accusing herself of the murder of the lay-sister, and thinking that she saw hell opening beneath her feet. I sought in vain to calm her; her grief increased, and at last she fell in a dead faint on the sack. I was extremely distressed, and not knowing what to do I called to the woman to bring some vinegar, as I had no essences about me. All at once I remembered the famous hellebore, which had served me so well with Madame and, taking the little box, I held it to her nostrils. It took effect just as the woman brought the vinegar. "Rub her temples," said I. She took off her cap, and the blackness of her hair was the only thing that convinced me it was not my fair Venetian. The hellebore having brought her to her senses, she opened her large black eyes, and from that moment I fell madly in love with her. The peasant woman, seeing that she was herself again and out of danger, went away, and taking her between my arms I covered her with fiery kisses, in spite of her continuous sneezes.

"Please let me put on my veil again," said she, "or else I shall be excommunicated."

I laughed at her fears, and continued to lavish my burning kisses on her face.

"I see you do not believe me, but I assure you that the abbess threatened me with excommunication if I let myself be seen by a man."

"Fear these bolts no longer, dear, they cannot hurt you."

But she sneezed more violently than ever, and fearing lest her efforts might bring on her delivery I called the woman again, and left the nun in her care, promising to return at the same hour on the next day.

It would not have been like me to leave this interesting creature in her distress, but my devotion to her cause had no merit, since I was madly in love with this new M—— M—— with black eyes; and love always makes men selfish, since all the sacrifices they make for the beloved object are always ultimately referable to their own desires.

I had determined, then, to do all in my power for her, and certainly not to allow her to return to the convent in the state she was in. I concluded that to save her would be an action pleasing to God, since God alone could have made her so like my beloved, and God had willed that I should win a good deal of money, and had made me find the Zeroli, who would serve as a shield to my actions and baffle the curiosity of spies. The philosophers and the mystics may perhaps laugh at me, but what do I care? I have always delighted in referring all the actions of my life to God, and yet people have charged me with Atheism!

343

Next morning I did not forget the Zeroli, and I went to her room at eight and found her asleep. Her maid begged me to go in quietly for fear of awakening her, and then left me and shut the door. I knew my part, for I remembered how, twenty years before, a Venetian lady, whose sleep I had foolishly respected, had laughed at me and sent me about my business. I therefore knew what to do; and having gently uncovered her, I gave myself up to those delicate preliminary delights which sweeten the final pleasure. The Zeroli wisely continued to sleep; but at last, conquered by passion, she seconded my caresses with greater ardour than my own, and she was obliged to laugh at her stratagem. She told me that her husband had gone to Geneva to buy a repeating watch, and that he would not return till next day, and that she could spend the night with me.

"Why the night, dearest, while we have the day before us? The night is for slumber, and in the day one enjoys double bliss, since the light allows all the senses to be satisfied at once. If you do not expect anybody, I will pass the whole morning with you."

"Very good; nobody will interrupt us."

I was soon in her arms, and for four hours we gave ourselves up to every kind of pleasure, cheating each other the better to succeed, and laughing with delight each time we convinced each other of our love. After the last assault she asked me, in return for her kindness, to spend three more days at Aix.

"I promise you," I said, "to stay here as long as you continue giving me such marks of your love as you have given me this morning."

"Let us get up, then, and go to dinner."

"In company, dearest? Look at your eyes."

"All the better. People will guess what has happened, and the two countesses will burst with envy. I want everybody to know that it is for me alone that you are remaining at Aix."

"I am not worth the trouble, my angel, but so be it; I will gladly oblige you, even though I lose all my money in the next three days."

"I should be in despair if you lost; but if you abstain from punting you will not lose, though you may let yourself be robbed."

"You may be sure that I know what I am about, and that I shall only allow ladies to rob me. You have had some money out of me yourself."

"Yes, but not nearly so much as the countesses, and I am sorry you allowed them to impose on you, as they no doubt put it down to your being in love with them."

"They are quite wrong, poor dears, for neither would have kept me here a day."

"I am delighted to hear it. But let me tell you what the Marquis of St. Maurice was saying about you yesterday."

"Say on. I hope he did not allow himself any offensive remarks."

"No; he only said that you should never have offered the Englishman to be off at eight cards, as you had as much chance as he, and if he had won he might have thought that you knew the card was there."

"Very good, but tell the marquis that a gentleman is incapable of such a thought, and besides I knew the character of the young nobleman, and I was almost sure he would not accept my offer."

When we appeared in the dining-room we were received with applause. The fair Zeroli had the air of regarding me as her property, and I affected an extremely modest manner. No one dared to ask me to make a bank after dinner; the purses were too empty, and they contented themselves with trente-quarante, which lasted the whole day, and which cost me a score of louis.

I stole away as usual towards evening, and after having ordered Le Duc not to leave my room for a moment during my stay at Aix, I went towards the cottage where the unfortunate nun was no doubt expecting me anxiously. Soon, in spite of the darkness, I thought I made out somebody following me. I stopped short, and some persons passed me. In two or three minutes I went on again, and I saw the same people, whom I could not have caught up if they had not slackened their pace. It might all be accidental, but I wanted to be sure about it. I left the road without losing my reckoning, feeling quite sure of finding my way when I ceased to be followed; but I soon felt sure that my steps were dogged, as I saw the same shadowy figures at a little distance off. I doubled my speed, hid behind a tree, and as soon as I saw the spies fired a pistol in the air. I looked round shortly after, saw no one, and went on my way.

I went upstairs and found the nun in bed, with two candles on the table.

"Are you ill?"

"I was ill for a time, but praised be God! I am now quite well, having given birth to a fine boy at two o'clock this morning."

"Where is the child?"

"Alas! I did but kiss him once, and my good hostess carried him away I know not where. The Holy Virgin heard my prayers, for my pains, though sharp, were soon over, and a quarter of an hour after my delivery I was still sneezing. Tell me whether you are a man or an angel, for I fear lest I sin in adoring you."

"This is good news indeed. And how about the lay-sister?"

"She still breathes, but we have no hope that she will recover. Her face is terribly distorted. We have sinned exceedingly, and God will punish me for it."

"No, dearest, God will forgive you, for the Most Holy judges by the heart, and in your heart you had no evil thoughts. Adore Divine Providence, which doeth all things well."

"You console me. The country-woman assures me that you are an angel, for the powder you gave me delivered me. I shall never forget you, though I do not know your name."

The woman then came, and I thanked her for the care she had taken of the invalid. I again warned her to be prudent, and above all to treat the priest well when the lay-sister breathed her last, and thus he would not take notice of anything that might involve leer in disaster.

"All will be well," said she, "for no one knows if the lay-sister is well or ill, or why the lady does not leave her bed."

"What have you done with the child?"

"I took him with my own hands to Anneci, where I bought everything necessary for the well-being of this lady and for the death of the other one."

"Doesn't your brother know anything about it?"

"Lord preserve us—no! He went away yesterday, and will not be back for a week. We have nothing to fear."

I gave her another ten louis, begging her to buy some furniture, and to get me something to eat by the time I came next day. She said she had still plenty of money left, and I thought she would go mad when I told her that whatever was over was her own. I thought the invalid stood in need of rest, and I left her, promising to return at the same hour on the following day.

I longed to get this troublesome matter safely over, and I knew that I could not regard myself as out of the wood till the poor lay-sister was under the sod. I was in some fear on this account, for if the priest was not an absolute idiot he must see that the woman had been poisoned.

Next morning I went to see the fair Zeroli, and I found her and her husband examining the watch he had bought her. He came up to me, took my hand, and said he was happy that his wife had the power to keep me at Aix. I replied that it was an easy task for her, and a "bravo" was all he answered.

The chevalier was one of those men who prefer to pass for good-natured than foolish husbands. His wife took my arm, and we left him in his room while we proceeded to the fountain. On the way she said she would be alone the next day, and that she would no longer indulge her curiosity in my nocturnal excursions.

"Oh! it is you who have had me followed, is it?"

"No, it is I who followed you, but to no effect. However, I did not think you were so wicked. You frightened me dreadfully! Do you know, sir, you might have killed me if your shot had not luckily missed."

"I missed on purpose, dearest; for though I did not suspect that it was you, I fired in the air, feeling certain that that would be enough to scare off the spies."

"You won't be troubled with them any more."

"If they like to follow me, perhaps I shall let them, for my walk is quite innocent. I am always back by ten."

While we were at table we saw a travelling carriage and six horses drawn up. It was the Marquis de Prie, with a Chevalier de St. Louis and two charming ladies, of whom one, as the Zeroli hastened to inform me, was the Marquis's mistress. Four places were laid, and while the newcomers were waiting to be served, they were told the story of my bet with the Englishman.

The marquis congratulated me, telling me that he had not hoped to find me at Aix on his return; and here Madame Zeroli put in her word, and said that if it had not been for her he would not have seen me again. I was getting used to her foolish talk, and I could only agree with a good grace, which seemed to delight her intensely although her husband was present, but he seemed to share her triumph.

The marquis said that he would make a little bank for me, and feeling obliged to accept I soon lost a hundred louis. I went to my room to write some letters, and at twilight I set out to see my nun.

"What news have you?"

"The lay-sister is dead, and she is to be buried tomorrow. To-morrow is the day we were to have returned to the convent. This is the letter I am sending to the abbess. She will dispatch another laysister, unless she orders the country-woman to bring me back to the convent."

"What did the priest say?"

"He said the lay-sister died of a cerebral lethargy, which super-induced an attack of apoplexy."

"Very good, very good."

"I want him to say fifteen masses for her, if you will let me?"

"Certainly, my dear, they will serve as the priest's reward, or rather as the reward of his happy ignorance."

I called the peasant woman, and gave her the order to have the masses said, and bade her tell the priest that the masses were to be said for the intention of the person who paid for them. She told me that the aspect of the dead sister was dreadful, and that she had to be guarded by two women who sprinkled her with holy water, lest witches, under the form of cats, should come and tear her limb from limb. Far from laughing at her, I told her she was quite right, and asked where she had got the laudanum.

"I got it from a worthy midwife, and old friend of mine. We got it to send the poor lay-sister to sleep when the pains of child-birth should come on."

"When you put the child at the hospital door, were you recognized?"

"Nobody saw me as I put it into the box, and I wrote a note to say the child had not been baptized."

"Who wrote the note?"

"I did."

"You will, of course, see that the funeral is properly carried out?"

"It will only cost six francs, and the parson will take that from two louis which were found on the deceased; the rest will do for masses to atone for her having had the money."

"What! ought she not to have had the two louis?"

"No," said the nun, "we are forbidden to have any money without the knowledge of the abbess, under pain of excommunication."

"What did they give you to come here?"

"Ten Savoy sols a day. But now I live like a princess, as you shall see at supper, for though this worthy woman knows the money you gave her is for herself she lavishes it on me."

"She knows, dear sister, that such is my intention, and here is some more to go on with."

So saying I took another ten louis from my purse, and bade the country-woman spare nothing for the invalid's comfort. I enjoyed the worthy woman's happiness; she kissed my hands, and told me that I had made her fortune, and that she could buy some cows now.

As soon as I was alone with the charming nun, whose face recalled to my memory the happy hours I had passed with M—— M——, my imagination began to kindle, and drawing close to her I began to talk of her seducer, telling her I was surprised that he had not helped her in the cruel position in which he had placed her. She replied that she was debarred from accepting any money by her vow of poverty and obedience, and that she had given up to the abbess what remained of the alms the bishop had procured her.

"As to my state when I was so fortunate as to meet you, I think he cannot have received my letter."

"Possibly, but is he a rich or handsome man?"

"He is rich but certainly not handsome. On the contrary, he is extremely ugly, deformed, and over fifty."

"How did you become amorous of a fellow like that?"

"I never loved him, but he contrived to gain my pity. I thought he would kill himself, and I promised to be in the garden on the night he appointed, but I only went there with the intention of bidding him begone, and he did so, but after he had carried his evil designs into effect."

"Did he use violence towards you, then?"

"No, for that would have been no use. He wept, threw himself on his knees, and begged so hard, that I let him do what he liked on the condition that he would not kill himself, and that he would come no more to the garden."

"Had you no fear of consequences?"

"I did not understand anything about it; I always thought that one could not conceive under three times at least."

"Unhappy ignorance! how many woes are caused by it! Then he did not ask you to give him any more assignations?"

"He often asked me, but I would not grant his request because our confessor made me promise to withstand him thenceforth, if I wished to be absolved."

"Did you tell him the name of the seducer?"

"Certainly not; the good confessor would not have allowed me to do so; it would have been a great sin."

"Did you tell your confessor the state you were in?"

"No, but he must have guessed it. He is a good old man, who doubtless prayed to God for me, and my meeting you was, perhaps, the answer to his prayers."

I was deeply moved, and for a quarter of an hour I was silent, and absorbed in my thoughts. I saw that this interesting girl's misfortune proceeded from her ignorance, her candour, her perfect innocence, and a foolish feeling of pity, which made her grant this monster of lubricity a thing of which she thought little because she had never been in love. She was religious, but from mere habit and not from reflection, and her religion was consequently very weak. She abhorred sin, because she was obliged to purge herself of it by confession under pain of everlasting damnation, and she did not want to be damned. She had plenty of natural common sense, little wit, for the cultivation of which she had no opportunities, and she was in a state of ignorance only pardonable in a nun. On weighing these facts I foresaw that I should find it a difficult task to gain those favours which she had granted to Coudert; her repentance had been too bitter for her to expose herself to the same danger over again.

The peasant woman returned, laid the table for two, and brought us our supper. Everything was new—napkins, plates, glasses, spoons, knives, etc., and everything was exquisitely clean. The wines were excellent, and the dishes delightful in their simplicity. We had roast game, fish, cheese with cream, and very good fruit. I spent an hour and a half at supper, and drank two bottles of wine as I talked to the nun, who ate very little.

I was in the highest spirits, and the woman, delighted with my praise of her provision, promised I should be served the same way every evening.

When I was alone with the nun, whose face filled me with such burning recollections, I began to speak of her health, and especially of the inconveniences attached to child-birth. She said she felt quite well, and would be able to return to Chamberi on foot. "The only thing that troubles me is my breasts, but the woman assures me that the milk will recede to-morrow, and that they will then assume their usual shape."

"Allow me to examine them, I know something about it."

"Look!"

She uncovered her bosom, not thinking it would give me any pleasure, but wishing to be polite, without supposing I had any concealed desires. I passed my hands over two spheres whose perfect shape and whiteness would have restored Lazarus to life. I took care not to offend her modesty, but in the coolest manner possible asked her how she felt a little lower down, and as I put the question I softly extended my hand. However, she kept it back gently, telling me not to go any further as she still felt a little uneasy. I begged her pardon, and said I hoped I should find everything quite right by the next day.

"The beauty of your bosom," I added, "makes me take a still greater interest in you."

So saying I let my mouth meet hers, and I felt a kiss escape as if involuntarily from her lips. It ran like fire through my veins, my brain began to whirl, and I saw that unless I took to a speedy flight I should lose all her confidence. I therefore left her, calling her "dear daughter" as I bade her farewell.

It poured with rain, and I got soaked through before I reached my lodging. This was a bath well fitted to diminish the ardour of my passion, but it made me very late in rising the next morning.

I took out the two portraits of M—— M——, one in a nun's dress, and the other nude, as Venus. I felt sure they would be of service to me with the nun.

I did not find the fair Zeroli in her room, so I went to the fountain, where she reproached me with a tenderness I assessed at its proper value, and our quarrel was made up in the course of our walk. When dinner was over the Marquis the Prie made a bank, but as he only put down a hundred louis I guessed that he wanted to win a lot and lose a little. I put down also a hundred louis, and he said that it would be better sport if I did not stake my money on one card only. I replied that I would stake a louis on each of the thirteen.

"You will lose."

"We will see. Here is my hand on the table, and I stake a louis on each of the thirteen cards."

According to the laws of probability, I should certainly have lost, but fate decided otherwise and I won eighty louis. At eight o'clock I bowed to the company, and I went as usual to the place where my new love dwelt. I found the invalid ravishing. She said she had had a little fever, which the country-woman pronounced to be milk fever, and that she would be quite well and ready to get up by the next day. As I stretched out my hand to lift the coverlet; she seized it and covered it with kisses, telling me that she felt as if she must give me that mark of her filial affection. She was twenty-one, and I was thirty-five. A nice daughter for a man like me! My feelings for her were not at all of a fatherly character. Nevertheless, I told her that her confidence in me, as shewn by her seeing me in bed, increased my affection for her, and that I should be grieved if I found her dressed in her nun's clothes next day.

"Then I will stop in bed," said she; "and indeed I shall be very glad to do so, as I experience great discomfort from the heat of my woollen habit; but I think I should please you more if I were decently dressed; however, as you like it better, I will stop in bed."

The country-woman came in at that moment, and gave her the abbess' letter which her nephew had just brought from Chamberi. She read it and gave it to me. The abbess told her that she would send two lay-sisters to bring her back to the convent, and that as she had recovered her health she could come on-foot, and thus save money which could be spent in better ways. She added that as the bishop was away, and she was unable to send the lay-sisters without his permission, they could not start for a week or ten days. She ordered her, under pain of the major excommunication, never to leave her room, never to speak to any man, not even to the master of the house, and to have nothing to do with anybody except with the woman. She ended by saying that she was going to have a mass said for the repose of the departed sister's soul.

"I am obliged to you for having shewn me this letter, but be pleased to tell me if I may visit you for the next week or ten days, without doing hurt to your conscience; for I must tell you I am a man. I have only stopped in this place because of the lively interest with which you have inspired me, but if you have the least objection to receive me on account of the singular excommunication with which you are threatened, I will leave Aix tomorrow. Speak."

"Sir, our abbess is lavish of these thunders, and I have already incurred the excommunication with which she threatens me; but I hope it will not be ratified by God, as my fault has made me happy and not miserable. I will be sincere with you; your visits are my only joy, and that joy is doubled when you tell me you like to come. But if you can answer my question without a breach of confidence, I should like to know for whom you took me the first time you saw me; you cannot imagine how you astonished and frightened me. I have never felt such kisses as those you lavished on me, but they cannot increase my sin as I was not a consenting party, and you told me yourself that you thought you were kissing another."

"I will satisfy your curiosity. I think I can do so as you are aware by this time that the flesh is weak, or rather stronger than the spirit, and that it compels the strongest intellects to commit faults against right reason. You shall hear the history of an amour that lasted for two years with the fairest and the best of all the nuns of Venice."

"Tell me all, sir. I have fallen myself, and I should be cruel and unjust if I were to take offence at anything you may tell me, for you cannot have done anything with her that Coudert did not do to me."

"I did much more and much less, for I never gave her a child. If I had been so unfortunate I should have carried her off to Rome, where we should have fallen at the feet of the Holy Father, who would have absolved her from her vows, and my dear M—— M—— would now be my wife."

"Good heavens M—— M—— is my name."

This circumstance, which was really a mere coincidence, rendered our meeting still more wonderful, and astonished me as much as it did her. Chance is a curious and fickle element, but it often has the greatest influence on our lives.

After a brief silence I told her all that had taken place between the fair Venetian and myself. I painted our amorous combats in a lively and natural manner, for, besides my recollections, I had her living picture before my eyes, and I could follow on her features the various emotions aroused by my recital. When I had finished she said,

"But is your M—— M—— really so like me, that you mistook me for her?"

Drawing from my pocket-book the portrait in which M—— M—— was dressed as a nun, I gave it to her, saying,

"Judge for yourself."

"She really is; it might pass for my portrait. It is my dress and my face; it is wonderful. To this likeness I owe all my good fortune. Thanks be to God that you do not love me as you loved her, whom I am glad to call my sister. There are indeed two M—— M—— s. Mighty Providence, all Thy least ways are wonderful, and we are at best poor, weak, ignorant mortals."

The worthy country-woman came up and have us a still better supper than on the previous night. The invalid only ate soup, but she promised to do better by the following evening.

I spent an hour with her after supper, and I convinced her by my reserve that she had made a mistake in thinking that I only loved her as a daughter. Of her own accord she shewed me that her breast had regained its usual condition. I assured myself of the fact by my sense of touch, to which she made no opposition, not thinking that I could be moved by such a trifle. All the kisses which I lavished on her lips and eyes she put down to the friendship for her. She said, smiling, that she thanked God she was not fair like her sister, and I smiled myself at her simplicity.

But I could not keep up this sort of thing for long, and I had to be extremely careful. As soon as I felt that passion was getting the upper hand, I gave her a farewell kiss and went away. When I got home Le Duc gave me a note from Madame Zeroli, who said she would expect me at the fountain, as she was going to breakfast with the marquis's mistress.

I slept well, but in my dreams I saw again and again the face of the new M——— M———. Next day, as soon as I got to the fountain, Madame Zeroli told me that all the company maintained that I ought to have lost in playing on thirteen cards at once, as it was not true that one card won four times in each deal; however, the marquis, though he agreed with the rest, had said that he would not let me play like that again.

"I have only one objection to make to that—namely, that if I wanted to play in the same way again he could only prevent me by fighting for it."

"His mistress swears she will make you play in the usual way."

I smiled, and thanked her for her information.

When I got back to the inn I played a game of quinze with the marquis, and lost fifty louis; afterwards I let myself be persuaded to hold a bank. I put down five hundred louis, and defied fortune. Desarmoises was my croupier, and I warned the company that every card must have the stake placed on it, and that I should rise at half-past seven. I was seated between two ladies. I put the five hundred louis on the board, and I got change from the inn-keeper to the amount of a hundred crowns, to amuse the ladies with. But something happened. All the cards before me were loose packs, and I called for new ones. The inn-keeper said he had sent to Chamberi for a hundred packs, and that the messenger would be back soon.

"In the meanwhile," said he, "you can use the cards on the table, which are as good as new."

"I want them new, not as good as new. I have my prejudices, and they are so strong as to be invincible. In the meanwhile I shall remain a spectator, though I am sorry to keep the ladies waiting."

Nobody dared say a word, and I rose, after replacing my money in my cash-box. The Marquis de Prie took the bank, and played splendidly. I stood beside Madame Zeroli, who made me her partner, and gave me five or six Louis the next day. The messenger who was to be back soon did not return till midnight, and I thanked my stars for the escape I had had, for in such a place, full of professional gamesters, there are people whose eyes are considerably sharper than a lynx's. I put the money back in my room, and proceeded on my usual way.

I found my fair nun in bed, and asked her,

"How do you feel to-day, madam?"

"Say daughter, that name is so sweet to me that I would you were my father that I might clasp you in my arms without fearing anyone."

"Well, my dear daughter, do not fear anything, but open your arms to me."

"I will; we will embrace one another."

"My little ones are prettier than they were yesterday let me suck them."

"You silly papa, you are drinking your daughter's milk."

"It is so sweet, darling, and the little drop I tasted has made me feel so happy. You cannot be angry at my enjoying this harmless privilege."

"Of course I am not angry; you delighted me. But I shall have to call you baby, not papa."

"How glad I am to find you in better spirits to-night!"

"You have 'given me back my happiness, and I feel at peace once more. The country-woman told me that in a few days I should be just the same as if I had never seen Coudert."

"That is not quite true; how about your stomach, for instance?"

"Be quiet; you can't know anything about such things, and I am quite astonished myself."

"Let me see."

"Oh, no; you mustn't see, but you may feel."

"All right."

"Oh! please don't go there."

"Why not? You can't be made differently from your sister, who would be now about thirty. I want to shew you her portrait naked."

"Have you got it with you? I should so like to see it."

I drew it out and gave it to her. She admired it, kissed it, and asked me if the painter had followed nature in all respects.

"Certainly," said I. "She knew that such a picture would give me pleasure."

"It is very fine. It is more like me than the other picture. But I suppose the long hair is only put in to please you?"

"Not at all. Italian nuns are allowed to wear their hair as long as they please, provided they do not shew it.

"We have the same privilege. Our hair is cut once, and then we may let it grow as long as we like."

"Then you have long hair?"

"As long as in the picture; but you would not like my hair as it is black."

"Why, black is my favourite colour. In the name of God, let me see it."

"You ask me in God's name to commit a sin; I shall incur another excommunication, but I cannot refuse you anything. You shall see my hair after supper, as I don't want to scandalize the countrywoman."

"You are right; I think you are the sweetest of your sex. I shall die of grief when you leave this cottage to return to your sad prison."

"I must indeed return and do penance for my sins."

"I hope you have the wit to laugh at the abbess's silly excommunications?"

"I begin not to dread them so much as I used to."

"I am delighted to hear it, as I see you will make me perfectly happy after supper."

The country-woman came up, and I gave her another ten louis; but it suddenly dawned upon me that she took me for a madman. To disabuse her of this idea I told her that I was very rich, and that I wanted to make her understand that I could not give her enough to testify my gratitude to her for the care she had taken of the good nun. She wept, kissed my hand, and served us a delicious supper. The nun ate well and drank indifferently, but I was in too great a hurry to see the beautiful black hair of this victim to her goodness of heart, and I could not follow her example. The one appetite drove out the other.

As soon as we were relieved of the country-woman's presence, she removed her hood, and let a mass of ebon hair fall upon her alabaster shoulders, making a truly ravishing contrast. She put the portrait before her, and proceeded to arrange her hair like the first M—— M——.

"You are handsomer than your sister," said I, "but I think she was more affectionate than you."

"She may have been more affectionate, but she had not a better heart."

"She was much more amorous than you."

"I daresay; I have never been in love."

"That is strange; how about your nature and the impulse of the senses?"

"We arrange all that easily at the convent. We accuse ourselves to the confessor, for we know it is a sin, but he treats it as a childish fault, and absolves us without imposing any penances."

"He knows human nature, and makes allowances for your sad position."

"He is an old man, very learned, and of ascetic habits, but he is all indulgence. It will be a sad day when we lose him."

"But in your amorous combats with another nun, don't you feel as if you would like her to change into a man?"

"You make me laugh. To be sure, if my sweetheart became a man I should not be sorry, but we do not desire such a miracle."

"That is, perhaps, through a coldness of temperament. In that your sister was better, for she liked me much more than C—— C——, and you do not like me as well as the sweetheart you left behind you at the convent."

"Certainly not, for with you I should violate my own chastity and expose myself to consequences I tremble to think of."

"You do not love me, then?"

"What are you saying? I adore you, and I am very sorry you are not a woman."

"I love you too, but your desire makes me laugh; for I would rather not be turned into a woman to please you, especially as I expect I should not think you nearly as beautiful. Sit down, my dear, and let me see your fine hair flowing over your beautiful body."

"Do you want me to take off my chemise?"

"Of course; how handsome you look without it. Let me suck your pretty breasts, as I am your baby."

She granted me this privilege, and looking at me with a face full of pleasure, she allowed me to press her naked body to my breast, not seeing, or pretending not to see, the acuteness of my enjoyment. She then said,

"If such delights as these were allowed friendship, I should say it is better than love; for I have never experienced so great pleasure as when you put your lips to my bosom. Let me do the same to you."

"I wish you could, but you will find nothing there."

"Never mind; it will amuse us."

After she had fulfilled her desire, we spent a quarter of an hour in mutual embraces, and my excitement was more than I could bear.

"Tell me truly," said I, "amidst our kisses, amidst these ecstacies which we call child-like, do you not feel a desire for something more?"

"I confess that I do, but such desires are sinful; and as I am sure that your passions are as high as mine, I think we had better stop our agreeable employment; for, papa dear, our friendship is becoming burning love, is it not?"

"Yes, love, and love that cannot be overcome."

"I know it."

"If you know it, let us perform to love the sweetest of all sacrifices."

"No, no; on the contrary, let us stop and be more prudent in the future, lest we become the victims of love. If you love me, you should say so too."

With these words she slipped gently from my arms, put back her beautiful hair under her cap, and when I had helped her on with her chemise, the coarseness of which horrified me, I told her she might calm herself. I told her how sorry I felt to see her delicate body frayed by so coarse a stuff, and she told me it was of the usual material, and that all the nuns wore chemises of the same kind.

My mind was in a state of consternation, for the constraint I had imposed on myself seemed much greater than the utmost pleasure I could have gained. I neither determined on persevering in nor on abandoning the pursuit; all I wanted was to be sure that I should not encounter the least resistance. A folded rose-leaf spoilt the repose of the famous Smindyrides, who loved a soft bed. I preferred, therefore, to go away, than to risk finding the rose-leaf which troubled the voluptuous Sybarite. I left the cottage in love and unhappy, and as I did not go to bed till two o'clock in the morning I slept till mid-day.

When I woke up Le Duc gave me a note which he should have given me the night before. He had forgotten it, and I was not sorry. The note came from Madame Zeroli, who said she would expect me at nine o'clock in the morning, as she would be alone. She told me that she was going to give a supper-party, that she was sure I would come, and that as she was leaving Aix directly after, she counted on my coming too—at any rate, as far as Chamberi. Although I still liked her, her pretensions made me laugh. It was too late now to be with her at nine, I could not go to her supper-party because of my fair nun, whom I would not have left just then for the seraglio of the Grand Turk; and it was impossible for me to accompany her to Chamberi, as when I came back I might no longer find the only object which kept me at Aix.

However, as soon as I had finished dressing, I went to see her and found her furious. I excused myself by saying that I had only had her letter for an hour, but she went away without giving me time to tell her that I could not sup with her or go to Chamberi with her. She scowled at me at table, and when the meal was over the Marquis de Prie told me that they had some new cards, and that everybody was longing to see me make a bank. I went for my money, and I made a bank of five hundred louis. At seven o'clock I had lost more than half that sum, but for all that I put the rest in my pocket and rose from the table.

After a sad glance in the direction of Madame Zeroli I went to the cottage, where I found my angel in a large new bed, with a small but pretty bed beside it which was meant for me. I laughed at the incongruity of these pieces of furniture with our surroundings, but by way of thanking the thoughtful country-woman I drew fifty louis from my purse and gave them to her, telling her it was for the remainder of the time the lady was with her, and I told her to spend no more money in furniture.

This was done in true gamester fashion. I had lost nearly three hundred louis, but I had risked more than five hundred, and I looked on the difference as pure profit. If I had gained as much as I had lost I should probably have contented myself with giving her ten louis, but I fancied I was losing the fifty louis on a card. I have always liked spending money, but I have never been careless with it except in gaming.

I was in an ecstasy to see the face of my M—— M—— light up with delight and astonishment.

"You must be very rich," said she.

"Don't think it, dearest, but I love you passionately; and not being able to give you anything by reason of your unfortunate vow of poverty, I lavish what I possess on this worthy woman, to induce her to spare nothing for your comfort while you are here. Perhaps, too—though it is not a definite thought—I hope that it will make you love me more."

"How can I love you more than I do? The only thing that makes me unhappy is the idea of returning to the convent."

"But you told me yesterday that it was exactly that idea which made you happy."

"I have changed my mind since yesterday. I passed a cruel night, for as soon as I fell asleep I was in your arms, and I awoke again and again on the point of consummating the greatest of crimes."

"You did not go through such a struggle before committing the same crime with a man you did—not love."

"It is exactly because I did not love him that my sin struck me as venial. Do you understand what I mean?"

"It's a piece of superstitious metaphysics, but I understand you perfectly."

"You have made me happy, and I feel very grateful to you, and I feel glad and certain of conquering when I reflect that your situation is different to mine."

"I will not dispute it with you, although I am sorry for what you say."

"Why?"

"Because you think yourself in duty bound to refuse caresses which would not hurt you, and which would give me new life and happiness."

"I have thought it over."

"Are you weeping?"

"Yes, and what is more, these tears are dear to me."

"I do not understand."

"I have two favours to ask of you."

"Say on, and be sure you will obtain what you ask."

CHAPTER XXI

End of My Adventure with the Nun from Chamberi—My Flight from Aix

"Yesterday," said the charming nun, "you left in my hands the two portraits of my Venetian sister. I want you to give them to me."

"They are yours."

"I thank you. My second favour is, that you will be good enough to take my portrait in exchange; you shall have it to-morrow."

"I shall be delighted. It will be the most precious of all my jewels, but I wonder how you can ask me to take it as a favour, whereas you are doing me a favour I should never have dared to demand. How shall I make myself worthy of giving you my portrait?"

"Ah, dearest! it would be a dear possession, but God preserve me from having it at the convent!"

"I will get myself painted under the costume of St. Louis of Gonzaga, or St. Anthony of Padua."

"I shall be damned eternally."

"We will say no more about it."

She had on a dimity corset, trimmed with red ribbon, and a cambric chemise. I was surprised, but politeness did not allow me to ask where they came from, so I contented myself with staring at them. She guessed my thoughts, and said, smilingly, that it was a present from the countrywoman.

"Seeing her fortune made, the worthy woman tries every possible way to convince her benefactor that she is grateful to him. Look at the bed; she was certainly thinking of you, and look at these fine materials. I confess I enjoy their softness extremely. I shall sleep better to-night if I am not plagued by those seductive dreams which tormented me last night."

"Do you think that the bed and the fine linen will deliver you from the dreams you fear?"

"No doubt they will have a contrary effect, for softness irritates the passions. I shall leave everything with the good woman. I do not know what they would say if I took them with me to the convent."

"You are not so comfortable there?"

"Oh, no! A straw bed, a couple of blankets, and sometimes, as a great favour, a thin mattress and two coarse sheets. But you seem sad; you were so happy yesterday."

"How can I be happy when I can no longer toy with you without making you unhappy."

"You should have said without giving me the greatest delight."

"Then will you consent to receive pleasure in return for that which you give me?"

"But yours is innocent and mine is not."

"What would you do, then, if mine and yours were the same?"

"You might have made me wretched yesterday, for I could not have refused you anything."

"Why wretched? You would have had none of those dreams, but would have enjoyed a quiet night. I am very sorry the peasant woman has given you that corset, as otherwise I might at least have seen my little pets without fear of bad dreams."

"But you must not be angry with the good woman, for she knows that a corset is easy to unlace. And I cannot bear to see you sad."

With these words she turned her ardent gaze upon me, and I covered her with kisses which she returned with interest. The country-woman came up to lay the pretty new table, just as I was taking off her corset without her offering the least resistance.

This good omen put me in high spirits, but as I looked at her I saw a shadow passing across her face. I took care not to ask her the reason, for I guessed what was the matter, and I did not wish to discuss those vows which religion and honour should have made inviolable. To distract her mind from these thoughts, I made her eat by the example I set, and she drank the excellent claret with as much pleasure as I, not thinking that as she was not used to it it would put her in a frame of mind not favourable to continence. But she did not notice this, for her gaiety made her look prettier than before, and aroused her passions.

When we were alone I congratulated her on her high spirits, telling her that my sadness had fled before her gaiety, and that the hours I could spend with her would be all too short.

"I should be blithe," said she, "if it were only to please you."

"Then grant me the favour you accorded me yesterday evening."

"I would rather incur all the excommunications in the world than run the risk of appearing unjust to you. Take me."

So saying, she took off her cap, and let down her beautiful hair. I unlaced her corset, and in the twinkling of an eye I had before me such a siren as one sees on the canvas of Correggio. I could not look upon her long without covering her with my burning kisses, and, communicating my ardour, before long she made a place for me beside herself. I felt that there was no time for thinking, that nature had spoken out, and that love bade me seize the opportunity offered by that delicious weakness. I threw myself on her, and with my lips glued to hers I pressed her between my amorous arms, pending the moment of supreme bliss.

But in the midst of these joys, she turned her head, closed her eyelids, and fell asleep. I moved away a little, the better to contemplate the treasures that love displayed before me. The nun slept, as I thought; but even if her sleep was feigned, should I be angry with her for the stratagem? Certainly not; true or feigned, the sleep of a loved one should always be respected by a delicate lover, although there are some pleasures he may allow himself. If the sleep is real there is no harm done, and if it is put on the lover only responds to the lady's desires. All that is necessary is so to manage one's caresses that they are pleasant to the beloved object. But M—— M—— was really asleep; the claret had numbed her senses, and she had yielded to its influence without any ulterior motives. While I gazed at her I saw that she was dreaming. Her lips uttered words of which I could not catch the meaning, but her voluptuous aspect told me of what she dreamt. I took off my clothes; and in two minutes I had clasped her fair body to mine, not caring much whether she slept on or whether I awoke her and brought our drama to a climax, which seemed inevitable.

I was not long uncertain, for the instinctive movements she made when she felt the minister that would fain accomplish the sacrifice at the door of the sanctuary, convinced me that her dream still lasted, and that I could not make her happier than by changing it into reality. I delicately moved away all obstacles, and gently and by degrees consummated this sweet robbery, and when at last I abandoned myself to all the force of passion, she awoke with a sigh of bliss, murmuring,

"Ah! it is true then."

"Yes, my angel! are you happy?"

For all reply she drew me to her and fastened her lips on mine, and thus we awaited the dawn of day, exhausting all imaginable kinds of pleasure, exciting each other's desires, and only wishing to prolong our enjoyment.

"Alas!" said she, "I am happy now, but you must leave me till the evening. Let us talk of our happiness, and enjoy it over again."

"Then you do not repent having made me a happy man?"

"No; it is you who have made me happy. You are an angel from heaven. We loved, we crowned our love; I cannot have done aught to offend God. I am free from all my fears. We have obeyed nature and our destinies. Do you love me still?"

"Can you ask me? I will shew you to-night."

I dressed myself as quickly as possible while we talked of our love, and I left her in bed, bidding her rest.

It was quite light when I got home. Le Duc had not gone to bed, and gave me a letter from the fair Zeroli, telling me that it had been delivered at eleven o'clock. I had not gone to her supper, and I had not escorted her to Chamberi; I had not had time to give her a moment's thought. I was sorry, but I could not do anything. I opened her letter which consisted of only six lines, but they were pregnant ones. She advised me never to go to Turin, for if I went there she would find means to take vengeance on me for the dastardly affront I had put upon her. She reproached me with having put her to public shame, said I had dishonoured her, and vowed she would never forgive me. I did not distress myself to any great extent; I tore up the friendly missive, and after I had had my hair done I went to the fountain.

Everybody flew at me for not having been at Madame Zeroli's supper. I defended myself as best I could, but my excuses were rather tame, about which I did not trouble myself. I was told that all was known, and this amused me as I was aware that nothing was known. The marquis's mistress took hold of my arm, and told me, without any circumlocution, that I had the reputation of being inconstant, and by way of reply I observed politely that I was wrongfully accused, but that if there was any ground for the remark it was because I had never served so sweet a lady as herself. She was flattered by my compliment, and I bit my lip when I heard her ask in the most gracious manner why I did not breakfast sometimes with the marquis.

"I was afraid of disturbing him," said I.

"How do you mean?"

"I should be interrupting him in his business."

"He has no business, and he would be delighted to see you. Come to-morrow, he always breakfasts in my room."

This lady was the widow of a gentleman of quality; she was young, undoubtedly pretty, and possessing in perfection the jargon of good society; nevertheless, she did not attract me. After recently enjoying the fair Zeroli, and finding my suit with the fair nun at the height of its prosperity, I was naturally hard to please, and in plain words—I was perfectly contented with my situation. For all that, I had foolishly placed myself in such a position that I was obliged to give her to understand that she had delighted me by her preference.

She asked the marquis if she could return to the inn.

"Yes," said he, "but I have some business in hand, and cannot come with you."

"Would you be kind enough to escort me?" said she to me. I bowed in assent.

On the way she told me that if Madame Zeroli were still there she would not have dared to take my arm. I could only reply by equivocating, as I had no wish to embark in a fresh intrigue. However, I had no choice; I was obliged to accompany her to her room and sit down beside her; but as I had had no sleep the night before I felt tired and began to yawn, which was not flattering for the lady. I excused myself to the best of my ability, telling her that I was ill, and she believed me or pretended to believe me. But I felt sleep stealing upon me, and I should have infallibly dropped off if it had not been for my hellebore, which kept me awake by making me sneeze.

The marquis came in, and after a thousand compliments he proposed a game of quinze. I begged him to excuse me, and the lady backed me up, saying I could not possibly play in the midst of such a sneezing fit. We went down to dinner, and afterwards I easily consented to make a bank, as I was vexed at my loss of the day before. As usual I staked five hundred louis, and about seven o'clock, though two-thirds of the bank had gone, I announced the last deal. The marquis and two other heavy gamesters then endeavoured to break the bank, but fortune turned, and I not only got back my losses but won three hundred Louis besides. Thereupon I rose, promising the company to begin again next day. All the ladies had won, as Desarmoises had orders to let them play as they liked up to a certain limit.

I locked up my money, and warning my faithful Spaniard that I should not be coming back, I went to my idol, having got wet through on the way, and being obliged to undress as soon as I arrived. The good woman' of the house took care to dry my clothes.

I found the fair nun dressed in her religious habit, and lying on the small bed.

"Why are you not in your own bed, dearest?"

"Because I feel quite well again, my darling, and I wished to sup with you at table. We will go to bed afterwards, if that will give you any pleasure."

"It will give me pleasure if you share in my delight."

"Alas! I am undone, and I shall doubtless die when I have to leave you."

"Do not leave me, sweetheart; come with me to Rome; and leave the matter in my hands. I will make you my wife, and we will live happily together ever after."

"That would be too great a bliss, but I could never make up my mind to it; say no more about it."

I was sure of spending a delicious night—in the possession of all her charms, and we stayed an hour at table, seasoning the dishes with sweet converse. When we had done, the woman came up, gave her a packet, and went away again, wishing us good night.

"What does this packet contain, darling?"

"It is the present I have got for you-my portrait, but you must not see it till I am in bed."

"I will indulge you in that fancy, although I am very curious to see the portrait."

"You will say I am right afterwards."

I wanted to undress her myself, and she submitted like a lamb. When she was in bed, she opened the packet, and shewed me her portrait, naked, and very like the naked portrait of M—— M——. I praised the painter for the excellence of the copy he had made; nothing was altered but the colour of the hair and eyes.

"It isn't a copy," she said, "there would not have been time. He only made the eyes and hair black, and the latter more abundant. Thus you have in it a portrait of the first and also of the second M—— M——, in whom you must forget the first. She has also vanished from the clothed portrait, for you see the nun has black eyes. I could shew this picture to anyone as my portrait."

"You do not know how precious your present is to me! Tell me, dearest, how you succeeded in carrying out your plan so well."

"I told the country-woman about it yesterday morning, and she said that she had a foster-son at Anneci, who was a miniature painter. Through him she sent the two miniatures to a more skilful painter at Geneva, who made the change you see for four or five Louis; he was probably able to do it in two or three hours. I entrusted the two portraits to him, and you see how well he did his work. The woman has no doubt just received them, and to-morrow she may be able to tell you more about it."

"She is really a wonderful woman. I will indemnify her for the expense. But now tell me why you did not want me to see the portrait before you were in bed?"

"Guess."

"Because I can now see you in the same posture as that in which you are represented."

"Exactly."

"It is an excellent idea; only love can have given it you. But you must wait till I am in the same state."

When we were both in a state of nature, exactly like Adam and Eve before they tasted the fatal apple, I placed her in the position of the portrait, and guessing my intention from my face she opened her arms for me to come to her; but I asked her to wait a moment, for I had a little packet too, which contained something she would like. I then drew from my pocket-book a little article of transparent skin, about eight inches long, with one opening, which was ornamented with a red rosette. I gave her this preventive sheath, and she looked, admired, and laughed loudly, asking me if I had used such articles with her Venetian sister. "I will put it on myself; you don't know how I shall enjoy it. Why didn't you use one last night? How could you have forgotten it? Well, I shall be very wretched if anything comes of it. What shall I do in four or five months, when my condition becomes past doubt?"

"Dearest, the only thing to do is not to think of it, for if the damage is done, there is no cure for it; but from my experience and knowledge of the laws of nature I expect that our sweet combats of last night will probably have no troublesome consequences. It has been stated that after child-birth a woman cannot conceive afresh without having seen something which I expect you have not seen."

"No, God be thanked!"

"Good. Then let us not give any thought to the dismal future lest we lose our present bliss."

"I am quite comforted; but I can't understand why you are afraid to-day of what you were not afraid yesterday; my state is the same."

"The event has sometimes given the lie to the most eminent physicians. Nature, wiser than they, has exceptions to her rules, let us not defy them for the future, but let us not trouble ourselves if we have defied there in the past."

"I like to hear you talk so sagely. Yes, we will be prudent whatever it costs. There you are, hooded like a mother abbess, but in spite of the fineness of the sheath I like the little fellow better quite naked. I think that this covering degrades us both."

"You are right, it does. But let us not dwell on these ideas which will only spoil our pleasure."

"We will enjoy our pleasure directly; let me be reasonable now, for I have never thought of these matters before. Love must have invented these little sheaths, but it must first have listened to the voice of prudence, and I do not like to see love and prudence allied."

"The correctness of your arguments surprises me, but we will philosophize another time."

"Wait a minute. I have never seen a man before, and I have never wished to enjoy the sight as much as now. Ten months ago I should have called that article an invention of the devil; but now I look upon the inventor as a benefactor, for if my wretched hump-back had provided himself with such a sheath he would not have exposed me to the danger of losing my honour and my life. But, tell me, how is that the makers of these things remain unmolested; I wonder they are not found out, excommunicated, or heavily fined, or even punished corporeally, if they are Jews as I expect. Dear me, the maker of this one must have measured you badly! Look! it is too large here, and too small there; it makes you into a regular curve. What a stupid the fellow must be, he can't know his own trade! But what is that?"

"You make me laugh; it's all your fault. You have been feeling and fondling, and you see the natural consequence. I knew it would be so."

"And you couldn't keep it back a minute. It is going on now. I am so sorry; it is a dreadful pity."

"There is not much harm done, so console yourself."

"How can I? you are quite dead. How can you laugh?"

"At your charming simplicity. You shall see in a moment that your charms will give me new life which I shall not lose so easily."

"Wonderful! I couldn't have believed it!"

I took off the sheath, and gave her another, which pleased her better, as it seemed to fit me better, and she laughed for joy as she put it on. She knew nothing of these wonders. Her thoughts had been bound in chains, and she could not discover the truth before she knew me; but though she was scarcely out of Egypt she shewed all the eagerness of an enquiring and newly emancipated spirit. "But how if the rubbing makes the sheath fall off?" said she. I explained to her that such an accident could scarcely happen, and also told her of what material the English made these articles.

After all this talking, of which my ardour began to weary, we abandoned ourselves to love, then to sleep, then to love again, and so on alternately till day-break. As I was leaving, the woman of the house told us that the painter had asked four louis, and that she had give two louis to her foster-son. I gave her twelve, and went home, where I slept till morn, without thinking of breakfasting with the Marquis de Prie, but I think I should have given him some notice of my inability to come. His mistress sulked with me all dinner-time, but softened when I allowed myself to be persuaded into making a bank. However, I found she was playing for heavy stakes, and I had to check her once or twice, which made her so cross that she went to hide her ill-temper in a corner of the hall. However, the marquis won, and I was losing, when the taciturn Duke of Rosebury, his tutor Smith, and two of his fellow-countrymen, arrived from Geneva. He came up to me and said, "How do you do?" and without another word began to play, inviting his companions to follow his example.

Seeing my bank in the last agony I sent Le Duc to my room for the cash-box, whence I drew out five rolls of a hundred louis each. The Marquis de Prie said, coolly, that he wouldn't mind being my partner, and in the same tone I begged to be excused. He continued punting without seeming to be offended at my refusal and when I put down the cards and rose from the table he had won two hundred louis; but all the others had lost, especially one of the Englishmen, so that I had made a profit of a thousand louis. The marquis asked me if I would give him chocolate in my room next morning, and I replied that I should be glad to see him. I replaced my cash-box in my room, and proceeded to the cottage, pleased with the day's work and feeling inclined to crown it with love.

I found my fair friend looking somewhat sad, and on my enquiring the reason she told me that a nephew of the country-woman's, who had come from Chamberi that morning, had told her that he had heard from a lay-sister of the same convent, whom he knew, that two sisters would start at day-break in two days' time to fetch her; this sad news, she said, had made her tears flow fast.

"But the abbess said the sisters could not start before ten days had expired."

"She must have changed her mind."

"Sorrow intrudes into our happy state. Will you be my wife? Will you follow me to Rome and receive absolution from your vows. You may be sure that I shall have a care for your happiness."

"Nay, I have lived long enough; let me return to my tomb."

After supper I told the good woman that if she could rely on her nephew, she would do well to send him at once to Chamberi with orders to return directly the lay-sisters started, and to endeavour to reach Aix two hours before them. She told me that I might reckon on the young man's silence, and on his carrying out my orders. I quieted in this way the charming nun's alarm, and got into bed with her, feeling sad though amorous; and on the pretext that she required rest I left her at midnight, as I wanted to be at home in the morning since I had an engagement with the marquis. In due course he arrived with his mistress, two other ladies, and their husbands or lovers.

I did not limit myself to giving them chocolate; my breakfast consisted of all the luxuries the place afforded. When I had got rid of my troublesome company, I told Le Duc to shut my door, and to tell everybody that I was ill in bed and could not see any visitors. I also warned him that I should be away for two days, and that he must not leave my room a moment till I came back. Having made these arrangements, I slipped away unperceived and went to my mistress, resolved not to leave her till half an hour before the arrival of the lay-sisters.

When she saw me and heard that I was not going to leave her till she went away, she jumped for joy; and we conceived the idea of not having any dinner that we might enjoy our supper the better.

"We will go to bed after supper," said she, "and will not get up till the messenger brings the fatal news that the lay-sisters have started."

I thought the idea an excellent one, and I called the woman of the house to tell her of our arrangements, and she promised to see that we were not disturbed.

We did not find the time long, for two passionate lovers find plenty to talk about since their talk is of themselves. And besides our caresses, renewed again and again, there was something so mysterious and solemn in our situation that our souls and our senses were engaged the whole time.

After a supper which would have pleased a Lucullus, we spent twelve hours in giving each other proofs, of our passionate love, sleeping after our amorous struggles, and waking only to renew the fight. The next day we rose to refresh ourselves, and after a good dinner, mashed down by some excellent Burgundy, we went to bed again; but at four the country-woman came to tell us that the lay-sisters would arrive about six. We had nothing now to look for in the future, the die was cast, and we began our farewell caresses. I sealed the last with my blood. My first M—— M—— had seen it, and my second rightly saw it also. She was frightened, but I calmed her fears. I then rose, and taking a roll containing fifty louis I begged her to keep them for me, promising to come for them in two years, and take them from her hands through the grating of her terrible prison. She spent the last quarter of an hour in tears, and mine were only restrained lest I should add to her grief. I cut off a piece of her fleece and a lock of her beautiful hair, promising her always to bear them next my heart.

I left her, telling the country-woman that she should see me again the next day, and I went to bed as soon as I got home. Next morning I was on the way to Chamberi. At a quarter of a league's distance from Aix I saw my angel slowly walking along. As soon as the lay-sisters were near enough they asked an alms in the name of God. I gave them a Louis, but my saint did not look at me.

With a broken heart I went to the good countrywoman, who told me that M—— M—— had gone at day-break, bidding her to remind me of the convent grating. I kissed the Worthy woman, and I gave her nephew all the loose silver I had about me, and returning to the inn I had my luggage put on to the carriage, and would have started that moment if I had had any horses. But I had two hours to wait, and I went and bade the marquis farewell. He was out, but his mistress was in the room by herself. On my telling her of my departure, she said,

"Don't go, stay with me a couple of days longer."

"I feel the honour you are conferring on me, but business of the greatest importance obliges me to be gone forthwith."

"Impossible," said the lady, as she went to a glass the better to lace herself, shewing me a superb breast. I saw her design, but I determined to baulk her. She then put one foot upon a couch to retie her garter, and when she put up the other foot I saw beauties more enticing than Eve's apple. It was nearly all up with me, when the marquis came in. He proposed a little game of quinze, and his mistress asked me to be her partner. I could not escape; she sat next to me, and I had lost forty Louis by dinner-time.

"I owe you twenty," said the lady, as we were going down.

At dessert Le Duc came to tell me that my carriage was at the door, and I got up, but under the pretence of paying me the twenty louis the marquis's mistress made me come with her to her room.

When we were there she addressed me in a serious and supplicating voice, telling me that if I went she would be dishonoured, as everybody knew that she had engaged to make me stay.

"Do I look worthy of contempt?" said she, making me sit down upon the sofa.

Then with a repetition of her tactics in the morning she contrived that I should see everything. Excited by her charms I praised her beauties, I kissed, I touched; she let herself fall on me, and looked radiant when her vagrant hand found palpable proof of her powers of attraction.

"I promise to be yours to-morrow, wait till then."

Not knowing how to refuse, I said I would keep her to her word, and would have my horses taken out. Just then the marquis came in, saying he would give me my revenge and without answering I went downstairs as if to come back again, but I ran out of the inn, got into my carriage, and drove off, promising a good fee to the postillion if he would put his horses at a gallop.

Echo Library
www.echo-library.com

Echo Library uses advanced digital print-on-demand technology to build and preserve an exciting world class collection of rare and out-of-print books, making them readily available for everyone to enjoy.

Situated just yards from Teddington Lock on the River Thames, Echo Library was founded in 2005 by Tom Cherrington, a specialist dealer in rare and antiquarian books with a passion for literature.

Please visit our website for a complete catalogue of our books, which includes foreign language titles.

The Right to Read

Echo Library actively supports the Royal National Institute of the Blind's Right to Read initiative by publishing a comprehensive range of large print and clear print titles.

Large Print titles are in 16 point Tiresias font as recommended by the RNIB.

Clear Print titles are in 13 point Tiresias font and designed for those who find standard print difficult to read.

Customer Service

If there is a serious error in the text or layout please send details to feedback@echo-library.com and we will supply a corrected copy. If there is a printing fault or the book is damaged please refer to your supplier.

Lightning Source UK Ltd.
Milton Keynes UK
15 December 2009
147549UK00002BC/16/A